# Securing Constitutional Democracy

# Securing Constitutional Democracy

*The Case of Autonomy*

JAMES E. FLEMING

THE UNIVERSITY OF CHICAGO PRESS    CHICAGO AND LONDON

JAMES E. FLEMING is the Leonard F. Manning Distinguished Professor of Law at Fordham University School of Law and coauthor of *American Constitutional Interpretation,* 3d ed. (2003, with Walter F. Murphy, Sotirios A. Barber, and Stephen Macedo).

The University of Chicago Press, Chicago 60637
The University of Chicago Press, Ltd., London
© 2006 by The University of Chicago
All rights reserved. Published 2006
Printed in the United States of America
15 14 13 12 11 10 09 08 07 06    1 2 3 4 5

ISBN: 0-226-25343-0 (cloth)

Library of Congress Cataloging-in-Publication Data

Fleming, James E.
    Securing constitutional democracy : the case of autonomy / James E. Fleming.
        p.   cm.
    Includes bibliographical references and index.
    ISBN 0-226-25343-0 (cloth : alk. paper)
        1. Constitutional law—United States. 2. Judicial review—United States. 3. Privacy,
Right of—United States. 4. Democracy. 5. Civil rights—United States. I. Title.
    KF4750.F535 2006
    342.7308'5—dc22

                                                                                2005036080

⊗ The paper used in this publication meets the minimum requirements of the American National Standard for Information Sciences—Permanence of Paper for Printed Library Materials, ANSI Z39.48-1992.

*For Linda, Sarah, and Katherine*

# Contents

**PART III**

*Adjusting, Preserving, and Perfecting the Scheme of Constitutional Democracy*

# Acknowledgments

In this book, I put forward a Constitution-perfecting theory, one that aspires to interpret the American Constitution so as to make it the best it can be. A number of friends and colleagues have questioned the prudence of calling my theory "Constitution-perfecting," suggesting that by doing so I am leading with my chin. I have disregarded their advice on that point but I have heeded many other suggestions that I hope have helped make this book the best it can be. Here I wish to acknowledge many debts.

First, I am grateful for the inspiration and encouragement of John Rawls and John Hart Ely. I had the good fortune to study with Rawls while I was a student at Harvard Law School. In his courses in political philosophy, I sketched the initial formulations of some of the core ideas that I develop in chapter 4. Rawls's work is inspiring and instructive as a model of how to construct a theory. Through his celebrated humility, he imparted wisdom in judging what we can expect from a theory. He was not daunted if a theory could not do everything that one might hope for it or that a critic might demand of it. This, too, was a great model, for it gave me confidence in proceeding even if I did not have definitive answers to every question. I never formally studied with Ely, though I was fortunate to be conceiving a Ph.D. dissertation topic at Princeton University just as he published *Democracy and Distrust.* It proved an inspiring and illuminating foil for my own work, for he heroically modeled what an elegant, comprehensive constitutional theory should look like. Both Rawls and Ely provided helpful encouragement and criticism of my project.

Special thanks go to Sot Barber, Sandy Levinson, Linda McClain, Frank Michelman, and Ben Zipursky. Linda and I coauthored a previous version of what appears here as chapter 7, and Sot and I coauthored a prior version of what appears here as chapter 9. Beyond that, Linda and Sot have aided this project through countless conversations and tireless engagement. And Linda gave careful and constructive readings of several drafts of the entire manuscript. I am indebted to Sandy for many fruitful conversations over the years about many questions in constitutional theory, especially the question concerning who may authoritatively interpret the Constitution. I have benefited from continuing and sustained conversations with Frank about the implications of Rawls's work for constitutional theory. Finally, Ben by his example provides the very definition of an ideal colleague. I always learn from his counsel and his criticism, and it helps that he is a Rawlsian and Dworkinian fellow traveler.

I also want to thank Cass Sunstein for writing a thoughtful response to what ultimately became chapter 3, Tim Scanlon for writing an insightful and incisive comment on what became chapter 8, and Ronald Dworkin for writing a sympathetic reply to what became the conclusion of chapter 10. I also am grateful to Michael Sandel for conversations about my criticisms of his work in chapter 7, and to Larry Sager and Bruce Ackerman for conversations about my critiques of their work in portions of chapter 10.

For helpful comments and instructive conversations about particular pieces in this project, I am grateful to Akhil Amar, Jack Balkin, Mike Dorf, Chris Eisgruber, Daniel Farber, John Finn, Martin Flaherty, Ned Foley, Willy Forbath, Mark Graber, Abner Greene, Tracy Higgins, Bob Kaczorowski, Greg Keating, Larry Kramer, Thomas Lee, Sharon Lloyd, Steve Macedo, Wayne Moore, Bill Treanor, Mark Tushnet, and Keith Whittington. For insightful comments and conversations about Rawls's work and its implications for constitutional theory, I am thankful to Samuel Freeman and Larry Solum.

I want to thank my editor, Alex Schwartz, for his support of the project, together with his assistant, Catherine Beebe. For constructive criticisms of my original book proposal, I am grateful to two reviewers, Mike Seidman and an anonymous reviewer. For helpful suggestions concerning the entire manuscript, I am indebted to two anonymous reviewers.

Over the years I have gotten valuable research assistance by my students in constitutional theory. I wish to reiterate my appreciation here to Anthony Cicia, Devon Filas, Mark Hagelin, Melissa Lawton, Larry McCabe, Alan Rabinowitz, Steven Shaw, Sabrena Silver, and Carrie

Tendler. I am especially grateful to Stacey Daniel and Matthew Raalf, who read the entire manuscript in its final stages and made innumerable helpful suggestions. Furthermore, reference librarian Paul Miller, also one of my former students in constitutional theory, provided remarkably intelligent, resourceful, and prompt assistance.

I would be remiss if I did not acknowledge Daniel Auld, Kim Holder, and Christian Steriti for their ingenuity and good cheer in providing secretarial assistance.

I owe great debts to three terrific communities of scholars. First, to Princeton University Department of Politics, where I began my critical engagement with the work of Ely, Dworkin, and Rawls in my Ph.D. dissertation, "Constitutional Constructivism," written under the supervision of Walter F. Murphy and Sandy Levinson. I shall be forever grateful to Walter for continuing and enriching Princeton's long-standing tradition of strength in constitutional theory and for fostering what has come to be known in some circles as the "Princeton school" of constitutional theory. This work is unmistakably a product of the Princeton school, however conceived. My early formulations also benefited immeasurably from the brilliant mind and incomparable wisdom of my fellow graduate student and sometime coauthor, Will Harris.

Second, to Harvard University, both the Law School and the Center for Ethics and the Professions. As a law student, I originally conceived some of the core ideas developed in this book in projects supervised by Frank Michelman, Lewis Sargentich, and Albert Sacks. In 1999–2000, I returned to Harvard as a faculty fellow in ethics at the Center for Ethics and the Professions. There I learned from instructive conversations concerning the arguments of this book with Arthur Applbaum, Dick Fallon, Bob Gordon, and Dennis Thompson. During that year, for the first time I saw how my entire project fit together.

Finally, to Fordham University School of Law. I am indebted to my colleagues who make up the vibrant Fordham community in constitutional theory that has sparked and informed my work, especially Martin Flaherty, Abner Greene, Tracy Higgins, Robert Kaczorowski, Bill Treanor, and Ben Zipursky, along with Matt Diller and Charles Kelbley. I also am grateful for the excellent students in my seminar in constitutional theory (many of whom I have acknowledged for research assistance). Fordham provided generous research support, not just for summer projects and sabbaticals but also for a series of major conferences and symposia in constitutional theory that have borne fruit in this book: "Fidelity in Constitutional Theory"; "The

Constitution and the Good Society"; "Rawls and the Law"; "Theories of Constitutional Self-Government"; and "Theories of Taking the Constitution Seriously Outside the Courts." For this support I am indebted to two stellar deans, John Feerick and Bill Treanor.

I benefited from presenting papers in workshops or conferences at a number of institutions: the American Political Science Association Annual Meeting, the Association of American Law Schools Annual Meeting, the Association of American Law Schools Conference on Constitutional Law, Fordham University School of Law, Georgetown/ Maryland Discussion Group on Constitutional Law (several iterations thereof, convened by Mark Tushnet and/or Mark Graber), Harvard University Center for Ethics and the Professions, New York University School of Law Colloquium on Constitutional Theory (thanks especially to Chris Eisgruber and Larry Sager), Ohio State University College of Law, Princeton University, University of Tulsa College of Law, Western New England College of Law Clason Speaker Series, William & Mary School of Law, and the Yale Legal Theory Workshop.

In the book, I draw on and revise material previously published in the following articles: *Constructing the Substantive Constitution,* 72 TEXAS LAW REVIEW 211 (1993); *Securing Deliberative Autonomy,* 48 STANFORD LAW REVIEW 1 (1995); (with Linda C. McClain) *In Search of a Substantive Republic,* 76 TEXAS LAW REVIEW 509 (1997); *Constitutional Tragedy in Dying: Or Whose Tragedy Is It, Anyway?* in CONSTITUTIONAL STUPIDITIES, CONSTITUTIONAL TRAGEDIES 162 (William N. Eskridge Jr. & Sanford Levinson eds., 1998); *Securing Deliberative Democracy,* 72 FORDHAM LAW REVIEW 1435 (2004); and (with Sotirios A. Barber) *War, Crisis, and the Constitution,* in THE CONSTITUTION IN WARTIME 232 (Mark Tushnet ed., 2005). I also incorporate revised versions of brief portions of *We the Exceptional American People,* 11 CONSTITUTIONAL COMMENTARY 355 (1994); *Fidelity to Our Imperfect Constitution,* 65 FORDHAM LAW REVIEW 1335 (1997); *Fidelity, Basic Liberties, and the Specter of* LOCHNER, 41 WILLIAM & MARY LAW REVIEW 147 (1999); *The Constitution Outside the Courts,* 86 CORNELL LAW REVIEW 215 (2000); *Lawrence's Republic,* 39 TULSA LAW REVIEW 563 (2004) (the Legal Scholarship Symposium: The Scholarship of Frank I. Michelman); and *Judicial Review without Judicial Supremacy: Taking the Constitution Seriously Outside the Courts,* 73 FORDHAM LAW REVIEW 1377 (2005).

Warm thanks go to the artist whose painting serves as the basis for the jacket of this book, my good friend Linda Hyatt Wilson. That painting has hung in my living room for more than fifteen years, and it now serves beautifully in graphically raising the question of what it means to secure conditions favorable to the pursuit of happiness.

I dedicate this book to my wife and our two daughters. Linda McClain and I have had a wonderful and fruitful collaboration: we have coauthored three law review articles (one of which appears here in revised form as chapter 7) and have two children, Sarah McClain Fleming and Katherine Amelia McClain Fleming. Sarah's and Katherine's clever sketches of me teaching my class in constitutional law never fail to amuse me. And they have given me hope that through the tireless, committed efforts of a critical, engaged constitutional citizenry, we might indeed ultimately interpret the Constitution so as to make it the best it can be.

## CHAPTER ONE

# Securing Constitutional Democracy

The makers of our Constitution undertook to secure conditions favorable to the pursuit of happiness. . . . They conferred, as against the Government, the right to be let alone—the most comprehensive of rights and the right most valued by civilized men. — Justice Louis D. Brandeis

## The Problem of Grounding Autonomy in Constitutional Law

Justice Brandeis's famous celebration of the constitutional right to privacy or autonomy as the "right to be let alone" sowed the seeds of paradox in constitutional law.[1] The right is "the most comprehensive of rights," yet constitutional scholars and jurists have devoted more effort to narrowing, bounding, or "cabining" it than they have given any other right. It is "the right most valued by civilized men," yet scholars and jurists have repeatedly claimed either that it is trivial or that it is wild, unruly, and dangerous. Indeed, controversy over the meaning, scope, and constitutional status of this right is so widespread and durable that it all but defines the post-1960s era of constitutional adjudication. Conservative Robert H. Bork calls the right to privacy "a loose canon in the law" and its announcement in *Griswold v. Connecticut* (1965) the "construction of a constitutional time bomb."[2] Feminist Catharine A. MacKinnon attacks it as "a right of men 'to be let alone' to oppress women one at a time" in private realms of sanctified isolation.[3] Civic republican Michael J. Sandel and communitarian Mary Ann Glendon contend that theorists who defend the right to autonomy conceive persons as "lone rights-bearers" who are "unencumbered" by the bonds of community.[4] And liberal John

Hart Ely belittles "the right to be different" as an upper-middle-class right: "the right of my son to wear his hair as long as he pleases."[5] The right to privacy or autonomy on the loose in these caricatured renditions is so unruly, dangerous, or rootless that one might wonder whether such a right can be grounded in constitutional law. Can a right with such prominent critics from across the ideological spectrum be a genuine constitutional right?

The most dramatic recent occasion for this question was *Lawrence v. Texas* (2003), in which a bitterly divided Supreme Court held that a law criminalizing same-sex sodomy violated a homosexual's right to privacy or autonomy.[6] Justice Anthony Kennedy's opinion for the Court proclaimed that decisions about sexual conduct and relationships involve "'the most intimate and personal choices a person may make in a lifetime, choices central to personal dignity and autonomy'" and that "'[b]eliefs about these matters could not define the attributes of personhood were they formed under compulsion of the state'"[7] (quoting *Planned Parenthood v. Casey* [1992], which reaffirmed the central holding of *Roe v. Wade* [1973] that the right to privacy encompasses the right to abortion).[8] Kennedy declared that it "demeans the lives" of homosexuals to respect the right of heterosexuals to autonomy without respecting an analogous right for them.[9]

In dissent, Justice Antonin Scalia ridiculed this "sweet-mystery-of-life passage" from *Casey* and chastised the Court for "mak[ing] no effort to cabin the scope of its decision." He castigated Kennedy's opinion for putting the Court on a slippery slope leading to "the end of all morals legislation." If, said, Scalia, states may not enact their moral disapproval of homosexual sodomy, they may not in principle enact their disapproval of "bigamy, same-sex marriage, adult incest, prostitution, masturbation, adultery, fornication, bestiality, and obscenity." For him, homosexuals' intimate sexual conduct is analogous to such traditional morals offenses, not to heterosexuals' autonomy regarding intimate associations. Scalia further scolded the Court for "tak[ing] sides in the culture war, departing from its role of assuring, as neutral observer, that the democratic rules of engagement are observed."[10]

As debated by Kennedy and Scalia, the question in *Lawrence* involved not merely the morality of homosexual sodomy but also important interpretive and institutional questions. The interpretive questions include: What does the Constitution mean? How are interpreters to decide what it means? What are the legitimate sources of constitutional meaning?

What form of democratic government does the Constitution as a whole embody—specifically, is it a scheme of constitutional democracy that guarantees substantive rights like autonomy or, to the contrary, a scheme of majoritarian representative democracy that guarantees neutral processes for representing conflicting interests but no such substantive rights? The institutional questions include: What should be the role of courts in protecting substantive rights such as autonomy? More generally, what should be the role of courts as compared with legislatures in deciding cases implicating substantive moral disagreement in our morally pluralistic polity?

Every significant case regarding privacy or autonomy to reach the Court in the last forty years—from contraception and abortion to euthanasia and sodomy—has implicated such interpretive and institutional questions, and, at bottom, the place of these substantive liberties in our constitutional order. These cases bring out two characteristic forms of uneasiness about privacy or autonomy: the flights from protecting substantive liberties to preserving original understanding of the Constitution (narrowly conceived) and to reinforcing procedural liberties in the Constitution (to the exclusion of substantive liberties). In *Lawrence* and *Casey,* the dissenters urged taking such retreats—and thus declining to recognize rights to privacy or autonomy because they are not specifically enumerated in the text of the Constitution or are not essential to traditional procedures—but the Court resisted hankerings to do so. To secure the rights to privacy or autonomy against these flights, we must construct an overarching substantive theory that can provide a better grounding for them in our constitutional order. We need a theory that firmly connects privacy or autonomy to the substance and structures of constitutional democracy and to the roles and responsibilities of courts and legislatures in protecting constitutional norms. Meeting this challenge is the object of this book.

I ground autonomy in a theory of securing constitutional democracy, a guiding framework with two fundamental themes: first, securing the basic liberties that are preconditions for *deliberative democracy,* to enable citizens to apply their capacity for a conception of justice to deliberating about and judging the justice of basic institutions and social policies as well as the common good, and second, securing the basic liberties that are preconditions for *deliberative autonomy*, to enable citizens to apply their capacity for a conception of the good to deliberating about and deciding how to live their own lives. Together, these themes afford everyone the status of free and equal citizenship in our morally pluralistic constitutional democracy. They reflect two bedrock structures of our constitutional scheme: deliberative political and personal self-government. As against charges that rights of autonomy like those defended in *Lawrence* and *Casey* are anomalous, unruly, or rootless, I show that deliberative autonomy is rooted, along with deliberative democracy, in the language and overall design of the Constitution. Each theme has a structural role to play in securing and fostering our constitutional democracy.

My conception of the structures and design of the Constitution stems from a "constitutional constructivism," which I mean in both a methodological sense—as a method of interpreting the Constitution—and a substantive sense—as the substantive political theory that best fits and justifies our constitutional document and our underlying constitutional order. I develop such a theory by analogy to John Rawls's political constructivism, a theory he developed in *Political Liberalism.*[11]

## Beyond Process-Perfecting Theories to a Constitution-Perfecting Theory

I put forward a "Constitution-perfecting" theory as an alternative to the well-known "process-perfecting" theories advanced by John Hart Ely in *Democracy and Distrust*[12] and Cass Sunstein in *The Partial Constitution.*[13] Ely's book, published in 1980, is undoubtedly the most celebrated book in the history of constitutional theory, and Sunstein's more recent book has close affinities to it. According to their theories, the Constitution's core commitment is to democracy, and judicial review is justified principally when the processes of democracy, and thus the political decisions resulting from them, are undeserving of trust. Many find such theories alluring because of their promise that judicial review might be supportive of rather than inconsistent with democracy. Process-perfecting theories, however, are vulnerable to the criticism that they reject certain substantive liberties (such as privacy, autonomy, liberty of conscience, and freedom of association) as anomalous in our scheme, except insofar as such liberties can be recast as procedural preconditions for democracy.

Yet process-perfecting theories persist,[14] notwithstanding such criticisms, because no one has done for "substance" what Ely has done for "process." That is, no one has developed an alternative substantive Constitution-perfecting theory[15]—a theory that would reinforce not only the procedural liberties (those related to deliberative democracy) but also the substantive liberties (those related to deliberative autonomy) embodied in our Constitution and presupposed by our constitutional democracy— with the elegance and power of Ely's process-perfecting theory.[16]

That is what I aspire to do in this book. I develop a Constitution-perfecting theory that secures both the substantive liberties associated with autonomy and the procedural liberties associated with democracy as fundamental, without deriving the former from the latter or, worse, failing to account for substantive liberties altogether. Unlike process theories, the book provides a firm grounding for rights to privacy and autonomy, along with liberty of conscience and freedom of association, as necessary to secure individual freedom and to promote a diverse and vigorous civil society. My theory also shows how basic liberties associated with personal autonomy, in conjunction with those related to democratic participation, fit together as a coherent scheme of basic liberties that are integral to our constitutional democracy. Finally, I show that competing theories rest on incomplete and inadequate conceptions of democracy. Throughout, I pose fresh challenges to critics who reject rights to privacy and autonomy like those recognized in *Lawrence* and *Casey*.

My defense of a Constitution-perfecting theory includes conceptions not only of *what* the Constitution is and *how* it ought to be interpreted, but also of *who* may authoritatively interpret it.[17] First, as for *what,* constitutional constructivism conceives our Constitution as a "constitution of principle" that embodies (or aspires to embody) a coherent scheme of equal basic liberties, or fair terms of social cooperation on the basis of mutual respect and trust, for our constitutional democracy. The Constitution is not merely a "constitution of detail" that enacts a discrete list of particular rights narrowly conceived by framers and ratifiers.[18] Nor does it simply establish a procedural framework of democracy.

Second, as regards *how,* constitutional constructivism conceives interpretation as the exercise of "reasoned judgment"[19] in quest of the account that best fits and justifies the constitutional document and underlying constitutional order.[20] Responsible interpretation is not merely exegesis of isolated clauses of the constitutional document or research into the concrete intentions or expectations of the framers and ratifiers.

Finally, with respect to *who* may interpret the Constitution, my theory entails a conception of the roles and responsibilities not only of courts but also of legislatures, executives, and citizens. I distinguish between the partial or judicially enforceable Constitution and the whole Constitution that is binding outside the courts on nonjudicial institutions and citizens.[21] In other words, constitutional constructivism is a theory of *the Constitution*, not merely a theory of *judicial review*.

My theory of constitutional constructivism charts a third way between a universalist view of human rights and legal positivism. Here I follow Rawls, who advances a political constructivism that seeks to construct principles of justice that provide fair terms of social cooperation on the basis of mutual respect and trust among free and equal citizens in a morally pluralistic constitutional democracy like ours; he does not try to discover principles of justice true for all times and places.[22] Similarly, my constitutional constructivism seeks to interpret our Constitution so as to make it the best it can be.[23] But it is a theory of constructing *our* Constitution, not one that is *perfectly just* (unmoored by the constraints of our constitutional text, history, and structure, or by those of our practice, tradition, and culture).

In other words, constitutional constructivism is not a theory of natural law or natural rights; it does not conceive constitutional principles and rights as prepolitical and given by a prior and independent order of moral values that is binding for all times and places. Instead, it is what Frank Michelman, analyzing Rawls's political constructivism, calls an "interpretative theory" drawn from the ongoing political practice of a constitutional democracy.[24] Constitutional constructivism draws our principles and rights from our constitutional democracy's ongoing practice, tradition, and culture.[25] These principles are aspirational—the principles to which we as a people aspire and for which we as a people stand—and though they have a firm footing in our scheme, they may not be fully realized in our historical practices, statute books, and common law. Accordingly, constitutional constructivism recognizes that while our principles may fit and justify most of our practices, they enable us to criticize some of those practices for failing to live up to our constitutional commitments.[26]

## Overview

*Part I: Constructing the Substantive Constitution*

In part I (chapters 2–4) I construct a substantive Constitution-perfecting theory with two fundamental commitments: deliberative democracy and deliberative autonomy. I argue that such a theory is superior in important respects to Ely's and Sunstein's process-perfecting theories, which recast substantive liberties as procedural liberties or neglect them altogether.

## THE FLIGHTS FROM SUBSTANCE IN CONSTITUTIONAL THEORY

A specter is haunting constitutional theory—the specter of *Lochner v. New York*.[27] In the *Lochner* era, the Supreme Court gave heightened judicial protection to substantive economic liberties through the Due Process Clauses.[28] In 1937, during the constitutional revolution wrought by the New Deal, *West Coast Hotel v. Parrish*[29] officially repudiated the *Lochner* era's special judicial protection for business interests, marking the first death of substantive due process.[30] Nevertheless, the ghost of *Lochner* has haunted constitutional theory ever since, manifesting itself in charges that judges are "Lochnering" by imposing their own substantive fundamental values in the guise of interpreting the Constitution.[31]

Charges of Lochnering have been most unrelenting with respect to *Roe v. Wade,*[32] which held that the Due Process Clause of the Fourteenth Amendment protects a realm of substantive personal liberty or privacy broad enough to encompass the right of a woman to decide whether to terminate a pregnancy. In a classic critique, *The Wages of Crying Wolf: A Comment on* Roe v. Wade, Ely argues that the Court, to avoid Lochnering, must confine itself to perfecting the processes of representative democracy,[33] as intimated in Justice Harlan Fiske Stone's famous footnote four of *United States v. Carolene Products Co.*[34]

Despite these cries, *Casey* reaffirmed the "central holding" of *Roe* instead of marking the second death of substantive due process by overruling it.[35] In an apoplectic dissent, Justice Scalia blasted the Court for continuing to engage in Lochnering, protesting that the Court must limit itself to giving effect to the original understanding of the Constitution, narrowly conceived.[36] Scalia made similar criticisms in his angry dissent in *Lawrence.*[37]

Ely's and Scalia's critiques illustrate the two responses to the specter of *Lochner* that have dominated constitutional theory since *West Coast Hotel*. Both strategies have been widely criticized for taking "pointless flights from substance": the flights to process and original understanding, respectively.[38] The substance from which these dominant responses are said to flee is not only substantive liberties like privacy or autonomy, but also the burden of formulating an overarching substantive political theory that can encompass these liberties—a general substantive theory of constitutional aspirations. These flights are said to be pointless because perfecting processes and enforcing original understanding inevitably require the very sort of substantive constitutional choices that these strategies are at pains to avoid.

After *Casey* and *Lawrence*, the long-anticipated second death of substantive due process through a repudiation of rights to privacy and autonomy is unlikely to come anytime soon (notwithstanding the 2004 presidential election and the dawn of the Roberts Court). We need a general substantive theory of the Constitution that would fend off the specter of *Lochner*, yet also resist the "temptations" to flee from substance to process or original understanding.[39] This book develops such a theory, in the form of a Constitution-perfecting theory.

## BEYOND PROCESS-PERFECTING THEORIES OF REINFORCING REPRESENTATIVE DEMOCRACY

In chapter 2 I reconsider Ely's elegant and alluring process-perfecting theory of reinforcing representative democracy, offering a new interpretation and critique of it. I assess the common charges that Ely's theory takes futile flights from substance: that it flees substantive political theory in interpreting the Constitution and that it avoids giving effect to certain substantive constitutional provisions. I argue, contrary to familiar interpretations, that Ely's theory does not in fact take the first flight: it is not a process-*based* theory at all, but rather a process-*perfecting* theory that perfects processes by virtue of its substantive basis in a political theory of representative democracy (a qualified utilitarianism rooted in equal concern and respect). I argue, however, that Ely's theory does take the second flight: his process-perfecting theory does not account for, and thus leaves out, certain substantive liberties that are manifested in our constitutional document and implicit in our underlying constitutional order. Still, I contend, his interpretive method—a methodological constructivism—shows the need for a Constitution-perfecting theory such as my substantive constructivism.

## BEYOND PROCESS-PERFECTING THEORIES OF SECURING DELIBERATIVE DEMOCRACY

In chapter 3 I consider Cass Sunstein's process-perfecting theory of securing deliberative democracy. (There I focus on his *The Partial*

*Constitution;* in chapter 7 I critique some of his other work.) Sunstein claims to avoid Ely's putative flight from substance by clearly grounding his own constitutional theory in a substantive theory of liberal republicanism or deliberative democracy.[40] Nevertheless, those who thought that Ely's theory was the grandest process-perfecting theory of them all, or that it had sounded the Hegelian death knell for such theories,[41] have been proven wrong by Sunstein's work. For Sunstein's liberal republicanism leads to a theory of judicial review whereby courts principally secure the preconditions for deliberative democracy, and the structure of his theory parallels that of Ely's theory.[42] I show that Sunstein's theory does not secure the preconditions for deliberative autonomy, and that it recasts certain substantive liberties such as privacy, autonomy, and liberty of conscience as preconditions for deliberative democracy or, worse, leaves them out entirely. Sunstein's theory, like Ely's, thus represents a flight from protecting substantive liberties. From the standpoint of a theory of securing constitutional democracy, Sunstein's theory proves, contrary to his intention, to be a theory of the "partial Constitution" in two ways. His theory is *partial*, not *whole*, because it would not fully secure the preconditions for deliberative autonomy. Furthermore, it is *partial*, not *impartial*, because it would not adequately protect citizens' divergent conceptions of the good from coercive political power.

AN OUTLINE FOR A CONSTITUTION-PERFECTING THEORY OF SECURING
CONSTITUTIONAL DEMOCRACY

Chapter 4 moves beyond process-perfecting theories to a Constitution-perfecting theory by outlining a theory of securing constitutional democracy. This is a substantive theory of the Constitution in the spirit of Rawls's political liberalism. My first theme, *deliberative democracy,* emphasizes political equality and freedom of thought. Here I overlap with Sunstein's principal theme of securing deliberative democracy and, to a lesser extent, Ely's dominant theme of reinforcing representative democracy. This theme is concerned with the preconditions for political self-government, conceiving our political system as a public facility for deliberation concerning the common good, not as a market for aggregating self-interested preferences. My theory aims to ensure that political decisions will be impartial in the sense that they are justifiable by public-regarding reasons (common good), not merely by the self-interested preferences of private groups or individuals. Such a theory forbids political decisions that deny equal citizenship on the basis of race, sex, or sexual orientation.

My second theme, *deliberative autonomy*, is underwritten by liberty of conscience and freedom of association. Here I do justice to substantive liberties that Ely and Sunstein recast or neglect: liberty of conscience, freedom of association, privacy, autonomy, and bodily integrity. I conceive these liberties as preconditions for personal self-government by citizens, individually and in association with others. Where constitutional essentials and matters of basic justice are at stake, my theory aspires to ensure that political decisions will be impartial in the sense that they are justifiable on the basis of public reasons (common ground)—grounds that citizens generally can reasonably be expected to accept, whatever their particular conceptions of the good, because they come within an overlapping consensus concerning a political conception of justice. These constitutional restrictions must be honored if free and equal citizens are to engage in social cooperation on the basis of mutual respect and trust in a constitutional democracy such as our own, which is characterized by reasonable moral pluralism.

My Constitution-perfecting theory is a theory of constitutional democracy and trustworthiness, an alternative to Ely's theory of representative democracy and distrust and to Sunstein's theory of deliberative democracy and impartiality. (To fix ideas, I use the term "constitutional democracy" to refer to my Rawlsian theory of our underlying constitutional order, "representative democracy" to refer to Ely's theory, and "deliberative democracy" to refer to Sunstein's.)[43] To be trustworthy, a constitutional democracy must secure and respect not only the procedural preconditions for deliberative democracy but also the substantive preconditions for deliberative autonomy.[44] Ely's and Sunstein's process-perfecting theories secure only the former type of precondition for trust or impartiality. Constitutional constructivism, because it neither flees substantive political theory nor flees protecting substantive liberties, promises to give both substance and process their due.[45]

*Part II: Securing Deliberative Autonomy Together*
*with Deliberative Democracy*

In part II (chapters 5–7) I elaborate the guiding framework for securing deliberative autonomy together with deliberative democracy. I develop the theoretical underpinnings and scope of deliberative autonomy, reconceive the doctrinal substantive due process inquiry in terms of the significance of an asserted liberty for deliberative autonomy, and defend the right to privacy or autonomy as deliberative autonomy against charges that it is either too thin or too thick to secure freedoms in circumstances of moral pluralism.

## SECURING DELIBERATIVE AUTONOMY

In chapter 5 I elaborate the theoretical underpinnings of deliberative autonomy in the matrix values of liberty of conscience and freedom of association. I show how a conception of deliberative autonomy can justify and impart coherence and structure to a list of familiar "unenumerated" fundamental rights commonly classed under privacy, autonomy, or substantive due process. This list includes liberty of conscience and freedom of thought; freedom of association, including both expressive association and intimate association, whatever one's sexual orientation; the right to live with one's family, whether nuclear or extended; the right to travel or relocate; the right to marry; the right to decide whether to bear or beget children, including the rights to procreate, to use contraceptives, and to terminate a pregnancy; the right to direct the education and rearing of children; and the right to exercise dominion over one's body, including the right to bodily integrity and ultimately the right to die. As against charges that autonomy is anomalous, rootless, or unruly, I argue that deliberative autonomy is integral to our scheme and is rooted, along with deliberative democracy, in the language and design of our Constitution.

## RECONCEIVING THE DUE PROCESS INQUIRY IN TERMS OF SIGNIFICANCE
## FOR DELIBERATIVE AUTONOMY: BETWEEN SCALIA AND CHARYBDIS

In chapter 6 I turn from the theoretical underpinnings of deliberative autonomy to the doctrinal heading of substantive due process, which has served as the primary textual basis for recognizing or rejecting such "unenumerated" fundamental rights as those just listed. First, I propose a reconception of the substantive due process inquiry that bases the recognition of "unenumerated" fundamental rights on their significance for deliberative autonomy. With this criterion of significance, constructivism's guiding framework would chart a middle course between Scylla (Scalia), the rock of liberty as "hidebound" historical practices, and

Charybdis, the whirlpool of liberty as unbounded license. Second, I attempt to bring a sense of order and discipline to (supposedly wild and unruly) judgments about the significance of certain rights for deliberative autonomy through exploring homologies between the structure of deliberative autonomy and that of deliberative democracy. I show that substantive due process and First Amendment jurisprudences are mirror images of one another with respect to the judgments that they make regarding significance for deliberative autonomy and deliberative democracy, respectively. Finally, I indicate what deliberative autonomy is not, distinguishing it from familiar understandings or caricatures of privacy, autonomy, or liberty.

CONSTITUTIONAL INTERPRETATION IN CIRCUMSTANCES OF MORAL
DISAGREEMENT AND POLITICAL CONFLICT

In chapter 7 I consider the problem of what form constitutional interpretation and judicial review should take in the face of moral disagreement and political conflict about basic liberties such as the right to privacy or autonomy. I take up two diametrically opposed republican challenges to liberal theories of the sort I propound. On the one hand, civic republican Sandel charges that such theories are too thin: they represent a "minimalist liberalism" and an impoverished vision of the "procedural republic."[46] He argues that in interpreting constitutional freedoms like privacy, courts should move beyond liberal autonomy arguments about protecting individual choices to republican moral arguments about fostering substantive human goods or virtues. For example, in *Lawrence v. Texas,* the Court should have justified protecting homosexuals' right to privacy not on the basis of homosexuals' freedom to make personal choices, but on the ground of the goods or virtues fostered by homosexuals' intimate associations.

On the other hand, minimalist republican Sunstein objects that liberal theories like mine are too thick: they sponsor "maximalist" constitutional interpretation by the judiciary and too deep a vision of the substantive Constitution.[47] He contends that courts should eschew both autonomy arguments about choices and moral arguments about goods in favor of seeking "incompletely theorized agreements" on particular outcomes and "leaving things undecided" in order to allow democratic deliberation to proceed. Thus, in *Lawrence,* the Court should have avoided deciding whether homosexuals, like heterosexuals, have a right to privacy and instead struck down the law banning same-sex sodomy (but not opposite-sex sodomy) on the ground of desuetude: "Without a strong justification, the state cannot bring the criminal law to bear on consensual sexual behavior if enforcement of the relevant law can no longer claim to have significant moral support in the enforcing state or the nation as a whole."[48]

In reply, I argue that Sandel's civic republicanism is too thick because it requires deeper agreement on goods or virtues than seems feasible, given the fact of reasonable moral pluralism, without intolerable state oppression. Conversely, Sunstein's minimalist republicanism is too thin because, in the face of such pluralism, it settles for shallower agreement than is necessary to secure fundamental constitutional freedoms. A theory like mine, with affinities to Rawls's political liberalism, is just right. Indeed, Sandel's and Sunstein's theories, through their diametrically opposed challenges and shortcomings, unwittingly show the superiority of my liberal republican constitutional theory, which would secure the basic liberties that are preconditions not only for deliberative democracy but also for deliberative autonomy.

## Part III: Adjusting, Preserving, and Perfecting the Scheme of Constitutional Democracy

In part III (chapters 8–10) I address problems of adjusting basic liberties in order to secure the family of basic liberties as a whole, preserving the constitutional order itself in circumstances of war and crisis, and perfecting the Constitution through the pursuit of "happy endings" in constitutional interpretation.

### SECURING THE FAMILY OF BASIC LIBERTIES AS A WHOLE

In chapter 8 I take up the problem of what is to be done when basic liberties conflict with one another. How are we to address clashes of rights, or more precisely, clashes of higher order values or interests that underlie rights? Constitutional constructivism accords priority to the whole family of equal basic liberties over pursuit of conceptions of the public good or the imposition of perfectionist values. This understanding of priority entails that it may be permissible to regulate certain basic liberties for the sake of securing other basic liberties or the whole family of such liberties. No single basic liberty by itself is absolute. There may be clashes between basic liberties or the interests or values underlying them, for example, between concern for protecting freedom of expression and concern for securing equal citizenship for all. I illustrate in chapter 8 how a constructivist guiding framework might help us frame and ultimately resolve such clashes in order to secure the family of basic liberties as a whole.

I also explore what the structure of First Amendment law would look like if we were committed not to protecting an absolutist First Amendment in isolation from the rest of the Constitution, but to securing a fully adequate scheme of the basic liberties as a whole. I consider four important Supreme Court cases that involve clashes between the First Amendment's protection of freedom of expression and the Equal Protection Clause's concern for equal citizenship. In three out of four of these cases, the Court protected freedom of expression to the exclusion (or indeed erasure) of equal citizenship. First, I present Rawls's own critique of *Buckley v. Valeo*[49] (striking down certain campaign finance regulations limiting expenditures) as an exemplar of how to secure equal protection or equal participation together with freedom of expression. Second, I sketch an analogous critique of *R.A.V. v. City of St. Paul*[50] (invalidating an ordinance prohibiting "bias-motivated crimes" including hateful racist expression) for privileging freedom of expression over equal protection. Third, I analyze *Roberts v. United States Jaycees*[51] (forbidding the Jaycees to exclude women) as a model of how the Supreme Court itself on occasion has taken equal citizenship seriously in the context of freedom of expression and association. Finally, with this example on hand, I criticize *Boy Scouts of America v. Dale*[52] (permitting the Boy Scouts to exclude homosexuals) for privileging freedom of association over equal protection.

Throughout chapter 8 my aim is to suggest that a constructivist guiding framework of basic liberties might help frame our judgments concerning what to do when confronting clashes between freedom of expression and equal protection. Those judgments would be guided by the aspiration to accord priority to the family of basic liberties as a whole, not to give priority to freedom of expression over equal protection.

SECURING CONSTITUTIONAL DEMOCRACY IN WAR AND CRISIS

In chapter 9 I turn to a fundamentally different aspect of securing constitutional democracy: preserving the constitutional order itself in circumstances of war and crisis. I consider whether it may be justifiable, in such circumstances, to violate the Constitution in order to save it.

Using the example of Abraham Lincoln's justification for suspending the writ of habeas corpus during the Civil War, I acknowledge the possibility that actions like Lincoln's may have been *constitutionalist,* that is, justifiable on the ground that they were necessary to preserve or restore the conditions for the constitutional order itself, but not strictly *constitutional,* which is to say justifiable in terms of fidelity to particular constitutional norms themselves. I then consider whether *Bush v. Gore*[53] might be justifiable along similar lines, as necessary to avert a constitutional crisis. I conclude that it is not. Beyond that, I argue that a Lincolnian constitutionalist jurisprudence opens the window to a conception of the Constitution as a charter of positive benefits (which the government is obligated to secure), as contrasted with the conception of it as a scheme of negative liberties (which protect people from government) that the Rehnquist Court embraced in cases like *DeShaney v. Winnebago County Department of Social Services.*[54] From the standpoint of such a jurisprudence, we would see securing constitutional democracy itself—together with its scheme of basic liberties—in terms of positive benefits that the government is obligated to afford. We would not conceive either the order itself or its basic liberties in terms of freedoms from government.

## CONSTITUTIONAL IMPERFECTIONS AND THE PURSUIT OF HAPPY ENDINGS: PERFECTING OUR IMPERFECT CONSTITUTION

Finally, in chapter 10 I discuss constitutional imperfections and the pursuit of what Sanford Levinson has called "happy endings" in constitutional interpretation.[55] Levinson and others have expressed skepticism about constitutional theories like mine on the ground that they always seem to lead to happy endings: that the Constitution, properly interpreted, requires the result that my normative political theory recommends. Henry Monaghan famously ridicules such theories as conceptions of "our perfect Constitution."[56] Christopher Eisgruber helpfully frames this type of criticism in terms of a "no pain, no claim" test.[57] The basic idea is that a constitutional theory has no serious claim on our attention unless the theorist putting it forward suffers some pain by acknowledging that the Constitution does not secure everything that she or he would protect in a perfect Constitution. In response to this challenge, many constitutional theorists have been at pains to demonstrate that their theories sanction all manner of imperfections, tragedies and stupidities, and unhappy endings.

My theory—which I present without apology as a Constitution-perfecting theory—invites perfect Constitution challenges more straight-forwardly than perhaps any other theory. In responding to such challenges I resist the peculiar trend in constitutional theory to prove my positivist mettle by making a virtue of all the constitutional imperfec-tions, tragedies and stupidities, and unhappy endings that my theory sanctions. Put another way, I question the wisdom of submitting consti-tutional theories to perfect Constitution challenges or a "no pain, no claim" test. Our Constitution is indeed imperfect in many ways. But we should strive to interpret it so as to mitigate its imperfections, to avoid interpretive tragedies or stupidities, and to make it the best it can be. That is, we should embrace a Constitution-perfecting theory of interpre-tation, which proudly aims at happy endings rather than reveling in the imperfections that the Constitution might be interpreted to embody. Instead of a "no pain, no claim" test, I embrace what Eisgruber calls a "no gain, no claim" test.[58] From this standpoint, a constitutional theory has no serious claim on our attention unless it promises some gain, in the sense that adhering to it might help us realize our constitutional aspirations. My Constitution-perfecting theory abundantly satisfies the latter test, for it promises the considerable gain of securing the basic liberties associated with deliberative democracy and deliberative auton-omy that are preconditions for the trustworthiness of our constitutional democracy.

# PART I

## *Constructing the Substantive Constitution*

## CHAPTER TWO

# Beyond Process-Perfecting Theories of Reinforcing Representative Democracy

*We . . . suffer ourselves . . . to be transported to [E]lysian regions. — Samuel Johnson*

In *Democracy and Distrust,* the pinnacle of the *Carolene Products* tradition, John Hart Ely famously argues that courts should perfect the processes of representative democracy rather than impose substantive fundamental values.[1] His renowned theory has two elegant, comprehensive themes: first, keeping the processes of political communication and participation open, and second, keeping those processes free of prejudice against discrete and insular minorities in order to ensure equal concern and respect for everyone alike.[2] Ely contends that such a representation-reinforcing or process-perfecting theory, not a theory of discovering substantive fundamental values, captures the "deep structure" of and justifies the Warren Court's constitutional revolution.[3]

Ely's process-perfecting theory is widely thought—by critics and supporters alike—to take flights from substance: both to flee substantive political theory in interpreting the Constitution and to avoid giving effect to certain substantive constitutional provisions. In *The Wages of Crying Wolf,* Ely criticizes *Roe v. Wade* for protecting the substantive fundamental right to privacy by telling a fable of the theorists who cried "*Lochner*" too often, that is, who charged the Court too indiscriminately with protecting substantive fundamental rights in many cases that were justifiable in terms of reinforcing the processes of representative democracy.[4] In assessing Ely's theory, I tell a parallel fable of the theorist who cried "substance" too indiscriminately, the wages of which are that he is fated to suffer reiterations of the mistaken charge that his theory flees substantive political theory in interpreting the Constitution. But I do charge Ely with taking the second flight: avoiding giving effect to certain substantive constitutional provisions.

I interpret Ely's project as a quest for a process-perfecting "ultimate interpretivism" that is based on a substantive political theory of representative democracy, a qualified utilitarianism rooted in equal concern and respect.[5] From that standpoint, I argue that Ely's own interpretive method shows the need for a Constitution-perfecting theory, such as a constitutional constructivism, that would give meaningful effect to— rather than avoiding—the substantive liberties embodied in our Constitution along with the procedural liberties that Ely's theory protects. Such a theory would move beyond process to substance.

## An Outline of Ely's Quest for the Ultimate Interpretivism

*The False Dichotomy between Interpretivism and Noninterpretivism*

At the outset, it is useful to sketch the terrain of constitutional theory as Ely sees it and indeed helped define it. Constitutional theory, on his view, is dominated by a false dichotomy between two theories of judicial review.[6] "Clause-bound interpretivists" (or "originalists") believe that "judges deciding constitutional issues should confine themselves to enforcing norms that are stated or clearly implicit in the written Constitution."[7] Advocates of this theory include Justice Hugo Black and, in more recent times and narrower forms, Judge Bork and Justice Scalia.[8] "Noninterpretivists" (or "nonoriginalists") contend, on the contrary, that "courts should go beyond that set of references and enforce norms that cannot be discovered within the four corners of the document."[9] Representatives of this theory, on Ely's view, include the majorities of the Supreme Court that decided *Roe v. Wade*[10] and *Lawrence v. Texas*,[11] along with proponents of protecting substantive fundamental values.[12]

Put another way, clause-bound interpretivists have claimed a monopoly on the classical, interpretive justification of judicial review put forward in *The Federalist* No. 78 and in *Marbury v. Madison:* courts are obligated to interpret the higher law of the Constitution and to preserve it against encroachments by the ordinary law of legislation.[13] They have accused other theorists of engaging in Lochnering, or attempting to impose their own visions of political utopia on the polity in the name of the Constitution. Moreover, they have insisted that the only way to avoid Lochnering is to flee from making substantive constitutional choices in favor of giving effect to the original understanding of the Constitution, narrowly conceived.[14]

By contrast, substantive fundamental values theorists typically have rejected or reconstructed the classical justification: courts should elaborate the substantive fundamental values embodied in the higher law of the Constitution and protect them against deprivations by the ordinary law of legislation. They have been at pains to distinguish their theories from Lochnering and to justify protecting certain substantive fundamental values rather than others.[15] Furthermore, they have charged clause-bound interpretivists with abdicating responsibility for making substantive constitutional choices by resorting to formalist, authoritarian pretexts to interpretive neutrality like original understanding.[16]

The genius of Ely's approach is that it leads to a middle ground, a "third theory" that aims to break out of this false dichotomy.[17] First, Ely argues that clause-bound interpretivism, notwithstanding its allure, is impossible.[18] Its allure is its evident rule-of-law virtues and democratic virtues. First, it supposedly fits our usual conceptions of what the Constitution is and how it should be interpreted. Second, it claims to dissolve what Alexander Bickel conceived as the "counter-majoritarian difficulty" posed by judicial review in a democracy through invoking the classical justification.[19] Its impossibility is that it dispositively fails on its own terms: "For the constitutional document itself, the interpretivist's Bible, contains several provisions whose invitation to look beyond their four corners—whose invitation, if you will, to become at least to that extent a noninterpretivist—cannot be construed away."[20] The three provisions that Ely argues are "open-ended" in this sense are the Ninth Amendment[21] and the Privileges or Immunities and Equal Protection Clauses of the Fourteenth Amendment (but not the Due Process Clauses of the Fifth and Fourteenth Amendments).[22] The language of these provisions, quoted in the endnotes, suggests that they were "delegation[s] to future constitutional decision-makers to protect certain rights that the document neither lists, at least not exhaustively, nor even in any specific way gives directions for finding."[23] The clause-bound interpretivists, Ely contends, in their zeal to flee substance and avoid Lochnering, engage in their own brand of Lochnering by trying to read these open-ended clauses out of the Constitution. In doing so, they forfeit their claim to a monopoly on the classical, interpretive justification of judicial review.[24]

Second, Ely contends that theories of protecting substantive fundamental values, despite their appeal, are illegitimate. These theories—which he claims fill in the open-ended provisions with values drawn from such "external" sources beyond the Constitution as natural law, tradition, or consensus—are frighteningly indeterminate and irredeemably undemocratic.[25] Therefore, they lack both the supposed rule-of-law virtues and democratic virtues of clause-bound interpretivism. Accordingly, they aggravate rather than resolve the counter-majoritarian difficulty. Worse yet, Ely maintains, these theories prove to be straightforward invitations to engage in Lochnering.

## Ely's Third Theory of Reinforcing Representative Democracy

Thus, Ely declines to embrace either a clause-bound interpretivism or a substance-unbound fundamental values theory. Instead, he puts forward a third theory of representative democracy and distrust, the outlines of which were prefigured in the famous footnote four of *Carolene Products*. There, Justice Stone suggested three situations in which representative democracy is not to be trusted and which therefore justify judicial scrutiny more intensive than ordinary deference to the political process:

> There may be narrower scope for operation of the presumption of constitutionality when legislation appears on its face to be within a specific prohibition of the Constitution, such as those of the first ten amendments, which are deemed equally specific when held to be embraced within the Fourteenth. . . .
>
> It is unnecessary to consider now whether legislation which restricts those political processes which can ordinarily be expected to bring about repeal of undesirable legislation, is to be subjected to more exacting judicial scrutiny under the general prohibitions of the Fourteenth Amendment than are most other types of legislation. . . .
>
> Nor need we enquire whether similar considerations enter into the review of statutes directed at particular religious, . . . or national, . . . or racial minorities . . . ; whether prejudice against discrete and insular minorities may be a special condition, which tends seriously to curtail the operation of those

political processes ordinarily to be relied upon to protect minorities, and which may call for a correspondingly more searching judicial inquiry.[26]

Hence courts should enforce the specific provisions of the Constitution (paragraph one) and should reinforce the processes of representative democracy by setting aside decisions of legislatures and executive officials when those processes are systematically malfunctioning and thus producing untrustworthy outcomes (paragraphs two and three)—namely, when "(1) the ins are choking off the channels of political change to ensure that they will stay in and the outs will stay out," or "(2) though no one is actually denied a voice or a vote, representatives beholden to an effective majority are systematically disadvantaging some minority . . . , and thereby denying that minority the protection afforded other groups by a representative system."[27]

Ely suggests that his third theory represents the "ultimate interpretivism" because it derives content for the open-ended provisions of the Constitution "from the general themes of the entire constitutional document and not from some source entirely beyond its four corners."[28] That is, it fills in the Constitution's open texture by deriving whatever rights are implicit in the constitutional document and underlying constitutional order of representative democracy.[29]

Ely argues that his third theory avoids the pitfalls and incorporates the strengths of the first two theories. By questing for the ultimate interpretivism rather than searching for an "external" source of substantive fundamental values in the nether world beyond the *Carolene Products* paradigm, the theory can lay claim to the supposed rule-of-law virtues as well as the democratic virtues of the classical, interpretive justification of judicial review.[30] By reinforcing the processes of representative democracy when their outcomes are unworthy of trust, the theory is consistent with and supportive of the underlying system, thereby minimizing the counter-majoritarian difficulty.[31] In both ways, he maintains, his theory avoids Lochnering.

Ely is right to focus on securing the basic liberties that are preconditions for the trustworthiness of the outcomes of the political process, and to quest for an ultimate interpretivism (a constructivist, holistic account of the general themes of the Constitution). Much of the enormous critical literature responding to Ely's provocative theory has focused on his supposed avoidance of substance for process, to the relative neglect of his claim to be the ultimate interpretivist.[32] Moreover, scholars who have addressed the latter claim typically have done little more than belittle it.[33] I instead take Ely's claim seriously, interpreting his project as a quest for a process-perfecting ultimate interpretivism that is based on a substantive political theory of representative democracy.

My interpretation suggests neglected affinities between Ely's theory and Ronald Dworkin's constructivist theory of constitutional interpreta- tion.[34] These affinities are significant for two reasons. First, they show that the common charge that Ely's theory takes a flight from substantive political theory to feigning interpretive neutrality is mistaken. Second, they indicate that although the other familiar charge—that his theory takes a flight from protecting certain substantive constitutional provisions to perfecting processes—is basically sound, Ely's theory itself shows the need for a Constitution-perfecting theory.

## Ely Does Not Flee Substantive Political Theory: The Flight Not Taken

### Ely's Substantive Political Theory: Ely as Hercules

The suggestion that Ely's theory bears affinities to Dworkin's may seem surprising, if not paradoxical, for Dworkin's theory appears to epitomize the substantive fundamental values theories that Ely rejects as illegitimate. By creating a mythical philosopher-judge Hercules, who constructs a substan- tive political theory underlying the constitutional document and constitu- tional order to decide hard cases,[35] Dworkin boldly invites critical invocation of Judge Learned Hand's or Judge Bork's objections to rule by Platonic guardians or philosopher-judges in a democracy.[36] Indeed, Dworkin's Hercules may seem to be the very incarnation of the Lochnering judge.

Nonetheless, Ely's quest for the ultimate interpretivism leads him, like Hercules, to attempt to construct the substantive political theory that best *fits* and *justifies* the Constitution as a whole, as it was originally framed and has developed.[37] First, like Hercules, Ely works back and forth between the constitutional document and an underlying political theory of the constitutional order, striving toward reflective equilibrium between them.[38] Thus, Ely's interpretive method resembles Dworkin's construc- tivist method of constitutional interpretation.[39]

Second, the affinities between Ely's and Dworkin's theories extend beyond their interpretive methods to the content of their substantive political theories. Ely argues that the substantive political theory that best fits and justifies our constitutional document and underlying constitutional order is a theory of representative democracy that is rooted in Dworkin's constitutive principle of equal concern and respect.[40] As Ely puts it, our system combines "actual representation" of majorities' interests[41] and "virtual representation" of minorities' interests,[42] and "preclude[s] a refusal to *represent* [minorities], the denial to [them] of what Professor Dworkin has called 'equal concern and respect in the design and administration of the political institutions that govern [majorities and minorities alike].'"[43]

Ely also characterizes his substantive political theory of representative democracy as an "applied utilitarianism" that is designed to realize Jeremy Bentham's utilitarian principle of the equal weighting of preferences, namely, "each to count for one and none for more than one."[44] He adds, though, that his theory is a qualified utilitarianism: paragraphs one and two of the *Carolene Products* framework, concerned with enforcing specific prohibitions of the Constitution and keeping political processes open, impose rights or "side constraints" on the utilitarian processes' pursuit of the general welfare, while paragraph three mandates "distributional corrections" where those processes are corrupted by prejudice against discrete and insular minorities.[45] His theory, however, does not embrace substantive fundamental rights or values that lie beyond the *Carolene Products* framework.

To be sure, Ely's substantive political theory rooted in equal concern and respect or qualified utilitarianism is hardly programmatic and certainly not fully elaborated; it is instead synthetic and eclectic. Thus, he presents it as compatible with both republicanism and qualified interest-group pluralism, not to mention utilitarianism and liberalism (pairs of theories commonly thought to conflict with one another). For example, Ely states that his theory attempts to secure "the republican ideal of government in the interest of the whole people," and that it does not endorse a pure interest-group pluralist vision of government in the interests of majority coalitions, "winner-take-all."[46] But his claim that his substantive political theory synthesizes or is compatible with several traditions of political thought does not make it any less substantive.

My interpretation of Ely's theory makes two things clear. Ely seeks to avoid Lochnering by condemning judicial enforcement of substantive fundamental values that lie beyond his *Carolene Products* framework. Equally clearly, however, he does not shy away from constructing the substantive political theory that he believes best fits and justifies our constitutional document and underlying constitutional order. Whether Ely's political theory actually provides the best interpretation of our Constitution is, of course, another question.

### The Mistaken Charge That Ely Flees Substantive Political Theory

Nevertheless, many constitutional theorists have charged that Ely flees substance for process—that he denies the need for substantive political theory or substantive constitutional choices in constitutional interpretation and feigns interpretive neutrality through perfecting processes. For example, in a well-known critique, Laurence Tribe responds immediately to Ely's *Democracy and Distrust* by expressing his puzzlement at the persistence of "process-based" constitutional theories, calling instead for a substance-based theory.[47] Tribe argues that process-based theories are radically indeterminate and fundamentally incomplete because they necessarily perfect processes by virtue of a basis in a "full theory of substantive rights and values—the very sort of theory the process-perfecters are at such pains to avoid."[48] Yet, he contends, Ely seeks to eschew making substantive constitutional choices in favor of being "neutral on matters of substantive value."[49] Notwithstanding Ely's use of certain aspects of Dworkin's theory, Dworkin himself makes a similar critique of Ely's theory.[50]

In *The Partial Constitution,* Sunstein reiterates this type of critique, charging Ely with claiming that it is possible to interpret the Constitution without making substantive arguments and, thereby, to attain interpretive neutrality.[51] Sunstein argues, to the contrary, that constitutional interpretation inevitably requires reliance on substantive principles, which must be justified in terms of moral or political theory through substantive arguments. He contends that Ely fails to make such substantive arguments to defend his conception of representative democracy.

My interpretation of Ely's theory, by emphasizing its affinities to the method and content of Dworkin's theory, shows that these common critiques are mistaken. Ely's theory of democracy and distrust, contrary to Tribe's puzzled suggestion, is not a process-*based* theory at all; rather, it is a process-*perfecting* theory that perfects processes by virtue of its substantive basis in a political theory of representative democracy, a qualified utilitarianism rooted in equal concern and respect. And so, it will not suffice even to meet, let alone to better, Ely's theory to belittle it as taking a pointless flight from substance to process, or to pontificate about the necessity of making substantive constitutional choices in constitutional interpretation. Instead, the battle with Ely must be at the level of substantive political theory.

Some critics have argued that Ely's theory is not liberal enough because it stems from too frail a vision of "liberal" substantive liberties like privacy and autonomy.[52] Others have argued that his theory is not republican enough because it reflects an impoverished vision of political processes as utilitarian and pluralist.[53] But what they miss is that to argue for a more liberal theory or a more republican theory is to engage with Ely's substantive political theory rather than to deny that he has such a theory or to charge him with fleeing from one.

Sunstein, unlike Tribe, engages with Ely at the level of substantive political theory, arguing for the superiority of his liberal republican theory of deliberative democracy over Ely's qualified pluralist theory of representative democracy.[54] My theory of constitutional constructivism also engages with Ely and Sunstein at that level, arguing for the superiority of a theory of securing constitutional democracy.[55]

All of this, however, poses a puzzle: Why have constitutional theorists persisted in mistakenly charging that Ely avoids substantive political theory in constitutional interpretation in favor of feigning interpretive neutrality? To try to account for this puzzle, in the section that follows, I construct a fable of the theorist who cried "substance" too indiscriminately in his critique of substantive fundamental values theories.

*The Wages of Crying "Substance"*
THE THEORISTS WHO CRIED "*LOCHNER*" TOO OFTEN

In *The Wages of Crying Wolf,* Ely advances a famous critique of *Roe* by analogy to the fable of the boy who cried "wolf."[56] The wolf, of course, is *Lochner.* I interpret Ely's fable as follows:

> Since *West Coast Hotel* officially repudiated *Lochner*'s special judicial protection for substantive economic liberties, every time the Supreme Court has given heightened judicial protection to any constitutional value in any decision, judges and commentators alike have cried "*Lochner.*" They have done so frequently and indiscriminately, regardless of whether the decisions in question could be justified, on the basis of inferences from the text, history, or structure

of the Constitution, as being within the *Carolene Products* paradigm and its underlying theory of representative democracy. Therefore, when a real case of Lochnering came along, in the form of *Roe,* judges and commentators ignored the cry of "*Lochner.*" They had heard that cry too often.

The point of Ely's fable is that judges and commentators should have reserved the cry of "*Lochner*" for cases that could not be justified within the *Carolene Products* paradigm and its underlying theory of representative democracy. On his view, what the Supreme Court did in *Lochner* that was so dreadful was to enforce substantive fundamental values drawn from a world beyond a *Carolene Products* jurisprudence. That, too, Ely argues, is what is wrong with *Roe.*[57] Thus, for him, the specter of *Lochner* is incarnate in *Roe* and any other decision that rests on such substantive fundamental values, not in substance or fundamental values as such.

To fix ideas, we must distinguish Ely's narrow sense of the substance or Lochnering that is out of bounds—because it is beyond a *Carolene Products* jurisprudence—from a generic sense of the substance that is not forbidden. Contrary to common misinterpretations, Ely does not argue that it is out of bounds and illegitimate for judges to enforce substance or fundamental values as such, in a generic sense of making substantive constitutional choices and thus not being neutral in deciding which values the Constitution especially protects. What he does argue to be out of bounds and illegitimate is protecting substantive fundamental rights like privacy or autonomy, which he views as lying outside a *Carolene Products* jurisprudence.

THE THEORIST WHO CRIED "SUBSTANCE" TOO INDISCRIMINATELY

In *Democracy and Distrust* Ely puts forward a famous critique of "noninterpretivist" (or "nonoriginalist") theories of "discovering" substantive fundamental values.[58] There he runs "the gamut of fundamental-value methodologies" that was "the odyssey of Alexander Bickel."[59] He rejects, on skeptical and democratic grounds, "external" sources of substantive fundamental values that such theorists have proffered: the judge's own values, natural law, neutral principles, reason, tradition, consensus, and the predicted values of the future.

Ely's explosive critique—a tour de force—is an indiscriminate rout of all these *sources* of values as such, irrespective of the *content* of the values derived from them and regardless of whether the content is plausibly manifested in our constitutional document or implicit in our underlying constitutional order. His no-holds-barred attack seems to have misled some readers into thinking that he was rejecting, as out of bounds and illegitimate, judicial enforcement of substance in a generic sense rather than in the narrower sense of substance or Lochnering just distinguished. These readers may have rejected his theory for that reason.

To suggest how this result may have occurred, I offer another fable, this one of the theorist who cried "substance" too indiscriminately:

> There once was a theorist who warned judges and commentators against crying *"Lochner"* too often. When what he viewed as a real case of Lochnering came along, in the form of *Roe,* he himself cried *"Lochner."* But the judges and commentators, who had heard that cry too often from others, did not heed him. Then the theorist ran the gamut of sources of substantive fundamental values, crying "substance" indiscriminately with respect to them all, regardless of their content. When he finished, the judges and commentators said that they had heard the cry of "substance" too often. Next, the theorist elaborated a *Carolene Products* theory of judicial review and tried to explain that he really had meant to cry "substance" only with respect to judicial imposition of substantive fundamental values lying beyond his *Carolene Products* jurisprudence. But he had cried "substance" so indiscriminately that the judges and commentators did not listen. Worse still, they chanted back "substance" at the theorist's own theory, and proclaimed that they were not afraid of substance. Finally, they criticized him for pointlessly trying to flee substance for process.

The moral of the fable—the wages of Ely's crying "substance" too indiscriminately—is that he is doomed to endure reiterations of the mistaken charge that his theory flees substance for process in the sense of denying the need for substantive political theory or substantive constitutional choices in interpreting the Constitution.

## Ely Does Flee Substantive Constitutional Provisions: The Flight Taken

*Ely's Interpretive Method Calls for a Constitution-Perfecting Theory*

We have seen that Ely's theory does not flee substantive political theory in interpreting the Constitution. It does, however, take a different flight from substance to process: it flees certain substantive provisions of the Constitution in the sense that his two process-perfecting themes do not account for them and thus do not give meaningful effect to them. Some constitutional theorists have argued that Ely ignores or seeks to deny the Constitution's openly substantive provisions by construing those provisions so as to reduce them to procedural protections or to read them out of the Constitution. But some of the Constitution's provisions, such as its protection of religious freedom and private property, as well as its prohibition of slavery, evince substantive commitments that cannot be reduced to procedural protections.[60] These theorists, as it were, argue that Ely flees the *whole*, substantive Constitution for a *partial,* procedural Constitution. This criticism is basically sound, but misplaced.

My tack concerning Ely's flight from substantive constitutional provisions is different, for I seize the opportunity to criticize his theory on its own terms. I take seriously Ely's quest for the ultimate interpretivism, understanding it as a commitment to a constructivist method of constitutional interpretation. My argument is that Ely's interpretive method shows the need for a Constitution-perfecting theory, not merely a process-perfecting theory, to give meaningful effect to both the substantive and the procedural liberties embodied in our Constitution.

Ely's argument for his theory of judicial review from "the nature of the United States Constitution" is that his political theory of representative democracy better fits and justifies the constitutional document and underlying constitutional order than do substantive fundamental values theories.[61] He takes a "brisk tour" of the Constitution, arguing that it is "principally" concerned with establishing a procedural framework and protecting procedural liberties rather than securing substantive liberties.[62] Yet Ely admits that there are numerous manifestations of substantive values, as distinguished from procedural values, on the face of the Constitution that are not accounted for in his two process-perfecting themes. Indeed, on the evidence of his brisk tour, one might doubt whether he—supposedly the process theorist *par excellence*—is a process theorist in any strong sense.

For example, Ely acknowledges manifestations of substantive values, in addition to procedural values, in the First Amendment's protection of freedom of expression and freedom of religion.[63] These values include religious liberty, liberty of conscience, freedom of association, and autonomy. He also concedes an admixture of substantive and procedural values in the Third, Fourth, and Fifth Amendments—prohibiting, respectively, nonconsensual peacetime quartering of soldiers, unreasonable searches and seizures, and compulsory self-incrimination—such as privacy, repose, and independence.[64] His analysis of the Thirteenth Amendment's prohibition of involuntary servitude is more complicated, but basically seems to be an admission that it is concerned with securing the substantive value of independence or autonomy.[65]

Furthermore, Ely grants that the syntax of the open-ended Privileges or Immunities Clause of the Fourteenth Amendment and the Ninth Amendment "is most naturally that of substantive entitlement."[66] He also makes an *ejusdem generis* analysis—reasoning from the character of the rights listed to argue that those not listed are of the same character—stating that these provisions "seem to have been included in a 'we must have missed something here, so let's trust our successors to add what we missed' spirit."[67] Hence, his *ejusdem generis* analysis of these open-ended provisions as substantive would seem to entail construing them to justify protecting implicit substantive entitlements as well as implicit procedural entitlements.[68]

If one were questing for the ultimate interpretivism, and thus striving for reflective equilibrium between the constitutional document and the underlying political theory of the constitutional order, one should be disconcerted by the presence of so many disequilibrating substantive value anomalies or mistakes in the document that even Ely concedes are not reflected in the process-perfecting theory he has constructed.[69] These manifestations of substantive values on the face of the Constitution, in Ely's words, "call for more,"[70] that is, for further movement back and forth between document and theory toward reflective equilibrium between them, and thus for a more acceptable fit and a better justification.

To attain the ultimate interpretivism and reflective equilibrium, one must elaborate a theory that would construe these provisions of the document to vindicate their substantive values as well as their procedural values. Instead of moving beyond perfecting procedural liberties to securing substantive liberties, Ely basically lops off the document's substantive members in order to fit it into the narrow bed of his process-perfecting theory. If Ely achieves a close fit between the admittedly substantive and procedural Constitution and his merely process-perfecting theory, it is a fit in the manner of Procrustes, not Hercules. (Procrustes was a mythical Greek giant who stretched or shortened captives to make them fit his beds. Hercules is Dworkin's mythical philosopher-judge who, in order to decide hard cases, constructs a substantive political theory that best fits and justifies the Constitution as a whole.)

And so, Ely takes a flight from perfecting the whole Constitution to merely perfecting its processes. But his own interpretive method calls for more, a Constitution-perfecting theory that would protect both the substantive liberties and the procedural liberties embodied in our Constitution. In chapter 4, I outline such a theory in the form of a constitutional constructivism.

### The Ninth Amendment: Constitutional Jester

The Ninth Amendment provides: "The enumeration in the Constitution, of certain rights, shall not be construed to deny or disparage others retained by the people."[71] Ely refers to it as "that old constitutional jester" and observes that "[i]n sophisticated legal circles mentioning [it] is a surefire way to get a laugh."[72] For example, "What are you planning to rely on to support that argument, Lester, the Ninth Amendment?"[73] The joke supposedly was that a litigant who had no plausible constitutional arguments to support a claim might as a last resort invoke the "unenumerated" constitutional rights contemplated by the Ninth Amendment. Nonetheless, Ely takes it seriously, arguing that "the conclusion that the Ninth Amendment was intended to signal the existence of federal constitutional rights beyond those specifically enumerated in the Constitution is the only conclusion its language seems comfortably able to support."[74] In his quest for the ultimate interpretivism, Ely uses the open-ended Ninth Amendment to show that clause-bound interpretivism is impossible.[75] Ironically, his analysis likewise shows that his own process-perfecting interpretivism is incomplete.

Ely's interpretive approach, understood as a constructivist method, leads to a conception of the Ninth Amendment as a rule of construction for the Constitution as a whole. As Tribe puts it, "[T]he Ninth Amendment is a uniquely central text in any attempt to take seriously the process of *construing* the Constitution."[76] Indeed, it has come to play a supporting role, if not a leading one, in the work of courts and scholars in constructing the Constitution to protect rights not specifically enumerated, such as the right to privacy or autonomy.[77] The Ninth Amendment not only textually authorizes but indeed calls for deriving "unenumerated" constitutional rights that are implicit in the particular provisions of the constitutional document, the general themes of the Constitution as a whole, and the underlying constitutional order.[78] Because the Constitution as a whole includes manifestations of substantive liberties such as liberty of conscience, privacy, and autonomy as well as procedural liberties, a constructivist conception of the Ninth Amendment would derive implicit substantive liberties along with implicit procedural liberties.

Ely, as we have seen, acknowledges numerous manifestations of substantive liberties in the Constitution. Yet he argues that the Constitution as a whole embodies a political theory of representative democracy, which entails a process-perfecting theory of judicial review that does not account for, and so leaves out, those substantive liberties. Thus, he attempts to limit the Ninth Amendment to justify recognizing only implied procedural liberties. But again, the Ninth Amendment requires that responsible constitutional interpretation derive not only the procedural liberties but also the substantive liberties that are implicit in the constitutional document and the underlying constitutional order.

This constructivist conception of the Ninth Amendment accords with Justice Arthur Goldberg's interpretation of it in his concurring opinion in *Griswold v. Connecticut*.[79] Goldberg argued that to fail to protect a substantive fundamental right such as privacy—which is implicit in "fundamental principles of liberty and justice which lie at the base of all our civil and political institutions" and is "so rooted in the traditions and conscience of our people as to be ranked as fundamental"—simply because "that right is not guaranteed in so many words" by the Constitution is "to ignore the Ninth Amendment and to give it no effect whatsoever."[80] Failing to do so, he contended, would violate *Marbury*'s interpretive principle that "[i]t cannot be presumed that any clause in the constitution is intended to be without effect."[81] If, to recall Chief Justice John Marshall's hermeneutic principles in *McCulloch v. Maryland*—we must seek a "fair construction of the whole instrument" and "we must never forget that it is *a constitution* we are expounding"[82]—we must never forget to expound the Ninth Amendment so as to give it meaningful effect.[83]

Ironically, the Ninth Amendment indeed may play the role of the constitutional jester, but it is the jester as truth-teller in Shakespearean drama. Like the fool in *King Lear,* who is free to speak the truth notwithstanding the king's authority,[84] the Ninth Amendment scoffs at any presumption of the sovereign's omnipotence and omniscience in enumerating specific constitutional rights. It mocks the pretensions of all theories of constitutional interpretation that try to reduce constitutional rights to a closed, enumerated list (as clause-bound interpretivism or originalism does).[85] But it also scoffs at the presumptuousness of theories that attempt to prune constitutional provisions of their substantive character by recasting them as procedural protections (as Ely's theory does). Thus, the Ninth Amendment shows that the Constitution itself calls for moving beyond a process-perfecting theory to a Constitution-perfecting theory that would give meaningful effect to both the substantive liberties and the procedural liberties embodied in the Constitution.

## Ely's Process-Perfecting Interpretivism: Its Allure and Incompleteness

Ely concludes his critique of Justice Black's clause-bound interpretivism by stating that "[t]he point of all this is this": one cannot be a clause-bound interpretivist because several open-ended provisions of the Constitution show that the theory dispositively fails on its own terms.[86] Likewise, to conclude my parallel critique of Ely's theory, the point of all this is this: one cannot be an ultimate interpretivist and at the same time remain a *Carolene Products* process-perfecting representative democrat because certain substantive provisions of the Constitution call for going beyond *Carolene Products* to a Constitution-perfecting theory. In the end, Ely abandons his quest for the ultimate interpretivism, choosing instead a process-perfecting theory and therewith only the penultimate interpretivism.[87]

That abandonment, not a failure to do substantive political theory in the first place, is Ely's flight from substance to process. In a sense, he builds a flight from substantive liberties such as liberty of conscience, privacy, and autonomy into the very substance of his process-oriented political theory of representative democracy, since it does not include such liberties. In trying to avoid the specter of *Lochner,* Ely's theory flees substance for process by recasting certain substantive liberties of the Constitution as procedural protections of his theory or, worse yet, repealing their substantive aspects by construction.[88]

In another sense, Ely flees substance for process when he shifts from his first two, *interpretive* arguments for his process-perfecting theory to his third, *institutional* argument for it.[89] His first two arguments stem from his analysis of the nature of the Constitution as a whole, and the type of theory that would be consistent with and supportive of the underlying system, as being principally concerned with process rather than substance. His third argument is based on his assessment that because of the differences in institutional positions or perspectives between courts and legislatures, courts should perfect processes and legislatures should pursue substantive fundamental values. Thus, his distinction between process and substance turns from being a principle about *what* the Constitution, properly interpreted, means to a principle about *who* should interpret its meaning.[90] Ely's distinction becomes a principle of role differentiation between courts and legislatures.

When Ely turns from his two interpretive arguments to his institutional argument, he shifts, as it were, from theory of the Constitution to theory of judicial review. He then basically names as "the Constitution" those values that are judicially enforceable, that is, procedural values, rather than arguing for a conception of the Constitution outside the courts that would include substantive values along with procedural values. By contrast, my theory of constitutional constructivism distinguishes between the partial, judicially enforceable Constitution and the whole Constitution that is binding outside the courts on legislatures, executive officials, and citizens generally.[91]

In conclusion, Ely's process-perfecting interpretivism, notwithstanding its allure, is incomplete. His theory falls short of a Constitution-perfecting approach because it fails to give both substance and process their due.

## Interlude: A Thayer for Our Time?

In *Democracy and Distrust,* Ely seeks to justify the Warren Court's constitutional revolution on the basis of a *Carolene Products* jurisprudence.[92] Beyond the two process-perfecting themes of his framework, Ely's argument becomes reminiscent of James Bradley Thayer's classic argument for judicial deference to the representative process.[93] Thayer argues that politically elected officials are the primary makers of policy and that easy resort to judicial review deadens the citizenry's sense of political responsibility.[94] Thayer's argument, along with Justice Harlan's and Justice Holmes's dissents in *Lochner,*[95] served as a rallying cry for progressives during the conservative era of *Lochner.*[96] In a symposium assessing his book, Ely published *Another Such Victory: Constitutional Theory and Practice in a World Where Courts Are No Different from*

*Legislatures.*[97] His article implies that those who have argued that courts should impose substantive fundamental values rather than merely perfect processes have won the battle, but at too great a cost: namely, courts are now in theory and practice no different from legislatures.[98] Indeed, Ely's article reads like a veiled plea to be the Thayer for the next generation, the proponent of a theory of judicial review for progressive voices crying in the wilderness during the conservative era of the Rehnquist Court and now the Roberts Court. Ely himself makes a principled argument, but there may also be strategic arguments for joining him. In 1993, at the centennial of the publication of Thayer's classic argument, Sunstein made his own plea to be the Thayer for the next generation.[99] I now turn to Sunstein's theory.

## CHAPTER THREE

# Beyond Process-Perfecting Theories of Securing Deliberative Democracy

In *The Partial Constitution,* Cass Sunstein might seem to provide a Constitution-perfecting theory that moves beyond John Hart Ely's process-perfecting theory of *Democracy and Distrust.*[1] Sunstein aspires to avoid certain shortcomings of Ely's theory. He promises both to beware of the legacy of *Lochner* and to resist taking a flight from substance. In his introduction, he proclaims the Warren Court's constitutional revolution—which Ely sought to justify through a *Carolene Products* theory—to be over, along with the disputes that animated it. The most important contemporary disputes about the meaning of the Constitution, he argues, reflect disagreement about the meaning of the requirement that government be impartial or neutral: status quo neutrality versus deliberative democracy.[2]

Sunstein contends that what is wrong with *Lochner* is not, as Ely thought, that the Court gave heightened judicial protection to substantive fundamental values.[3] Rather, it is the Court's use of status quo neutrality and existing distributions as the baseline from which to distinguish unconstitutionally partisan political decisions from impartial ones.[4] Ironically, the implication of this interpretation is that certain contemporary justices, such as Scalia, who protest most adamantly against Lochnering (as protecting substantive fundamental rights) in fact engage most actively in it (as treating status quo neutrality as a baseline for constitutional interpretation).[5]

Furthermore, Sunstein claims to avoid Ely's putative flight from substance by clearly grounding his own constitutional theory in a substantive political theory of liberal republicanism or deliberative democracy.[6] His theory appears at once more liberal and more republican than Ely's.

Yet the structure of Sunstein's theory parallels that of Ely's *Carolene Products* theory, and his liberal republicanism leads to a theory of judicial review under which courts principally should secure the preconditions for deliberative democracy.[7] Although Sunstein moves somewhat beyond Ely's theory of reinforcing representative democracy, he falls short of offering a full Constitution-perfecting theory.

In this chapter I first outline Sunstein's theory along with his interpretation of what is wrong with *Lochner*. Second, I argue that Sunstein's liberal republicanism represents a flight from substance to process in the sense that it emphasizes "republican" deliberative democracy to the neglect of "liberal" deliberative autonomy (and such substantive liberties as liberty of conscience, privacy, and autonomy). Third, I illustrate this argument by criticizing Sunstein's analysis of *Bowers v. Hardwick*,[8] showing that Sunstein's theory, somewhat like Ely's, flees substantive due process and the preconditions for deliberative autonomy in favor of equal protection and the preconditions for deliberative democracy. (Even though *Lawrence v. Texas*[9] overruled *Bowers*, it remains worthwhile to critique Sunstein's analysis of *Bowers* because of what it reveals about the structure of his theory.) Finally, I suggest that, to the extent Sunstein's theory lacks a theme of securing the preconditions for deliberative autonomy, it is indeed, contrary to his hope, a theory of securing the *partial* Constitution.

## An Outline of Sunstein's Theory of Deliberative Democracy

*Sunstein's Political Theory of Deliberative Democracy*

Sunstein argues that the substantive political theory that best fits and justifies the Constitution is a theory of deliberative democracy or liberal republicanism.[10] This theory reflects a commitment to the "impartiality principle," which requires government to provide public-regarding reasons concerning the common good for its actions and forbids government from acting solely on the basis of the self-interest or "naked preferences" of private groups or individuals. In this sense, the Constitution is an impartial constitution, to be distinguished from a partial constitution of pure interest-group pluralism. It establishes "a republic of reasons," not a political market of naked preferences. Sunstein argues that this commitment to deliberative democracy, central to the founding, has been deepened by the Civil War Amendments and the New Deal.[11]

Deliberative democracy has four core commitments.[12] First, and most important, is a belief in political deliberation.[13] Political decisions should not simply reflect aggregations of the self-interested preferences of well-organized private groups or individuals. Nor should they consist merely of protections of status quo neutrality or "prepolitical" private rights. Instead, political decisions should be produced by an extended process of deliberation and discussion concerning the common good, in which new information and new perspectives are brought to bear, and the decisions should reflect public-regarding reasons. Moreover, politics should not simply implement existing preferences, as a market might; it should reflect on and sometimes transform such preferences in light of aspirations. Sunstein rejects any close analogy between consumers in a market and citizens in a polity, or between "consumer sovereignty" and the political sovereignty of We the People.

Second, the belief in political deliberation entails a commitment to citizenship and to widespread political participation by the citizenry.[14] It also requires that people have a large degree of security and independence from the will of others and from the state. For example, the commitment to citizenship implies a sphere of autonomy into which the state may not enter, such as that protected by the Fourth Amendment's prohibition on unreasonable searches and seizures. It further implies both property rights and social programs that attack poverty, such as the New Deal's "second Bill of Rights."[15] The Civil War Amendments deepened the original commitment to citizenship by abolishing involuntary servitude and casting doubt on "all efforts at political exclusion of identifiable groups on the basis of morally irrelevant characteristics," for example, race, sex, and sexual orientation.[16]

Third, deliberative democracy is committed to agreement as a regulative ideal for politics.[17] It seeks to reach agreement among equal citizens through deliberation concerning public-regarding reasons and the common good, not simply to register the different tastes or the different perspectives of disagreeable people.[18]

The final commitment is to political equality, which forbids not only disenfranchisement but also large disparities in political influence held by different social groups.[19] It presupposes freedom of speech and access to a good education. Political equality does not require economic equality, but it does entail (1) freedom from desperate conditions; (2) opposition to caste systems (e.g., racism, sexism, and heterosexism); and (3) rough equality of opportunity, including roughly equal educational opportunity.

*Sunstein's Theory of Judicial Review as Securing Deliberative Democracy*

This political theory of deliberative democracy, Sunstein argues, entails a theory of judicial review under which courts principally should secure the preconditions for deliberative democracy.[20] But he stresses that the judicially enforceable Constitution is not coextensive with the Constitution that is binding outside the courts on legislatures, executive officials, and citizens generally (unless and until they amend it).[21] Theory of the Constitution is broader than theory of judicial review. Accordingly, Sunstein sensibly and sensitively elaborates certain institutional limits on the role of courts in social reform.[22] For example, he argues that although deliberative democracy entails freedom from desperate conditions and imposes obligations on government to provide a minimum of goods and services to meet people's basic needs for subsistence, such obligations are not judicially enforceable in the absence of legislative or executive action.[23] Beyond securing judicially enforceable preconditions for deliberative democracy, Sunstein's argument becomes somewhat reminiscent of Thayer's plea for judicial deference to political decisions on the ground that easy resort to judicial review deadens the citizenry's sense of political responsibility.[24]

Nonetheless, Sunstein argues for an aggressive role for courts in two categories of cases. The first involves "rights that are central to the democratic process and whose abridgement is therefore unlikely to call up a political remedy."[25] Courts should protect the preconditions for political deliberation, political equality, and citizenship. The second involves "groups or interests that are unlikely to receive a fair hearing in the legislative process."[26] Courts should vindicate an anticaste principle of equal citizenship.

Sunstein acknowledges that these two categories of cases parallel the two themes of Ely's *Carolene Products* theory.[27] Furthermore, he observes that both his and Ely's theories of judicial review secure preconditions for democracy. But Sunstein argues that his conception of democracy—liberal republicanism—better fits and justifies the American system than does Ely's conception, which he characterizes as interest-group pluralism.[28] However, he overstates this contrast. As shown above, Ely's theory is one of qualified pluralism, and it is concerned with securing the "republican ideal of government in the interest of the whole people."[29] But there is no question that Sunstein's theory is a richer republican theory than Ely's. After all, Ely's theory derives from a political theory of qualified utilitarianism that ultimately seeks to aggregate individual preferences, whereas Sunstein's theory builds on anti-utilitarian liberal and republican political theories that emphasize respect for individual persons and for their capacity to deliberate about the common good.

### The Legacy of Lochner: Status Quo Neutrality versus Unenumerated Substantive Fundamental Rights

The best illustrations of the differences between Sunstein's and Ely's theories—at least with respect to the two categories of cases calling for an aggressive role for courts—are their approaches to *Buckley v. Valeo*[30] and *Roe v. Wade*.[31] I contrast their analyses of these cases in light of their different understandings of what is wrong with *Lochner:* status quo neutrality and unenumerated substantive fundamental rights, respectively.

In *Buckley,* the Court struck down certain campaign finance regulations imposing limitations on expenditures on the ground that "the concept that government may restrict the speech of some elements of our society in order to enhance the relative voice of others is wholly foreign to the First Amendment."[32] For Sunstein, *Buckley* is an incarnation of *Lochner* because it evinces status quo neutrality.[33] The Court treated the existing distribution of wealth and political power as a prepolitical state of nature or baseline, and therefore held that interfering with it is an impermissible, partisan objective.

Moreover, for Sunstein, *Buckley* stems from a flawed conception of democracy as a veritable marketplace of preferences rather than a republic of reasons. He draws on Rawls's analysis of *Buckley* and analogy between *Buckley* and *Lochner*.[34] As Rawls puts it:

> The First Amendment no more enjoins a system of representation according to influence effectively exerted in free political rivalry between unequals than the Fourteenth Amendment enjoins a system of liberty of contract and free competition between unequals in the economy, as the Court thought in the *Lochner* era.[35]

Thus, according to Sunstein and Rawls, what is wrong with *Buckley* is that the Court failed to see that such campaign finance regulations can be justified on the basis of a liberal republican commitment to securing political equality[36] or the fair value of the equal political liberties.[37] Cases like *Reynolds v. Sims*[38] and *Wesberry v. Sanders,*[39] in affirming the principle of one person, one vote, presuppose that the Constitution as a whole guarantees "a political procedure which secures for all citizens a full and equally effective voice in a fair scheme of representation."[40]

For Ely, by contrast, *Buckley* is unrelated to *Lochner* because it did not involve unenumerated substantive fundamental rights. Unlike Sunstein and Rawls, Ely conceives our system as being "programmed, at least roughly, to register the intensities of preference that utilitarianism makes crucial."[41] On his view, what is "questionable" about *Buckley* is that it allows money to distort the reflection of such intensities of preference and thus may thwart realization of Bentham's utilitarian principle of the equal weighting of preferences, namely, "each is to count for one, and none for more than one."[42] This principle itself is a principle of impartiality, Ely's alternative to status quo neutrality.[43] Thus, the differences between Ely's and Sunstein's analyses of *Buckley* stem from the differences between their utilitarian and liberal republican political theories.

For Ely, *Roe* is an incarnation of *Lochner* because it involved judicial protection of a substantive fundamental right drawn from beyond his *Carolene Products* jurisprudence.[44] Ely emphatically rejects substantive due process arguments for a right to abortion, whether framed in terms of liberty, privacy, or autonomy. But his classic critique also rejects the argument that women constitute a discrete and insular minority, and therefore he does not make an argument for a right to abortion based on equal protection or an anticaste principle.[45]

For Sunstein, by contrast, *Roe* is unrelated to *Lochner* because it did not evince status quo neutrality.[46] Sunstein, like Ely, rejects substantive due process arguments for a right to abortion, whether rooted in privacy, decisional autonomy, or bodily integrity.[47] But Sunstein, unlike Ely, argues for a right to abortion grounded in equal protection and an anticaste principle, contending that abortion restrictions turn a morally irrelevant characteristic, sex (like race), into a systemic source of social disadvantage. On his view, restrictive abortion laws are invalid because they are "an impermissibly selective co-optation of women's bodies," and they "turn women's reproductive capacities into something for the use and control of others."[48] Sunstein defends *Roe* and *Planned Parenthood v. Casey* as necessary to secure equal citizenship for women, indeed as tantamount to a *Brown v. Board of Education*[49] for women, not analogous to *Lochner* or *Dred Scott v. Sandford.*[50]

Thus, Sunstein's liberal republicanism cogently satisfies one line of criticism of Ely's theory by providing a more republican theory. However, it does not satisfy another line of criticism, for it does not offer a significantly more liberal theory than Ely's. My theory of constitutional constructivism, which I preview in my critique of Sunstein, answers both lines of criticism of Ely's theory and is more liberal than Sunstein's theory.

## Sunstein's Liberal Republicanism: A Flight from Substance?

*Beyond the False Antithesis of Liberalism and Republicanism*

There is a long-standing conflict in political and constitutional theory between the traditions of republicanism and liberalism. This conflict is encapsulated in Benjamin Constant's famous contrast between, respectively, the tradition associated with Jean-Jacques Rousseau, which gives primacy to the *liberties of the ancients,* such as the equal political liberties and the values of public life, and the tradition associated with John Locke, which gives greater weight to the *liberties of the moderns,* such as liberty of conscience, certain basic rights of the person and of property, and the rule of law.[51] Despite arguments that liberalism triumphed over republicanism at the founding,[52] the conflict has resurfaced periodically in various guises throughout our constitutional history by way of attempts to recover the civic aspirations of the republican tradition and to critique the individualist presuppositions of the liberal tradition.[53]

Some political philosophers, including Rawls, and some constitutional theorists, most prominently Sunstein and Frank Michelman, have sought to break the stranglehold of this false antithesis.[54] Sunstein proposes to move beyond the revival of classical republicanism, and beyond the clash between certain versions of liberalism and republicanism, to a synthesis he calls "liberal republicanism."[55] He also claims that his synthesis would resolve other familiar tensions in political and constitutional theory, for example, between constitutionalism and democracy and between understandings of liberty and equality.[56]

Does Sunstein's liberal republicanism represent an adequate synthesis of these traditions and liberties? Or does it instead take a flight from substance to process—namely, from the substantive liberties of the moderns to the procedural liberties of the ancients? First, I defend Sunstein's synthesis against Richard A. Epstein's version of the charge, arising from the standpoint of classical liberalism, that he flees substance for process.[57] Second, I critique Sunstein's synthesis from the standpoint of Rawls's resolution, political constructivism or political liberalism. I charge Sunstein with taking a different, problematic flight from substance to process.

### *Epstein's Antithesis: Status Quo Neutrality over Deliberative Democracy*

Epstein argues that Sunstein's liberal republicanism represents an indefensible flight from substance. He contends that "[n]o political theory can concentrate on process and deliberation to the exclusion of substantive concerns," yet Sunstein's theory tries to do precisely that.[58] At first glance, Epstein's critique of Sunstein looks like familiar critiques of Ely for taking a flight from substance to process.[59] On careful examination, however, it proves to be quite different, amounting to nothing more than an emphatic argument that the antithesis between liberalism and republicanism is real, and that in this clash classical liberalism should totally vanquish republicanism. In Sunstein's terms, Epstein basically argues that status quo neutrality should prevail over and constrain deliberative democracy.

What is Sunstein's supposed flight from substance? Epstein contends that Sunstein flees the substance of both republicanism and liberalism. First, he argues that Sunstein embraces the procedural and deliberative elements of classical republicanism while fleeing its substantive components—for example, by disavowing its militarist, elitist, sexist, racist, and religious sentiments.[60] As a result, he suggests, Sunstein's theory is selective, seductive, and incoherent. But traditions of political and constitutional theory are not all-or-nothing packages of ideas that one must accept or reject as a whole, and there is hardly anything more commonplace in the history of ideas than attempting to synthesize elements of more than one tradition while rejecting other elements.[61] Sunstein's flight from objectionable substantive components of classical republicanism does not render his project incoherent or doomed to fail.

Second, Epstein contends that Sunstein flees the substantive concerns of classical liberalism and thereby fails to respond to the major challenge of modern constitutional law: "the development of a substantive theory which demarcates the zone of collective legislative control from the zone of entrenched individual rights."[62] Epstein himself answers this challenge with a putatively Lockean theory of limited governmental powers and entrenched individual rights.[63] That is, he defends a strong version of precisely the sort of liberalism that is said fundamentally to oppose republicanism. Epstein would flee from the deliberation and process of Sunstein's liberal republicanism to the substance of classical liberalism. He would constrain deliberative democracy with a "natural" or "prepolitical" conception of status quo neutrality of the very sort that Sunstein is at pains to throw off.

Thus, unlike Rawls and Sunstein, who perceive the clash between liberalism and republicanism as a false opposition to be transcended through a synthesis, Epstein perceives that clash as a real opposition to be resolved through a total victory of classical liberalism over republicanism. But to charge, as Epstein does, that Sunstein's liberal republicanism flees from certain substantive concerns of classical liberalism is to comprehend that Sunstein rejects substantive political theories such as Epstein's and aims to synthesize liberalism and republicanism in the aftermath of the New Deal and the rise of the welfare state. That charge does not derail Sunstein's project.

There is nothing objectionable in Sunstein's rejection of Epstein's substantive political theory. We should flee the substance of Epstein's theory, with its scheme of limited governmental powers over the economy and its zone of entrenched economic liberties, for it would unduly constrain deliberative democracy and would fail to fit and justify much of our constitutional practice. Sunstein's theory gives adequate protection to property and liberty of contract; there is neither need nor good argument for aggressive judicial protection of such economic liberties in our constitutional order.[64] Epstein's theory is the very incarnation of status quo neutrality; indeed, it is *Lochner*'s revenge on constitutional theory since *West Coast Hotel v. Parrish* and the New Deal repudiated it.[65]

### A Rawlsian Synthesis: Deliberative Autonomy along with Deliberative Democracy

Sunstein's liberal republicanism does, however, take a different, objectionable flight from substance—namely, a flight from judicial protection of such substantive liberties as liberty of conscience, freedom of association, privacy, and autonomy, which I unify around a theme of securing deliberative autonomy. A constitutional theory grounded in Rawls's resolution of the conflict between liberalism and republicanism would not take a flight from process to substance that would unduly constrict the procedural liberties of the ancients (as Epstein does). Nor would it take a flight from substance to process that would not fully account for the substantive liberties of the moderns (as Sunstein does).

Like Sunstein's theory, Rawls addresses the impasse thrown up by the conflict between the traditions of the liberties of the ancients and the liberties of the moderns, and between understandings of equality and liberty. Rawls tries to dispel that conflict and to reconcile equality and liberty by combining the liberties of both traditions into a single coherent scheme of equal basic liberties that is grounded on a conception of citizens as free and equal persons.[66]

In chapter 4 I outline my proposed synthesis, a constitutional constructivism, by analogy to Rawls's political constructivism. For now, the main idea to note is that constitutional constructivism has two fundamental themes that correspond roughly to the liberties of the ancients and the liberties of the moderns, respectively. First, a republican theme secures the preconditions for *deliberative democracy,* to enable citizens to apply their capacity for a conception of justice to deliberations about and judgments regarding the justice of basic institutions and social policies as well as the common good. Second, a liberal theme secures the preconditions for *deliberative autonomy,* to enable citizens to apply their capacity for a conception of the good to deliberations about and decisions regarding how to live their own lives. Together, these two themes afford everyone the common and guaranteed status of free and equal citizenship in our constitutional democracy.[67]

To put the idea schematically, each tradition in the synthesis of republicanism and liberalism has a principal theme. Furthermore, the two themes correspond to aspects of self-government: political self-government and personal self-government (or self-determination), respectively. While this formulation may seem overly dualistic insofar as it may appear to deny that democracy and autonomy are complementary aspects of one unified vision, it has the virtue of emphasizing that an adequate unified account requires two themes.[68]

Constitutional constructivism's first theme, securing deliberative democracy, protects such basic rights as the equal political liberties and freedom of thought. Its second theme, securing deliberative autonomy, protects such basic rights as liberty of conscience and freedom of association, including decisional autonomy, privacy, and freedom of intimate association.

Here I merely mention familiar understandings of deliberative autonomy; in chapter 5 I elaborate them. As Justice Kennedy's opinion of the Court in *Lawrence v. Texas* explained: "[L]iberty presumes an autonomy of self that includes freedom of thought, belief, expression, and certain intimate conduct."[69] *Lawrence* evoked the joint opinion in *Casey,* which spoke of a woman's liberty at stake in the decision whether to have an abortion as

> involving the most intimate and personal choices a person may make in a lifetime, choices central to personal dignity and autonomy. . . . At the heart of liberty is the right to define one's own concept of existence, of meaning, of the universe, and of the mystery of human life. Beliefs about these matters could not define the attributes of personhood were they formed under compulsion of the State.[70]

Similarly, Justice Stevens wrote in dissent in *Bowers* that the Court's "privacy" decisions had been animated by fundamental concerns for "the individual's right to make certain unusually important decisions that will affect his own, or his family's, destiny" and "the abiding interest in individual liberty that makes certain state intrusions on the citizen's right to decide how he will live his own life intolerable."[71] As he put it in concurrence in *Casey:* "Decisional autonomy must limit the State's power to inject into a woman's most personal *deliberations* its own views of what is best because a woman's decision to terminate her pregnancy is nothing less than a matter of conscience."[72] All of these formulations evince deliberative autonomy.

## Sunstein's Synthesis: Deliberative Democracy to the Neglect of Deliberative Autonomy

Sunstein likens his synthesis, liberal republicanism, to Rawls's theory.[73] Moreover, he claims that his theory of deliberative democracy is entirely compatible with the liberal theories of constitutional democracy defended by John Stuart Mill and Rawls.[74] Sunstein's principal theme of securing the preconditions for deliberative democracy is indeed largely compatible with constructivism's first theme.[75] But his theory lacks a principal theme of securing the preconditions for deliberative autonomy corresponding to constructivism's second theme. Indeed, he is remarkably silent concerning certain substantive liberties such as liberty of conscience, privacy, autonomy, and freedom of association. To the extent that Sunstein addresses them, he tries conclusorily (and unconvincingly) to recast them as preconditions for deliberative democracy. Constitutional constructivism better fits and justifies these substantive liberties—which are manifested on the face of our constitutional document and implicit in our underlying constitutional order—than does Sunstein's theory.

For example, in his presentation of the four core commitments of deliberative democracy, Sunstein makes no reference whatever to liberty of conscience or religious liberty.[76] To be sure, in *Beyond the Republican Revival,* he states that "liberty of expression and conscience and the right to vote . . . are the basic preconditions for republican deliberation," citing Rawls.[77] But he does not justify this conclusory statement, nor does he elaborate the relationship between liberty of conscience and republican deliberation.

Sunstein explains that the exclusion of religion from politics is a precondition for republican deliberation in an "ironic sense": "[R]emoval of religion from the political agenda protects republican politics by ensuring against stalemate and factionalism."[78] Here Sunstein analyzes religious liberty in terms of a "gag rule" to remove divisive, factional issues from the political agenda so that republican deliberation can go on.[79] He does not treat religious liberty and liberty of conscience as shields to protect citizens against oppressive republican deliberators wielding coercive political power in enforcing the republic's collective judgments concerning the good. Hence, he recognizes the potential divisiveness of protecting religious liberty, which results in citizens' holding divergent conceptions of the good, but he ignores the potential oppressiveness of not protecting it.[80]

Sunstein's liberal republican theory also gives remarkably little attention to principles of liberty, privacy, or autonomy that have been vindicated through substantive due process cases from *Meyer v. Nebraska* and *Pierce v. Society of Sisters* to the present. In *Meyer,* the Court struck down a statute forbidding the teaching of a modern language other than English to elementary school children as an infringement of parents' right to direct the education of their children. The Court wrote: "[T]he ideas touching the relation between individual and state [in ancient Sparta and Plato's ideal commonwealth, which 'submerge the individual and develop ideal citizens'] were wholly different from those upon which our institutions rest."[81] In *Pierce,* which invalidated a statute requiring parents to send their children to public schools on the ground that it violated parents' right to direct the upbringing and education of their children, the Court wrote: "The fundamental theory upon which all governments in this Union repose excludes any general power of the state to standardize its children by forcing them to accept instruction from public teachers only. The child is not the mere creature of the state."[82]

These landmark cases, however controversial, reflect fundamental principles of our underlying constitutional order. Any constitutional theory, to be persuasive, must account for them and for the principles that they embody. Yet Sunstein does not consider whether these cases from the *Lochner* era, not to mention their progeny—including *Griswold v. Connecticut*,[83] *Loving v. Virginia*,[84] *Roe v. Wade*,[85] *Moore v. East Cleveland*,[86] *Planned Parenthood v. Casey*,[87] and subsequently *Lawrence v. Texas*[88]—evince status quo neutrality or, to the contrary, stem from an alternative baseline in liberty.[89] Jed Rubenfeld argues persuasively that such cases reflect the latter, an antitotalitarian principle of privacy: they are concerned with the danger of "creeping totalitarianism, an unarmed *occupation* of individuals' lives."[90]

In constitutional constructivism, a similar antitotalitarian principle of liberty, privacy, or autonomy is intertwined with an anticaste principle of equality like Sunstein's. Moreover, all these cases are justifiable on the basis of a constructivist principle of deliberative autonomy, or a conception of liberty and personhood, that constrains the republic's enforcement of its collective judgments concerning the good. Instead of developing an antitotalitarian principle of liberty as a precondition for deliberative autonomy, Sunstein neglects cases like *Meyer, Pierce,* and *Moore,* and justifies cases like *Loving, Roe,* and *Casey* on the basis of an anticaste principle of equality as a precondition for deliberative democracy. And he attempts to justify *Griswold* and *Lawrence* by recasting them from the ground of autonomy to the ground of desuetude—striking down old morals laws forbidding use of contraceptives and certain sexual conduct on the ground that there are reasons to doubt that there is contemporary democratic support for them.[91] Such use of desuetude, he argues, will enable democratic deliberation to proceed.

In his presentation of the four core commitments of deliberative democracy, Sunstein refers to autonomy only once, mentioning "a sphere of autonomy into which the state may not enter" that is created by the Fourth Amendment's prohibition of unreasonable searches and seizures.[92] Clearly, he is referring to "spatial privacy" as distinguished from "decisional privacy" or decisional autonomy (though cases such as *Lawrence* involve "liberty of the person both in its spatial and more transcendent dimensions [concerned with 'autonomy of self'])."[93] Furthermore, Sunstein is critical of both doctrinal strands on which the joint opinion in *Casey* relied in reaffirming the right of a woman to decide whether to have an abortion—namely, decisional autonomy and bodily integrity. He instead would base that right on equal protection grounds.[94]

Despite his neglect of liberty of conscience, privacy, and autonomy, Sunstein does state that "no democracy should impose on citizens a particular or unitary conception of what their lives ought to be like."[95] His theory, however, does not provide or entail any limits on deliberative democracy to protect citizens against the republic's doing just that and thus encroaching on deliberative autonomy. He claims that the rights that are preconditions for deliberative democracy impose constraints on collective judgments, adding that "other rights fundamental to individual autonomy or welfare—such as consensual intimate sexual activity—ought generally to be off-limits to government."[96] Yet he offers this statement almost as a throwaway line. He does not articulate any reason why such activity should be off limits to government, for example, because this sort of individual autonomy or welfare is a precondition for deliberative autonomy or even for deliberative democracy.

At this point in his argument, Sunstein conclusorily states that "the notions of autonomy and welfare would be defined by reference to the ideal of free and equal persons acting as citizens in setting up the terms of democratic life," echoing Rawls's idea that basic liberties are grounded on a conception of citizens as free and equal persons.[97] Prior to this point, though, Sunstein had not grounded his theory of deliberative democracy on such a conception of the person, nor does he proceed at this juncture to develop this sort of a conception. But Sunstein's reference to Rawls's theory suggests what is needed in his own theory: a theme of securing deliberative autonomy that, together with his theme of securing deliberative democracy, is grounded on a conception of citizens as free and equal persons. The former theme would protect citizens' pursuit of their divergent conceptions of the good from coercive political power, even that of a well-functioning deliberative democracy. The constitutional constructivism that I outline in chapter 4 includes these two themes and is based on such a conception of citizens as free and equal persons.

In sum, Sunstein's elaboration of the preconditions for deliberative democracy includes several references to substantive liberties of the

moderns such as religious liberty, liberty of conscience, freedom of intimate association, and autonomy. But he does not elaborate the role or
significance of these liberties in relation to securing the preconditions for
deliberative democracy, much less develop a principal theme of securing
the preconditions for deliberative autonomy. Nor does he adequately
ground either deliberative democracy or deliberative autonomy on a
conception of citizens as free and equal persons.

The architecture of Sunstein's theory in *The Partial Constitution* forces
or leads him to recast, as preconditions for deliberative democracy, certain substantive liberties that are better understood as preconditions for
deliberative autonomy. Worse yet, his theory ignores such liberties. In this
sense, Sunstein's liberal republicanism, somewhat like Ely's qualified
utilitarianism, represents a flight from giving effect to substantive liberties
to perfecting processes.

## Sunstein's Flight from Substantive Due Process to Equal Protection

Bowers: *Analogous to* West Coast Hotel *or to* Lochner?

To illustrate what is at stake in Sunstein's emphasis on deliberative
democracy to the neglect of deliberative autonomy, I explore his conception of the relationship between due process and equal protection in
general, and how that understanding shapes his analysis of *Bowers
v. Hardwick* in particular.[98] (Fortunately, *Lawrence v. Texas*[99] overruled
*Bowers,* but Sunstein's analysis of *Bowers* clearly expresses certain features of his theory that still warrant scrutiny.) My critique of Sunstein's
theory in this respect shows that a theme of securing deliberative autonomy, along with a theme of securing deliberative democracy, is necessary
to secure the basic liberties essential to free and equal citizenship
for everyone in our constitutional democracy. Sunstein, like Ely, flees
substantive due process for equal protection.

In *Bowers,* the Supreme Court held that the Due Process Clause of
the Fourteenth Amendment does not protect "a fundamental right to engage in homosexual sodomy."[100] Writing for the Court, Justice White
acknowledged that many cases have interpreted that clause to protect
not only procedural rights but also substantive rights that "have little or
no textual support in the constitutional language," including substantive

rights to heterosexual intimate association.[101] But White expressed wari-
ness, fearing that the ghost of *Lochner* was incarnate in those decisions.[102]
The opinion stated that heightened judicial protection under the Due
Process Clause had been limited to those fundamental rights that are, in
*Palko*'s formulation, "implicit in the concept of ordered liberty,"[103] or, in
*Moore*'s formulation, "deeply rooted in this Nation's history and tradi-
tion."[104] Although White said that these two formulations were different
descriptions, he treated them as if they were the same.

Understanding substantive due process as basically confined to protecting traditions conceived as *historical practices,* White's opinion rudely
concluded that the claim that the Due Process Clause protects a fundamental right of homosexuals to engage in acts of consensual sodomy "is,
at best, facetious."[105] The opinion ignored the fact that the claim instead
was being made in all earnestness on the basis of an understanding of
substantive due process as extending to protecting traditions and a
scheme of ordered liberty conceived as *aspirational principles* that are
critical of our historical practices. (Below, I sketch this contrast between
two basic understandings of what a tradition is and of what due process
requires.) What is more, White's opinion ignored that Hardwick was not
asking the Court to recognize a "new" right, but rather was asking the
Court to apply its precedents protecting heterosexual intimate association
to protecting analogous homosexual intimate association.

*Bowers* was and remains an emblematic, defining case.[106] Some
decried it as marking a second death of substantive due process, at any
rate as a principled doctrine of constitutional law applicable to all citizens.[107] Others, including Justice Scalia in *Michael H. v. Gerald D.* and
Judge Bork in *The Tempting of America,* celebrated it as signaling a
restoration of legitimacy in constitutional law.[108] Both reactions suggest
an analogy between *Bowers* and the watershed case of *West Coast Hotel v.
Parrish,*[109] which officially repudiated the era of *Lochner.* But *Bowers,*
unlike *West Coast Hotel,* did not overrule substantive due process precedents. Rather, it refused to extend those precedents from protecting
heterosexual intimate association to protecting homosexual intimate
association.[110]

Sunstein's analysis, however, suggests that *Bowers,* far from signaling the
end of Lochnering, is analogous to *Lochner* itself and indeed to *Plessy v.
Ferguson.*[111] Like those egregious precedents, *Bowers* evinced status quo
neutrality concerning long-standing historical practices. The Court simply
pointed to historical practices, common law, and statutes condemning

sodomy (whether heterosexual or homosexual) to justify refusing to recognize the asserted right to homosexual intimate association.[112] Similarly, in *Plessy,* the Court refused to invalidate a statute enacted "with reference to the established usages, customs, and traditions of the people."[113] Sunstein argues that the Due Process Clause is backward-looking—grounded in a principle of status quo neutrality that operates largely as a baseline for protecting historical practices against ill-considered or short-term departures.[114] From that standpoint, he suggests that the decision in *Bowers* as a matter of due process is not altogether surprising, even if it is unprincipled in relation to precedents protecting heterosexual intimate association.[115] For due process on his view does not reflect an aspirational principle that is critical of historical practices.

By contrast, Sunstein contends, the Equal Protection Clause is forward-looking: it is grounded in a principle of equality that operates largely as a baseline for criticizing historical practices that deny equality, protecting against such practices however long-standing and deeply rooted. Equal protection is largely an anticaste principle, criticizing historical practices that manifest second-class citizenship, whether founded on racism, sexism, or heterosexism.[116] From that standpoint, laws of the sort upheld in *Bowers* on due process grounds nevertheless should be struck down on equal protection grounds.[117] For equal protection on his view does reflect an aspirational principle. Sunstein puts forward this conception of the relationship between due process and equal protection, not simply as a litigation strategy in the aftermath of *Bowers* or as a strategy of damage control in trying to protect our basic liberties while Justice Scalia sits, but as a general constitutional theory. It may have some merit as such strategies, but it should be rejected as such a theory.[118]

## The Relationship between Due Process and Equal Protection

Thus, Sunstein, like Ely, eschews substantive due process in favor of equal protection as a ground for deriving basic liberties implicit in deliberative democracy and representative democracy, respectively. Instead, Sunstein emphasizes an anticaste principle of equality, Ely a conception of equal concern and respect.[119] In order to explicate Sunstein's flight from substantive due process and deliberative autonomy, I examine three conceptions of the relationship between due process and equal protection, or liberty and equality: those illustrated by Ronald Dworkin, Scalia, and Sunstein.

### DWORKIN: FREE AND EQUAL CITIZENS

First, one might argue that due process and equal protection in large part overlap and are intertwined. Dworkin, for example, contends that the Constitution embodies an abstract conception of justice, "a political ideal . . . of a society of citizens both equal and free."[120] On his view, both equality and liberty are comprehensive principles: the Constitution requires both that government treat everyone with equal concern and respect and that it not infringe their most basic liberties, those liberties essential to a scheme of "ordered liberty," to use Justice Cardozo's famous formulation in *Palko*.[121]

And so, Dworkin continues, "particular constitutional rights that follow from the best interpretation of the Equal Protection Clause, for example, will very likely also follow from the best interpretation of the Due Process Clause."[122] As Chief Justice Warren put it in *Bolling v. Sharpe:* "[T]he concepts of equal protection and due process, both stemming from our American ideal of *fairness,* are not mutually exclusive."[123]

Thus, Dworkin, like Justice Stevens, justifies *Roe* and *Casey* on grounds of equal concern and respect as well as of liberty of conscience and decisional autonomy.[124] Furthermore, he criticizes *Bowers* not only on the ground that it fails to accord equal concern and respect to homosexuals, but also on the ground that it denies them liberty of conscience and decisional autonomy.[125]

Hence, for Dworkin, both due process and equal protection stem from principles of justice that provide alternative baselines to status quo neutrality. They provide overlapping and intertwined bases for criticizing historical practices that fail to realize our ideals, or aspirational principles, of liberty and equality.

### JUSTICE SCALIA: DESTRUCTION AND SALVATION

Second, one might argue that due process and equal protection, instead of overlapping, in large part perform separate functions. Both Justice Scalia and Sunstein, from different perspectives, advance versions of this conception. Scalia's *Michael H.* jurisprudence held that the Due Process Clause ensures procedural due process and, to the extent that it includes substantive restrictions, prohibits only deprivations of "substantive" rights "historically and traditionally protected against State interference"[126] and conceived at a highly specific level of generality.[127] If the Court uses the Due Process Clause to try to protect the citizenry from "irrationality and oppression," he warned, "it will destroy itself."[128] After all, the ghost of *Lochner* lurks. By contrast, Scalia declaimed, "Our salvation is the Equal Protection Clause, which requires the democratic majority to accept for themselves and their loved ones what they impose on you and me."[129]

For example, Scalia argued that *Roe* and *Casey* are the *Lochner* and the *Dred Scott* of our time.[130] For in all of these cases the Court protected "unenumerated" substantive rights. He contended, on the other hand, that *Bowers* signaled a restoration of legitimacy in constitutional law.[131] For there the Court declined to recognize an "unenumerated" substantive right that had not been historically protected by statutes or common law.

Therefore, for Scalia, neither the Due Process Clause nor the Equal Protection Clause offers a baseline beyond status quo neutrality for criticizing historical practices. Due process requires status quo neutrality and grows out of a Burkean deposit of historical practices.[132] Equal protection requires neutrality in the sense of generality, and reflects a Thayerian[133] or Frankfurterian[134] faith in salvation through democratic processes rather than a ready resort to judicial review.

Two caveats regarding Scalia's theory are in order. First, it is very likely that Scalia, for his own part, would limit due process to procedural due process and overrule the whole line of substantive due process cases. At present, however, he does not have the votes on the Court to bring about that result. His *Michael H.* gloss on substantive due process as tradition understood as historical practices, and his argument for conceiving rights at a highly specific rather than abstract level of generality, would narrow the analysis of *Bowers* even further. *Michael H.* was his effort to engage in damage control: to limit the reach of the substantive due process cases as narrowly as he could and to deprive them of critical force or generative power.

Second, the salvation that Scalia contemplated through the Equal Protection Clause is not heightened judicial protection for fundamental rights or from prejudice against discrete and insular minorities, under either the fundamental rights or the suspect classifications strand of equal protection analysis. It is merely the political safeguard that requires neutrality, even in the context of classifications based on race.[135]

Hence, for Scalia, due process is not an antitotalitarian principle of liberty or a principle of deliberative autonomy, nor is equal protection an anticaste principle. Equal protection is merely a principle of neutrality.

## SUNSTEIN: JANUS

Like Scalia, Sunstein argues that due process and equal protection in large part operate along different tracks and serve different purposes. But according to his analysis, the Fourteenth Amendment, like Janus, has two faces looking in opposite directions. The Due Process Clause is backward-looking and largely evinces status quo neutrality as a baseline. The Equal Protection Clause, by contrast, is forward-looking and centrally embodies an anticaste principle of equal citizenship as a baseline. Thus, Sunstein's Due Process Clause looks backward somewhat like Scalia's, and his Equal Protection Clause looks forward somewhat like Dworkin's. For example, Sunstein justifies *Roe* and *Casey* on the ground of an anticaste principle of equality, but not on the ground of an antitotalitarian principle of liberty or a principle of deliberative autonomy. Likewise, he criticizes *Bowers* primarily on the former ground (in subsequent work he criticizes *Bowers* on the ground of desuetude).[136]

Sunstein's account of the relationship between due process and equal protection has two fundamental problems. First, it gives insufficient attention to the possibility that the Due Process Clause might reflect an antitotalitarian principle of liberty that would serve as a baseline for criticizing historical practices that deny deliberative autonomy, much as the Equal Protection Clause expresses an anticaste principle of equality that provides a baseline for criticizing historical practices that deny equal citizenship.

Second, Sunstein ignores or downplays that equal protection alone, without a substantive conception of citizens as free and equal persons from which to derive fundamental rights or fundamental interests, may not be a sufficient ground for securing even equal citizenship, let alone free citizenship. Without such a conception, Sunstein cannot satisfactorily answer the question "Equality with respect to what?" Ely's theory of equal protection needs to be complemented by a principle like deliberative autonomy to accomplish all that he claims for it with respect to discrimination on the basis of race and sexual orientation.[137] Similarly, Sunstein's anticaste principle of equality must be supplemented with an explicit principle like deliberative autonomy to support all that he attempts to derive from it, for it inevitably smuggles in such a principle.[138] Sunstein's theory in this sense takes flight from substantive due process and deliberative autonomy to equal protection and deliberative democracy. Constitutional constructivism more comfortably grounds such basic liberties on both liberty and equality, and on a conception of citizens as free and equal persons.

In some respects, Sunstein's theory may be more appealing as a strategy of damage control than it is as a general constitutional theory. Scalia, from the right, is trying to control the damage caused by expansive substantive due process holdings—such as those in *Griswold, Roe, Casey,* and *Lawrence*—by narrowly confining the due process inquiry. Perhaps Sunstein, from the left, is trying to control the damage brought about by narrow substantive due process opinions—such as that in *Bowers*—by resorting to equal protection arguments. The upshot of Sunstein's analysis is that he all but cedes the Due Process Clause and liberty, as a ground for basic liberties, to Scalia. *Lawrence,* which overruled *Bowers* and held that the liberty protected by the Due Process Clause included the right to autonomy or freedom of intimate association for homosexuals,[139] suggested that Sunstein's strategy is imprudent and unnecessary. Moreover, *Lawrence* substantiated the conception of liberty and equality as overlapping, as against Sunstein's Janus-faced conception, by richly intertwining concern for homosexuals' liberty with concern for not "demean[ing] their existence" and status as equal citizens.[140] In any event, such efforts at damage control may not work, because just as the Rehnquist Court tried to read status quo neutrality—rather than an antitotalitarian principle of liberty or a principle of deliberative autonomy—into the Due Process Clause, it attempted to read racial neutrality—rather than an anticaste principle of equality—into the Equal Protection Clause.[141] We may expect much the same from the Roberts Court.

### Sunstein's Janus-Faced Fourteenth Amendment

Sunstein's backward-looking conception of due process concedes too much to the *Bowers* formulation of the due process inquiry or, worse still, to Scalia's formulation of it in *Michael H.* Sunstein basically goes along with Scalia in his flight from aspirational principles to historical practices. But substantive due process and liberty are better understood as furthering aspirational principles, not merely as safeguarding backward-looking historical practices. The Rehnquist Court and now the Roberts Court may well be Burkean, but our Constitution and our constitutional democracy are not.

Ironically, Sunstein's analysis of due process as backward-looking and evincing status quo neutrality carries forward the legacy of *Lochner.* Yet our due process precedents such as *Meyer, Pierce, Bolling, Griswold, Loving, Roe, Casey,* and *Lawrence* repudiated status quo neutrality in favor of a normative baseline rooted in an aspirational principle of liberty. These cases vindicated an antitotalitarian principle of liberty or a principle of deliberative autonomy. Such landmark precedents pose serious problems for Sunstein's general conception of due process as backward-looking. Indeed, he concedes that there is "some" aspirational element to due process and that there is nothing about the Due Process Clause itself that compels a reading of it as backward-looking.[142]

To recapitulate, Sunstein's Janus-faced conception of the relationship between due process and equal protection allows substantive due process and liberty to do too little of the necessary work in grounding basic liberties; equal protection and equality, however, are unreasonably expected to do too much. But equal protection and equality alone, to the exclusion of substantive due process and liberty, need not, cannot, and should not do all of the work in grounding basic liberties essential to free and equal citizenship for everyone in our constitutional democracy.

My more general contention is that the architecture of Sunstein's theory of deliberative democracy forces or leads him to recast issues of liberty and equality as issues of equality alone, and to recast preconditions for deliberative autonomy as preconditions for deliberative democracy or, worse yet, to leave them out entirely. Sunstein's Janus-faced conception of the relationship between due process and equal protection is mirrored in the architecture of his general theory: It unwittingly reflects the false antithesis between the liberties of the moderns and the liberties of the ancients, despite all his attempts at synthesis.

Constitutional constructivism instead combines due process and equal protection, liberty and equality, the liberties of the moderns and the liberties of the ancients, and liberalism and republicanism into a coherent scheme of equal basic liberties with two themes: securing the preconditions for deliberative autonomy as well as those of deliberative democracy. Together, these two themes secure aspects of the justice that is due free and equal citizens within our constitutional democracy. As Chief Justice Warren put it in *Bolling:* "[T]he concepts of equal protection and due process, both stemming from our American ideal of *fairness,* are not mutually exclusive."[143] Constitutional constructivism combines both in a conception of justice as fairness.

Constitutional constructivism grounds basic liberties in a conception of citizens as free and equal persons or, in Dworkin's terms, "a political ideal . . . of a society of citizens both equal and free."[144] From that standpoint, *Bowers* was wrongly decided not only because it ignored an anticaste principle of equality and thus failed to secure the preconditions for deliberative democracy, as Sunstein argues. It also was wrongly decided because it applied a stunted conception of liberty of conscience and freedom of intimate association and thus failed to secure the preconditions for deliberative autonomy that are essential to our scheme of ordered liberty. Appropriately, *Lawrence* overruled *Bowers* on the basis of the principle of deliberative autonomy—that "[l]iberty presumes an autonomy of self that includes freedom of thought, belief, expression, and certain intimate conduct."[145]

Put another way, within constitutional constructivism, if the Fourteenth Amendment is indeed Janus-faced, perhaps the Equal Protection Clause is an entrance, a gate that opens the polity to everyone with respect to deliberative democracy, whereas the Due Process Clause serves as an exit, one that allows persons "to be let alone" from the polity with respect to deliberative autonomy.[146] Constitutional constructivism, unlike Sunstein's theory, does not take a flight from substantive due process to equal protection, or from deliberative autonomy to deliberative democracy.

## Sunstein's Partial Constitution

The title of Sunstein's book, *The Partial Constitution,* is richly ambiguous in ways that he largely leaves implicit.[147] I focus on two senses of his title. Sunstein's theory of judicial review as principally securing preconditions for deliberative democracy proves, contrary to his intention, to secure the *partial* Constitution—as compared with both the *whole* Constitution and the *impartial* Constitution.

First, one might speak of the *partial* Constitution as distinguished from the *whole* Constitution—for example, the partial, judicially enforceable Constitution as contrasted with the whole Constitution that is binding outside the courts on legislatures, executive officials, and citizens generally (unless and until they amend it). Sunstein intends his theory of judicial review to be a theory of the partial Constitution in this sense.

Constitutional constructivism's theory of judicial review is likewise partial in this respect.

But Sunstein's theory is partial rather than whole in another sense that he does not intend. It does not fully account for important aspects of our constitutional document and underlying constitutional order that are concerned with protecting substantive liberties such as liberty of conscience, freedom of association, and decisional autonomy. From the standpoint of constitutional constructivism, Sunstein's theory of securing deliberative democracy to the neglect of securing deliberative autonomy is partial rather than whole in this sense.

Second, one might distinguish between the *partial* Constitution and the *impartial* Constitution—for example, between the partial, self-interested marketplace of preferences and the impartial, public-regarding republic of reasons. Sunstein intends his theory to be a theory of the impartial Constitution in this sense. Constitutional constructivism is similarly impartial in this respect.

But Sunstein's theory is partial rather than impartial in another, unintended sense. It does not adequately secure preconditions for deliberative autonomy that constrain the government's enforcement of collective judgments concerning the good. Constitutional constructivism's theme of securing deliberative autonomy requires the government to be impartial with respect to citizens' pursuit of their divergent conceptions of the good in a certain sense. That is, it more fully prevents the government from imposing comprehensive religious, philosophical, or moral conceptions of the good, which are outside the limits of public reason, and thus it more fully secures toleration of citizens' pursuit of their divergent conceptions of the good. From the standpoint of constitutional constructivism, Sunstein's theory of securing deliberative democracy to the neglect of securing deliberative autonomy is not sufficiently impartial in this respect.

I now turn to my argument that constitutional constructivism is a fuller theory of perfecting the whole, impartial Constitution than is Sunstein's theory. Its theme of securing deliberative democracy requires that political decisions be justifiable on the basis of public-regarding reasons. And its theme of securing deliberative autonomy aspires to ensure that such decisions are justifiable on grounds of public reasons.

# An Outline for a Constitution-Perfecting Theory of Securing Constitutional Democracy

To move beyond process-perfecting theories to a Constitution-perfecting theory, I outline a constitutional constructivism by analogy to John Rawls's political constructivism, a theory he developed in *Political Liberalism*.[1] I mean "constitutional constructivism" in both a methodological sense, as a way to interpret our Constitution, and a substantive sense, by which I mean the substantive political theory that best fits and justifies our constitutional document and underlying constitutional order. Constitutional constructivism is, however, a theory of perfecting the Constitution and securing the preconditions for constitutional democracy through constructing *our* substantive Constitution. It is distinguished from a theory of constructing *a perfectly just* constitution unmoored by the constraints of our constitutional text, history, and structure, or of our tradition, practice, and culture.

Constitutional constructivism entails a theory of judicial review with two fundamental themes: first, securing the preconditions for deliberative democracy, and second, securing the preconditions for deliberative autonomy, in order to afford everyone the common and guaranteed status of free and equal citizenship in our constitutional democracy. Such a theory flees neither substantive political theory nor substantive constitutional provisions. The first theme, deliberative democracy, closely resembles Cass Sunstein's principal theme of securing deliberative democracy (which itself draws on Rawls's theory). The second theme, deliberative autonomy, secures substantive liberties such as liberty of conscience, freedom of association, privacy, and autonomy, which John

Hart Ely's and Sunstein's theories flee or recast as preconditions for representative or deliberative democracy. Constitutional constructivism does for substance and process what Ely's and Sunstein's theories have done for process.[2]

In this chapter I put forward an outline for a constitutional constructivism and argue that such a theory resists the temptations to take flights from substantive liberties like those taken by Ely's and Sunstein's theories. Indeed, I suggest that constitutional constructivism better satisfies Ely's criteria for an acceptable theory than does his own theory, and that it offers a better synthesis of the traditions of liberalism and republicanism than does Sunstein's liberal republicanism. Finally, I defend constitutional constructivism against charges that it represents a boundless flight to substance beyond the Constitution, or that it is the very incarnation of the specter of *Lochner*.

## An Outline for a Constitutional Constructivism

### Political and Constitutional Constructivism

In *Political Liberalism,* Rawls reformulates his well-known theory— justice as fairness—as a political constructivism.[3] What is a political constructivism? How might it provide a framework for a constitutional constructivism?

Rawls's political constructivism seeks to construct a shared basis of reasonable political agreement in a morally pluralistic constitutional democracy such as our own, or to construct principles of justice that provide fair terms of social cooperation on the basis of mutual respect and trust among free and equal citizens.[4] He distinguishes his project from theories of moral realism and natural law, which seek to discover principles of justice that are true to a prior and independent order of moral values binding for all times and all places.[5] Rawls seeks to construct the principles of justice that are "most reasonable for us," given our conceptions of the person and society and our principles of practical reason.[6] "[W]hat," he asks, "is the most appropriate conception of justice for specifying the fair terms of social cooperation between citizens regarded as free and equal, and as fully cooperating members of society over a complete life, from one generation to the next?"[7] Rawls conceives justification in political philosophy not as a search for truth and objectivity from the point of view of the universe, but as a quest for reflective equilibrium between our considered judgments and underlying principles of justice.[8]

Now, what is a constitutional constructivism? By way of an answer, I first propose a general methodological sense of constructivism, illustrated by Ronald Dworkin's conception of constitutional interpretation as constructing schemes of principles that best fit and justify our constitutional document and underlying constitutional order as a whole.[9] Dworkin originally put forth this conception by analogy to Rawls's conception of justification in political philosophy as a quest for reflective equilibrium between our considered judgments and underlying principles of justice. Dworkin argues, by analogy, that constitutional interpretation proceeds back and forth between extant legal materials and underlying principles toward reflective equilibrium between them.[10] Constitutional constructivism embraces a methodological constructivism that is similar, though not identical, to Dworkin's.[11]

Second, I propose a specific substantive sense of constructivism, exemplified by Rawls's conception of the equal basic liberties in a constitutional democracy such as our own as being grounded on a conception of citizens as free and equal persons, together with a conception of society as a fair system of social cooperation. As shown below, constitutional constructivism employs a substantive constructivism that is analogous, though not identical, to Rawls's.

In chapter 2 I previewed constructivism in the methodological sense, arguing that Ely's interpretive method, understood as a quest for the ultimate interpretivism, has affinities to Dworkin's constructivist conception of constitutional interpretation and Rawls's notion of reflective equilibrium. I contended that Ely's interpretive method shows the need for a Constitution-perfecting theory, like a constructivism in the substantive sense, to better fit and justify the constitutional document and underlying constitutional order as a whole than does his own process-perfecting theory, which does not account for certain substantive liberties.

In chapter 3 I previewed constructivism in the substantive sense, pointing out that Sunstein's liberal republicanism has affinities to Rawls's political constructivism. But it lacks a theme of securing the preconditions for deliberative autonomy. Constitutional constructivism combines this theme with a theme of securing the preconditions for deliberative democracy (much like that of Sunstein's theory). For that reason, I suggested, it better fits and justifies our constitutional document and underlying constitutional order as a whole than does his theory.

In this chapter I more fully present constitutional constructivism. It is important to clarify two things at the outset. First, this theory does not entail that everything Rawls argues is required by justice is also, for that reason, mandated by our Constitution. Nor do I rely on Rawls as an authority for what the Constitution means. Second, one need not be persuaded to adopt Rawls's political constructivism in order to embrace constitutional constructivism, which only uses Rawls's guiding framework of equal basic liberties to help orient our deliberations, reflections, and judgments about our Constitution and constitutional democracy. To explain that framework, I must put forth several abstract conceptions from Rawls's theory.

## The Constitution of Political Liberalism

Aristotle remarked that a common understanding of justice makes a *polis*.[12] Similarly, Rawls says that a shared conception of justice as fairness makes a constitutional democracy.[13] Aristotle, however, conceived such a common understanding as being based on a single conception of the good—that is, a single comprehensive religious, philosophical, or moral doctrine concerning what is valuable in human life.[14] By contrast, Rawls argues that, at least since the Wars of Religion in the sixteenth and seventeenth centuries and the Protestant Reformation, a shared basis of reasonable political agreement in a morally pluralistic constitutional democracy such as our own cannot be grounded on a single conception of the good without intolerable state oppression. Instead, such a shared basis can be grounded only on an overlapping consensus concerning a political conception of justice.[15]

### POLITICAL CONCEPTION OF JUSTICE

Rawls offers justice as fairness as an example of a political liberalism or a political conception of justice, as distinguished from a comprehensive religious, philosophical, or moral conception of the good.[16] First, political liberalism accepts "the fact of reasonable pluralism"—the fact that a diversity of reasonable yet conflicting and irreconcilable comprehensive religious, philosophical, and moral doctrines may be affirmed by citizens in the free exercise of their capacity for a conception of the good—as a feature of the political culture of a constitutional democracy not to be regretted and not soon to pass away.[17] Second, political liberalism emphasizes the related "fact of oppression"—the fact that a single comprehensive religious, philosophical, or moral doctrine could be established as a shared basis of political agreement or public justification in a constitutional democracy only through the intolerably oppressive use of coercive political power—as an entailment of accepting the fact of reasonable pluralism.[18] Political liberalism generalizes the principle of religious toleration to apply to reasonable conceptions of the good.[19]

Despite these two related facts, Rawls argues that citizens in a constitutional democracy who hold opposing and irreconcilable conceptions of the good—comprehensive religious, philosophical, or moral doctrines, for example—may be able to find a shared basis of reasonable political agreement or public justification through an overlapping consensus concerning a political conception of justice. This sort of consensus would obtain where different persons, from the standpoint of their own divergent conceptions of the good, affirmed a shared political conception of justice.[20] Such a conception, with the following scheme of basic liberties embodied in a constitution, would provide fair terms of social cooperation on the basis of mutual respect and trust that citizens might reasonably be expected to endorse, whatever their particular conceptions of the good. It would have priority over and would constrain the polity's pursuit of conceptions of the public good and its imposition of perfectionist values.[21] This is what is meant by the common notion that the right, or justice, is prior to and constrains the good.[22]

## THE TWO PRINCIPLES OF JUSTICE

Rawls presents justice as fairness as an illustration of a political conception of justice that might provide a shared basis of reasonable political agreement in a constitutional democracy such as our own. It has two principles of justice:

1. Each person has an equal claim to a fully adequate scheme of equal basic rights and liberties, which scheme is compatible with the same scheme for all; and in this scheme the equal political liberties, and only those liberties, are to be guaranteed their fair value.
2. Social and economic inequalities are to satisfy two conditions: first, they are to be attached to positions and offices open to all under conditions of fair equality of opportunity; and second, they are to be to the greatest benefit of the least advantaged members of society [the "difference principle"].[23]

The equal basic rights and liberties of the first principle of justice are specified by a list as follows: "freedom of thought and liberty of conscience; the political liberties and freedom of association, as well as the freedoms specified by the liberty and integrity of the person; and finally, the rights and liberties covered by the rule of law."[24] This list is drawn up from both historical and theoretical analysis. It includes the basic liberties that the constitutions of successful constitutional democracies, such as our Constitution, historically have protected. It also includes the basic liberties that such systems analytically presuppose as necessary for the development and exercise of the two moral powers of citizens, conceived as free and equal persons, in the two fundamental cases to be explained below.[25]

Again, within Rawls's political constructivism these equal basic liberties are not conceived as prepolitical or given by a prior and independent order of moral values, as in theories of moral realism, natural law, or natural rights. Rather, they are conceived as those that are "most reasonable for us,"[26] and are worked up from the way citizens are regarded in the public political culture of a constitutional democracy, in the basic political texts (for example, the Constitution and the Declaration of Independence), and in the tradition and practice of the interpretation of those texts.[27] Thus, political constructivism does not attempt to impose claims to philosophical truth on an unwilling people.[28] Instead, it is an "interpretative theory" drawn from the ongoing political practice of a constitutional democracy.[29]

Rawls envisions an ideal four-stage sequence for incorporating the two principles of justice into the basic institutions and social policies of a constitutional democracy: the original position and the constitutional, legislative, and judicial stages.[30] At the constitutional stage, two kinds of constitutional essentials are embodied in the constitution: the general structure of government and the political process, and the equal basic liberties of the first principle of justice.[31] The latter constitutional essentials include the equal basic liberties listed above; due process of law and equal protection of the laws; and rights and liberties protecting the security and independence of citizens, such as freedom of movement and free choice of occupation, the right to hold and have exclusive use of personal property, and a guaranteed provision of a social minimum of goods and services to meet the basic needs of all citizens.[32]

But the second principle of justice, including the principle of fair equality of opportunity and the difference principle, is not among the constitutional essentials in a constitutional democracy, and it is not incorporated in the constitution.[33] "Indeed," Rawls observes, "the history of successful constitutions suggests that principles to regulate economic and social inequalities, and other distributive principles, are generally not suitable as constitutional restrictions."[34] The history to which Rawls refers includes the era of *Lochner.*[35] Instead, it is only at the legislative stage that the second principle of justice, to the extent that it is accepted by the citizenry, is incorporated into legislation.

Constitutional democracy is in a general way "dualist": it distinguishes the constituent power of We the People from the ordinary power of officers of government and, accordingly, distinguishes the higher law of We the People from the ordinary law of legislative bodies.[36] At the judicial stage, courts may serve as one of the institutional devices to protect the higher law of the constitution against encroachments by the ordinary law of legislation.[37]

## CONCEPTION OF CITIZENS AS FREE AND EQUAL PERSONS: THE TWO MORAL POWERS

Constitutional constructivism, like Rawls's political liberalism, understands our basic liberties to be grounded on a conception of citizens as free and equal persons, together with a conception of society as a fair system of social cooperation.[38] It views those persons who engage in such cooperation as having *two moral powers.* The first is *the capacity for a sense of justice*—the capacity to understand, apply, and act from (and not merely in accordance with) the political conception of justice that characterizes the fair terms of social cooperation in a constitutional democracy. Citizens apply this capacity in deliberating about and judging the justice of basic institutions and social policies, as well as the common good.[39]

The second moral power is *the capacity for a conception of the good*— the capacity to form, revise, and rationally pursue a conception of the good, individually and in association with others, over the course of a complete life. A conception of the good is a conception of what is valuable in human life. It typically consists of ends and aims derived from religious, philosophical, or moral doctrines, as well as attachments to other persons and loyalties to various groups and associations. Citizens apply this capacity, their power of deliberative reason, in deciding how to live their own lives.[40]

The basic idea is that by virtue of their two moral powers persons are free and that their having these powers makes them equal. Possession of the two moral powers constitutes the basis of the status of free and equal citizenship.[41] The basic liberties are understood as preconditions for the development and exercise of the two moral powers.[42] It is important to comprehend that this conception of the person as free and equal, and as having the two moral powers, is a normative, political conception of the person as a citizen in a constitutional democracy; it is not a biological or psychological conception of the human being as such.[43]

DELIBERATIVE DEMOCRACY AND DELIBERATIVE AUTONOMY:
THE TWO FUNDAMENTAL CASES

Constitutional constructivism arranges our basic liberties so as to show their relation to the *two fundamental cases* in which citizens exercise their two moral powers. The first fundamental case is that of *deliberative democracy:* the equal political liberties and freedom of thought enable citizens to develop and exercise their first moral power (their capacity for a sense of justice) in understanding, applying, and acting from their conception of justice in deliberating about and judging the justice of basic institutions and social policies as well as the common good.[44] In the first instance, the Constitution is understood to establish a just and workable political procedure without imposing any explicit constitutional restrictions on legislative outcomes.[45] It incorporates the equal political liberties and seeks to guarantee their fair value so that the processes of political decision will be open to all on a roughly equal basis.[46] It also protects freedom of thought (including freedom of speech and press, freedom of assembly, and the like) so that the exercise of those liberties in those processes will be free and informed.[47]

The second fundamental case is that of *deliberative autonomy:* liberty of conscience and freedom of association enable citizens to develop and exercise their second moral power (their capacity for a conception of the good) in forming, revising, and rationally pursuing their conceptions of the good, individually and in association with others, over the course of a complete life—that is, to apply their power of deliberative reason in deciding how to live their own lives.[48] In the second instance, the Constitution is seen as establishing constitutional restrictions on the grounds for political decisions.[49] It protects liberty of conscience and freedom of association both to secure citizens' free exercise of deliberative autonomy and to ensure that political decisions will not be justifiable solely on the basis of comprehensive religious, philosophical, or moral conceptions of the good.[50]

Finally, constitutional constructivism connects the remaining (and supporting) basic liberties to the two fundamental cases by noting that it is necessary to secure them in order properly to guarantee the preceding basic liberties associated with deliberative democracy and deliberative autonomy. These liberties include "the liberty and integrity of the person (violated, for example, by slavery and serfdom, and by the denial of freedom of movement and occupation) and the rights and liberties covered by the rule of law."[51] The constitutional essentials also include due process of law, equal protection of the laws, the right to personal property, and the right to basic necessities. In other words, guarantees of these remaining and supporting basic liberties and constitutional essentials are preconditions for securing both deliberative democracy and deliberative autonomy.

Possession of this whole family of basic liberties constitutes the common and guaranteed status of free and equal citizenship.[52] Moreover, the preconditions for both deliberative democracy and deliberative autonomy are preconditions for the sovereignty of free and equal citizens.[53]

*Constitutional Constructivism: A Guiding Framework for Securing Deliberative Democracy and Deliberative Autonomy*

Constitutional constructivism, as we have seen, builds on the architecture of Rawls's political constructivism. Rawls states that although his political conception of justice "is not to be regarded as a method of answering the jurist's questions," it may provide "a guiding framework, which if jurists find it convincing, may orient their reflections, complement their knowledge, and assist their judgment."[54] He also states that it is "a guiding framework of deliberation and reflection" concerning constitutional essentials.[55] In putting forth a constitutional constructivism, I use the guiding framework because it suggests certain interpretive strategies to help orient our deliberations, reflections, and judgments about our Constitution and constitutional democracy.[56] The usefulness of the framework should be assessed by applying the ordinary criteria for an acceptable theory of constitutional interpretation and judicial review.[57]

WHAT, HOW, AND WHO?

In general, constitutional constructivism is a conception of *what* the Constitution is, *how* it ought to be interpreted, and *who* may authoritatively interpret it.[58] First, as for *what,* constitutional constructivism conceives our Constitution as a "constitution of principle," which embodies (or aspires to embody) a coherent scheme of equal basic liberties, or fair terms of social cooperation on the basis of mutual respect and trust, for our constitutional democracy. The Constitution is not merely a "constitution of detail" that enacts a discrete list of particular rights narrowly conceived by framers and ratifiers.[59] Nor does it simply establish a procedural framework for democracy. Furthermore, constitutional constructivism views interpreting the Constitution as specifying basic liberties in terms of the significance of an asserted liberty for the development and exercise of one (or both) of the two moral powers in one (or both) of the two fundamental cases.

Second, regarding *how,* constitutional constructivism conceives interpretation as the exercise of "reasoned judgment"[60] in quest of the interpretation that best fits and justifies the constitutional document and underlying constitutional order.[61] Responsible interpretation is not a quest for a formula or bright-line rule. Neither is it merely exegesis of isolated clauses of the constitutional document or research into the concrete intentions or expectations of the framers and ratifiers. In short, the theory is committed to a methodological constructivism.

Finally, with respect to *who* may interpret, constitutional constructivism holds that although the Supreme Court generally is the final (but not the exclusive) institutional interpreter in any given case, We the People are the ultimate interpreters of the Constitution.[62] Furthermore, it distinguishes between the partial, judicially enforceable Constitution and the whole Constitution that is binding outside the courts on legislatures, executive officials, and citizens generally in our constitutional democracy (unless and until they amend it).[63] As Rawls puts it, the Supreme Court is an "exemplar of public reason" in a forum of principle. But it is not the exclusive voice of such reason, nor is it the sole forum of principle: "While the Court is special in this respect, the other branches of government can certainly, if they would but do so, be forums of principle along with it in debating constitutional questions."[64] In other words, constitutional constructivism is a theory of the Constitution, not merely a theory of judicial review. Certain constitutional norms, including aspects of deliberative democracy and deliberative autonomy, may be judicially underenforced because of the institutional limits of courts, and left to the political processes for fuller enforcement. For example, the Constitution might impose affirmative obligations on the legislative and executive branches to provide basic necessities for all citizens, but it might not afford a judicially enforceable right to these necessities in the absence of legislative or executive measures.[65]

## THE TWO FUNDAMENTAL CASES OR THEMES OF DELIBERATIVE
## DEMOCRACY AND DELIBERATIVE AUTONOMY

Constitutional constructivism entails a theory of judicial review with an active role for courts with respect to the two fundamental cases or corresponding themes: securing the basic liberties that are preconditions for *deliberative democracy,* and securing the basic liberties that are preconditions for *deliberative autonomy.* Both themes are necessary to afford everyone the common and guaranteed status of free and equal citizenship in our constitutional democracy. Courts should exercise stringent review to strike down political decisions that do not respect the two types of basic liberties because both are preconditions for the trustworthiness of such decisions. The remaining and supporting basic liberties, as stated above, also must be guaranteed in order to secure these preconditions.

Constitutional constructivism's first theme emphasizes the equal political liberties and freedom of thought. It resembles Sunstein's principal theme of securing deliberative democracy and, to a lesser extent, Ely's dominant commitment to reinforcing representative democracy. It seeks to secure the preconditions for political self-government, conceiving our political system as a public facility for deliberation concerning the common good, not a veritable political market for aggregation of self-interested preferences.[66] This theme aims to ensure that political decisions will be impartial in the sense that they are justifiable on the basis of public-regarding reasons (common good), not merely the self-interested preferences of private groups or individuals. Also, it forbids political decisions that violate the constraints of impartiality by denying equal citizenship on the basis of such morally irrelevant characteristics as race, sex, or sexual orientation.[67]

I have previewed this first theme, along with its central notion of securing political equality and the fair value of the equal political liberties, in presenting Sunstein's theory of securing deliberative democracy. The equal political liberties are *primus inter pares,* first among the equal basic liberties. Constitutional constructivism in this respect parallels the doctrine of "preferred freedoms" outlined in footnote four of *United States v. Carolene Products Co.*[68] and elaborated in Ely's theory, not to mention Sunstein's. It also incorporates their two *Carolene Products* categories of cases warranting stricter judicial scrutiny, that is, to keep the political processes open and to prevent the corruption of the political processes through prejudice against discrete and insular minorities. Finally, it largely accepts Sunstein's insightful analysis of the legacy of *Lochner* and is wary of status quo neutrality—without further justification—as a baseline for judging the justice of basic institutions and social policies and as a constraint on deliberative democracy.

Constitutional constructivism's second theme is underwritten by liberty of conscience and freedom of association. It articulates and unifies the concerns for substantive liberties that process-perfecting theories such as those of Sunstein and Ely recast or neglect: liberty of conscience, freedom of intimate association, decisional autonomy, decisional privacy, spatial privacy, bodily integrity, and an antitotalitarian principle of liberty. It seeks to secure these preconditions for personal self-government or for deliberation and decision by citizens—individually and in association with others—about how to lead their own lives. Moreover, at least where constitutional essentials and matters of basic justice are at stake, this theme aspires to assure that political decisions will be impartial in the sense that they are justifiable on the basis of public reasons (common ground)—on grounds that citizens generally can reasonably be expected to accept, whatever their particular conceptions of the good, because they come within an overlapping consensus concerning a political conception of justice.[69] These constitutional restrictions must be honored if free and equal citizens are to engage in social cooperation on the basis of mutual respect and trust in a constitutional democracy such as our own, which is characterized by the fact of reasonable pluralism and which recognizes the related fact of oppression. Constitutional constructivism conceives our polity to be subject to the limits of public reason, rather than free to make collective judgments founded solely on comprehensive religious, moral, or philosophical conceptions of the good.[70]

I have previewed this second theme in criticizing Sunstein's theory for emphasizing deliberative democracy to the neglect of deliberative autonomy. I also have shown, through critiquing his analysis of *Bowers,* that constitutional constructivism, unlike Sunstein's theory, applies both substantive due process and equal protection as bases for securing the status of free and equal citizenship for everyone. It embraces conceptions like decisional autonomy, decisional privacy, spatial privacy, and freedom of intimate association as aspects of deliberative autonomy, not merely an anticaste principle of equal citizenship as an aspect of deliberative democracy.[71] The architecture of constitutional constructivism, unlike that of Sunstein's theory, would not force or lead it to recast such basic liberties, better understood as preconditions for deliberative autonomy, as preconditions for deliberative democracy or to disregard them entirely.

Constitutional constructivism accords priority to the whole family of equal basic liberties over the pursuit of conceptions of the public good or the imposition of perfectionist values.[72] This understanding of priority entails that it may be permissible to regulate certain basic liberties for the sake of securing other basic liberties or the whole family of such liberties. No single basic liberty by itself is absolute.[73] For example, *Buckley* was wrongly decided with respect to limitations on campaign expenditures, among other reasons, because the Court failed to see the Constitution as a whole. Therefore, it failed to see that freedom of political expression may be regulated (though not restricted) through campaign finance laws in order to try to assure political equality, or the fair value of the equal political liberties, for equal citizens in a fair scheme of representation.[74] The Court's single-minded focus on the First Amendment without regard to such preconditions for deliberative democracy blinded it to that compelling governmental objective.

Constitutional constructivism bears a certain similarity to Alexander Meiklejohn's well-known view concerning the overriding value of self-government and political freedom.[75] But it gives the kind of primacy that Meiklejohn gives to political liberties instead to the family of political and personal liberties as a whole[76] and thus seeks to secure both deliberative democracy and deliberative autonomy. It aspires to be a theory of self-government in both a political and a personal sense.

## CONSTITUTIONAL DEMOCRACY AND TRUSTWORTHINESS

I have shown that constitutional constructivism is concerned with securing preconditions for processes of deliberation and decision with respect to both deliberative democracy and deliberative autonomy. By virtue of these concerns, it is a theory of constitutional democracy and trustworthiness, an alternative to Ely's theory of representative democracy and distrust. I mean trustworthiness in the sense of Rawls's remark: "By publicly affirming the basic liberties citizens . . . express their mutual respect for one another as reasonable and trustworthy, as well as their recognition of the worth all citizens attach to their way of life."[77] Each of constitutional constructivism's two themes seeks to secure a type of precondition for the trustworthiness of political decisions in our constitutional democracy. To be trustworthy, a constitutional democracy must secure and respect a scheme of basic liberties that guarantees not only the preconditions for deliberative democracy, but also the preconditions for deliberative autonomy. Ely's and Sunstein's process-perfecting theories secure only the former type of precondition for trust or impartiality. Hence constitutional constructivism is a fuller theory of perfecting the trustworthy and impartial Constitution than are Ely's and Sunstein's process-perfecting theories.

I elsewhere develop the implications of my theory for the project of taking the Constitution seriously outside the courts—that is, by legislatures, executive officials, and citizens generally. I do so by grappling with arguments for popular constitutionalism like those in Mark Tushnet's book *Taking the Constitution Away from the Courts.*[78] Tushnet argues against judicial supremacy in constitutional interpretation and advances the best arguments to date for the proposition that the Constitution is self-enforcing through the political processes rather than through judicial review. I show, however, that Tushnet does not establish that taking the Constitution seriously outside the courts requires, in his terms, "taking the Constitution *away from* the courts." Rather, I contend, it requires taking the Constitution *to* legislatures, executives, and citizens generally in order that its principles and aspirations might better frame and guide their decisions. My approach, like Ely's, calls for (1) judicial enforcement of constitutional norms in situations where the political processes are systematically untrustworthy, but for (2) enforcement of constitutional norms outside the courts in situations where the political processes are systematically trustworthy. Unlike Ely, again, I argue that the former situations include restriction and regulation of basic liberties that are preconditions for deliberative autonomy as well as deliberative democracy. The latter situations include enforcement of commitments to federalism, states' rights, and separation of powers as well as commitments to property rights and economic liberties.

## The Theoretical Architecture of Constitutional Constructivism

*The Value of the Apparatus of the Guiding Framework*

It may be asked why I stress using the apparatus of the guiding framework with two fundamental themes. I do so because the guiding framework underscores that the basic liberties associated with the second theme of deliberative autonomy, like those related to the first theme of deliberative democracy, have a "structural role to play" in securing and fostering our constitutional democracy.[79] Together, their structural roles are to secure the preconditions for deliberative self-governance in both political and personal senses. The guiding framework helps keep in view that the basic liberties that are preconditions for deliberative autonomy are rooted in the language and design of our constitutional document and underlying constitutional order, not usurpations by illegitimate philosopher-judges who roam beyond process or narrowly conceived original understanding.[80]

The guiding framework also demonstrates that constitutional constructivism's conception of citizens (with two moral powers) is writ large in its conception of our Constitution (with two fundamental themes). Here I mean to echo Plato's idea that the constitution of individuals is writ large in the constitution of a state.[81] Constitutional constructivism presents our Constitution as embodying (or aspiring to embody) a coherent scheme of basic liberties fit for use by free and equal citizens, rather than as enacting an antique list appropriate for ancestor worship.[82] And it frames questions of constitutional interpretation in terms of the significance of an asserted liberty for such citizens' application of their two moral powers in the two fundamental cases that arise in our constitutional scheme.

Finally, by putting these two fundamental themes of deliberative democracy and deliberative autonomy side by side as reflecting two bedrock structures, the guiding framework invites us to inquire whether homologies exist between these structures (and between the doctrines of constitutional law that they undergird).[83] As Charles Black might put it, rubbing these two stones together may generate some illuminating sparks.[84] In chapter 6, I use the guiding framework to suggest such homologies and thus to bring a sense of order and discipline to deliberative autonomy.

*Constitutional Constructivism Is Dualist*

Constitutional constructivism embraces both deliberative autonomy and deliberative democracy as integral to our scheme of government because it conceives that scheme as "dualist" in three ways. Many claims that rights of autonomy are anomalies or mere add-ons[85] stem from impoverished views of our scheme as a "monist" or majoritarian representative democracy. Constitutional constructivism provides a richer and better account, normatively and historically, of our constitutional tradition, practice, and culture than do such views.

First, constitutional constructivism is dualist in the general sense that it distinguishes between the constituent power of We the People, expressed in the higher law of the Constitution, and the ordinary power of officers of government, expressed in the ordinary law of legislative bodies.[86] Moreover, it reconstructs the classical, dualist justification of judicial review: to preserve the fundamental rights ordained and established by the higher law of the Constitution against encroachments by ordinary law.[87] Thus, it rejects monist views of our scheme, which emphasize popular sovereignty and majoritarianism over and against fundamental rights, and therefore tend to equate popular sovereignty with the British model of parliamentary sovereignty.[88]

Second, constitutional constructivism is dualist in the substantive sense that it conceives the content of the higher law of the Constitution as a synthesis of the conflicting traditions of civic republicanism and liberalism. As noted in chapter 3, this conflict is encapsulated in Benjamin Constant's famous contrast between the tradition associated with Jean-Jacques Rousseau, which gives primacy to the *liberties of the ancients,* such as the equal political liberties and the values of public life, and the tradition associated with John Locke, which gives greater weight to the *liberties of the moderns,* such as liberty of conscience, certain basic rights of the person and of property, and the rule of law.[89] The conflict has appeared throughout our history in attempts to recover the civic aspirations of the republican tradition and to critique the individualist presuppositions of the liberal tradition. Constitutional constructivism seeks to resolve this conflict by combining a "republican" theme of securing the preconditions for deliberative democracy (or the liberties of the ancients) with a "liberal" theme of securing the preconditions for deliberative autonomy (or the liberties of the moderns).

Third, constitutional constructivism is dualist in yet another substantive sense: it understands our scheme of government as a hybrid of the competing traditions of constitutionalism and democracy, or a constitutional democracy. In their purest forms, constitutionalism is concerned with limited government and democracy with unfettered majority rule.[90] Democracy gives primacy to open political processes, while constitutionalism insists that limits exist on what government may do. The tradition of constitutionalism was sounded, for example, in the landmark cases of *Calder v. Bull,* where Justice Chase contended that the Constitution includes "certain vital principles in our free republican governments, which will determine and overrule an apparent and flagrant abuse of legislative power,"[91] and *Corfield v. Coryell,* where Justice Washington proclaimed that the Constitution embraces "those privileges and immunities which are fundamental; which belong, of right, to the citizens of all free governments."[92]

Constitutional constructivism melds these competing traditions into a conception of constitutional democracy, rejecting the understanding of our system as a majoritarian representative democracy. A constitutional democracy is a system in which a constitution imposes limits on the content of legislation: to be valid, a law must be consistent with fundamental rights and liberties embodied in the constitution. A majoritarian representative democracy, by contrast, is a system in which there are no constitutional limits on the content of legislation: whatever a majority enacts is law, provided the appropriate procedural preconditions are met.[93] Thus, a constitutional democracy combines the democratic notion that "the people should govern through those whom they elect" with the constitutionalist idea that "there are critical limitations on what government—however democratically chosen—may validly do and on how it may carry out its legitimate powers."[94] And so, within a scheme of constitutional democracy, constitutional limitations such as the basic liberties associated with deliberative autonomy are indeed "countermajoritarian" but they are not for that reason anomalous or "deviant."[95]

Thus, constitutional constructivism, with its two themes of deliberative democracy and deliberative autonomy, synthesizes our traditions and practices of higher law and ordinary law, civic republicanism and liberalism, and democracy and constitutionalism in a conception of dualist constitutional democracy. That conception better fits and justifies our constitutional scheme than do views of the scheme as a monist or majoritarian representative democracy.

*Is Constitutional Constructivism Too Dualistic?*

Is my formulation of constitutional constructivism's two fundamental themes overly dualistic, dichotomous, or schematic? Does it imply that the realms of political self-government and personal self-government are entirely distinct?[96] I do not mean to suggest this implication. Nor do I intend to deny what Frank Michelman has cogently emphasized—that democracy and autonomy are complementary aspects of one unified vision that coexist in a dialectical relation of mutuality, reciprocity, and entailment.[97] Nonetheless, I do contend that an adequate unified account in constitutional theory requires both of these themes instead of just one principal theme of democracy.

The first reason is prophylactic: articulating a constitutional constructivism with these two themes protects us against fleeing from substance to process or to narrowly conceived original understanding by recasting or neglecting substantive liberties. Even if imaginative process-perfecting theorists can recast some of the substantive liberties that are preconditions for deliberative autonomy as preconditions for deliberative democracy, renditions of those liberties in such terms fail to capture what is at stake in some instances or leave out something important in the translation. Constitutional constructivism is not driven to undertake such reductive flights in the first place, for it does not entertain any (untenable) presupposition that the idea of democracy is relatively uncontroversial and a matter of stable consensus while the idea of autonomy is hopelessly contested and a matter of profound disagreement. It understands that both are normatively contested and can be elaborated only through substantive political theory or substantive constitutional choices.[98]

A second, related reason is architectonic: presenting our basic liberties by way of the guiding framework illustrates that the two fundamental themes of deliberative democracy and deliberative autonomy are "co-original and of equal weight."[99] For both themes derive from a common substrate—namely, a conception of citizens as free and equal persons (with two moral powers) and a conception of society as a fair system of social cooperation. Thus, the guiding framework may help meet such long-standing objections as those stemming from the traditions of civic republicanism and discourse ethics—that liberal theories treat the liberties of the moderns (associated with autonomy) as being "prepolitical" or "prior to all political will formation" and thus as having "priority" over the liberties of the ancients (related to democracy).[100] Similarly, it may rebut objections that the basic liberties associated with autonomy are anomalies while the basic liberties related to democracy are integral.[101] For it shows that both themes are constitutive of, and articulate preconditions for, the sovereignty of free and equal citizens.

The third, more general reason is heuristic: articulating our basic liberties through the abstract, simplifying device of the guiding framework with two themes keeps in view that our constitutional scheme is a dualist constitutional democracy, not a monist or majoritarian representative democracy. Doing so fortifies us against being fooled by the tyranny of simple labels like "democracy" into thinking that there is something illegitimate or embarrassing about arguing for rights related to autonomy (or that there is nothing illegitimate or problematic about majoritarian representative democracy).[102] It also wards off any illusion that we can accomplish an easy resolution between democracy and autonomy through a unified account of democracy such as "Democracy and autonomy are one and that one is democracy."[103]

A final reason is elegance: the importance of being elegant (though not too reductive) in constructing a constitutional theory.[104] A major reason for the attractiveness of Ely's theory of reinforcing representative democracy is its elegance. Ely provides an elegant account of judicial review as perfecting the processes of representative democracy through two intelligible, comprehensive themes: first, keeping the processes of political communication and participation open, and second, keeping those processes free of prejudice against discrete and insular minorities in order to ensure equal concern and respect for everyone alike.[105] In chapter 1 I suggested that an important reason for the persistence of process-perfecting theories such as Ely's, notwithstanding the resistance to them, is that no one has done for "substance" what Ely has done for "process." That is, no one has developed an alternative substantive Constitution-perfecting theory—a theory that would reinforce not only the procedural liberties (those related to deliberative democracy) but also the substantive liberties (those related to deliberative autonomy) embodied in our Constitution and presupposed by our constitutional democracy—with the elegance and power of Ely's process-perfecting theory. By developing a Constitution-perfecting theory with two fundamental themes of deliberative democracy and deliberative autonomy, I attempt to emulate the elegance of Ely's theory without taking a reductive flight from substance to process like that which he takes.

## Constitutional Constructivism Does Not Take a Pointless Flight from Substance

I have claimed that constitutional constructivism resists the temptations to take flights from substantive liberties like those taken by Ely's and Sunstein's theories. Here I pull together several strands of the analysis.

### Constitutional Constructivism Avoids Ely's Flight from Substance

In chapter 2 I intimated that constitutional constructivism avoids Ely's flight from giving effect to certain substantive provisions of the Constitution to merely perfecting processes. Here I suggest three arguments for the superiority of constitutional constructivism over Ely's theory of reinforcing representative democracy. These arguments parallel Ely's three arguments for his theory of judicial review, which imply his three criteria for an acceptable theory.

Ely's first argument for his process-perfecting theory is that it better fits and justifies the constitutional document and underlying constitutional order than do substantive fundamental values theories.[106] I contended, though, that his own quest for the ultimate interpretivism showed the need for a Constitution-perfecting theory. Constitutional constructivism is such a theory. Its second theme of securing deliberative autonomy fits and justifies the substantive liberties manifested in our constitutional document and implicit in our underlying constitutional order that elude the reach of the two process-perfecting themes of Ely's *Carolene Products* framework. Its first theme of securing deliberative democracy better fits and justifies our constitutional democracy's political processes than does Ely's qualified utilitarian and pluralist theory of representative democracy. Accordingly, constitutional constructivism better satisfies Ely's first criterion than does his own theory.

Ely's second argument is that his theory, unlike substantive fundamental values theories, "is not inconsistent with, but on the contrary is entirely supportive of, the American system of representative democracy."[107] This argument assumes that, or begs the question whether, the political theory that best fits and justifies the American system is Ely's theory of representative democracy as an applied utilitarianism.[108] By constructing such a conception of our system, which cannot account for certain substantive liberties, Ely has built a flight from such liberties into the very substance of his process-oriented political theory of representative democracy. His theory, however, is not consistent with nor supportive of the substantive liberties that it cannot account for and that are better fit and justified by constitutional constructivism.

Constitutional constructivism, by contrast, argues that our underlying system is better interpreted as a constitutional democracy and a synthesis of liberalism and republicanism. Unlike Ely's theory, it aspires to perfect both our constitutional democracy's substantive preconditions for deliberative democracy and its procedural preconditions for deliberative autonomy, and thus to reinforce that system on its own terms. Accordingly, constitutional constructivism is more consistent with and more effective at reinforcing our underlying system, constitutional democracy, than is Ely's theory. Therefore, it is superior to Ely's theory on his second criterion.

Ely's third argument is that his representation-reinforcing theory, again unlike substantive fundamental values theories, "assigns judges a role they are conspicuously well situated to fill" as compared with politically elected officials: perfecting political processes rather than discovering society's substantive fundamental values.[109] His argument is not so much about relative institutional competence as it is about institutional position or perspective.

Constitutional constructivism agrees with Ely that courts are different from legislatures, but it draws the opposite conclusion: precisely because of their differences from legislatures, and because of their relative independence from politics, courts are well situated to protect basic liberties against encroachment by the ordinary political processes. To use Dworkin's term, courts should be a "forum of principle," vindicating fundamental rights.[110] That is not to say, however, that legislative and executive branches should not also be forums of principle, deliberating concerning matters of principle.[111]

This argument, like Ely's, is less one of competence than of institutional position. It is an argument about the entailments of judges' responsibility to render their decisions according to law, understanding law on a constructivist model of principles rather than a positivist model of rules.[112] As Justice Jackson put it in the second flag-salute case (invalidating a required salute), responding to Justice Frankfurter in the first flag-salute case (upholding a required salute): rather than deferring to the "vicissitudes" of the political processes, courts vindicate fundamental rights "not by authority of their competence but by force of their commissions."[113]

Constitutional constructivism combines a conception of courts as exemplars of public reason in a forum of principle, vindicating fundamental rights in our constitutional democracy, with a recognition of certain institutional limits of courts. Ely basically uses the notion of "substance" versus "process" as a principle of role differentiation between legislatures and courts, so again he builds his flight from certain substantive liberties into his argument for a process-perfecting theory of judicial review.[114] Constitutional constructivism, then, is also superior to Ely's theory on his third criterion.

And so, constitutional constructivism better satisfies Ely's three criteria for an acceptable theory of judicial review than does his own theory. It also is at once more liberal and more republican than Ely's qualified utilitarian and pluralist theory. Finally, it is a fuller Constitution-perfecting theory.

### Constitutional Constructivism Avoids Sunstein's Flight from Substance

I contended in chapter 3 that constitutional constructivism avoids Sunstein's flight from deliberative autonomy to deliberative democracy and, in particular, from substantive due process to equal protection. Now that I have outlined my theory more fully, I reprise those arguments.

First, constitutional constructivism does not flee deliberative autonomy for deliberative democracy. Rather, it offers a better synthesis of the traditions of liberalism and republicanism than does Sunstein's liberal republicanism, for it combines a "republican" theme of securing the preconditions for deliberative democracy with a "liberal" theme of securing the preconditions for deliberative autonomy. Sunstein's synthesis emphasizes the republican liberties of the ancients to the neglect of the liberal liberties of the moderns. Furthermore, constitutional constructivism better fits and justifies certain substantive liberties manifested on the face of our constitutional document and implicit in our underlying constitutional order than does Sunstein's theory.

Second, constitutional constructivism does not flee substantive due process for equal protection. It aspires to secure both free and equal citizenship for everyone by providing both liberty- and equality-rooted baselines for criticizing existing practices that fail to satisfy the preconditions for deliberative autonomy and deliberative democracy. It offers a better combination of liberty and equality in one coherent scheme of equal basic liberties than does Sunstein's theory. In sum, constitutional constructivism is a fuller Constitution-perfecting theory than is Sunstein's theory of the partial Constitution.

## Constitutional Constructivism Does Not Take a Boundless Flight to Substance: The Specter of *Lochner*

Constitutional constructivism does not take flight from substance to process like Ely's or Sunstein's theories. But does it take a boundless flight from process to substance beyond the Constitution? That is, does it put aside the legal materials of our constitutional order and succumb to the temptation to remake our Constitution in the image of a perfect liberal utopia?[115] Indeed, is constructivism the very incarnation of the specter of *Lochner?*

Constitutional constructivism must be prepared to confront the inevitable paraphrase of Justice Holmes's dissenting opinion in *Lochner:* if the Constitution does not enact Mr. Herbert Spencer's *Social Statics,* neither does it enact Mr. John Rawls's *A Theory of Justice* or his *Political Liberalism.*[116] What responses can it give to this paraphrase?

Most important, a first response is to recall that constitutional constructivism simply deploys the constructivist framework as a guiding framework to help orient our reflections, deliberations, and judgments about our Constitution and constitutional democracy as embodying (or aspiring to embody) a coherent scheme of equal basic liberties, rather than merely enacting a "laundry list of particular rights."[117] It does not make an absurdly anachronistic claim that the constitutional framers and ratifiers in 1791 enacted a book published by Rawls in 1971, much less 1993.[118] Nor does it make a far-fetched Panglossian claim that our Constitution establishes a perfect liberal utopia. It simply conceives our equal basic liberties to be centrally concerned with two fundamental cases or themes—those of deliberative democracy and deliberative autonomy.

A second response to the paraphrase of Holmes is in terms of economic liberties and particular economic theories: to grant that it would aptly dispose of any attempt to read Rawls's difference principle, like liberty of contract during the *Lochner* era, into our Constitution. But we need to recall that Rawls himself argues that the difference principle is not among the constitutional essentials that would be incorporated into a constitution in the ideal four-stage sequence (let alone into our Constitution).[119] He observes that history, including the era of *Lochner,* reveals that principles to regulate economic and social inequalities and other distributive principles are not among the constitutional essentials that are incorporated as constitutional restrictions. "Rather," he suggests, "just legislation seems to be best achieved by assuring fairness in representation and by other constitutional devices."[120] In this respect, Rawls sounds more like Ely or Sunstein than like either Justice Peckham of the *Lochner* era[121] or Richard A. Epstein or Randy E. Barnett of the age of *Roe* and *Buckley*.[122]

A third, more general response is in terms of the legacy of *Lochner*. Constitutional constructivism accepts Sunstein's insightful analysis of what is wrong with *Lochner* and rejects status quo neutrality—without further justification—as a baseline that imposes constraints on deliberative democracy. It decidedly does not enact status quo neutrality, whereas *Lochner* in effect did.

A final response is in terms of interpretive method: to argue that the terms of Holmes's dissent in *Lochner*, such as whether the Constitution "enacts" the text of "a particular economic theory" or a particular political theory, are the wrong terms. Instead, the right terms are what substantive political theory best fits and justifies the constitutional document and underlying constitutional order as a whole—taking the Constitution's text, history, and structure as "fixed points" that a theory must acceptably fit and justify.[123] These terms are those of a methodological constructivism.

Constitutional constructivism holds that interpreting the Constitution with fidelity and integrity to its text, history, and structure requires elaborating the substantive political theory (or competing theories) that best fits and justifies the constitutional document and underlying constitutional order that were originally framed and have developed.[124] Thus, substantive political theory in constitutional interpretation is bounded by the criteria of fit with and justification of the extant legal materials. Courts are exemplars of public reason in a forum of principle, not seminars of boundless philosophical speculation.[125] The character of the Constitution, as an embodiment of a coherent scheme of general principles rather than merely an enactment of a discrete list of particular rights, establishes the need for substantive political theory in interpreting it faithfully and with integrity. These terms are those not only of a methodological constructivism, but also of the joint opinion in *Casey* along with the majority opinion in *Lawrence*, which conceive interpretation as a quest not for a formula or bright-line rule, but for "reasoned judgment."[126] On this view, to echo *The Federalist* No. 78, courts have "neither force nor will but merely [reasoned] judgment."[127]

In conclusion, it would be profoundly beside the point to protest, against constitutional constructivism, that the Constitution does not enact Rawls's *Political Liberalism.* One might practically as well complain that it does not enact the *Carolene Products* framework, or Scalia's *Michael H.* framework,[128] or indeed Holmes's dissent in *Lochner,* to say nothing of Bork's *The Tempting of America*[129] or Scalia's *A Matter of Interpretation.*[130] All of this should go without saying. The inevitable paraphrase of Holmes's dissent in *Lochner* is hardly dispositive of the project of constitutional constructivism.

## Conclusion: Constitutional Democracy and Trustworthiness

We need to move beyond Ely's and Sunstein's process-perfecting theories to a Constitution-perfecting theory, one which would reinforce not only the procedural liberties, but also the substantive liberties embodied in our Constitution. In this chapter, I have outlined a constitutional constructivism, a theory that secures the preconditions for trustworthiness of political decisions in our constitutional democracy by reinforcing both the procedural preconditions for deliberative democracy and the substantive preconditions for deliberative autonomy. Constitutional constructivism is wary of the specter of *Lochner* and takes neither a pointless flight from substance to process nor a boundless flight from process to substance beyond the Constitution. It provides a guiding framework to help orient our reflections, deliberations, and judgments in interpreting and justifying our constitutional document and underlying constitutional order. Unlike Ely's theory of representative democracy and distrust, and Sunstein's theory of deliberative democracy and impartiality, constitutional constructivism is a theory of constitutional democracy and trustworthiness.

PART II

*Securing Deliberative Autonomy Together with*
*Deliberative Democracy*

## CHAPTER FIVE

# Securing Deliberative Autonomy

My theory of securing constitutional democracy, in the spirit of Justice Brandeis's famous formulation concerning the right to privacy, undertakes to "secure conditions favorable to the pursuit of happiness" by securing the preconditions for deliberative autonomy.[1] The right is, as Brandeis put it, "the most comprehensive of rights and the right most valued by civilized [persons]" in our constitutional democracy; yet scholars and jurists have repeatedly claimed either that it is trivial or that it is wild, unruly, and dangerous (as witnessed by the criticisms and caricatures of it in the opening paragraph of chapter 1). Indeed, anxiety about recognizing rights to privacy or autonomy, more than any other right, has prompted charges of "Lochnering" and has animated flights from protecting substantive liberties to preserving original understanding (narrowly conceived) or to reinforcing procedural liberties in the Constitution (to the exclusion of substantive liberties).

I ground the right to privacy or autonomy in a constitutional constructivism, a guiding framework for constitutional theory with two fundamental themes: deliberative democracy and deliberative autonomy. These themes reflect the two bedrock structures of our constitutional document and underlying constitutional order: deliberative political and personal self-government, respectively. The second theme bounds the right to autonomy by limiting it to the protection of basic liberties that are significant preconditions for persons' development and exercise of deliberative autonomy in making certain fundamental decisions affecting their destiny, identity, or way of life.

My aim in developing a constitutional constructivism is not to unveil a new package of basic liberties that We the People never knew we had. Nor is it to provide a new justification for any particular liberty. Rather, I aim to advance deliberative autonomy as a unifying theme that shows the coherence and structure of certain substantive liberties on a list of familiar "unenumerated" fundamental rights (commonly classed under privacy, autonomy, or substantive due process)[2] and to argue that deliberative autonomy is rooted, along with deliberative democracy, in the language and design of our Constitution.

To the extent this project succeeds, responsible constitutional interpreters may become less vulnerable to the temptation to flee protecting such substantive liberties to merely perfecting processes of democracy or preserving original understanding, narrowly conceived—in the name of avoiding "Lochnering."[3] Furthermore, interpreters may become less likely to lapse into constitutional illiteracy concerning deliberative autonomy, as the Supreme Court did in *Bowers v. Hardwick*[4] and as Justice Scalia did in his apoplectic dissents in *Planned Parenthood v. Casey*[5] and *Lawrence v. Texas.*[6] Finally, the right to autonomy may become less susceptible to caricature.

## Carrying Forward the "Unfinished Business of Charles Black"

I conceive securing deliberative autonomy within a constitutional constructivism as carrying forward the "unfinished business of Charles Black": constructing a structure of fundamental rights integral to free and equal citizenship, and showing its coherence. In his classic book *Structure and Relationship in Constitutional Law,* Black demonstrates that responsible constitutional interpretation requires not mere textual exegesis and historical research concerning isolated clauses, but reasoning from structures and relationships manifested in the constitutional document and implicit in the underlying constitutional order as a whole.[7] In his well-known article *The Unfinished Business of the Warren Court,* Black applies a similar analysis to resolve the "methodological crisis" precipitated by *Griswold v. Connecticut*'s recognition of an "unenumerated" right to privacy. He calls for the construction of a structure or *corpus juris* of fundamental rights essential to full citizenship.[8] Black devoted the rest of his life to building that structure, arguing for protection of "unenumerated" rights that are analogous to or presupposed by already recognized rights and using neglected "stones" such as the Ninth Amendment to justify their protection.[9]

Black's project of persuading scholars, judges, and lawyers that constitutional interpretation requires drawing inferences from structures and relationships has been more successful with regard to institutional structures (for example, separation of powers and federalism) and procedural liberties (for example, the right to vote) than it has been with respect to substantive liberties (for example, the right to privacy or autonomy). Even such narrow originalists as Robert Bork and Antonin Scalia today accept the trilogy of "text, history, and structure" as legitimate sources of constitutional values. They readily engage in structural reasoning concerning separation of powers, federalism, and a republican form of government, yet continue to attack as "Lochnering" the drawing of inferences from a structure of ordered liberty, privacy, or autonomy.[10] The same can be said of process-perfecting theorists like John Hart Ely[11] and, to a lesser extent, Cass R. Sunstein.[12] Much work remains to be done in articulating such substantive liberties as stemming from coherent structures or patterns rooted in the language and design of our Constitution, rather than as representing nothing more than episodic "ukases" by roving philosopher-judges.[13]

In this chapter I take up this unfinished business of Charles Black by showing the coherence and structure of certain familiar basic liberties (commonly grouped under the rubrics "privacy," "autonomy," or "substantive due process") on the basis of a fundamental theme of securing deliberative autonomy. I certainly aspire to make substantial progress in this project, but I recognize, with Black, that the structure of fundamental rights integral to free and equal citizenship "will always be building," whether through reasoning by analogy or through working toward reflective equilibrium.[14] Accordingly, I do not expect to finish that business. Bork may think of the project as the construction of a constitutional time bomb.[15] Black terms it "decision according to law."[16] I call it "constructing the substantive Constitution."

In the second section of this chapter I sketch the contours of deliberative autonomy, presenting it as a unifying theme that shows the coherence and structure of a list of familiar "unenumerated" fundamental rights. In the third section I elaborate the idea of deliberative autonomy, exploring its underpinnings in liberty of conscience and freedom of association. Now that the literal frontier has largely vanished, I suggest that deliberative autonomy in effect provides an "exit" option from majoritarian oppression to a figurative "frontier." I also show that its scope is limited to significant basic liberties. In chapter 6 I indicate what deliberative autonomy is not, distinguishing it from the familiar under-standings or caricatures of privacy, autonomy, or liberty mentioned in the opening paragraph of chapter 1.

## What Deliberative Autonomy Is

*Constructing Deliberative Autonomy from a List of Familiar "Unenumerated" Fundamental Rights*

Imagine that you are a constitutional archaeologist who digs up the following bones and shards of a constitutional culture:

liberty of conscience and freedom of thought
freedom of association, including both expressive association and intimate associ-
    ation, whatever one's sexual orientation
the right to live with one's family, whether nuclear or extended
the right to travel or relocate
the right to marry
the right to decide whether to bear or beget children, including the rights to
    procreate, to use contraceptives, and to terminate a pregnancy
the right to direct the education and rearing of children
the right to exercise dominion over one's body, including the right to bodily
    integrity and ultimately the right to die[17]

You may recognize this as a list of familiar "unenumerated" fundamental rights. The Supreme Court has recognized most of these rights under the categories of privacy, autonomy, or substantive due process.[18] The chal-lenge that you face is to decide whether these bones and shards fit together into, and are justifiable within, a coherent structure.[19]

Let us consider how originalist, process-perfecting, and constructivist archaeologists might view these materials. Generally, originalists hold that interpreters must limit themselves to giving effect to the specifically enumerated provisions or narrowly conceived original understanding of the Constitution. Process-perfecters believe that interpreters must con-fine themselves to perfecting the processes of democracy rather than imposing substantive fundamental values. Constructivists contend that interpreters should perfect the whole Constitution by reinforcing not only the procedural liberties of democracy, but also the substantive liberties of autonomy embodied in it.

If you were an originalist archaeologist you might conclude that, because these bones and shards were not specifically enumerated in the constitutional document, you had unearthed the junk pile of the constitutional culture. From that viewpoint, the only thing these relics have in common is that they are anomalies that have nothing to do with the language and design of the Constitution. Or you might decide that what they have in common is that they evince the hubris and futility of judges episodically succumbing to the temptation of imposing their personal visions of utopia on the polity in the guise of interpreting the Constitution. Indeed, you might speculate that you had exhumed a ghost town, and that these shards were lying here together because judicial protection of them culminated in the destruction of the Supreme Court and the Constitution.[20]

If you were a process-perfecting archaeologist you might conclude, from the fact that many of these bones do not readily fit the procedural mold of representative or deliberative democracy, that they were alien substances, malformed growths on the body of the Constitution. Yet, if you were imaginative, you might reconstruct or recast some of these substantive growths as legitimate procedural appendages to the skeleton. In performing that reconstruction, however, you would have to force fit these bones into the body of the Constitution, lopping them off where necessary and leaving out some of them altogether. Thus, the fit would be Procrustean, not Herculean.[21]

But if you were a constructivist archaeologist, you would accept these bones as stipulated features (or fixed points) of a skeleton that you had a responsibility to construct. You would be able to construct the unity of these bones in a structure of deliberative autonomy that, along with a framework of deliberative democracy, is an integral part of the body of the Constitution. From that standpoint, you would comprehend that all of these bones constitute rights that reserve to persons the power to deliberate about and decide how to live their own lives, with respect to certain matters unusually important for such personal self-governance, over the course of a complete life (from cradle to grave). Put another way, the bones represent basic liberties that are significant preconditions for persons' development and exercise of deliberative autonomy in making certain fundamental decisions affecting their destiny, identity, or way of life, and spanning a complete lifetime. Hence, constructivists would fit these bones together and justify them within a coherent structure of deliberative autonomy in a Constitution that embodies both deliberative autonomy and deliberative democracy as aspects of "a political ideal . . . of a society of citizens both equal and free."[22]

## Familiar Understandings of Deliberative Autonomy in Our Constitutional Culture

Returning from this imaginary archeological excavation to our constitutional culture, we can find many familiar understandings of deliberative autonomy with respect to the "unenumerated" fundamental rights listed above. For example, it is illustrated by Justices Stevens's and Blackmun's dissents in *Bowers v. Hardwick*.[23] Stevens wrote that the Court's "privacy" decisions had actually been animated by fundamental concerns for "'the individual's right to make certain unusually important decisions that will affect his own, or his family's, destiny'" and "'the abiding interest in individual liberty that makes certain state intrusions on the citizen's right to decide how he will live his own life intolerable.'"[24] In *Whalen v. Roe,* Stevens described this right as an "interest in independence in making certain kinds of important decisions."[25] In his dissent in *Bowers,* Blackmun characterized this liberty in terms of "freedom of intimate association" and the "decisional and the spatial aspects of the right to privacy."[26] His discussion built on Justice Brennan's powerful analysis of the right to intimate association in *Roberts v. United States Jaycees:* "The Court has long recognized that, because the Bill of Rights is designed to secure individual liberty, it must afford the formation and preservation of certain kinds of highly personal relationships a substantial measure of sanctuary from unjustified interference by the State."[27] This protection, Brennan stated, "safeguards the ability independently to define one's identity that is central to any concept of liberty."[28]

Similar conceptions of deliberative autonomy appear in *Planned Parenthood v. Casey,* not only in the opinions of Justices Stevens and Blackmun, but also in the joint opinion of Justices O'Connor, Kennedy, and Souter. As Stevens put it, "Decisional autonomy must limit the State's power to inject into a woman's most personal *deliberations* its own views of what is best," because a woman's decision to terminate her pregnancy "is nothing less than a matter of conscience."[29] He emphasized liberty of conscience and decisional autonomy (as well as equal dignity and respect for women and men).[30] Likewise, Blackmun's opinion in *Casey* emphasized that cases protecting the fundamental right to privacy embody "the principle that personal decisions that profoundly affect bodily integrity, identity, and destiny should be largely beyond the reach of government."[31] He, too, stressed personal self-government or self-determination (along with gender equality).[32]

The joint opinion in *Casey* spoke of a woman's liberty at stake in the decision whether to have an abortion as

> involving the most intimate and personal choices a person may make in a lifetime, choices central to personal dignity and autonomy. . . . At the heart of liberty is the right to define one's own concept of existence, of meaning, of the universe, and of the mystery of human life. Beliefs about these matters could not define the attributes of personhood were they formed under compulsion of the State.[33]

The joint opinion's explication of this personal liberty, rooted in decisional autonomy and bodily integrity, evinces deliberative autonomy. (Like the opinions of Stevens and Blackmun, the joint opinion intertwines concerns for personal liberty and gender equality.)[34]

Justice Kennedy's opinion of the Court in *Lawrence* likewise illustrated deliberative autonomy by quoting this passage from *Casey* and stating that "[l]iberty presumes an autonomy of self that includes freedom of thought, belief, expression, and certain intimate conduct" and by invoking "liberty of the person both in its spatial and more transcendent dimensions."[35] Finally, *Lawrence* intertwined concern for liberty as autonomy with concern for the equal citizenship of gays and lesbians. We see this most clearly in Kennedy's arguments that it "demeans the lives" of homosexuals to respect the right of heterosexuals to autonomy without respecting an analogous right for them.[36]

Landmark substantive due process cases such as *Meyer v. Nebraska*,[37] *Pierce v. Society of Sisters*,[38] *Griswold v. Connecticut*,[39] *Loving v. Virginia*,[40] *Eisenstadt v. Baird*,[41] *Moore v. City of East Cleveland*,[42] *Carey v. Population Services International*,[43] and *Roe v. Wade*[44] also illustrate deliberative autonomy. Perhaps its most stirring expression was by Justice Jackson in *West Virginia State Board of Education v. Barnette:*

> [W]e apply the limitations of the Constitution with no fear that freedom to be intellectually and spiritually diverse or even contrary will disintegrate the social organization. . . . [F]reedom to differ is not limited to things that do not matter much. That would be a mere shadow of freedom. The test of

its substance is the right to differ as to things that touch the heart of the existing order.[45]

Jed Rubenfeld argues persuasively that such cases reflect an antitotalitarian principle of privacy: they are concerned with the danger of "creeping totalitarianism, an unarmed *occupation* of individuals' lives."[46] Constitutional constructivism incorporates a similar antitotalitarian principle of liberty, along with a parallel anticaste principle of equality, as aspects of the free and equal citizenship that is due everyone in our morally pluralistic constitutional democracy.

The eloquent formulations of deliberative autonomy in *Lawrence* and *Casey* and in the dissents in *Bowers* aptly distill the core of the cases involving decisional autonomy, bodily integrity, and dignity. They have consolidated a framework of "reasoned judgment" concerning our Constitution's "promise" of a "rational continuum" of liberty,[47] rather than just recapitulating doctrines. These formulations, expressed in the contexts of abortion and intimate association, also apply to the other types of personal decisions encompassed by the rights on the foregoing list. They succinctly capture what is at stake in these unusually important decisions profoundly affecting persons' destiny, identity, or way of life, and why such decisions lie in "a realm of personal liberty which the government may not enter."[48] In other words, these rights represent basic liberties that are significant preconditions for deliberative autonomy.

Notwithstanding the cogency and coherence of these formulations, Bork asserts that the recognition in *Griswold* of a right to privacy amounted to "the construction of a constitutional time bomb" whose full extent we still do not know many years later.[49] One thing that we do know, however, is that for Bork *Griswold* indeed proved to be a constitutional time bomb, for it blew up in his face during his Supreme Court nomination hearings in 1987, when it became apparent that he still had not articulated or embraced a theory of constitutional interpretation that could justify it.[50]

Bork's hearings, and all the subsequent confirmation hearings of Supreme Court nominees, suggest that *Griswold*, far from being a constitutional time bomb, has become a "fixed star in our constitutional constellation."[51] *Brown v. Board of Education*[52] in the 1950s and *Griswold* in the 1960s provoked "methodological crises" in constitutional law.[53] Yet like *Brown, Griswold* today is a case that any nominee to the Supreme Court, to stand any chance of being confirmed, must say was rightly decided. Thus, Justices Kennedy, Souter, and Thomas, as well as Chief Justice Roberts were as scrupulous about saying that they recognized a constitutional right to privacy and accepted *Griswold* as they were about declining to say whether they recognized a right to abortion and accepted *Roe;* even Justice Scalia strained, in *Michael H.*, to say that *Griswold* was rightly decided according to his conception of the due process inquiry while maintaining that *Roe* was wrongly decided.[54] Justices Ginsburg and Breyer accepted both *Griswold* and *Roe* as settled law.[55] So it is in our constitutional culture that the most controversial cases of earlier decades become litmus tests for later decades.

Constructing a fundamental theme of deliberative autonomy does not entail constructing a constitutional time bomb. Nor does it involve drawing bright lines around privacy, autonomy, or liberty. Instead, it entails tethering the right to autonomy, and what *Casey* called "*Griswold* liberty,"[56] to a bedrock structure in our constitutional democracy.

### Constitutional Constructivism Can Fit and Justify Familiar Understandings of Deliberative Autonomy

I now turn to situating these familiar understandings of deliberative autonomy and "unenumerated" fundamental rights in the framework of constitutional constructivism. As discussed in chapter 2, John Hart Ely argues that the Constitution is principally concerned with establishing a procedural framework of democracy and protecting procedural liberties rather than securing substantive liberties.[57] Nonetheless, he admits that there are on the face of the Constitution numerous expressions of substantive values, in addition to procedural values, for which his process-perfecting theory does not account.[58] These substantive values (manifested in the First, Third, Fourth, Fifth, Ninth, Thirteenth, and Fourteenth Amendments) include liberty of conscience, freedom of association, autonomy, privacy, and independence.[59] Yet Ely suggests that to represent such concerns for substantive liberties "as a dominant theme of our constitutional document one would have to concentrate quite single-mindedly on hopping from stone to stone and averting one's eyes from the mainstream."[60]

Notwithstanding Ely, constitutional constructivism concentrates on constructing the unity or structure of these substantive "stones." These stones do not necessitate hopping; they form a bedrock structure of

deliberative autonomy. This fundamental theme powerfully fits and justifies these substantive liberties, and shows them to be integral to the
language and design of the Constitution. In the words of Charles Black,
"[t]he stone[s] the builders rejected may yet be the cornerstone of the
temple."[61] Ely's and Sunstein's process-perfecting theories recast such
substantive liberties as procedural preconditions for democracy or omit
them altogether. Narrow originalists like Scalia and Bork are even less
faithful to the constitutional scheme, in effect repealing these substantive
liberties by construction. In short, these two types of theories flee from
substance to process and narrowly conceived original understanding.[62]
Constitutional constructivism instead treats these substantive liberties
reflected on the face of the Constitution and these "unenumerated"
fundamental rights recognized in landmark cases as crucial features
(or fixed points) of our constitutional practice, tradition, and culture. It
accepts the responsibility to fit and justify these materials in constructing a
constitutional theory.

In other words, constitutional constructivism is not a theory of natural
law or natural rights, and does not conceive the substantive liberties—of
conscience, association, autonomy, privacy, and independence—as prepolitical or given by a prior and independent order of moral values that
is binding for all times and all places.[63] Instead, constitutional constructivism is an "interpretative theory"[64] that draws our principles and
substantive liberties from our constitutional democracy's ongoing practice, tradition, and culture.[65] These principles are aspirational—the principles to which we as a people aspire, and for which we as a people stand—
and may not be fully realized in our historical practices, statute books, and
common law.[66] Accordingly, constitutional constructivism recognizes that
our principles may fit and justify most of our practices or precedents, but
may also criticize some of them for failing to live up to our constitutional
commitments to principles such as liberty and equality.[67]

## Constituting Deliberative Autonomy

In this section I further elaborate the constitution (or Constitution) of
deliberative autonomy. After first sketching the idea of deliberative
autonomy and defending it against certain misconceptions, I take up its
underpinnings and scope.

## The Idea of Deliberative Autonomy
### THE TERM "DELIBERATIVE AUTONOMY"

Why do I use the term "deliberative autonomy" instead of simply "autonomy"? In a word, I do so to differentiate it from the welter of usages of the term "autonomy" in contemporary discourse. Gerald Dworkin has observed:

> [Autonomy] is used sometimes as an equivalent of liberty (positive or negative in [Isaiah] Berlin's terminology), sometimes as equivalent to self-rule or sovereignty, sometimes as identical with freedom of the will. It is equated with dignity, integrity, individuality, independence, responsibility, and self-knowledge. It is identified with qualities of self-assertion, with critical reflection, with freedom from obligation, with absence of external causation, with knowledge of one's own interests. It is even equated by some economists with the impossibility of interpersonal comparisons. It is related to actions, to beliefs, to reasons for acting, to rules, to the will of other persons, to thoughts, and to principles.[68]

Nevertheless, the etymology of the term suggests its basic meaning: *autos* (self) and *nomos* (rule or law).[69] Familiar formulations such as "self-rule," "self-determination," "self-government," "independence," or "sovereignty" express this underlying meaning.[70] Moreover, commentators apply such terms as these both to nation-states and to individuals, or to refer to self-government in a political sense and a personal sense.[71]

I speak of "deliberative autonomy" for four reasons: (1) to emphasize that it builds on Rawls's idea of persons' second moral power, the capacity for a conception of the good, as the power of "deliberative reason";[72] (2) to recognize its similarity to Justice Stevens's analysis of "decisional autonomy" in terms of "deliberation" about important decisions concerning how to live one's own life;[73] (3) to suggest parallels between the structure of "deliberative" autonomy and that of "deliberative" democracy; and (4) to acknowledge affinities between constitutional constructivism and other theories that conceive our Constitution as a scheme of deliberative or reflective self-government.[74]

I should clarify that constitutional constructivism deploys ecumenical or "thin" conceptions of both "deliberation" and "autonomy." They are compatible with, and have affinities to, a number of "thicker" conceptions drawn from diverse constitutional and political theories, whose common concern is the centrality of freedom to form, revise, and pursue a conception of the good.[75] Nevertheless, the principal reason for developing the theme of deliberative autonomy is to articulate a structure that houses basic liberties associated with autonomy, not to advance a sectarian or "thick" conception of autonomy.

## THE IDEA OF DELIBERATION

What, in general, is "deliberative" about deliberative democracy and deliberative autonomy? In what senses do the basic liberties associated with both themes secure preconditions for deliberation? First, the two fundamental cases in which persons apply their two moral powers involve deliberation: deliberation about justice or the common good and deliberation about their own good or way of life, respectively. Second, deliberation in each fundamental case is a process whereby persons engage in self-governance, realizing their freedom and, indeed, their sovereignty. Thus, both themes safeguard processes for deliberation rather than impose outcomes. To acknowledge this structural affinity between constitutional constructivism and process-perfecting theories—while also recognizing that the former theory secures two types of preconditions for deliberation rather than just one—I have characterized it as a "Constitution-perfecting" theory.

In our scheme of deliberative self-governance, some matters are committed to resolution through the process of democratic deliberation and others are reserved to resolution through the process of personal deliberation, individually and in association with others. For example, just as the right to vote is justified as an essential precondition for the process of deliberation about the common good, so too are liberty of conscience and the right to procreative autonomy justified as essential preconditions for deliberation in forming, revising, and pursuing one's conception of the good.

Both deliberative democracy and deliberative autonomy may involve individual or collective deliberation. "Deliberative democracy" may conjure up for us a citizen making her decision in the secrecy of the voting booth; here, self-government manifests itself through an individual act of deliberation. Or we might picture a citizen participating in a town meeting, speaking or listening at a political rally, or discussing matters of public concern with fellow citizens; here, we see a collective dimension of deliberation. Similarly, the term "deliberative autonomy" may connote a person making a decision, deemed private and intimate, about her sexual or reproductive life. Although "deliberative autonomy" in this sense stresses that the individual person is the locus of deliberation and decisionmaking, it also allows room for a social dimension.[76] Deliberative autonomy may, for example, include consulting with others, taking their views into account, and associating with them. The crucial point, however, is that in an important way the individual person is the locus of moral agency, responsibility, and independence.[77]

What, in particular, is deliberative about liberty of conscience and freedom of association, along with the other fundamental rights listed earlier? How do these basic liberties fit within a structure of deliberative autonomy? For one thing, they all implicate deliberations, or the capacity to deliberate, concerning certain fundamental decisions affecting persons' identity, destiny, or way of life. They reserve to persons the power to deliberate about and decide how to live their own lives, including certain matters that are unusually important or significant for such personal self-governance, over the course of a lifetime.

Furthermore, the landmark cases and powerful dissents that I have offered as illustrations of deliberative autonomy reflect an anti-totalitarian principle concerned with safeguarding against the danger of "creeping totalitarianism, an unarmed *occupation* of individuals' lives,"[78] or coercion of conformity concerning "the most intimate and personal choices a person may make in a lifetime."[79] If persons do not have the freedom to deliberate about and make such decisions, they are not free.

The meaning of "deliberation" in deliberative autonomy does not stem from an abstract philosophical conception that lacks roots in our constitutional practice. Rather, our constitutional practice has identified basic liberties such as those listed earlier as involving central "attributes of personhood"[80] and as being "essential to the orderly pursuit of happiness"[81] by free persons. The deliberations and decisions encompassed by the list typically figure prominently in conflicting and irreconcilable comprehensive religious, philosophical, and moral conceptions of the good that reside in the background culture of our constitutional democracy and that are fervently held by individual persons and groups. These basic liberties are and will remain controversial, precisely because of the centrality of such matters in conflicting comprehensive views and in the lives of individual persons and groups. Governmental restriction or regulation of such personal decisions triggers the risk of majoritarian oppression and transgression of the limits of public reason. As the Supreme Court put it in *Lawrence:* "The issue is whether the majority may use the power of the

State to enforce these views on the whole society through operation of the criminal law." The Court continued, quoting from the joint opinion in *Casey:* "'Our obligation is to define the liberty of all, not to mandate our own moral code.'"[82]

The basic liberties we have been talking about do not define or exhaust deliberative autonomy. My goal here is not to delineate the exact scope of this structure, but simply to outline its parameters in order to tether the right to autonomy in constitutional law. Its general scope is limited to securing significant basic liberties. As explained in chapter 6, deliberative autonomy is much narrower than comprehensive libertarian or liberal principles of liberty, autonomy, or individuality.

## AVOIDING MISCONCEPTIONS ABOUT THE IDEA OF
## DELIBERATIVE AUTONOMY

It is important to recognize that deliberative autonomy is concerned with securing basic liberties that are *preconditions* for the development and exercise of persons' capacity for a conception of the good when deliberating about and making decisions concerning certain fundamental matters. It does not *guarantee* or *require* actual conscientious deliberation in applying that capacity. This theme reflects general assumptions about persons' second moral power, and does not call for or require an inquiry by the government into the actual deliberations, responsibility, and judgment of particular exercises of that power.[83] Indeed, such an inquiry would be intolerably intrusive or oppressive.

To be sure, military conscription statutes might direct draft boards to interview draftees seeking conscientious exemption from service in order to ensure that their objections are rooted in conscience.[84] But restrictive abortion laws may not require a pregnant woman to demonstrate that her decision to have an abortion is for her a matter of conscience or a responsible exercise of her reproductive freedom.[85] Even if the government tries to *encourage* a pregnant woman to deliberate conscientiously or responsibly about her decision through such measures as the twenty-four-hour waiting period and informed consent requirements upheld in *Casey*,[86] it may not *compel* her to give testimony proving that she has done so or to provide reasons for her decision.[87]

Perhaps this feature of deliberative autonomy—that it secures basic liberties as preconditions for deliberation without guaranteeing or requiring actual deliberation—will seem less peculiar or problematic if

I draw an analogy between a basic liberty associated with deliberative autonomy and one related to deliberative democracy. The "unenumerated" right to vote is justified because it is a significant precondition for deliberative democracy,[88] just as the "unenumerated" right to abortion is justified on the ground that it is a significant precondition for deliberative autonomy. This justification for the right to vote is not undercut by the observation that not everyone who votes actually conscientiously or responsibly deliberates about the common good before casting a vote. Nor is the justification for the right to abortion undermined by the objection that not every woman who has an abortion conscientiously or responsibly deliberates about a conception of the good life before undergoing the procedure.[89] The best justification for each right is still framed in terms of securing the preconditions for deliberation, even if that justification cannot vouchsafe the deliberativeness, much less the responsibility, of each individual decision.

Furthermore, constitutional constructivism does not stem from an overly rationalistic or romantic conception of the person that presupposes or demands too much deliberation to be attractive, realistic, or useful. First, its conception of the person is a political one that is advanced to provide a ground for justifying basic liberties in our constitutional democracy; it is not a biological or psychological conception of the human being as such.[90] Second, this political conception of the person is not part of what Rawls calls a comprehensive moral view with respect to either democracy or autonomy.[91] Thus, constitutional constructivism does not subject the first moral power (and the theme of deliberative democracy) to the demands, rigors, and commitments of comprehensive moral views like those associated with civic humanism, which idealize taking part in politics "as the privileged locus of the good life."[92] Nor does it subject the second moral power (and the theme of deliberative autonomy) to the challenges, reflectiveness, and experiments of comprehensive moral views like those of Kant or Mill, which idealize autonomy or individuality as a way of life.[93] In sum, constitutional constructivism's political conception of the person is simply an abstract device to model the capacities of citizens that are most salient to grounding our basic liberties and interpreting our constitutional order. It does not glorify a life of deliberation.

Finally, deliberative autonomy does not entail that every governmental exercise of the police power concerning fundamental decisions affecting persons' identity, destiny, or way of life is presumptively illegitimate.

Far from it. Precisely because those matters are so important or significant, a government dedicated to securing the preconditions for deliberative autonomy and deliberative democracy would enact many legislative
measures to foster the development and exercise of persons' moral
powers.[94] Deliberative autonomy hardly rules out such measures; it
does, however, safeguard against legislation that coercively standardizes
persons with respect to such matters. Justice Jackson's famous words in
*Barnette* remind us that freedom embraces "the right to differ as to things
that touch the heart of the existing order."[95]

## *The Underpinnings and Scope of Deliberative Autonomy*
### THE MATRIX VALUES UNDERWRITING DELIBERATIVE AUTONOMY:
### LIBERTY OF CONSCIENCE AND FREEDOM OF ASSOCIATION

Why stress liberty of conscience and freedom of association in developing the fundamental theme of deliberative autonomy instead of just
using the more common ideas of privacy, autonomy, or liberty? I do
so because those basic liberties are matrix values that underwrite deliberative autonomy.

First, I emphasize liberty of conscience to make clear that this theme
involves persons' deliberations and decisions concerning unusually
important matters of conscience or basic decisions implicating beliefs
that "could not define the attributes of personhood were they formed
under compulsion of the State."[96] Liberty of conscience is more abstract
than freedom of religion (or the religion clauses of the First Amendment)
and so it undergirds free exercise not only of religion, but also of deliberative autonomy as to certain fundamental decisions.

Thus, constitutional constructivism generalizes liberty of conscience
from a narrow principle applicable only to religious persons to a general
principle applicable to all. It generalizes the principle of religious toleration to apply not only to traditional religious conceptions of the good but
also to reasonable moral and philosophical conceptions of the good.[97]
Given the fact of reasonable pluralism, conceiving liberty of conscience
narrowly would unfairly privilege traditional religious conceptions.[98] In a
morally pluralistic constitutional democracy such as our own, liberty of
conscience secures preconditions for the development and exercise of
each person's capacity to pursue her or his *conception of the good;* it
does not merely confer a privilege on religious persons to obey the
commands or dictates of their *conception of a God.*[99]

To be sure, some religious persons may view liberty of conscience not as involving deliberation about their conception of the good at all, but instead as involving obedience to God. That fact does not undermine the justification for liberty of conscience as a precondition for deliberative autonomy—any more than the fact that such persons may view themselves as voting the commands and dictates of conscience, rather than engaging in deliberation about the common good, undercuts the justification for the right to vote as a precondition for deliberative democracy.

Second, I emphasize freedom of association to highlight that deliberative autonomy relates to persons' deliberations and decisions in pursuing their conceptions of the good, individually and in association with others. It is not, contra Michael J. Sandel and Mary Ann Glendon, merely a right of "unencumbered selves" or "lone rights-bearers" to be "let alone."[100] *Roberts v. United States Jaycees* helpfully distinguished between freedom of expressive association and freedom of intimate association. The former (which I would link principally to deliberative democracy) is "a right to associate for the purpose of engaging in those activities protected by the First Amendment." Of freedom of intimate association (which I would connect primarily with deliberative autonomy), the Court writes: "to secure individual liberty" and "the ability independently to define one's identity," the Constitution protects "choices to enter into and maintain certain intimate human relationships . . . against undue intrusion by the State."[101] Freedom of association also comprehends the whole realm of voluntary memberships in associations in civil society, which may be important for both political and personal self-government. Furthermore, constitutional constructivism recognizes the human goods promoted through freedom of association and not simply the individual choices protected by that freedom.[102]

Third, the fundamental theme of deliberative autonomy, underwritten by liberty of conscience and freedom of association, may provide a more secure basis for certain "unenumerated" fundamental rights[103] deemed "essential to the orderly pursuit of happiness"[104] than does privacy or due process. Even narrow originalists, deeply skeptical about rights of privacy, autonomy, or liberty when unconnected to specific provisions of the Constitution or when connected to the Due Process Clauses, are hard pressed to deny that liberty of conscience and freedom of association have firm First Amendment roots.[105] Ronald Dworkin and Charles Black argue persuasively that the distinction between "enumerated" and "unenumerated" rights in our constitutional practice is largely "spurious" or "bogus," and that objections to recognizing asserted rights on the ground that they are "unenumerated" are often overstated or off the mark.[106] Nonetheless, the incubus of such objections does (for some people) encumber the ideas of privacy, autonomy, and liberty. Liberty of conscience and freedom of association may offer a fresh start in undergirding those basic liberties that are "'so rooted in the traditions and conscience of our people as to be ranked as fundamental.'"[107]

It may be instructive to revisit *Griswold,* the first case explicitly to recognize the "unenumerated" right to privacy. There Justice Douglas recast *Meyer* and *Pierce*—two substantive due process cases from the *Lochner* era invalidating state laws on the ground that they infringed the substantive liberty of parents to direct the upbringing and education of their children—as securing First Amendment freedoms.[108] Justice Harlan did likewise in dissent in *Poe v. Ullman.*[109] Indeed, even Bork, for whom substantive due process and the right to privacy are anathema, concedes that *Meyer* and *Pierce* were justifiable on First Amendment grounds.[110] Also, an early draft of Justice Douglas's opinion in *Griswold* framed the right in question as freedom of association secured by the First Amendment.[111] With the specter of *Lochner* haunting constitutional law, grounding the right to privacy in freedom of association might have seemed less frightening or spooky to some people than summoning forth penumbras and emanations from the First, Third, Fourth, Fifth, and Ninth Amendments.[112]

Finally, I should explain what I mean when I state that liberty of conscience and freedom of association "underwrite" the theme of deliberative autonomy rather than, say, "enumerate" it. These basic liberties underwrite deliberative autonomy in the sense that they are, in Justice Cardozo's terms in *Palko v. Connecticut,* "matrix values," or "indispensable conditions" for nearly every other form of freedom associated with it.[113] Similarly, the equal political liberties and freedom of thought are matrix values underwriting deliberative democracy, for they are "preservative of all rights."[114] Both types of basic liberties are rooted in "fundamental principles of liberty and justice which lie at the base of all our civil and political institutions."[115]

To contend that liberty of conscience and freedom of association underwrite deliberative autonomy is not necessarily to argue that they or the First Amendment provide a new "textual home" or doctrinal basis for every hitherto "unenumerated" fundamental right associated with deliberative autonomy that has been protected through the Due Process or the Equal Protection Clauses.[116] These basic liberties instead provide a matrix, or undergirding structure, for such rights. Therefore, such rights have a deeper basis in our constitutional "scheme of ordered liberty"[117] than is acknowledged by proponents of a "constitution of detail," who demand to know where these rights are "enumerated" in the expressions "liberty" or "equal protection."[118]

Furthermore, even if as a doctrinal matter the textual home of "unenumerated" fundamental rights associated with deliberative autonomy largely remains the "liberty" of the Due Process Clause, that does not mean that deliberative autonomy rests on that clause alone. The clauses of the Constitution are not isolated, self-contained units. Within our "constitution of principle," as Dworkin argues, we should not be surprised to find underpinnings for basic liberties in more than one clause.[119] Conceiving liberty of conscience and freedom of association as matrix values in an underlying structure shows that "unenumerated" fundamental rights such as those excavated by our imaginary constitutional archeologist "emanate[] from the totality of the constitutional scheme under which we live,"[120] even if they are not dictated by a particular clause. Put another way, the basic liberties associated with deliberative autonomy are implicit in a "transcendent structure" embodied in the scheme as a whole.[121]

## DELIBERATIVE AUTONOMY CONSTITUTES AN "EXIT" OPTION:
## THE VANISHING FRONTIER AND THE GROWING RIGHT TO AUTONOMY

Another structural argument for securing deliberative autonomy is rooted in the idea that the basic liberties associated with it constitute an "exit" option from majoritarian oppression. This argument invokes the tradition of dissident or different individuals and groups having the right to pull up stakes and move to the frontier to escape prejudice, intolerance, and oppression, and to pursue their own conceptions of the good.[122]

Ely is at pains to maintain, as against arguments for the right to autonomy, that the Constitution does not protect "the right to be different."[123] But he does derive a right of "dissenting or 'different'" individuals and groups to relocate through an analysis of the general contours of the Constitution.[124] Ely points out that in *Crandall v. Nevada,* the Supreme Court justified the "unenumerated" right to travel on the ground that "the right to travel freely through the various states is critical to the exercise of our more obviously political rights." This structural justification links the right to travel with "the idea that it is some kind of handmaiden of majoritarian democracy," or the "voice" option.[125] Ely constructs an alternative structural justification, which associates such a right with "the notion that one should have an option of escaping an incompatible majority," or the "exit" option. Referring to the tradition of the frontier, he submits that "a dissenting member for whom the 'voice' option seems unavailing should have the option of exiting and relocating in a community whose values he or she finds more compatible."[126] Thus, Ely claims, the right manifests a structural concern for protecting "process rights, minority style."[127]

Following Ely's analysis, we should interpret provisions and themes of the Constitution that relate to the right to relocate, and to the plight of dissenting or different individuals and groups, in light of a line of growth or development.[128] Thus, we should ponder whether, to the extent that the frontier has diminished, the right to autonomy has grown and developed. At the present time, the literal frontier has largely vanished, and we have a plurality of divergent conceptions of the good in our morally diverse society that individuals and groups might reasonably entertain and pursue. In such circumstances, an increasingly important analogue to the "exit" option and the tradition of the frontier is the protection of basic liberties that are preconditions for deliberative autonomy.[129] These basic liberties constitute a partial "exit" option from majoritarian oppression because they set aside a figurative "frontier" in which persons, individually and in association with others, may deliberate about and decide how to lead their own lives.[130] Indeed, historical studies have shown that the development of the right to privacy has closely tracked the receding line of the frontier.[131]

This structural argument by analogy to the tradition of the frontier does not itself settle the question of what basic liberties we should protect to secure an "exit" option. It might appear that the liberties would be as wild and unruly as the frontier itself. But the argument is self-limiting in the sense that it supports protecting only basic liberties that are significant for deliberative autonomy. After all, it was typically the denial of such significant liberties, not trivial ones, that prompted individuals and groups to pull up stakes and "exit" to the frontier. In our constitutional democracy, there are limits on the extent to which the government may engage in perfectionist statecraft as soulcraft:[132] our imperfect souls are our own to craft, at least with respect to certain fundamental decisions profoundly affecting our destiny, identity, or way of life.

## THE SCOPE OF DELIBERATIVE AUTONOMY: LIMITED TO SIGNIFICANT
BASIC LIBERTIES

Why do only the foregoing "unenumerated" fundamental rights appear on the list that illustrates deliberative autonomy? Constitutional constructivism's answer, and its criterion for specifying the basic liberties in interpreting the Constitution as a coherent scheme, is in terms of the *significance* of such liberties for deliberative autonomy or deliberative democracy. Rawls explains the criterion of significance: "[A] liberty is more or less significant depending on whether it is more or less essentially involved in, or is a more or less necessary institutional means to protect, the full and informed and effective exercise of the moral powers in one (or both) of the two fundamental cases."[133] Constitutional constructivism limits the scope of autonomy to protecting basic liberties that are significant preconditions for deliberative autonomy in this sense. All of the liberties listed earlier satisfy this criterion. In chapter 6 I distinguish deliberative autonomy from comprehensive libertarian and liberal principles of liberty, autonomy, or individuality, which are broader and encompass liberties that are not significant in this sense.

This criterion for specifying the basic liberties is not one of significance *simpliciter,* that is, simply whether an asserted "unenumerated" fundamental right is significant or important in the abstract (or in someone's "subjective" scheme of values). Rather, the criterion frames the inquiry in terms of whether an asserted liberty is significant for the development and exercise of one (or both) of the two moral powers in one (or both) of the two fundamental cases. This criterion requires reasoned judgment rather than providing a formula or bright-line rule, but it structures the inquiry along constitutionally appropriate lines.[134]

Furthermore, applying the criterion of significance does not call for judgments based on subjective interpersonal comparisons of incommensurable values. Within constitutional constructivism, basic liberties are conceived as primary goods (or all-purpose goods) that in principle are significant for all persons, whatever their conceptions of the good.[135] And so, the question framed by the criterion of significance is not: "What liberties does a particular person need to enable him or her to pursue his or her particular conception of the good?" It is, instead: "What liberties in principle are significant for everyone, regardless of their particular conceptions of the good and irrespective of whether particular persons happen to value those liberties?" In recognizing the significance of the basic liberties on the foregoing list and of the rights of persons to make fundamental decisions of the sort encompassed by them, we need not embrace any particular view of the ultimate meaning or importance of such decisions within any specific comprehensive conception of the good (though we might well find considerable overlap among a variety of such conceptions).

Admittedly, "unenumerated" liberties such as those listed earlier are controversial, but that is not because they are merely subjective, insignificant, or readily disparaged as "liberty as license." To the contrary, they are controversial precisely because they are significant for deliberative autonomy. The criterion of significance is double-edged, for a government may have obligations with respect to certain matters because of their importance for deliberative autonomy, or for the ordered reproduction of society over time, but nonetheless be prohibited from standardizing people with respect to such matters precisely because they are so important.

In contemporary American society, where "rights talk" is pervasive, persons may try to dress up relatively insignificant liberty claims in the garb of "unenumerated" fundamental rights to privacy, autonomy, or liberty.[136] This fact poses no special difficulty for constitutional constructivism. First, many such claims are frivolous as constitutional claims. And second, many of the claims that could pass that threshold still would not trump the government's compelling, important, or even merely legitimate interests. According to constitutional constructivism, the constitutional protection afforded such liberty claims is merely that of "a general presumption against imposing legal and other restrictions on conduct without sufficient reason,"[137] generally requiring that political decisions be justifiable on the basis of public-regarding reasons and public reasons. Only significant basic liberties, including those on the foregoing list and others of similar significance for one or both of the two fundamental cases, have the much-vaunted priority over the polity's pursuit of conceptions of the public good or imposition of perfectionist virtues.[138] Those are the basic liberties to which the call for "taking rights seriously" applies.[139]

Rawls issues an important caveat concerning the application of the criterion of significance in specifying basic liberties in a constitutional democracy such as our own: "It is wise, I think, to limit the basic liberties to those that are truly essential in the expectation that the liberties which are not basic are satisfactorily allowed for by the general presumption [referred to above]."[140] He explains: "Whenever we enlarge the list of basic liberties we risk weakening the protection of the most essential ones and recreating within the scheme of liberties the indeterminate and unguided balancing problems we had hoped to avoid by a suitably circumscribed notion of priority."[141] Some champions of the right to autonomy have advocated constitutional protection for liberties that are not essential or significant in this sense. But constitutional constructivism heeds this caveat.

By accepting this caveat, I do not mean to imply that the basic liberties analyzed above and the "unenumerated" fundamental rights on the foregoing list make up a complete, closed list of basic liberties that are significant for deliberative autonomy. For the unfinished business of Charles Black will never be completed; the structure or *corpus juris* of fundamental rights significant for deliberative autonomy "will always be building."[142] But tethering the right to autonomy by limiting it to protecting basic liberties that are significant for deliberative autonomy may render it less vulnerable to the caricatures mentioned in the opening paragraph of chapter 1, to say nothing of making autonomy less frightening to the jurists and scholars who are tempted to flee it.[143] Limiting deliberative autonomy to significant basic liberties may also provide a partial response to the exaggerated complaints that "rights talk" has led to the "impoverishment" of political and constitutional discourse and to the debilitation of the responsible citizenry on which our institutions depend.[144]

# Reconceiving the Due Process Inquiry in Terms of Significance for Deliberative Autonomy: Between Scalia and Charybdis

In this chapter I turn from the theoretical underpinnings of deliberative autonomy to the doctrinal heading of substantive due process, which has served as the primary textual basis for recognizing or rejecting "un-enumerated" fundamental rights that are preconditions for deliberative autonomy, such as those excavated by our imaginary archeologist in chapter 5: liberty of conscience and freedom of thought; freedom of association, including both expressive association and intimate association, whatever one's sexual orientation; the right to live with one's family, whether nuclear or extended; the right to travel or relocate; the right to marry; the right to decide whether to bear or beget children, including the rights to procreate, to use contraceptives, and to terminate a pregnancy; the right to direct the education and rearing of children; and the right to exercise dominion over one's body, including the right to bodily integrity and ultimately the right to die.[1]

I first trace the trajectory of the substantive due process inquiry from *Palko v. Connecticut* (1937) to *Lawrence v. Texas* (2003), showing how the Court and individual justices have gone through three available conceptions regarding what constitutes a tradition and therefore of the baseline for what due process requires: (1) *abstract aspirational principles* (for example, Justice Cardozo's opinion of the Court in *Palko*[2] and Justice Brennan's dissenting opinion in *Michael H. v. Gerald D.*)[3]—principles to which we as a people aspire, and for which we as a people stand, whether or not we have always realized them in our historical practices, statute books, or common law; (2) *concrete historical practices* (for example, Justice Scalia's plurality opinion in *Michael H.*)[4]—liberty includes whatever liberties were protected specifically in the statute books or recognized concretely in the common law when the Fourteenth Amendment was adopted in 1868; and (3) a *"rational continuum"* and a *"living thing"* or evolving consensus (for example, Justice Harlan's dissenting opinion in *Poe v. Ullman*)—liberty is a "rational continuum," a "balance struck by this country, having regard to what history teaches are the traditions from which it developed as well as the traditions from which it broke. That tradition is a living thing."[5] Embracing the aspirational principles conception and recasting the rational continuum conception, I propose a reconception of the substantive due process inquiry that bases the recognition of "unenumerated" fundamental rights on their significance for deliberative autonomy. With this criterion of significance, constructivism's guiding framework charts a middle course between Scylla (Scalia)—the rock of liberty as "hidebound" historical practices—and Charybdis—the whirlpool of liberty as unbounded license.

Second, I attempt to bring a sense of order and discipline to (supposedly wild and unruly) judgments about the significance of certain rights for deliberative autonomy. To do so, I explore homologies between the structures of deliberative autonomy and deliberative democracy, and show that substantive due process and First Amendment jurisprudences are mirror images of one another with respect to the judgments that they make regarding significance for deliberative autonomy and deliberative democracy, respectively. Finally, I indicate what deliberative autonomy is not, distinguishing it from the familiar understandings or caricatures of privacy, autonomy, or liberty mentioned in the opening paragraph in chapter 1.

## The Rational Continuum of Ordered Liberty

*The Trajectory of Due Process from* Palko *to* Lawrence

DUE PROCESS FROM *PALKO* TO *BOWERS* TO *CASEY:* THE FLIGHT FROM ASPIRATIONAL PRINCIPLES TO HISTORICAL PRACTICES AND BACK

Between *Palko, Griswold v. Connecticut,* and *Roe v. Wade* on the one hand and *Bowers v. Hardwick* on the other, an important change occurred in the Supreme Court's conception of the due process inquiry. The Court moved from considering whether an asserted "unenumerated" fundamental right is "of the very essence of a scheme of ordered liberty,"[6] or is required by a "principle of justice so rooted in the traditions and conscience of our people as to be ranked as fundamental,"[7] to considering only whether it historically has been protected against governmental interference.[8] The former cases call for an inquiry into traditions conceived as *aspirational principles,* while the latter makes an inquiry into traditions understood as *historical practices,* narrowly conceived.[9] That is, between *Palko* and *Bowers,* the Court took flight from aspirational principles to historical practices in its understanding of what constitutes a tradition and therefore of the baseline for what due process requires. Between these two conceptions of the due process inquiry lies a third: Justice Harlan's formulation in his dissent in *Poe,* a "rational continuum" of liberty that views tradition as a "living thing."[10] In *Planned Parenthood v. Casey* and *Lawrence,*[11] the Court returned to this conception, which is closer to aspirational principles than to historical practices.

*Palko, Griswold,* and *Roe* conceived due process as encompassing the basic liberties implicit in a scheme of ordered liberty embodied in our Constitution—or the fundamental principles of justice to which we as a people aspire and for which we as a people stand ("aspirational principles")—whether or not we actually have realized them in our historical practices, common law, and statute books (collectively, "historical practices").[12] On this view, our aspirational principles may be critical of our historical practices, and our basic liberties and traditions are not merely the Burkean deposit of historical practices. Cases such as *Griswold* and *Roe,* as well as *Bolling v. Sharpe* and *Loving v. Virginia,* broke from historical practices in pursuit of due process and traditions in the sense of aspirational principles.[13]

In *Bolling,* Chief Justice Warren wrote that "[c]lassifications based solely upon race must be scrutinized with particular care, since they are contrary to our traditions and hence constitutionally suspect."[14] Warren's argument necessarily presupposes a conception of traditions as aspirational principles, given our shameful history of slavery and historical practices of enacting laws that drew classifications based solely on race, even after the ratification of the Civil War Amendments and Reconstruction. Similarly, Warren's statement in *Loving* that "[t]he freedom to marry has long been recognized as one of the vital personal rights essential to the orderly pursuit of happiness by free men"[15] necessarily reflects a conception of aspirational principles, given our shameful historical practices of enacting statutes forbidding interracial marriage.

In *Bowers,* by contrast, the Court per Justice White narrowly conceived the due process inquiry as a backward-looking question concerning historical practices, stripped of virtually any aspirational force or critical bite with respect to the status quo. White simply recounted our nation's historical practices disapproving homosexual sodomy and rudely dismissed the claim that the Due Process Clause protects "a fundamental right of homosexuals to engage in acts of consensual sodomy" as, "at best, facetious."[16] In fact, Justice White's view of history was narrow and selective. As Justice Stevens stressed in dissent, White flagrantly ignored that the common law and statutes historically condemned all sodomy, both homosexual and heterosexual.[17]

Justice Scalia's plurality opinion in *Michael H.* was an attempt to narrow the *Bowers* due process inquiry even further, to limit substantive due process to include only those rights that actually have been protected through historical practices, common law, and statutes.[18] Scalia also argued against conceiving protected rights abstractly, insisting on framing them at "the most specific level [of generality] at which a relevant tradition protecting, or denying protection to, the asserted right can be identified."[19] For example, in *Michael H.* itself, in rejecting an unwed biological father's assertion of parental visitation rights, Scalia framed the right at issue not in abstract terms of rights of parenthood (as Justice Brennan would have done), but as the right of "the natural father to assert parental rights over a child born into a woman's existing marriage with another man," or the right to have a state "award substantive parental rights to the natural father of a child conceived within, and born into, an extant marital union that wishes to embrace the child."[20] Scalia pitched the issue in apocalyptic terms of destruction. If the Court used the Due Process Clause to try to protect the citizenry from "irrationality and oppression," he warned, "it will destroy itself."[21] For the ghost of *Lochner* lurks.[22]

To avoid the destruction that he feared would follow in the wake of engaging in reasoned judgment concerning aspirational principles— veering into the whirlpool of liberty as unbounded license—Scalia steered into the rock of liberty as "hidebound" historical practices and narrowly conceived original understanding. As Justice Brennan aptly put it in his dissent in *Michael H.:* "The document that the plurality [opinion of Justice Scalia] construes today is unfamiliar to me. It is not the living charter that I have taken to be our Constitution; it is instead a stagnant, archaic, hidebound document steeped in the prejudices and superstitions of a time long past."[23] Brennan had taken our Constitution to be one of aspirational principles.

In *Casey,* the joint opinion rejected Scalia's *Michael H.* jurisprudence, resisting the "temptation" to flee from substantive liberties to original understanding, narrowly conceived, or from aspirational principles to historical practices.[24] It instead accepted Justice Harlan's approach to due process in his dissent in *Poe* and concurrence in *Griswold.*[25]

## RECONCEIVING JUSTICE HARLAN'S RATIONAL CONTINUUM OF ORDERED LIBERTY IN TERMS OF DELIBERATIVE AUTONOMY

Justice Harlan conceived the liberty guaranteed by the Due Process Clause as a "rational continuum" of ordered liberty, not merely as a "series of isolated points pricked out" in the constitutional document. Furthermore, he understood judgment in this area as a "rational process" that views tradition as a "living thing"—"[w]hat history teaches are the traditions from which [this country] developed as well as the traditions from which it broke"—not as a mechanical process of formulas or bright-line rules.[26] The joint opinion in *Casey* conceived the due process inquiry as requiring "reasoned judgment" in interpreting the Constitution, under-stood as a "covenant" or "coherent succession" whose "written terms embody ideas and aspirations that must survive more ages than one" and guarantee "the promise of liberty." It stated: "We accept our responsibil-ity not to retreat from interpreting the full meaning of the covenant in light of all of our precedents."[27] As shown below, Justice Kennedy's majority opinion in *Lawrence* reflected a similar conception of the due process inquiry and of the character of interpretation of the Constitution.

Constitutional constructivism provides a guiding framework for fulfill-ing the responsibility not to retreat from interpreting the full meaning of our covenant of aspirational principles. Only through such a holistic reading of the Constitution can we guarantee the promise of liberty rather than merely enforcing historical practices that may have failed to live up to that promise. In particular, we should reconceive Harlan's, the *Casey* joint opinion's, and *Lawrence*'s approach to due process along the lines of a constructivist criterion of significance for deliberative autonomy or deliberative democracy. Here, I focus on deliberative autonomy.

Justice Harlan's dissent in *Poe* represents a classic formulation of the due process inquiry. In recent years, liberal and conservative funda-mental rights theorists alike, from Laurence Tribe to Charles Fried, have celebrated it,[28] perhaps because it offers a safe harbor from the narrow originalism of Justice Scalia or Robert Bork. Put another way, Harlan's approach epitomized a *preservative conservatism* as distinguished from the *counter-revolutionary conservatism* of Scalia and Bork. Preservative conservatives (like Justices Harlan, Powell, O'Connor, Kennedy, and Souter) mostly attempt to preserve precedents and principles—rather than immediately overruling decisions that they, as an original matter, might have decided differently—perhaps conservatively developing those precedents and principles in subsequent cases rather than liberally expanding them. Counter-revolutionary conservatives (like Justices Scalia and Thomas and Chief Justice Rehnquist) seek to purge constitutional law of precedents and principles manifesting liberal error at the earliest available opportunity or—if they do not have the votes to do so—to reinterpret decisions so as to extirpate any generative force from them. Indeed, consider this dramatic testimony concerning how far constitutional law and theory have traveled since Harlan died in 1971: he, the most conservative member of the Warren Court, has become the last best hope of liberal theorists such as Tribe during the era of the Rehnquist Court and now the Roberts Court, as well as the target of an acerbic attack in *Casey* by Justice Scalia,[29] one of the two most conservative members of the Court (the other being Justice Thomas). *Casey* was a battleground between the preservative conservatives in the joint opinion who embraced Harlan's formulation of the due process inquiry and the counter-revolutionary conservatives in dissent who rejected it.

With all due respect, Justice Harlan's formulation of the due process inquiry suffers from two fundamental shortcomings. Consider his conceptions of *what* the Constitution is and *how* it ought to be interpreted. Harlan rightly conceived the Constitution as a "constitution of principle" (for him, basically common law principles) as opposed to a "constitution of detail."[30] And he rightly understood interpretation of the Constitution as a rational process of reasoned judgment as opposed to a mechanical process of bright-line rules. But his "common law constitution" was not fully a constructivist "constitution of principle."[31]

First, as for *what* the Constitution is, Harlan believed that a rational continuum of ordered liberty embodied in the Constitution provided the baseline for deciding what our "living" traditions are. But Harlan conceived ordered liberty by reference to those liberties that have been protected through the historical deposit of common law principles (the "common law constitution"). Thus he insufficiently appreciated that our Constitution reflects a scheme of ordered liberty that provides an alternative baseline of aspirational principles, which may fit and justify most of our historical practices, common law, and statutes but will criticize some of them. The basic reason for this shortcoming is that Harlan's understanding of what constitutes a tradition was too traditionalist and not sufficiently aspirational or critical. Harlan's analysis proves that tradition is too important to be left to the traditionalists.

Second, as for *how* to interpret the Constitution, Harlan believed that judgment in the due process inquiry is a rational process concerning tradition as a "living thing." But he did not adequately frame the questions concerning what our traditions are and what are those from which we have broken as distinguished from those that have survived. The basic guideline that he offered is the promise of the ineffable sound judgment or reason of a "first-rate common lawyer."[32] Alexander Bickel hardly did any better in formulating such questions, asking "Which values . . . qualify as sufficiently important or fundamental or what have you."[33] Harlan and Bickel were thus relatively easy prey for John Hart Ely's well-known critique of tradition, consensus, and reason as sources of substantive fundamental values in constitutional interpretation.[34]

Constitutional constructivism would reconceive the due process inquiry to redress these two shortcomings. First, it would reconstruct Harlan's idea of the rational continuum of ordered liberty embodied in the common law constitution, using a constructivist constitution of principle underwritten by a substantive political theory that best fits and justifies the constitutional document and underlying constitutional order as a whole. That substantive political theory articulates a scheme of ordered liberty to which our Constitution aspires through the two fundamental themes of deliberative autonomy and deliberative democracy. Thus the constructivist constitution of principle reflects a scheme of ordered liberty that provides a baseline of aspirational principles, centering on those two themes, which may fit and justify most of our historical practices, common law, and statutes but will criticize some of them for failing to live up to our constitutional commitments. If equal protection embodies a forward-looking anticaste principle, criticizing historical practices that flout our aspirations to equality, due process should secure a forward-looking antitotalitarian principle, criticizing historical practices that deny the promise of liberty, instead of merely safeguarding backward-looking historical practices.[35]

Second, constitutional constructivism would reconstruct Harlan's idea of judgment as a rational process concerning tradition as a "living thing" with a criterion of the significance of an asserted "unenumerated" fundamental right for deliberative autonomy. Such a criterion better frames the due process inquiry—concerning what our "living" traditions are and what are the historical practices from which we have broken or are breaking—by focusing on what are the significant preconditions for deliberative autonomy in our scheme of ordered liberty. Harlan's more formal and traditionalist formulation basically looked to common law principles for the sake of carrying them forward without offering a substantive account of what our basic liberties are or what they are for. Also, the criterion of significance for deliberative autonomy better fits and justifies the "unenumerated" fundamental rights listed in chapter 5 than does Harlan's formulation. For example, it is more plausible to argue that we should protect the right to decide whether to terminate a pregnancy (*Roe* and *Casey*), the right to homosexual intimate association (*Lawrence*), and the right to die (at least to the extent of a right to refuse unwanted medical treatment that would keep one alive, *Cruzan*) in order to secure deliberative autonomy than it is to contend that we should do so to safeguard long-standing yet evolving common law principles.

The joint opinion in *Casey* embraced Harlan's formulation of the due process inquiry in accounting for what the Court has done in this area. But we should distinguish Harlan's formulation both from how he himself would have applied it and from how the joint opinion in *Casey* in fact used it. For it is unlikely that he would have applied his method to reach many of the due process decisions that the Court handed down between *Griswold* and *Casey* and beyond to *Lawrence*.[36] Yet the joint opinion in *Casey* used his formulation to make sense of those decisions. Indeed, the joint opinion's account of decisions protecting substantive liberties such as decisional autonomy and bodily integrity has more in common with the justification that constitutional constructivism provides for them—that they secure significant preconditions for deliberative autonomy—than with the view that Harlan's more formal and traditionalist methodology would offer. Put another way, the practice of applying a method like Harlan's, over time, has led to lines of cases that are themselves better fit and justified, retrospectively, on the basis of a criterion of significance for deliberative autonomy. In sum, constitutional constructivism's criterion for framing the due process inquiry is superior, retrospectively and prospectively, to Harlan's more formal and traditionalist methodology.

REHNQUIST'S AND SCALIA'S METHODOLOGIES FOR INTERPRETING THE DUE
PROCESS CLAUSE IN *GLUCKSBERG, MICHAEL H.,* AND *CRUZAN:* THE
WHIPSAW OF LIBERTY BETWEEN SPECIFICITY AND ABSTRACTION

In *Washington v. Glucksberg,* in which the Court declined to extend the
right to die to include the right to physician-assisted suicide, Rehnquist
sought to rein in the *Poe-Casey* formulation of the due process inquiry. If
Harlan's methodology in *Poe* and the joint opinion's approach in *Casey*
represented a "rational continuum" of liberty, Rehnquist's methodology
in *Glucksberg* represents a "whipsaw" of liberty between specific and
abstract levels of generality in the characterization of asserted rights: it
rigs the description narrowly or broadly in order to make it easy for the
Court to reject any given right. The same argument applies to Scalia's
methodology in *Michael H.* and *Cruzan.* To substantiate this claim, I
examine these three cases in some depth.

In *Glucksberg,* Rehnquist wrote that the Court's "established method
of substantive due process analysis has two primary features"[37]:

> First, we have regularly observed that the Due Process Clause specially pro-
> tects those fundamental rights and liberties which are, objectively, "deeply
> rooted in this Nation's history and tradition," . . . and "implicit in the concept
> of ordered liberty." . . . Second, we have required . . . a "careful description" of
> the asserted fundamental liberty interest.[38]

Rehnquist continued: "Justice Souter, relying on Justice Harlan's dissenting opinion in [*Poe,*] would largely abandon this restrained methodology. . . . True, the Court relied on Justice Harlan's dissent in *Casey,* but . . .
we did not in so doing jettison our established approach."[39]

In calling for a "careful description" of the asserted right and an
inquiry into "[o]ur Nation's history, legal traditions, and practices,"
Rehnquist called to mind Scalia's formulation of the due process inquiry
in his plurality opinion in *Michael H.* and in his concurring opinion
in *Cruzan.* In *Michael H.,* Scalia famously offered the following methodology for selecting the level of generality in deciding whether an asserted
right has been traditionally protected: "We refer to the most specific level
at which a relevant tradition protecting, or denying protection to, the
asserted right can be identified."[40] Clearly, he conceived tradition as
"historical practices," not as "aspirational principles." In *Cruzan,* Scalia
similarly wrote: "[N]o 'substantive due process' claim can be maintained

unless the claimant demonstrates that the State has deprived him of a right historically and traditionally protected against state interference."[41]

In *Glucksberg,* however, Rehnquist did not officially follow, or even cite, Scalia's *Michael H.* opinion. It is reasonable to conclude that Rehnquist was wary of doing anything that might have prompted O'Connor and Kennedy to concur separately with respect to due process methodology. For one thing, O'Connor, with Kennedy joining the opinion, concurred in *Michael H.,* rejecting pointedly Scalia's "mode of historical analysis" because it "may be somewhat inconsistent with our past decisions in this area"[42] and referring favorably to Harlan's dissent in *Poe.*[43] For another, both O'Connor and Kennedy participated with Souter in the joint opinion in *Casey,* which rejected Scalia's *Michael H.* methodology as "inconsistent with our law" and embraced Harlan's *Poe* methodology.[44]

Even though Rehnquist did not officially follow Scalia's *Michael H.* opinion, the question arises whether he, in applying his formulation in *Glucksberg,* carried out a *Michael H.* analysis. At first, Rehnquist's call for a "careful description" sounded like Scalia's call in *Michael H.* for a specific or narrow, rather than abstract or broad, formulation of the asserted right. We should examine Rehnquist's actual description of the right asserted in *Glucksberg,* however. Here it is useful to bear in mind Rehnquist's rather specific formulation in *Cruzan* of the right asserted. Instead of framing it *abstractly,* as the right to die or the right to commit suicide, he framed it *specifically,* as the right of a competent adult to refuse unwanted medical treatment including lifesaving hydration and nutrition.[45] Notably, in *Cruzan,* Scalia himself eschewed any such specific formulation in favor of highly abstract formulations—the right to die and the right to commit suicide.[46]

In *Glucksberg,* however, Rehnquist did not formulate the asserted right specifically or narrowly, as he did in *Cruzan.* Rather, he framed it highly abstractly, as "a right to commit suicide which itself includes a right to assistance in doing so."[47] That is, he took the approach that Scalia took in concurrence in *Cruzan,* even though several more specific formulations were readily available to him, formulations that arguably have greater support in our traditions whether they are understood as historical practices or aspirational principles. For example, Rehnquist did not frame the asserted right as the court of appeals did in its *en banc* decision: the right of terminally ill, competent adults to control the manner and timing of their deaths by using medication prescribed by their physicians.[48] Nor did he frame it as Breyer did in concurrence: "a right to die with dignity" (which he characterized as "a different formulation, for which our legal tradition may provide greater support").[49] Nor did he heed Stevens's objections in concurrence that, even if "[h]istory and tradition provide ample support for refusing to recognize an open-ended [or 'categorical'] constitutional right to commit suicide," our Constitution protects a "basic concept of freedom" that "embraces not merely a person's right to refuse a particular kind of unwanted treatment, but also her interest in dignity, and in determining the character of the memories that will survive long after her death."[50]

We can now see that both Rehnquist and Scalia resort to a whipsaw between specificity and abstraction in formulating the level of generality of an asserted right. Sometimes Scalia rejects assertions of rights after framing them highly specifically, as in *Michael H.:* the right of "the natural father to assert parental rights over a child born into a woman's existing marriage with another man," or the right to have a state "award substantive parental rights to the natural father of a child conceived within, and born into, an extant marital union that wishes to embrace the child."[51] At other times Scalia rejects assertions of rights after framing them in highly abstract forms, as in *Cruzan:* the right to die and the right to commit suicide. This whipsaw pinches from both sides, specificity and abstraction. Scalia always frames the right in the manner that makes it appear to have the least support in our traditions (understood as historical practices).

Rehnquist's whipsaw is more complex in how it pinched from both sides. He joined Scalia's plurality opinion in *Michael H.* and thus embraced Scalia's highly specific formulation. In *Cruzan,* he framed the asserted right specifically, *Michael H.* style, and "assumed" that it was protected, while Scalia framed it highly abstractly and rejected it. Then, in *Glucksberg,* Rehnquist framed the asserted right highly abstractly and rejected it. Both Rehnquist's and Scalia's resorts to this whipsaw between specificity and abstraction showed that their search for a "careful description" involved taking care to describe the asserted right in a manner that made it easiest for the Court to conclude that there was no support for it in tradition and thus to reject it. Rehnquist's and Scalia's methodologies for interpreting the Due Process Clause are rigged against protecting basic liberties and are not faithful to the abstract moral principles embodied in our constitution of principle.

We should ask which methodology, Rehnquist's or Harlan's and Souter's, is more "[]consistent with our law" in the area of substantive due process. That is, which account better fits with and justifies cases such as *Meyer*,[52] *Pierce*,[53] *Griswold*,[54] *Loving*,[55] *Roe*,[56] *Moore*,[57] *Cruzan*, and *Casey?* The Harlan-Souter methodology wins hands down over Rehnquist's methodology. The former can account for all of these cases—as the joint opinion in *Casey* did through the framework of "reasoned judgment"—while the latter can account for none of them. None of these cases protected a right as a matter of vindicating long-standing, concrete historical practices as Rehnquist and Scalia conceive them, that is, historical practices embodied in and specifically protected by statutes and common law; but all of them are justifiable on the basis of realizing aspirational principles that are critical of such practices. This should come as no surprise, for it is very likely that, as an original matter, Rehnquist as well as Scalia would have dissented in all of these cases; in fact, Rehnquist and Scalia did dissent in some of them.[58] It is also very likely that, had they the votes to do so, they would have overruled these cases. Through his methodology, Rehnquist, like Scalia, was engaged in damage control; his concerns were not merely to decline to extend this line of cases, but also to gut the cases of any vitality or generative force. Again, both Rehnquist and Scalia showed themselves to be counter-revolutionary conservatives, not preservative conservatives like Harlan.

## *LAWRENCE:* A RETURN TO ASPIRATIONAL PRINCIPLES

Justice Kennedy's opinion in *Lawrence*[59] strikingly repudiated the framework of *Glucksberg* in favor of the framework of *Casey*. In so doing, it signaled a return to a conception of tradition as a rational continuum or evolving consensus of aspirational principles. In fact, one reason Scalia was so furious in dissent in *Lawrence* is his belief that *Glucksberg* had "'eroded'" *Casey*'s conception of the due process inquiry.[60] Kennedy wrote in *Lawrence*:

> Had those who drew and ratified the Due Process Clauses of the Fifth Amendment or the Fourteenth Amendment known the components of liberty in its manifold possibilities, they might have been more specific. They did not presume to have this insight. They knew times can blind us to certain truths and later generations can see that laws once thought necessary and proper in

fact serve only to oppress. As the Constitution endures, persons in every generation can invoke its principles in their own search for greater freedom.[61]

Thus Kennedy, unlike Rehnquist and Scalia, did not attribute arrogance and authoritarianism to the founders: "They did not presume" to enumerate specifically the components of constitutionally protected liberty. This passage underscores that the Court conceived the Constitution as an abstract scheme of principles to be elaborated over time—in a "search for greater freedom"—not as a specific code of detailed rules and enumerated rights (or an expression of the founders' intentions, understandings, and meanings or a deposit of historical practices) to be discovered and preserved.

If Kennedy did not claim to ground the right to privacy or autonomy in original understanding, where did he ground it? The answer is in the line of privacy or autonomy cases beginning with *Griswold* and running through *Eisenstadt v. Baird*,[62] *Carey v. Population Services International*,[63] *Roe*, and *Casey*[64] (along with *Romer v. Evans*,[65] which is grounded in equal protection),[66] and in an understanding of tradition as an evolving consensus of aspirational principles. Kennedy conceived tradition not as a positivist, historicist, or traditionalist deposit of "millennia of moral teaching"[67] (to quote Chief Justice Burger's concurring opinion in *Bowers*), but as an evolving consensus about how best to realize liberty (and by implication equality).

This evolving consensus reaches beyond "this Nation's history and tradition" to that of a wider, Western civilization, as evidenced by *Lawrence*'s citation of *Dudgeon v. United Kingdom*, a decision of the European Court of Human Rights holding that laws proscribing consensual homosexual sexual conduct are invalid under the European Convention on Human Rights.[68] Similarly, in *Roper v. Simmons*, which abolished the death penalty for juveniles as cruel and unusual punishment under the Eighth Amendment, the Court referred to the laws of other countries, observing that "the United States now stands alone in a world that has turned its face against the juvenile death penalty."[69] This is not the place fully to weigh in on the emerging and fascinating debate about the Court's invocation of international authorities and the laws of other countries in constitutional decisions like *Lawrence* and *Roper*.[70] Here I simply would suggest that the due process inquiry under *Palko* (whether an asserted liberty is essential to "a scheme of ordered liberty," such that "a fair and enlightened system of justice would be impossible" without it)[71] and the cruel and unusual punishment inquiry under *Trop v. Dulles* applied in *Roper* (whether a practice accords with "the evolving standards of decency that mark the progress of a maturing society")[72] invite comparative constitutional law inquiries reckoning with the practices of other "enlightened" and "maturing" societies.

Furthermore, in *Lawrence,* Kennedy carefully scrutinized history to determine what the statutes, common law, and historical practices actually prohibited.[73] He found that they prohibited sodomy generally, not same-sex sodomy as such or even non-procreative sexual conduct. In this respect, his opinion was markedly different from White's and Burger's opinions in *Bowers,* and more like Stevens's dissenting opinion there.[74] The Court in *Lawrence* practically accepted the very unauthoritarian notion of "[t]he [i]nvention of [h]eterosexuality,"[75] and thus the invention of homosexuality, as against the idea that it is just there as a natural and moral fact of the matter and that it has been condemned through millennia of Judeo-Christian moral teaching.

What exactly was the role of history in Kennedy's opinion? The Court critiqued *Bowers*'s invocation of history as an obstacle to recognizing the right of homosexuals to privacy or autonomy, a right that principled elaboration of the precedents protecting privacy or autonomy (mentioned above) would lead one to recognize. That is, the Court cleared away White's and Burger's use of history in *Bowers* as representing "millennia of moral teaching" that precluded recognizing the right. So, Kennedy analyzed history to debunk their monolithic and traditionalist claims about history. Thus, the Court used history negatively to show that history does not foreclose a just interpretation of our Constitution to protect the right of homosexuals to privacy or autonomy.

The Court also made a positive use of history, applying a Harlan-like notion of tradition as a "living thing" to direct attention to recent evolving consensus. Under this view, we have regard for the traditions from which we have broken—here, the Court looked at the states' evolving repudiation of statutes outlawing sodomy differently than White did in *Bowers*[76]—as well as the traditions we carry forward. Kennedy's opinion in *Lawrence* implied that, on a proper understanding of tradition as a living thing or evolving consensus of aspirational principles, the pattern of the repeal of laws proscribing sodomy between 1961 and 1986 should have supported the opposite holding in *Bowers.*[77] *Lawrence* represented a return to a *Casey*-like understanding of aspirational principles and a repudiation of Scalia's and Rehnquist's conceptions of historical practices.

*Between Scalia and Charybdis*

Constitutional constructivism's guiding framework, with its criterion of significance for deliberative autonomy, charts a middle course between Scalia—the rock of liberty as hidebound historical practices—and Charybdis—the whirlpool of liberty as unbounded license—in the due process inquiry.[78] Haunted by the ghost of *Lochner,* Scalia wrote ominously about the dangers that judicial protection of basic liberties through the Due Process Clause, which he found dangerously unbounded, posed for destruction.[79] But we need to recall that veering into either the rock or the whirlpool brings destruction. Tethering the due process inquiry to the structure of deliberative autonomy might help stem the Court's characteristic temptation to flee from aspirational principles to historical practices in this area, as well as steady its return to aspirational principles.

Constitutional constructivism does not advocate writing on a blank slate concerning significance for deliberative autonomy. It calls for working within our ongoing constitutional democracy, which has a long-standing practice and tradition of protecting "unenumerated" fundamental rights that are essential to our "scheme of ordered liberty"[80] or to the "orderly pursuit of happiness."[81] In the first instance, my project here is retrospective, contending that a criterion such as significance for deliberative autonomy accounts for why the categories of personal decisions encompassed by the foregoing list of "unenumerated" fundamental rights are indeed fundamental and should be on the list.[82] Put simply, it fits and justifies the cases. That established, my proposal is prospective, arguing for using such a criterion in further specifying the basic liberties presupposed by our constitutional document and underlying constitutional order. Needless to say, offering a criterion of significance will not resolve all questions concerning the scope and content of the basic liberties associated with deliberative autonomy, or concerning the governmental interests that may justify regulating such liberties in particular circumstances. It will, however, help frame and guide our reflections and judgments regarding those questions, which can be resolved only as they arise.

And so, applying the constructivist guiding framework in giving content to our rational continuum of ordered liberty, we should interpret the Constitution to secure the basic liberties that are significant preconditions for deliberative autonomy (as well as of deliberative democracy). By interpreting the Constitution in this manner, to recall the joint opinion in *Casey,* we would face up to the responsibility to give full meaning to our constitution of principle, a covenant of aspirations and ideals that guarantee the promise of liberty and that must survive more ages than one.[83] And, to recall Justice Kennedy's opinion in *Lawrence,* we would not "presume"—any more than the framers and ratifiers of the Constitution did—exhaustively to specify "the components of liberty in its manifold possibilities."[84]

## Exploring Homologies regarding Significance for Deliberative Democracy and Deliberative Autonomy

*Homologies between the Structures of First Amendment and Substantive Due Process Jurisprudences*

Many constitutional theorists and judges assume that democracy and the First Amendment are relatively grounded and settled compared to autonomy and substantive due process, which they regard as free-for-alls that are anathema to constitutional law. They may fear that engaging in "reasoned judgment" concerning which "unenumerated" fundamental rights are significant for deliberative autonomy is, as Scalia put it in dissent in *Casey,* indistinguishable from "Lochnering" or imposing one's own "philosophical predilection[s] and moral intuition[s]" in the guise of interpreting the Constitution.[85] Using constitutional constructivism's guiding framework with two fundamental themes, however, I attempt to domesticate supposedly wild and unruly judgments about significance for deliberative autonomy to constitutional law through exploring homologies between the structure of First Amendment jurisprudence and that of substantive due process jurisprudence.[86] I contend that the refusal on the part of First Amendment jurisprudence to protect certain categories of expression while protecting other areas of expression is a mirror image of substantive due process jurisprudence's protection of certain categories of decision but refusal to protect other decisions. These jurisprudences are illuminatingly seen as efforts to cabin comprehensive principles of autonomy by constructing frameworks that require judgments concerning significance for deliberative democracy and deliberative autonomy, respectively. For autonomy theories in these areas of constitutional law push toward protecting all expression and all decisions.

Using the guiding framework to bring out such homologies between the First Amendment and substantive due process, or between deliberative democracy and deliberative autonomy, will not itself decide any concrete cases. But it will suggest coherence and structure in the substantive due process inquiry, an area where many have persisted in seeing only periodic interventions by free-wheeling philosopher-judges. Moreover, using the framework will illuminate the structural role of deliberative autonomy in our constitutional democracy in relation to that of deliberative democracy.

## FIRST FUNDAMENTAL CASE: THE INSIGNIFICANCE OF CATEGORIES OF UNPROTECTED EXPRESSION FOR DELIBERATIVE DEMOCRACY

Our First Amendment jurisprudence has distinguished two levels of expression—high value and low value speech—on the basis of judgments about its significance for securing a scheme of deliberative democracy.[87] Rather than making case-by-case judgments about the value of particular expression, however, the Supreme Court has recognized certain categories of *unprotected expression,* in advance, as relatively *insignificant.*[88] These categories include fighting words, obscenity, libel, and incitement to imminent lawless action.[89] All of them are relatively insignificant for securing a scheme of deliberative democracy (or for the development and exercise of the first moral power in the first fundamental case discussed in chapter 4).

Under such a two-level framework, the Court has applied most exacting scrutiny to laws that restrict or regulate expression that is *outside* these categories of unprotected or insignificant expression: This is the domain of the "absolute" (or at least stringently protected) First Amendment.[90] Within the unprotected categories, the Court has generally applied less stringent scrutiny to laws that restrict or regulate expression.[91] Moreover, Ely and Cass Sunstein, leading theorists advocating reinforcing representative democracy or securing deliberative democracy, have advanced such two-tier frameworks, arguing that they serve the central function of the First Amendment: maintaining democracy.[92] Thus, a criterion like significance for deliberative democracy has informed First Amendment jurisprudence.

## SECOND FUNDAMENTAL CASE: THE SIGNIFICANCE OF CATEGORIES OF PROTECTED DECISIONS FOR DELIBERATIVE AUTONOMY

Likewise, our substantive due process jurisprudence has distinguished two levels of decisions on the basis of judgments about their significance for securing a scheme of deliberative autonomy: unusually important decisions, which are significant for that purpose, and less important decisions, which are relatively insignificant or of no significance for it. Rather than making case-by-case judgments about the value of particular decisions, however, the Court has recognized certain categories of *protected decisions,* in advance, as relatively *significant.* These categories have included most if not all of the decisions encompassed by the foregoing list of "unenumerated" fundamental rights. All of them are unusually important or significant for securing a scheme of deliberative autonomy (or for the development and exercise of the second moral power in the second fundamental case).

Applying such a two-level framework, the Court has applied more stringent scrutiny to laws that restrict or regulate decisions that come *within* (most of) these categories of protected or significant decisions: This is the realm of personal sovereignty to make certain fundamental decisions, reserved to or retained by persons, that the government may not enter.[93] Outside these protected categories, the Court has generally applied relatively lenient scrutiny to laws that restrict or regulate liberty and conduct.[94] Thus, a criterion like significance for deliberative autonomy has informed substantive due process jurisprudence.

## The Language and Design of Deliberative Democracy and Deliberative Autonomy

Some narrow originalists might object to my sketch of First Amendment and substantive due process jurisprudences as mirror images of each other. They might argue that the former secures "enumerated" rights, whereas the latter protects "unenumerated" rights.

Constitutional constructivism has two main responses. First, as argued in chapter 5, the basic liberties that underwrite deliberative autonomy—liberty of conscience and freedom of association—like freedom of expression, have well-established First Amendment roots. Second, none of the categories of unprotected expression, for example, obscenity, is "enumerated" in the language of the First Amendment; the judgments that these types of expression are relatively insignificant for deliberative democracy are instead rooted in inferences of substantive political theory from the underlying structure or design of deliberative democracy.[95] Likewise, none of the categories of protected decisions is "enumerated" in the language of the Due Process Clauses; but the judgments that these types of decisions are significant for deliberative autonomy are rooted in inferences of substantive political theory from the underlying structure or design of deliberative autonomy.[96]

Overblown distinctions between "enumerated" and "unenumerated" rights aside, are there any relevant differences between the First Amendment and substantive due process with respect to judgments regarding significance? Some narrow originalists summon the specter of *Lochner* in an attempt to frighten us away from substantive due process, as Justice White did in *Bowers,* arguing that asserted liberties associated with deliberative autonomy have "little or no cognizable roots in the language or design of the Constitution."[97] They claim that the specter of *Lochner* haunts substantive due process but not the First Amendment.[98] That putative difference, however, is deeply problematic. For those, such as Scalia, who most vociferously decry "Lochnering" in substantive due process jurisprudence are often the ones who most vigorously engage in "Lochnering" in First Amendment jurisprudence.[99] Obviously, complex issues lurk here concerning what is wrong with *Lochner:* that the judiciary gave heightened protection to "unenumerated" fundamental rights as such (White's and Scalia's view), or that the judiciary treated the status quo of existing distributions of wealth and political power as a prepolitical state of nature, or neutral baseline, and therefore held that interfering with it was an impermissibly partisan objective (Sunstein's and my view). I pursued these matters in chapter 3, arguing that securing deliberative autonomy does not involve "Lochnering."[100]

Thus, First Amendment jurisprudence and substantive due process jurisprudence do not differ in any way that undercuts my homology. Both are derived from "enumerated" rights along with underlying structures. Constitutional interpretation in both areas involves structural reasoning, not just textual exegesis or historical research concerning isolated clauses. Carrying forward the unfinished business of Charles Black, we would become more literate concerning the language and design of the Constitution by comprehending that the basic liberties associated with both deliberative democracy and deliberative autonomy have structural roles to play in our constitutional scheme.[101]

Furthermore, this analysis illustrates that carving out categories of unprotected expression, like recognizing categories of protected decisions, requires judgments of significance grounded in substantive political theory. It simply is not the case that the former judgments are unproblematically neutral or "process-oriented" while the latter judgments are problematically normative or "substantive." The structure of deliberative democracy and the First Amendment is hardly more determinate, neutral, or uncontroversial than the structure of deliberative autonomy and substantive due process. We make judgments of significance for deliberative democracy all the time in the context of the First Amendment. We should not be overly anxious about making judgments of significance for deliberative autonomy in the context of substantive due process.

## The Homologous Frameworks for Cabining Autonomy in First Amendment and Substantive Due Process Jurisprudences

The constructivist guiding framework suggests another homology between the two fundamental themes of deliberative democracy and deliberative autonomy: the jurisprudences of both the First Amendment and substantive due process, by requiring judgments regarding significance, provide frameworks for cabining comprehensive principles of autonomy that otherwise press toward protecting all expression and all decisions. Indeed, the two main areas of constitutional law where autonomy theories abound are the First Amendment and substantive due process.[102]

Autonomy as a comprehensive principle, brought to bear on First Amendment jurisprudence, tends to erode if not obliterate all of the categories of unprotected insignificant expression and thus to protect virtually all expression. It abhors empowering the government, including courts, to make judgments about the significance of expression for deliberative democracy. All that it would leave of First Amendment jurisprudence would be generally "absolute" freedom of expression, grounded on something like a comprehensive Millian principle of the autonomy or individuality of citizens. Autonomous individuals could hear all expression, no matter how insignificant the government might think it for deliberative democracy, and decide for themselves the significance of that expression[103] (subject, perhaps, to a Millian harm principle or the like).[104]

Likewise, autonomy as a comprehensive principle, brought to bear on substantive due process jurisprudence, tends to expand the categories of protected significant decisions and thus to protect virtually all decisions that persons might make in exercising their capacity for a conception of the good. It dreads allowing the government, including courts, to make judgments about the significance of decisions for deliberative autonomy. Substantive due process would become something like a comprehensive

Millian principle of the autonomy or individuality of citizens. Autonomous individuals, making decisions according to their own consciences, would become virtually a law unto themselves (subject again, perhaps, to a Millian harm principle or the like).[105]

Constitutional constructivism embraces neither comprehensive Millian principle of autonomy or individuality—either in First Amendment jurisprudence or in substantive due process jurisprudence. Its guiding framework with two fundamental themes cabins comprehensive principles of autonomy with a criterion of significance for deliberative democracy and deliberative autonomy, and prevents such principles of autonomy from unduly constraining deliberative democracy.

The constructivist guiding framework thus provides a lens through which we can see that judgments about significance regarding categories of decisions for deliberative autonomy are neither anomalous in constitutional law nor especially unruly, but are like judgments about significance regarding categories of expression for deliberative democracy. Put another way, it shows that the Constitution is Janus-faced: the first theme provides an entrance, opening up deliberative democracy with regard to significant expression, while the second theme offers an exit, an escape from deliberative democracy with respect to significant decisions.[106]

## What Deliberative Autonomy Is Not

I have observed that scholars and jurists have either belittled the right to privacy or autonomy as trivial or portrayed it as wild, unruly, and dangerous. In this section, I briefly distinguish deliberative autonomy from certain familiar understandings and caricatures of privacy, autonomy, or liberty. Doing so will both defend deliberative autonomy against common criticisms of such ideas and further elaborate its boundaries and content.

### Deliberative Autonomy Is Not a Comprehensive Liberal "Right to Be Different"

Ely mocks the right to autonomy as "the right to be different," belittling it as being an "upper-middle-class right"—"the right of my son to wear his hair as long as he pleases"[107]—or as reflecting the values of the "reasoning class."[108] Moreover, because the best-known liberal conception of autonomy or individuality is that of Mill, Ely rolls out the inevitable paraphrase of Justice Holmes's dissenting opinion in *Lochner* protesting resort to political or economic theory in constitutional interpretation: "If the Constitution does not enact Herbert Spencer's *Social Statics,* does it enact John Stuart Mill's *On Liberty?*"[109]

Constitutional constructivism does not embrace a comprehensive liberal "right to be different" that extends constitutional protection to everyone's pursuit of individuality or autonomy in a broad sense.[110] Indeed, as discussed above, there are affinities between my structural argument for deliberative autonomy as an "exit" option and Ely's own analysis of the right of "dissenting or 'different'" individuals to relocate.[111] I do not consider a right to wear one's hair as long as one pleases (which Ely mocks) or a right to loaf to be illustrations of deliberative autonomy. With all due respect to Justices Marshall and Douglas, who argued during the early years of the Burger Court that the Constitution does protect such rights,[112] I fear that they may have extended the idea of autonomy too far, well beyond constitutional essentials to a romantic ideal of self-fulfillment or the development of one's individuality, tastes, and personality.[113] Constitutional constructivism limits the scope of autonomy to protecting significant basic liberties. The "unenumerated" fundamental rights listed earlier, which I have characterized as significant for deliberative autonomy, do not have an elitist cast.

I do not mean to trivialize the significance of hair length or loafing in any particular conception of the good or ideal of self-fulfillment[114] or to deny that there may be good arguments against regulations that encroach on such liberty claims. But advancing such claims as constitutional rights has provided fodder for those who would trivialize the more significant "unenumerated" fundamental rights mentioned above, making it too easy to caricature arguments for such significant rights. Perhaps notions of autonomy or self-fulfillment like those expressed by Justices Marshall and Douglas frightened the conservative Burger and Rehnquist Courts and fueled their flight from aspirational principles to historical practices in the due process inquiry.

My response to Ely's paraphrase of Holmes's dissent in *Lochner* involves a strategy of confession and avoidance. The confession is to admit that the first wave of Rawlsian constitutional theorists, after the 1971 publication of Rawls's *A Theory of Justice,*[115] may have zealously extended arguments for constitutional rights of autonomy too far: going beyond essential basic liberties that are significant within a political conception of justice to something like a comprehensive moral view, such as Millian individuality or autonomy. They may have embraced what Rawls later calls a "comprehensive liberalism" as distinguished from a "political liberalism."[116] However attractive such comprehensive moral views may be from a normative standpoint, they cannot fit and justify, but must criticize as mistaken, a great deal of our constitutional law that fails to recognize rights to develop one's individuality or autonomy.

The avoidance is to contend that the second wave of Rawlsian constitutional theorists, following the 1993 publication of his *Political Liberalism,* should tether constitutional rights of autonomy to the structure of basic liberties that are significant for deliberative autonomy within a political conception of justice (or political liberalism). They should not try to secure, as constitutional rights, whatever liberties are entailed by comprehensive moral views of individuality or autonomy. Understandably, the first wave of Rawlsian constitutional theorists did not appreciate the distinction between a political liberalism and a comprehensive liberalism; in fact, Rawls himself did not.[117] In working out a constitutional constructivism, I invoke this distinction to avoid or deflect Ely's criticism and paraphrase of Holmes's dissent in *Lochner* by basically agreeing with it. The Constitution no more enacts Mill's comprehensive moral view of individuality or autonomy than it establishes the Catholic Church or a Christian Nation or any other comprehensive conception of the good. (Nor, as I noted in chapter 4, does it enact John Rawls's *A Theory of Justice* or his *Political Liberalism.*)

### Deliberative Autonomy Is Not a Comprehensive Libertarian Principle of Autonomy

Some libertarians might object that deliberative autonomy is too bounded or does not go far enough in securing autonomy. Indeed, deliberative autonomy is not a comprehensive libertarian principle of autonomy or limited government that deems every exercise of the police power of the state presumptively illegitimate. Here I differentiate deliberative autonomy from libertarian theories like that of Randy E. Barnett, who argues for stringent judicial protection of liberties (including economic liberties) against the baseline of a presumption of liberty and against governmental regulation.[118]

First, constitutional constructivism is not a libertarian view but instead a synthesis of liberalism and civic republicanism. It accords priority not to a libertarian right to liberty as such, but rather to the scheme of basic liberties that is articulated through the two fundamental themes of deliberative democracy and deliberative autonomy.[119] This contrast entails two further contrasts. Second, constitutional constructivism, like John Hart Ely's *Carolene Products* theory of *Democracy and Distrust,* in general presumes the constitutionality of legislation. It identifies specific situations in which the political processes are not trustworthy, and only in those situations does it call for a more searching judicial scrutiny. Barnett reverses this presumption. He begins with a presumption of liberty and practically presumes every governmental regulation to be illegitimate. Thus, his theory is generally distrustful of the political processes. Third, deliberative autonomy is a conception of autonomy—and of the basic liberties that are preconditions for the exercise of the second moral power (the capacity for a conception of the good) in the second fundamental case (that of applying that capacity to deliberating about and deciding how to live their own lives)—not a conception of liberty as such. Barnett's libertarian conception, by contrast, is a conception of liberty as such, and only incidentally a conception of autonomy.

Fourth, accordingly, constitutional constructivism conceives "unenumerated" rights as implicit in our practice of constitutional democracy, rights that are significant for the development and exercise of one (or both) of the two moral powers in one (or both) of the two fundamental cases. Unlike Barnett, it does not conceive these rights as natural rights. After all, again, it is a constructivism, not a theory of moral realism, natural law, or natural rights. Finally, unlike Barnett, who ultimately eschews providing a criterion for identifying our "unenumerated" fundamental rights in favor of a procedural presumption of liberty and against governmental regulation, constitutional constructivism offers the criterion of significance for deliberative democracy or deliberative autonomy.

For example, as noted in chapter 4, the right to personal property is a constitutional essential and indeed a precondition for both deliberative democracy and deliberative autonomy. But constitutional constructivism does not justify special judicial protection of economic liberties. In fact, economic liberties and property rights are so significant and fundamental in our constitutional scheme, and so sacred in our constitutional culture, that there is neither need nor good argument for aggressive judicial protection of them. Rather, such liberties are properly judicially under-enforced, for their fuller enforcement and protection is secure with legislatures and executives in the Constitution outside the courts. There is every indication that they can and do fend well enough for themselves in the political process. The regulation of such liberties does not present a situation of distrust that would warrant more searching judicial protection. Therefore, deferential scrutiny of economic regulation is appropriate.[120] Thus, despite the views of libertarians like Barnett and Richard Epstein, the opportunity for consenting adults to perform capitalistic acts in private without governmental regulation is not among the stringently judicially enforced preconditions for deliberative autonomy, any more than for deliberative democracy.[121] Much regulation that would be, as *Lochner* put it, "meddlesome interferences with the rights of the individual"[122] in a libertarian private society would be legitimate, important, or even compelling in our constitutional democracy.

Nor does deliberative autonomy rule as off limits certain common-place, minimal forms of paternalism to which some libertarians might object, such as social insurance, drug laws, and automobile safety requirements.[123] Unlike laws regulating or restricting the "unenumerated" fundamental rights on the foregoing list, such paternalistic laws typically do not implicate the concerns of the antitotalitarian principle of liberty or infringe on significant basic liberties. There may well be forceful libertarian autonomy arguments (as well as pragmatic arguments) against some laws of this sort. But no plausible principle of autonomy secured by our Constitution prohibits them, for too much of our practice does not square with such a principle. Moreover, the liberty claims infringed by such measures do not satisfy the constructivist criterion of significance for deliberative autonomy.

Indeed, a constitutional democracy dedicated to securing deliberative autonomy might adopt many legislative measures aimed at preventing or discouraging persons from "destroying those basic rational capacities that make them moral beings worthy of respect."[124] It certainly would pass many legislative programs designed to promote the development and exercise of those capacities.[125] There are limits to what measures legislatures may take, but minimal forms of paternalism such as those mentioned do not transgress those limits.

Finally, deliberative autonomy does not put us on a slippery slope leading to "the end of all morals legislation."[126] In *Lawrence,* Scalia protested in dissent that if states may not enact their moral disapproval of homosexual sodomy, they may not in principle enact their disapproval of "bigamy, same-sex marriage, adult incest, prostitution, masturbation, adultery, fornication, bestiality, and obscenity."[127] For him, homosexuals' intimate sexual conduct is analogous to such traditional morals offenses, not to heterosexuals' autonomy regarding intimate associations. Deliberative autonomy is not a libertarian conception of liberty as such that condemns all "morals legislation," nor does *Lawrence*'s embrace of deliberative autonomy put us on a slippery slope. The reason is that *Lawrence*'s argument for protecting homosexual intimate association is grounded in the recognition that it is closely analogous to heterosexual intimate association, which is already constitutionally protected. The argument is not grounded in a libertarian view that it is illegitimate for the state to pass laws based on moral judgments as such. The latter argument, if it had been accepted in *Lawrence,* might have put the Court on a slippery slope. But the former argument, which was accepted there, does not.

In sum, deliberative autonomy protects a right of homosexuals to autonomy or intimate association that is analogous to that already protected for heterosexuals. And it does so not to enable individuals to partake of immoral activities, but to secure the significant preconditions for deliberative autonomy and the status of free and equal citizenship for homosexuals and heterosexuals alike. Hence, deliberative autonomy would not unduly constrain deliberative democracy with a comprehensive libertarian right to autonomy.[128]

### Deliberative Autonomy Is Not a "Right of Men 'To Be Let Alone' to Oppress Women"

Some progressives and feminists are wary of such ideas as privacy, autonomy, or liberty because they believe them to mask abuse and oppression. Instead, they emphasize deliberative democracy and an anticaste principle of equality in grounding basic liberties. For example, Catharine A. MacKinnon famously argues that rights to privacy, autonomy, and liberty may readily prove, for women, to be "an injury got up as a gift"[129] or a "right of men 'to be let alone' to oppress women one at a time."[130] On this view, such constitutional rights are not only illusory for women, but indeed are a hindrance to—rather than a precondition for—securing equal citizenship for them.[131] More generally, feminists draw attention to the social costs of rights (not only privacy but also rights protected by the First Amendment) to women's equality and liberty, as well as their physical security.[132]

These concerns are important. They do not, however, warrant neglecting the preconditions for deliberative autonomy or overlooking the vital importance of such autonomy to women's, as well as men's, free and equal citizenship.[133] Constitutional constructivism's theme of deliberative autonomy does not secure a private realm or "hellhole" of sanctified isolation wherein men may oppress women.[134] I have two responses to MacKinnon's critique.

First, MacKinnon mistakenly conflates different senses of privacy, confusing "territorial privacy" with "sovereignty over personal decisions" (or deliberative autonomy).[135] Consequently, she mistakenly views the right to privacy that justifies *Roe* as also shielding a realm of male-perpetrated domestic violence and oppression. As against that right, she supports an antisubordination principle of sex equality that would protect and secure equal citizenship for women.[136] MacKinnon persuasively illustrates the problematic history of treating a private realm of family life as beyond state intervention. But she does not persuasively link constitutional protection of the right of privacy to such wrongs. As feminist defenders of privacy including Linda McClain point out, courts have not invoked the constitutional right to privacy or autonomy, or cited cases such as *Griswold, Eisenstadt,* or *Roe,* to defend marital rape exemptions or to shield domestic violence from state intervention.[137] To the contrary, courts have invoked the right to privacy or autonomy, and cited such cases, to justify invalidating marital rape exemptions and to protect against domestic violence.[138] The idea of deliberative autonomy has affinities with the latter notions of privacy or autonomy, which emphasize women's dignity, decisional autonomy, and bodily integrity. Deliberative autonomy is an antitotalitarian principle of liberty that works in tandem with, rather than as a shield against, an antisubordination or anticaste principle of equality.

Second, MacKinnon erroneously conflates the right to privacy with the idea of the Constitution as a charter of negative liberties. (By "negative liberties," I mean rights that limit what government may do to persons, as distinguished from "affirmative liberties," or rights that impose obligations on government to provide certain services to persons.)[139] On her view, the right to privacy recognized in *Roe* led directly to decisions denying rights to affirmative liberties, such as a right to abortion funding in *Harris v. McRae*[140] and ultimately a right to protection against domestic violence in *DeShaney v. Winnebago County Department of Social Services.*[141] It is quite telling against MacKinnon's critique that the greatest champions of the right to privacy on the Supreme Court, Justices Blackmun, Brennan, and Marshall, have been the greatest critics of the idea of the Constitution as a charter of negative liberties. All of them wrote or joined in powerful dissents in *Harris* and *DeShaney.*[142] Furthermore, the greatest critics of the right to privacy, Chief Justice Rehnquist and Justice Scalia, have been the greatest champions of the idea of the negative Constitution.[143] In any event, MacKinnon's critique does not apply here because the idea of deliberative autonomy does not entail the idea of the negative Constitution.

Progressives and feminists correctly argue that the Constitution, interpreted as a charter of negative liberties, does not secure the affirmative liberties needed fully to guarantee free and equal citizenship for women and men. But that deficiency is one of a negative Constitution, not a shortcoming of deliberative autonomy. Within Rawls's political constructivism, the protection of basic liberties includes protecting individuals not only from the government, but also from each other, including within families.[144] Furthermore, I concur with Lawrence Sager that the government is constitutionally obligated "to make reasonable efforts to undo structurally entrenched social bias against . . . women."[145] Both women and men are due the status of free and equal citizenship. Progressives and feminists should not and need not flee deliberative autonomy for deliberative democracy, or liberty for equality, but should pursue basic liberties that are grounded in both.

## Conclusion

In chapter 5 and this chapter I have sought to secure deliberative autonomy as a bedrock structure of our constitutional document and underlying constitutional order. I have argued that both deliberative democracy and deliberative autonomy have structural roles to play in our scheme of deliberative self-governance, and that both are integral to our dualist constitutional democracy. By tethering the right to autonomy in a constitutional constructivism, I have shown that it is not unruly, dangerous, and rootless as some of its critics have charged. Furthermore, by limiting the right to autonomy to protection of basic liberties that are significant preconditions for deliberative autonomy, I have charted a middle course between Scalia and Charybdis in the due process inquiry. Constitutional constructivism seeks, in the spirit of Justice Brandeis's famous formulation, to "secure conditions favorable to the pursuit of happiness"[146] by securing the preconditions for deliberative autonomy. I have not tried to resolve all questions of the scope and content of the basic liberties associated with deliberative autonomy, but to outline a structure to help frame and guide our reflections and judgments concerning such questions along constitutionally appropriate lines.

In calling for the construction of a coherent scheme of fundamental rights essential to the pursuit of happiness, Charles Black observed: "[Justice] Holmes once remarked of the first Justice Harlan that the latter's mind resembled a powerful vise, the jaws of which could not be brought closer than two inches apart."[147] Black's rejoinder to Holmes was that "in constitutional-law work, jewelers' vises are well enough for tasks of detail, but the lack tremblingly to be feared is the lack of a vise whose jaws can be got more than two inches apart, because if you lack such a vise you cannot handle the big beams."[148] Constitutional constructivism, with its guiding framework of two fundamental themes of deliberative democracy and deliberative autonomy, provides a vise for handling the big beams. It enables us to interpret our Constitution not as a constitution of detail, but as a constitution of principle that aspires to secure for everyone the common and guaranteed status of free and equal citizenship.

# Constitutional Interpretation in Circumstances of Moral Disagreement and Political Conflict

What form should constitutional interpretation and judicial review take in the face of moral disagreement and political conflict about basic liberties such as the right to privacy or autonomy? John Rawls's political constructivism seeks to construct a shared basis of reasonable political agreement in a morally pluralistic constitutional democracy such as our own, or to construct principles of justice that provide fair terms of social cooperation on the basis of mutual respect and trust that citizens might reasonably be expected to endorse, whatever their particular conceptions of the good.[1] I have presented constitutional constructivism, like Rawls's political constructivism, as being well suited to circumstances of reasonable moral pluralism.

In this chapter I take up two diametrically opposed republican challenges to liberal theories of the sort Rawls and I propound. On the one hand, Michael Sandel charges that such theories are too thin: they represent a "minimalist liberalism" and an impoverished vision of the "procedural republic."[2] He exhorts us to embrace a robust civic republicanism and a richer conception of a substantive republic. Sandel argues that in interpreting constitutional freedoms like privacy, courts should move beyond liberal autonomy arguments about protecting individual choices to republican moral arguments about fostering substantive human goods or virtues. For example, in *Lawrence v. Texas*,[3] the Court should have justified protecting homosexuals' right to privacy not on the basis of homosexuals' freedom to make personal choices, but on the ground of the goods or virtues fostered by homosexuals' intimate associations.

On the other hand, Cass Sunstein objects that liberal theories like mine are too thick: they sponsor "maximalist" constitutional interpretation by the judiciary and too deep a vision of the substantive Constitution.[4] He develops a "minimalist" republican constitutional theory and advocates judicial reinforcement of the procedural preconditions for deliberative democracy, his version of the procedural republic. For Sunstein, the domain of any substantive republic is outside the courts in the realm of deliberative democracy. He contends that courts should eschew both autonomy arguments about choices (such as those liberals like Ronald Dworkin and I make) and moral arguments about goods (such as those civic republicans like Sandel make) in favor of seeking "incompletely theorized agreements" on particular outcomes and "leaving things undecided" in order to allow democratic deliberation to proceed. Thus, in *Lawrence*, the Court should have avoided deciding whether homosexuals, like heterosexuals, have a right to privacy or autonomy and instead struck down the law banning same-sex sodomy (but not opposite-sex sodomy) on the ground of desuetude: "Without a strong justification, the state cannot bring the criminal law to bear on consensual sexual behavior if enforcement of the relevant law can no longer claim to have significant moral support in the enforcing state or the nation as a whole."[5]

Notwithstanding Sandel's and Sunstein's critiques of liberal theories, the Court's opinion in *Lawrence* resoundingly embraced a conception of liberty as deliberative autonomy—"[l]iberty presumes an autonomy of self that includes freedom of thought, belief, expression, and certain intimate conduct"—and waxed eloquent about "liberty of the person both in its spatial and more transcendent dimensions."[6]

Sandel's and Sunstein's theories, with their diametrically opposed challenges and shortcomings, unwittingly show the superiority of a liberal republican constitutional theory like mine, which would secure the basic liberties that are preconditions for self-government in two senses: deliberative democracy and deliberative autonomy. In reply, I argue that Sandel's civic republicanism is too thick because it requires deeper agreement on goods or virtues than seems feasible, given the fact of reasonable moral pluralism, without intolerable state oppression.[7] Conversely, Sunstein's minimalist republicanism is too thin because, in the face of such pluralism, it settles for shallower agreement than is necessary to secure fundamental constitutional freedoms. A theory like mine, with affinities to Rawls's theory, is just right.

## Moral Disagreement, Liberalism, and Sandel's and Sunstein's Forms of Republicanism

Sandel argues that our democracy is engulfed by discontent because our public philosophy—"the political theory implicit in our practice, the assumptions about citizenship and freedom that inform our public life"—is impoverished and inadequate to the challenges of self-government. That public philosophy, he contends, is a form of "minimalist liberalism" whose central idea is that, since citizens disagree about the best way to live, the government should be neutral and not affirm in law any particular conception of the good life. Instead, it should provide a framework of rights that respects persons as free and independent selves, capable of choosing their own values and ends. Because this liberalism "asserts the priority of fair procedures over particular ends," Sandel suggests, "the public life that it informs might be called the procedural republic."[8]

Sandel sharply contrasts such liberalism with republicanism. The most salient contrast concerns their respective conceptions of freedom and of the role of government in fostering such freedom. For liberalism, freedom consists of the "capacity to choose our ends."[9] Accordingly, "government should be neutral toward the moral and religious views its citizens espouse," take existing preferences as given, and merely "provide a framework of rights" within which citizens may pursue the ends and values that they choose.[10] In contrast, to be free within the republican tradition is to be capable of sharing in self-government, which involves "deliberating with fellow citizens about the common good and helping to shape the destiny of the political community."[11] Because self-government requires certain qualities of character, or civic virtues, government cannot be neutral but instead must engage in a formative project to cultivate such qualities. Sandel contends that the liberal conception of freedom is attractive as a response to the circumstances of moral pluralism, but flawed because it gives up too much—the republican formative project and its ideal of self-government.[12]

In *The Partial Constitution*, Sunstein claimed to move beyond the clash between liberalism and republicanism to a synthesis—namely, liberal republicanism.[13] In *Legal Reasoning and Political Conflict* and *One Case at a Time*, he further develops his theory, advancing a model of legal reasoning appropriate to a deliberative democracy as he understands it. He calls for courts to avoid moral arguments about the good as well as autonomy arguments about the right in constitutional law. Indeed, Sunstein recommends that courts eschew arguments about abstract moral principles generally. On his view, it cheats deliberative democracy when courts, conceiving themselves to be "the forum of principle," grandly theorize and reach "maximalist" decisions that take issues of moral principle off the political agenda.[14] Instead, Sunstein argues for judicial "minimalism." He claims that law's distinctive approach to the problem of political conflict and moral pluralism is to seek "incompletely theorized agreements" on particular outcomes, accompanied by "agreements on the narrow or low-level principles that account for them."[15] Courts should engage in reasoning by analogy from case to case, deciding cases narrowly (or "leaving things undecided") so as to leave room for political deliberation.[16]

In this chapter I assess Sandel's approach to the form constitutional interpretation should take in circumstances of moral disagreement and political conflict in a pluralistic polity by considering his critique of the privacy cases from *Griswold v. Connecticut*[17] to *Planned Parenthood v. Casey.*[18] This cluster of Supreme Court decisions concerns the proper scope of substantive liberty protected by the Due Process Clause with respect to intimate association and reproductive freedom.

Sandel rejects the type of liberal constitutional theory exemplified by the work of Dworkin and by this book, especially insofar as it interprets the Due Process Clause as embracing abstract principles of liberty, privacy, and autonomy.[19] Sandel claims that such "minimalist liberalism," because it attempts to stay on the surface, philosophically speaking, is too shallow to attain agreement on the justification for and the scope of constitutional rights such as intimate association and reproductive freedom. To attain such agreement, we have to go beyond liberalism's appeal to "autonomy rights alone," and its attempt to bracket questions of the good, to a deeper form of argument that directly engages the moral permissibility of the social practices to be protected by rights.[20] Thus, under Sandel's model of interpretation, we should flee from the substance of autonomy rights to the substance of moral argument about the goods or ends or virtues protected by rights.

Sunstein also rejects abstract liberal principles of liberty, privacy, and autonomy, but he proceeds in the opposite direction from Sandel. Sunstein finds theories like Dworkin's and mine too deep and contends that to attain agreement in the face of moral conflict, we have to stay nearer to the surface. He advocates that we flee the substance of autonomy rights for process and for such lawyerly methods as incompletely theorized agreements, reasoning by analogy, and leaving things undecided. He claims that these methods permit judges to make shallower and narrower decisions and thus to avoid deep and controversial issues, leaving those issues open for democratic deliberation.[21] Sandel thus calls for a civic republicanism that engages in substantive moral argument, while Sunstein advocates a minimalist republicanism that avoids such argument.

## Sandel's Call for a Civic Republicanism that Engages in Substantive Moral Argument

### Sandel's Analysis of the Privacy Cases

Sandel uses the line of privacy cases from *Griswold* to *Casey* to chronicle the ascent of the procedural republic and its flawed model of liberal toleration or autonomy.[22] For him, the tale involves the Court's unfortunate move from the "old" privacy to the "new" one, and from a justification rooted in substantive moral goods to one based on autonomy.[23] The Court began promisingly enough in *Griswold*, identifying a right to privacy of married couples as limiting the government's authority to ban their use of contraceptives.[24] On Sandel's account, *Griswold* did not rest on the flawed tenets of liberal toleration: the justification of rights premised on a "voluntarist" conception of the self and on the value of autonomy, independent of the moral goods it secures.[25] Sandel praises the *Griswold* Court for resting the justification for a right to privacy on a substantive moral judgment about the value of marriage (which it characterized as "intimate to the degree of being sacred," "a harmony in living . . . a bilateral loyalty," and "an association for [a] noble . . . purpose").[26]

But from this substantive republican justification for a right to privacy, the Court took a dramatic and fateful turn toward the liberal procedural republic in later cases by construing *Griswold* as enshrining the decisional autonomy of the individual—and the value of choice itself—as the core justification.[27] No longer limited to guarding the precincts of the "sacred" marital bedroom, privacy became in *Eisenstadt v. Baird* the "right of the *individual,* married or single, to be free from unwarranted governmental intrusion into matters so fundamentally affecting a person as the decision whether to bear or beget a child."[28] That individual right to privacy served as the basis for striking down, in *Eisenstadt,* a law restricting the distribution of contraceptives to unmarried persons and, in *Roe v. Wade,* a law forbidding women to terminate their pregnancies.[29] Then, in *Carey v. Population Services International,* another contraception case, the Court expressly cast the right to privacy as a right to "individual autonomy in matters of childbearing"[30] that extends to individuals independently of their roles or attachments (for example, in marriage). So transformed, Sandel observes, privacy protects certain kinds of individual decisions rather than certain kinds of morally valuable social practices.

Sandel interprets *Casey,* which reaffirmed the central holding of *Roe,*[31] as offering the "fullest expression" of this notion of privacy as autonomy, pointing to *Casey*'s language about the relationship between the abortion decision and a woman's personal "dignity and autonomy."[32] He uses the language of *Casey* concerning the scope of "*Griswold* liberty" to show an explicit link between this notion of privacy and the voluntarist conception of the person: "At the heart of liberty is the right to define one's own concept of existence, of meaning, of the universe, and of the mystery of human life. Beliefs about these matters could not define the attributes of personhood were they formed under compulsion of the State."[33]

How should a republican court have decided these cases interpreting the scope of *Griswold* liberty? Sandel offers us clues in his critique of *Bowers v. Hardwick.*[34] (Fortunately, *Lawrence v. Texas,* discussed below,[35] overruled *Bowers,* but Sandel's critique of *Bowers* still warrants analysis for what it reveals about his conception of the form that constitutional interpretation should take in circumstances of moral disagreement.) For Sandel, *Bowers* starkly illustrates that liberal toleration arguments cannot adequately ground rights. Writing for the majority, Justice White rejected a challenge, rooted in the right to privacy, to the application of Georgia's sodomy statute to private, consensual homosexual sexual conduct. He summarily found no analogy or "resemblance" between homosexual sodomy and the choices and conduct protected under *Griswold* and its progeny. Instead, he analogized homosexual sexual conduct to adultery, incest, and other sexual crimes committed in the home that are properly subject to governmental regulation. Moreover, with no critical evaluation of such belief, White concluded that "the presumed belief of a majority of the electorate in Georgia that homosexual sodomy is immoral and unacceptable" provided a rational basis for the statute.[36] Sandel points to *Bowers* as an evident anomaly among the Court's new privacy cases in its rejection of the liberal ideal of the neutral state and its acceptance of the state's proper authority to express through criminal law a moral judgment about sexual conduct.[37]

But Sandel does not embrace Justice White's opinion in *Bowers* as exemplifying republican moral discourse. To the contrary, he suggests that the challenge to Georgia's statute should have directly engaged the question of morality by drawing analogies between the human goods of homosexual intimacy and those of heterosexual intimacy previously protected by the Court.[38] Such a justification for a right to homosexual intimate association would eschew the liberal ideal of state neutrality concerning citizens' conceptions of the good because it would rest on the good of the practices that the right protects. Rather than pursue this moral high ground, Sandel contends, the dissenting opinions in *Bowers* by Justices Blackmun and Stevens relied wholly on bare autonomy arguments, drawing an analogy to *Griswold* not as to the goods of marriage, but only as to the importance of choice to the voluntarist self. Worse, he contends, those defending or upholding privacy rights for gays and lesbians frequently bracket the issue of the morality of homosexual intimate association and draw an analogy to *Stanley v. Georgia*, which upheld the right to possess obscene materials in one's home.[39] Here, for Sandel, is the epitome of the shortcomings of liberal toleration arguments: like obscenity, homosexuality is defended wholly independent of its moral worth and is demeaned as a "base thing that should nonetheless be tolerated so long as it takes place in private."[40]

Sandel contends that such bare autonomy arguments, because they avoid substantive moral discourse, may fail even to secure toleration. As a practical matter, "it is by no means clear that social cooperation can be secured on the strength of autonomy rights alone, absent some measure of agreement on the moral permissibility of the practices at issue." Even if such arguments for rights succeed in court, they are unlikely to win more than a "thin and fragile toleration."[41] Because these arguments leave unchallenged the negative views about gays and lesbians, they forego the opportunity to move citizens beyond empty toleration of private, disfavored conduct to respect and appreciation of the lives that homosexuals lead.[42]

The republican alternative of grounding rights in the substantive moral good of social practices, Sandel argues, makes possible genuine respect and appreciation among citizens. Republicanism interprets rights in light of their relation to its conception of the good society as a self-governing republic. This link to republican self-government suggests that the full republican argument for a right would go along these lines: the social practice protected by a right allows the realization of something that citizens (through engaging in moral discourse) can recognize to be substantive moral goods, which in turn foster the citizens' engagement in republican self-government. Exactly what this means depends on the scope that Sandel gives to the term "self-government." His rejection of liberal notions of autonomy implies that he would construe the term to refer to deliberative democracy to the exclusion of deliberative autonomy.

## A Critique of Sandel's Analysis of the Privacy Cases

Is Sandel's critique of the "voluntarist" conception said to be dominating the privacy cases persuasive? Is his alternative republican justification altogether missing from such cases? And is it more attractive or persuasive than a liberal justification? I offer three responses.

First, Sandel's critique of the new privacy accurately identifies the emergence of a strong autonomy justification but overstates the supposed dichotomy between the liberal appeal to choice and the republican appeal to moral goods. Sandel points to the central role that the appeal to a principle of autonomy plays in liberal constitutional argument, a principle that Blackmun and Stevens in dissent correctly concluded should have led the Court to strike down the statute before it in *Bowers.* Yet his critique of the *Bowers* dissents in particular, and of liberal toleration arguments in general, draws too sharp a contrast between protection of rights for the sake of choice in itself and protection of them because of the moral good of what is chosen.

A more complete, less selective reading of the dissents in *Bowers* reveals the argument that the protection of choice is important precisely because of the good of such things as marriage, family, and intimate association in persons' lives. As Justice Blackmun put it: "[o]nly the most willful blindness could obscure the fact that sexual intimacy is 'a sensitive, key relationship of human existence, central to family life, community welfare, and the development of human personality.'"[43] This is an admittedly and inescapably liberal argument in the following sense: it is precisely because these matters are so important or significant in persons' lives, and for their pursuit of moral goods, that we protect, in Justice Stevens's words, an "individual's right to make certain unusually important decisions that will affect his own, or his family's, destiny."[44] Arguably, there is an analogical argument here in the contention that homosexual intimate association, like heterosexual sexual intimacy, is central to persons' lives, sense of place in society, identity, and happiness.

Of course, Sandel would find this fuller account of liberal toleration unsatisfying, for it is undeniably "voluntarist" in emphasizing the relationship between autonomy and personal identity. Here Sandel's analysis highlights that there is an undeniable and unbridgeable gap between liberal and republican justifications for rights of the sort he advocates. This gap has one basic source: Sandel's rejection of the moral principle of autonomy and its value (as liberals understand it) and his apparent exclusion of such autonomy from his conception of self-government. Notwithstanding Sandel, liberal justifications for rights such as privacy can and do make recourse to substantive moral goods, but they do so to augment rather than to supplant the appeal to autonomy. Furthermore, if, as Sandel argues, rights are to be justified with regard to their facilitation of self-government, a liberal argument should insist on a conception of self-government that includes not only deliberative democracy but also deliberative autonomy. This liberal commitment to a more complete conception of self-government reflects a moral judgment about the centrality of self-determination in securing the status of free and equal citizenship for everyone, and here liberals can only plead guilty to Sandel's charge.

Rather than flee the liberal commitment to autonomy, I would turn the tables on Sandel and ask: Is there no room in a republican justification of rights for a principle of protecting individual choice and autonomy? Sandel's republican model artificially separates moral goods from the process of choosing them. For example, marriage is an association and a social practice, but (absent a regime of arranged marriages) we do not just find ourselves in a marriage; we make a choice. While there are often constraints on choices, and social norms and roles may shape choices, it is generally the case that procreation, parenthood, and other practices protected under the rubric of privacy or autonomy entail some element of choice.[45] If republicanism's concern is simply that citizens engage in morally worthy social practices, then a regime that places no value on choice could simply assign citizens to engage in those practices. If Sandel objects that forcing persons into particular relationships and practices compromises the moral worth of those practices, he must implicitly assume that there is some value attached to the element of choice, autonomy, or personal self-government.[46] And if so, the gap narrows between Sandel and Justice Blackmun, who contended that "much of the richness of a relationship will come from the freedom an individual has to *choose* the form and nature of these intensely personal bonds."[47]

The justification for the right to abortion also illustrates that liberalism can move closer to Sandel's republicanism than he allows. Sandel offers *Casey* as the fullest expression of the notion of privacy as autonomy. He ignores, however, the role that substantive moral discourse played in that case. In articulating a pregnant woman's liberty, the joint opinion spoke of the "unique" condition of pregnancy, stressing not only the moral good that women may bestow on children through childbirth and motherhood, but also the moral harm of denying women choice, due to the deeply personal nature of the pain and suffering of pregnancy, childbirth, and motherhood.[48] *Casey* sounded themes of self-government both in the liberal sense of autonomy, when it spoke of the role that procreation plays in a woman's self-definition and self-determination, and in a more republican sense, when it noted the vital role that the "ability to control their reproductive lives" has played in facilitating the "ability of women to participate equally in the economic and social life of the Nation."[49] Sandel's analysis of *Casey* also completely leaves out any discussion of sex equality as a component of women's full citizenship, a principle that Sunstein emphasizes in justifying the right to abortion.[50]

Most interesting, Sandel does not comment on perhaps the most republican aspect of the joint opinion in *Casey:* the latitude it gives to the state to shape women's decisionmaking process in favor of childbirth as a way to encourage "wise" or responsible decisions, in part because of the "consequences" of the abortion decision for women, the community, and prenatal life.[51] Contrary to Sandel's characterization of the abortion cases as minimalist in their bracketing of the moral issues regarding abortion, *Casey* acknowledges that abortion is a matter as to which "men and women of good conscience" may always disagree[52] and yet does not require that the state be neutral because of this moral conflict. Rather, that case permits the state, due to its "profound interest in potential life," to take sides by seeking to persuade women to choose childbirth, so long as its measures aim to enhance informed decisionmaking rather than to impose an undue burden on decisionmaking.[53]

Furthermore, it is telling against Sandel's critique of liberal conceptions of autonomy that he fails to acknowledge Dworkin's praise of the *Casey* joint opinion for recognizing a proper role for government in encouraging responsibility, in the sense of reflective decisionmaking, when such intrinsic values as respect for the sanctity of life are at issue.[54] Dworkin contends that the constitutional right to procreative autonomy rests on a right to make essentially religious decisions for ourselves; yet such a right entails a moral responsibility of reflective exercise, which government may encourage. Dworkin's analysis may remain too liberal for Sandel because it holds to a strong principle of ethical individualism, a right to decide for ourselves, and even to make an immoral, or wrong, decision. Yet his argument is notable as an attempt within liberalism to reconcile a principle of ethical individualism with a proper governmental role of shaping citizens and encouraging them to exercise their rights responsibly. Dworkin's attempt to give some credence to arguments about the ethical environment and a community's interest in its members' decisions suggests some common ground with a republican formative project. Moreover, Dworkin's argument for toleration on the issue of abortion seems far from minimalist, for it attempts to move citizens beyond pale civility and grudging toleration by recasting the abortion debate as a conscientious disagreement as to the interpretation of how best to respect the intrinsic value of the sanctity of life in particular circumstances.

My second response to Sandel's critique is that, even assuming that his republican alternative offers a better justification for rights than liberal models, Sandel may overestimate the power of analogy about moral goods to move citizens from grudging toleration to respect and appreciation. To be sure, some critics of liberal toleration may find Sandel's critique, and his plea to move from toleration to respect and appreciation, inspiring and sound. For example, proponents of gay and lesbian rights might wager that engaging in and winning a substantive moral debate could lead to full citizenship and acceptance more readily than making toleration arguments.[55] But Sandel tells us little about how the appeal to moral goods should actually be made and how judges, legislators, and citizens should evaluate such goods. Using his critique of *Bowers* as illustrative, I presume that his approach would encourage advocates of same-sex marriage to draw analogies between the goods realized in heterosexual marriage and those attained in same-sex relationships. *Griswold* spoke of the goods of bilateral loyalty and a harmony in living; contemporary accounts of marriage identify many goods, such as companionship, security, emotional commitment, and children. *Goodridge v. Department of Public Health*, the Massachusetts decision extending the right to marry to same-sex couples, spoke of the following goods of marriage: most centrally, "commitment" but also "the ideals of mutuality, companionship, intimacy, fidelity, and family."[56] Similar analogical arguments could be made concerning the moral goods of gay and lesbian families in order to secure rights to procreation and parenting.

Sandel may underestimate the intensity of moral disagreement about how persuasive these analogical arguments are, especially in the absence of any clear criteria for what counts as a moral argument. Witness the reaction throughout the United States to *Goodridge*'s holding regarding same-sex marriage, the resulting inflammatory discussions of "moral values" in the 2004 presidential campaign, the rush in many states to adopt state constitutional amendments or statutes defining marriage to exclude same-sex unions,[57] and President George W. Bush's pledge of support for a federal constitutional amendment to "protect marriage in America" and to prevent change to "the most fundamental institution of civilization."[58] Such an amendment would define marriage throughout the United States as a male-female union and would bar any state or federal court from extending marriage-like rights and responsibilities to same-sex couples. Suppose proponents of same-sex marriage offer numerous testimonials concerning the goods of gay and lesbian intimate association, along with psychological and sociological studies confirming such goods and further supporting gay and lesbian parenthood. And suppose opponents argue against the moral worth of such unions and contend that they are harmful to the participants and threaten the institution of marriage on these bases: biblical verses and religious teachings and convictions; philosophical arguments that the goods of marriage are realizable only by heterosexuals (for example, Catholic natural law arguments)[59]; arguments about gay male promiscuity and the fear of AIDS; and arguments about alleged gender role confusion in children raised in same-sex marriages.

Sandel offers no guidance as to any requirements that his model would place on citizens concerning what would count as a moral argument or as to any criteria to be used by judges or legislators in evaluating moral arguments. For example, he is critical of Rawls's idea of public reason: that political and legal decisions be justifiable on grounds that citizens generally can reasonably be expected to accept.[60] Without knowing more about how the moral reasoning process is to unfold—whether judges or legislators may reasonably reject arguments rooted in homophobia, ignorance, and fear, and how they ultimately are to resolve matters of genuine moral conflict—I find Sandel's alternative to be perilous. He seeks to open the "naked" public square to persons' substantive moral and religious convictions, but he gives little guidance about how to guard against the triumph of "intolerant moralisms."[61] As the unfolding battle over same-sex marriage suggests, moral argument in service of gay and lesbian rights may prevail in some judicial and legislative arenas—for example, initially in the Hawaii Supreme Court and ultimately (more modestly) in the Hawaii legislature, in the Vermont Supreme Court and legislature, in Canada,[62] most famously, in the Massachusetts Supreme Judicial Court's decision in *Goodridge*, and, most recently, in the legislature in Connecticut—but its success depends critically on the framing of the moral debate.

My third and final response to Sandel's critique is that he may be right that it is difficult to secure public support for constitutional freedoms on the strength of the appeal to autonomy alone. Yet, to jettison autonomy arguments entirely, rather than to supplement them with arguments based on substantive moral goods, may prove an even more difficult strategy for securing such freedoms. For example, the idea that even if one believes it is morally wrong for a pregnant woman to have an abortion, it is wrong for government to prevent her from making that decision, has a powerful hold on the public.[63]

In some cases of persistent moral conflict, liberal toleration is a necessary starting point and may even be the most that can be achieved. But toleration need not be grudging and fragile if its proponents persuasively make a moral argument for it and its possible tempering of the formative project of cultivating civic virtue: autonomy is a human good, as are diversity, equal citizenship, and toleration itself. A commitment to protecting those goods should often (but not always) constrain government from coercively acting to make citizens lead good lives by compelling "moral" and prohibiting "immoral" choices.[64] To the extent toleration, by its very definition, is empty in that it does not require respect and appreciation, liberalism itself may be said to attempt to go beyond what Linda McClain calls a model of "empty toleration" to what she calls a model of "toleration as respect" (and even appreciation) through the appeal to such a moral argument.[65] In concurrence in *Goodridge*, Justice Greaney expressed such an idea in terms that bear quotation in full:

> I am hopeful that our decision will be accepted by those thoughtful citizens who believe that same-sex unions should not be approved by the State. I am not referring here to acceptance in the sense of grudging acknowledgment of the court's authority to adjudicate the matter. My hope is more liberating. The plaintiffs are members of our community, our neighbors, our coworkers, our

friends. As pointed out by the court, their professions include investment advisor, computer engineer, teacher, therapist, and lawyer. The plaintiffs volunteer in our schools, worship beside us in our religious houses, and have children who play with our children, to mention just a few ordinary daily contacts. We share a common humanity and participate together in the social contract that is the foundation of our Commonwealth. Simple principles of decency dictate that we extend to the plaintiffs, and to their new status, full acceptance, tolerance, and respect. We should do so because it is the right thing to do.[66]

Thus, securing agreement on a principle of autonomy does not rule out more ambitious moral argument and attempts to persuade citizens concerning the moral goods realized through different choices and ways of life. Nor does it preclude an appeal in democratic arenas for expanded protections of rights premised on moral goods.

## Lawrence: *Liberal, Republican, or a Synthesis?*

To illustrate a case in which liberal and republican arguments are intertwined in a way encouraged by my liberal republican theory of securing deliberative autonomy, I analyze *Lawrence v. Texas,* which overruled *Bowers.* To what extent did Justice Kennedy's opinion in *Lawrence* reflect liberalism? Republicanism? A synthesis of republicanism and liberalism? Not surprisingly, Kennedy's opinion lends itself to a number of interpretations, for instead of reflecting one coherent theory it weaved together elements of several theories. Sunstein has written a thoughtful article examining what *Lawrence* held, distinguishing four strands of the opinion: (1) autonomy, (2) rational basis, (3) desuetude (which Sunstein offers as the best justification), and (4) equality.[67] Indeed, the opinion intertwined concerns for autonomy and equality in a way encouraged by my theory of securing constitutional democracy.

I intend to do "a Sandel" on Kennedy's opinion in *Lawrence.* (I coined this term—"a Sandel"—with the greatest appreciation and respect for Michael Sandel.) That is, I shall go through the opinion and single-mindedly differentiate the liberal strains from the republican strains. Let us say that the liberal elements bespeak concern for choice, autonomy, toleration, and bracketing moral arguments and disagreement, while the republican elements bespeak concern for justifying freedoms on the basis of substantive moral arguments about the goods or virtues they promote, or on the basis of their significance for citizenship.[68] Carrying out such a Sandel will oversimplify somewhat, but it may be illuminating. The opinion opened with a ringing declaration of deliberative autonomy (and what Sandel calls the "voluntarist self")—"Liberty presumes an autonomy of self that includes freedom of thought, belief, expression, and certain intimate conduct"—and waxed eloquent about "liberty of the person both in its spatial and more transcendent dimensions."[69] But there is more, as we shall see.

### THE LIBERAL STRAINS OF KENNEDY'S OPINION IN *LAWRENCE*

***Mill's Harm Principle.*** In *Lawrence* Kennedy evoked or echoed John Stuart Mill's "harm principle": "That the only purpose for which power can be rightfully exercised over any member of a civilized community, against his will, is to prevent harm to others."[70] The following passage is an illustration: "This, as a general rule, should counsel against attempts by the State, or a court, to define the meaning of the relationship or to set its boundaries absent injury to a person or abuse of an institution the law protects."[71] And Kennedy deemed it significant to note that the case involves conduct in private by consenting adults: "It does not involve persons who might be injured or coerced or who are situated in relationships where consent might not easily be refused."[72] These passages may lend some credence to Randy Barnett's interpretation of Kennedy's opinion as libertarian.[73]

***"Sweet-Mystery-of-Life" Liberalism.*** Kennedy's opinion in *Lawrence,* quoting from the joint opinion in *Casey,* also proclaimed that decisions about sexual conduct and relationships involve "the most intimate and personal choices a person may make in a lifetime, choices central to personal dignity and autonomy."[74] He continued: "At the heart of liberty is the right to define one's own concept of existence, of meaning, of the universe, and of the mystery of human life. Beliefs about these matters could not define the attributes of personhood were they formed under compulsion of the State."[75] In dissent, Scalia ridiculed Kennedy's invocation of what he called this "sweet-mystery-of-life passage"[76] from *Casey.* Sandel no less than Scalia would cringe at these passages, and he would see them as exalting choice itself, without regard to the good of what is chosen.[77] Sandel had argued that these passages in *Casey* reflect a liberal conception of the unencumbered, freely choosing voluntarist self.[78]

*Liberal Privacy or Autonomy.* Kennedy's opinion emphasized liberty as autonomy to make certain decisions fundamentally affecting one's destiny and the like.[79] This is the rationalist as opposed to voluntarist or existentialist interpretation of passages like those derided by Scalia. Again, the opinion resoundingly embraced a conception of liberty as deliberative autonomy.[80]

Sandel commends *Griswold,* which he views as resting on the "old" privacy: (1) the privacy of the home and (2) the goods or virtues of protecting the institution of marriage or the marital relationship.[81] At first glance, he might be thought to see *Lawrence* as embodying the "new" privacy: namely, individual autonomy to make certain decisions.[82] Yet *Lawrence,* like *Griswold,* emphasizes (1) the privacy of the home in the sense that it observes that it is protecting private conduct rather than conduct in public and (2) the goods of protecting and respecting homosexual intimate association and relationships by analogy to heterosexual intimate association and relationships.[83]

*Liberal Toleration.* Sandel, in his critique of liberal toleration arguments against *Bowers,* contends that such arguments actually demean homosexuals by bracketing the morality of homosexual intimate association.[84] He argues that such arguments win at best a "thin" and "fragile" or empty toleration; they fall far short of attaining the appreciation or respect necessary to secure important freedoms.[85]

Kennedy did not make this form of empty liberal toleration argument. To be sure, he noted the long-standing religious and moral disapproval of homosexual intimate conduct and relationships.[86] And he quoted the passage from *Casey:* "Our obligation is to define the liberty of all, not to mandate our own moral code."[87] But Kennedy pointedly argued that it "demeans" the lives of homosexual persons not to accord them a right to privacy or autonomy analogous to that accorded heterosexual persons.[88] He emphasized that homosexuals are entitled to respect. So, if in *Lawrence* Kennedy made or presupposed a liberal toleration argument, it is not "empty toleration" but "toleration as respect."[89]

THE REPUBLICAN STRAINS OF KENNEDY'S OPINION IN *LAWRENCE*

Is *Lawrence* republican in ways that accord with Sandel's analysis? Strikingly, unlike Sunstein's republican theory, Kennedy's opinion did not eschew privacy or autonomy for equality: it squarely grounded its holding in the Due Process Clause rather than the Equal Protection Clause.[90] The equality route certainly was available to Kennedy, given that *Romer v. Evans* held that legislation reflecting animus against homosexuals violated the Equal Protection Clause[91] (and, indeed, Justice O'Connor urged an equality route in concurrence in *Lawrence*).[92] Sandel might see this holding as evidence of liberalism, but we might view it in a republican light. Frank Michelman, after all, highlights the political and republican significance of privacy.[93] I argue that Kennedy's privacy or autonomy holding evinces an understanding that free and equal citizenship is a status due to all. Let me work up to this claim through a discussion of five points: (1) "demeans"; (2) analogies; (3) the "homosexual agenda"; (4) the "invention of heterosexuality"; and (5) the goods and virtues of relationships, not just individual choices.

*"Demeans."* What are we to make of Kennedy's arguments that it "demeans the lives"[94] of homosexuals to respect the right of heterosexuals to autonomy without respecting an analogous right for them?[95] Should we view these arguments as liberal or republican? On one reading, these passages simply reflect a liberal principle of respect and dignity, as distinguished from a liberal principle of empty toleration. But on the better reading, I believe "demeans" also connotes a republican recognition of a status of free and equal citizenship due to all. The Court packed such a notion into its due process analysis by recognizing that homosexual intimate association is analogous to heterosexual intimate association (rather than, say, to the "traditional 'morals' offenses"[96] on Scalia's parade of horribles). This brings us to the next point.

*Analogies.* Kennedy's opinion recognized that homosexual intimate association is analogous to heterosexual intimate association rather than, as Scalia would have it, to bestiality and the like.[97] In this regard, the opinion is certainly the opposite of White's opinion in *Bowers:* White said that none of the rights recognized in precedents from *Meyer v. Nebraska*[98] through *Griswold, Eisenstadt,* and *Roe* "bears any resemblance" to the right asserted in *Bowers.*[99] In dissent, Scalia castigated Kennedy's opinion for putting the Court on a slippery slope leading to "the end of all morals legislation."[100] If, said Scalia, states may not enact their moral disapproval of homosexual sodomy, they may not in principle enact their disapproval of "bigamy, same-sex marriage, adult incest, prostitution, masturbation, adultery, fornication, bestiality, and obscenity."[101] For him, homosexuals' intimate sexual conduct is analogous to such traditional morals offenses, not to heterosexuals' autonomy regarding intimate associations. Not so Kennedy: his argument for protecting homosexual intimate association is grounded in the recognition that it is closely analogous to heterosexual intimate association, which is already constitutionally protected. The argument is not grounded in a libertarian view that it is illegitimate for the state to pass laws based on moral judgments as such. The latter argument, had it been accepted in *Lawrence,* might have put the Court on a slippery slope as envisioned by Scalia. But the former argument, which was accepted there, did not.

*"Homosexual Agenda."* Scalia complained that Kennedy's opinion "has largely signed on to the so-called homosexual agenda."[102] He wrote: "One of the most revealing statements in today's opinion is the Court's grim warning that the criminalization of homosexual conduct is 'an invitation to subject homosexual persons to discrimination both in the public and in the private spheres.'"[103] He continued: "It is clear from this that the Court has taken sides in the culture war, departing from its role of assuring, as neutral observer, that the democratic rules of engagement are observed."[104] I can envision this passage launching a thousand liberal and progressive fundraising ships. Just imagine fundraising solicitations from gay and lesbian rights organizations quoting Scalia's formulation and retorting "We do have an agenda: to establish that homosexuals are people, too, and to secure the status of free and equal citizenship for gays and lesbians." Kennedy's opinion in *Lawrence,* like his opinion in *Romer* rejecting the idea that gays and lesbians were seeking "special rights,"[105] recognized the significance of such a status in protecting gays and lesbians against discrimination.

*"Invention of Heterosexuality."* *Bowers* presumed that moral disapproval of homosexuality is simply an historical given and a moral fact of the matter and that majorities may enact their moral disapproval of homosexuality for no better reason than that they are majorities.[106] I never thought I would see the day when the Supreme Court would use the phrase "invention of heterosexuality," and by implication the idea of the invention of homosexuality, much less practically embrace the idea. Well, that day has come. Kennedy wrote in *Lawrence:* "The absence of legal prohibitions focusing on homosexual conduct may be explained in part by noting that according to some scholars the concept of the homosexual as a distinct

category of person did not emerge until the late 19th century,"[107] citing a book titled *The Invention of Heterosexuality.*[108] Here, Kennedy's opinion made clear that it is implicitly what Michelman calls republican or "jurisgenerative" rather than authoritarian in the way that *Bowers* was: *Lawrence* recognized that homosexuality is socially and legally constructed rather than simply an historical given and a moral fact of the matter.[109] This recognition helped clear the path to a republican argument for securing the status of free and equal citizenship for homosexuals along with heterosexuals (rather than treating them as outcasts or second-class persons by nature).

**The Goods and Virtues of Relationships, Not Just Individual Choices.** Did Kennedy's opinion make (or at least point toward) substantive moral arguments about the goods or virtues fostered through protecting homosexual intimate conduct and relationships that even a civic republican like Sandel could acknowledge or praise? There is no doubt that Kennedy did not make such arguments as fully, thickly, and explicitly as Sandel would. And Sandel might say that just goes to show the limits of privacy or autonomy arguments and indeed indicates why the opinion stops short of implicitly embracing same-sex marriage.[110] Still, there are notions of goods or virtues implicit in Kennedy's acceptance of the analogy between homosexual and heterosexual intimate association.[111] Moreover, Kennedy recognized not merely analogies of choice but also analogies regarding relationships.[112] He understood that *Lawrence* was not simply about the right to homosexual sodomy any more than *Griswold* was simply about the right to heterosexual intercourse.[113] More generally, Kennedy's opinion signaled a return from the "new" privacy to the "old" privacy of *Griswold* in two respects: (1) concern for privacy of the home (in the sense of protecting private conduct rather than conduct in public) and (2) concern for protecting not only choices but also relationships. Finally, there is implicit in Kennedy's passages about how *Bowers* "demeans the lives" of homosexual persons a concern for securing their status as free and equal citizens. These passages are not simply about permitting choice and autonomy.

A justification for *Lawrence* that emphasizes the goods of relationships and not simply the right to choose may prompt the question whether both "casual sex" and "relational sexuality" are entitled to constitutional protection. They are—just as casual, uninformed voting is entitled to protection along with responsible, informed voting. Why? The fact that some persons who vote may be casual and uninformed rather than responsible and informed does not undercut the justification for the right to vote as a precondition for deliberative democracy; nor does the fact that some persons who have sex may be casual and not in committed relationships undercut the justification for the right to intimate association as a precondition for deliberative autonomy.

*Lawrence* reflects an intertwining of liberal and republican concerns, putting respecting autonomy front and center but also emphasizing securing the status of free and equal citizenship. My liberal republican theory, concerned with securing deliberative autonomy, is tailor made to fit and to support arguments and decisions weaving together such strands. Sandel's civic republican theory calls for substantive moral arguments to the exclusion of liberal autonomy or toleration arguments.

## Sunstein's Call for a Minimalist Republicanism that Avoids Substantive Moral Argument

*Sunstein's Analysis of the Privacy Cases*

Unlike Sandel, who seeks to replace the "new" privacy in the line of cases from *Griswold* to *Casey* (and beyond to *Lawrence*) with a republican justification for privacy rooted in substantive moral argument about goods, Sunstein would abandon the privacy justification entirely. For him, judicial enforcement of broad privacy rights is too "adventurous" because the Due Process Clause too readily engenders expansive, anti-democratic rights of autonomy.[114]

Sunstein's justification for *Griswold* would look to neither the old nor the new privacy, and to neither substantive moral goods nor autonomy. Instead, Sunstein believes that the Court was too ambitious in *Griswold*. Here he seeks to build on and invigorate the idea of desuetude as a constitutional basis for courts to invalidate statutes. Rather than recognize a right to privacy, the Court should have struck down Connecticut's contraceptive ban on the ground that "citizens need not comply with laws, or applications of laws, that lack real enforcement and that find no support in anything like common democratic conviction."[115] Sunstein contends that enforcement of the statute at issue in *Griswold* against a married couple would have lacked contemporary democratic support; the real function of the statute was to deter birth control clinics from assisting poor people.[116] He argues that a judgment based on desuetude "would have had the large advantage of producing a narrow and incompletely theorized outcome. It might have obtained a range of agreement from people who reject any 'right of privacy' or are uncertain about its foundations and limits."[117] His minimalist approach, under which courts decide the case before them on the narrowest ground available, would seek and secure agreement on the result—invalidation of the statute—based on the low-level or narrow principle against the enforcement of obsolescent and underenforced or selectively enforced laws, and would avoid recourse to abstract, broad, and contested rights.

Sunstein finds a ready analogy between *Griswold* and *Bowers*. Like *Griswold*, *Bowers* involved an old, unenforced law—a ban on sodomy. Indeed, the law mainly served as a tool for harassment through selective enforcement on "invidious grounds."[118] The Court could therefore have invalidated the statute on the narrow ground of desuetude. By doing so, it could have avoided abstract moral reasoning about the right or the good, and avoided even an anticaste principle of equality, and simply struck down the old law.

Furthermore, in *Lawrence*, Sunstein argues, the Court should have avoided deciding whether homosexuals, like heterosexuals, have a right to privacy or autonomy and instead struck down the law banning same-sex sodomy (but not opposite-sex sodomy) on the ground of desuetude: "Without a strong justification, the state cannot bring the criminal law to bear on consensual sexual behavior if enforcement of the relevant law can no longer claim to have significant moral support in the enforcing state or the nation as a whole."[119]

Obviously, the principle of desuetude cannot justify invalidating laws in cases in which a legal prohibition does not lack real enforcement or in fact has contemporary democratic support. Restrictive abortion laws prior to *Roe v. Wade* and current bans on same-sex marriage offer two illustrations. Sunstein's approach to abortion and same-sex marriage suggests just how much his commitment to deliberative democracy constrains his conception of judicial role and legal reasoning. In each case, Sunstein believes that the Equal Protection Clause, properly interpreted to incorporate an anticaste principle, forbids such laws as impermissible discrimination on the basis of sex or sexual orientation.[120] However, in both cases, Sunstein contends that it would be wrong for a court to give full vindication to that principle, because that would rob the democratic process of a chance to "participate[] in the evolving interpretation of the Constitution."[121]

Restrictive abortion laws, Sunstein argues, selectively impose on women a duty to devote their bodies to render aid to the vulnerable (fetuses), a burden that the state does not impose on men (parents, for example, are not required to donate kidneys to their children).[122] This selective imposition stems from stereotyped "conceptions of women's proper role" and perpetuates their "second-class citizenship."[123] Thus, abortion restrictions are a form of sex discrimination. Moreover, Sunstein argues in an earlier work that just as miscegenation laws, rooted in an ideology of white supremacy, impermissibly perpetuated a racial caste system, so bans on same-sex marriage serve to perpetuate a gender caste system or gender hierarchy based on the "natural" and unequal roles of men and women.[124]

Nonetheless, Sunstein concludes that, in each instance, courts should proceed incrementally, narrowly, and cautiously. In the case of abortion, he critiques the ambitious "maximalist" decision of *Roe*, which invalidated the abortion laws of almost every state, and suggests that the Court should have proceeded slowly and incrementally, beginning with striking down laws that did not permit abortion in cases of rape and incest. Meanwhile, democratic bodies could wrestle independently with the moral questions and come to resolutions, possibly ultimately protecting a more expansive right to reproductive freedom, rooted in sex equality, than that recognized by the Court in *Roe*.[125]

Similarly, with respect to state statutes excluding gays and lesbians from marrying, it would be wrong for the Court to announce the unconstitutionality of such laws "now or as soon as it can"; such a broad ruling would be inconsistent with deliberative democracy.[126] (Nor would Sunstein invoke any fundamental constitutional right to marry, a right that he argues the Court, had it been properly minimalist, would not have recognized.)[127] Because the debate over the legal treatment of sexual orientation, including same-sex marriage, involves a fundamental moral conflict, courts should not rob the people of their right to deliberate by purporting to settle the issue and remove it from the political agenda. Instead, courts should proceed cautiously and narrowly, and allow the democratic process to come to terms with the broader and deeper issues. (Nonetheless, Sunstein praised the Massachusetts Supreme Judicial Court's decision in *Goodridge*, holding that the prohibition of same-sex marriage violated the state constitution: "We should . . . celebrate *Goodridge*, not only because it ends a form of second-class citizenship for gays and lesbians but also because it exemplifies the federal system at its best.")[128]

For such reasons, Sunstein generally applauds the judicial minimalism of the Supreme Court's decision in *Romer,* which invalidated Colorado's Amendment 2, a categorical proscription of protection against discrimination aimed at gays, lesbians, and bisexuals.[129] *Romer* rests on the principle that the Equal Protection Clause does not permit a state to make a class of citizens a "stranger to its laws," and the conclusion that the very sweep of Amendment 2 belied any assertion of legitimate interests and suggested that "a bare . . . desire to harm a politically unpopular group" underlay it.[130] Sunstein suggests that, by its "narrow and shallow" decision, the Court proceeded incrementally, perhaps in recognition of the need for democratic rather than judicial conclusions, and left unanswered the question whether a more closely tailored prohibition justified in terms of legitimate public purposes could pass muster.[131] Similarly, while Sunstein's analysis of what *Lawrence* held acknowledges autonomy as an important strand, he approves and justifies the decision on the minimalist ground of desuetude.[132]

## *A Critique of Sunstein's Analysis of the Privacy Cases*

Is Sunstein's argument for judicial minimalism persuasive and sound, or does it amount to a troubling withering away of the proper role and responsibility of courts as vindicators of constitutional rights? Sunstein's minimalism represents a significant and disturbing retreat from what began, in *The Partial Constitution*, as a potentially robust interpretation of the Equal Protection Clause, assigning courts a role to play in protecting citizens from laws perpetuating second-class citizenship. There, he argued for an anticaste principle of equal citizenship pursuant to which society may not turn morally irrelevant characteristics—most obviously race and sex, but also sexual orientation—into systemic sources of social disadvantage.[133] To be sure, from the outset he contended that the legislative and executive branches should play the primary role in enforcing the anticaste principle because courts have limited capacities to implement any general attack on such systemic disadvantage. Nonetheless, he clearly contemplated some role for courts, leading to the reasonable conclusion that, although he rejected any broad principle of autonomy or privacy as a basis for rights, his principle of equality might secure similar protections.[134] Thus, Sunstein defended *Roe* not on privacy grounds but by analogy to *Brown v. Board of Education*[135] and through a link between race and sex discrimination: like *Brown, Roe* was a "judicial invalidation of a law contributing to second-class citizenship for a group of Americans defined in terms of a morally irrelevant characteristic."[136] And he hinted that an analogy to *Loving v. Virginia*[137] offered a foundation for judicial invalidation of bans on same-sex marriage (an analogy he now calls "highly controversial").[138]

In his more recent writings, however, Sunstein's position is that courts should not fully enforce such constitutional principles or give full scope to such analogies, even if they are sound; rather, courts should apply those principles very narrowly and make far more modest use of analogical reasoning.[139] Such morally ambitious constitutional interpretation is simply not in the judge's tool box of lawyerly methods. Sunstein's view seems to be that so long as deliberative democracy will eventually vindicate constitutional principles, courts should defer to the democratic process. In contrast with Dworkin's liberal model of courts as aggressive vindicators of constitutional rights, Sunstein's model of judicial minimalism comes perilously close to sacrificing such rights for the sake of deliberative processes. For how long should the courts stay their hand? What of the human cost to the individuals who may have legitimate claims to constitutional protection but whose rights are underenforced by the courts and who must await protection in the democratic arena? Justice delayed is not, for Sunstein, justice denied. Or justice delayed, all things considered (especially the benefits to deliberative democracy of such a delay), is justifiably denied.

Sunstein, of course, does recognize that the democratic process may have flaws and that courts have an appropriate role in protecting persons who are disadvantaged in that process. Yet his strong commitment to judicial minimalism leads to a judicial incrementalism that appears to undercut that protection for the sake of democratic process. To return to the example of abortion, women, he argues, are a group who suffer disadvantage in the democratic process, and the courts should play a role in striking down restrictive abortion laws. But Sunstein suggests that judicial incrementalism (for example, beginning with invalidating laws that prohibited abortion even in cases of rape and incest) would have been a better course than the "maximalist" approach of *Roe,* and he justifies it with the wager that it might have led to legislatures fashioning a broader and more accepted right of sex equality and reproductive freedom than *Roe*.[140] It is a point of considerable controversy whether, without *Roe*, state legislatures would have done so.[141] In any event, abortions sought because of rape and incest are a tiny portion of all abortions, and such a limited right would leave most pregnant women who seek to terminate their pregnancies with no legal recourse. And here, justice delayed, given the temporal nature of pregnancy, is certainly justice denied. If there are, as Sunstein contends, strong arguments for abortion rights rooted in an anticaste principle of sex equality (under the Equal Protection Clause), why must women wait for democratic vindication? This is an especially troubling prescription, given that the abortion issue has illustrated repeatedly that highly mobilized minorities opposing abortion rights can have dramatic effects on legislatures.[142]

Perhaps the Court should be praised for judicial minimalism in cases like *Romer*. But *Romer*'s utter silence about *Bowers,* in which the Court concluded that the majority's presumed belief in the immorality of homosexual sodomy afforded a rational basis for its proscription, is problematic. (Fortunately, *Lawrence* subsequently overruled *Bowers,* and cited *Romer* together with *Casey* as undermining *Bowers*,[143] but that happy ending was by no means a foreordained conclusion; *Romer* still warrants scrutiny.) *Romer* may be read either as an implicit overruling of *Bowers* or as a postponement of the evident conflict between these two decisions. For, as Justice Scalia pointed out in dissent, the "mere animus" that the Court condemned as inadequate to justify civil disabilities in *Romer* was the very moral condemnation that justified criminal penalties in *Bowers*.[144] Sunstein seeks to reconcile these cases by drawing an unpersuasive distinction (which, he suggests, a minimalist decision in *Romer* could have drawn) between the "forward-looking" or critical function of the Equal Protection Clause and the "backward-looking" or status-quo-preserving function of the Due Process Clause.[145] But surely Dworkin has a point—that, from the standpoint of a concern for principle and integrity, the Court should have reached more directly the underlying question whether moral condemnation of gay and lesbian sexual orientation affords a sufficient justification for unequal treatment of citizens on the basis of such orientation or offends constitutional principles of liberty and equality.[146]

I conclude this section with two points. First, Sunstein's commitment to judicial minimalism cannot be understood simply as an entailment of his theory of legal reasoning, with its advocacy of such tools as analogical reasoning. To the contrary, it constrains even the process of analogical reasoning. As Sunstein explains, the crucial step in analogical reasoning comes at the point where a court must interpret the principle, rule, or standard that accounts for the result in the prior case and apply it to the new case. This is an act of creativity, for the "meaning of an analogous case may be inexhaustible."[147] It is this very openness that allows for moral evolution within the law in light of new facts, ideas, and values. Whether analogical reasoning takes a conservative or a critical view of social practices depends, he says, not on the method itself, but on the "principles brought to bear on disputed cases."[148] Yet Sunstein concludes that while it would be possible for a court to use analogical reasoning to conclude that bans on abortion and same-sex marriage are unconstitutional, courts should instead resist the full import of such analogies and decide cases as narrowly as possible. This constraint on the use of analogy is puzzling given that Sunstein also claims that courts interpret high-level principles like equal protection by drawing analogies between race and other classifications without recourse to abstract moral theory about the meaning of equality.[149]

As Sunstein's ambiguous treatment of the race-sex analogy suggests, there is reason to doubt that a court really could engage in analogical reasoning or use a tool box of legal methods without recourse to some broader principle or grander theory in interpreting the proper scope of equality, whether it be an anticaste principle (like Sunstein's) or a principle of equal concern and respect (like Dworkin's). If I am correct, then, equality is not necessarily less "adventurous" than privacy or autonomy as a constitutional ground for invalidating statutes. Arguably, constitutional theory that deploys abstract principles developed, as a discipline, in part due to a recognition that the lawyers' tool box conception of law is inadequate.

Second, the justification for Sunstein's judicial minimalism rests both on his argument concerning legitimacy—that judicial resolution of pressing moral conflicts robs the people of their right to deliberate about them—and on an argument about the limited institutional competence of courts. He offers a number of prudential reasons concerning the likelihood that courts will get things wrong and the lack of any special qualities making judges better suited than citizens or legislatures to resolve moral conflicts.[150] He embraces the "hollow hope" argument that courts usually cannot effectively bring about social change and that, even if they seek to vindicate constitutional rights, political and social resistance will weaken those rights and render their efforts ineffectual.[151]

Thus, judicial minimalism is appropriate given the relative institutional capacities of courts as compared with politically elected officials.

There are two opposed traditions in constitutional theory concerning the relative institutional capacities or positions of courts and legislatures. On one account, courts' independence from politics is their greatest weakness or disqualification for performing a function like elaborating and protecting substantive constitutional freedoms against encroachment through the political process. Sunstein has fully developed a version of this view. On another account, courts' independence from politics is their greatest strength or qualification for discharging such a responsibility. Dworkin has advanced a well-known version of such a view.[152] It is not possible to resolve the long-standing dispute between these traditions here. But it is worth recalling Justice Jackson's formulation in the second flag-salute case (invalidating a required salute), responding to Justice Frankfurter in the first such case (upholding a required salute): rather than deferring to the "vicissitudes" of the political process, courts vindicate constitutional freedoms "not by authority of [their] competence but by force of [their] commissions."[153] If the commission of the courts is to preserve the Constitution, including substantive liberties, against encroachment through the political process, they arguably would be abdicating their responsibility were they to side with Sunstein and against Dworkin on this dispute.

## A Critique of Sunstein's Theory of the Constitution Outside the Courts

Sunstein's development of judicial minimalism can be interpreted, in part, as an answer to his own earlier call (in *The Partial Constitution*) for taking seriously the idea of "the Constitution outside the courts."[154] But it is not clear that judicial minimalism will promote democratic deliberation, much less conscientious constitutional interpretation, outside the courts. It may simply permit the political processes to proceed, such as they are, and to trample on or neglect basic principles of liberty and equality. For one thing, for courts to leave matters undecided in order to permit democratic deliberation to proceed is not necessarily the same thing as to promote, or reinforce, or force democratic deliberation. To the extent that Sunstein's theory simply entails judicial deference to democracy—such as it is—rather than judicial reinforcement of democracy—in order to secure the preconditions for the trustworthiness of political decisions—it may have more in common with Thayer's deferential view[155] than with Ely's representation-reinforcing view. For another, promoting democratic deliberation is not necessarily the same thing as promoting conscientious constitutional interpretation outside the courts. For example, democratic deliberation about the common good is not the same as deliberation about the meaning and realization of constitutional principles and obligations, and it may well lead to flouting the Constitution outside the courts. Indeed, the Constitution properly interpreted outside as well as inside the courts may trump the common good and preclude deliberation about certain matters.

Sunstein's call for taking the Constitution seriously outside the courts began sensibly enough (in *The Partial Constitution*) by emphasizing certain institutional limitations of courts, especially where spending money and restructuring large institutions were concerned.[156] I worry that he may have added the circumstance of moral disagreement (especially about basic liberties) as an institutional limitation of courts. This development is troubling because moral disagreement about basic liberties may signal a situation of distrust that should trigger the need for judicial review; it should not be viewed as a situation that disqualifies courts and relegates basic liberties to the Constitution outside the courts.

In the wake of the Warren Court, constitutional law scholars with misgivings about judicial interpretation and enforcement of the Constitution by the Burger and Rehnquist Courts have repeatedly called for taking the Constitution seriously outside the courts, and thus looking to legislatures and executives for fuller protection of constitutional norms (and no doubt will continue to do so with respect to the Roberts Court).[157] Mark Tushnet's *Taking the Constitution Away from the Courts*[158] is the most comprehensive, thoughtful, and provocative answer to those calls to date. It travels beyond a judicial minimalism like Sunstein's in order to argue that constitutional interpretation belongs outside the courts and directly in the hands of the people themselves. Tushnet offers powerful arguments against judicial supremacy in constitutional interpretation and advances the best arguments to date for the proposition that the Constitution is self-enforcing through the political processes rather than through judicial review. But Tushnet does not establish that taking the Constitution seriously outside the courts requires, in his terms, "taking the Constitution *away from* the courts." Rather, I contend, it requires taking the Constitution *to* legislatures, executives, and citizens generally in order that its principles and aspirations might better frame and guide their decisions.

Tushnet's analysis, like Sunstein's, suggests some of the things we should do if we are to take the Constitution seriously outside the courts. First, we should develop, or reinvigorate, a rigorous and coherent notion of political questions—that is, questions the resolution of which the Constitution commits to institutions besides the courts. Second, we should generalize the notion of political questions in service of arguments that nonjudicial actors have an obligation to take the Constitution seriously outside the courts and that courts should defer to such actors in certain circumstances. Many arguments for judicial deference to the judgments of legislatures and executives simply emphasize the respect that courts owe the coordinate branches of government. Those arguments should go deeper, and ask why respect should be due those branches. The most defensible answer to that question is that the coordinate branch of government, like courts, is under the obligation conscientiously to interpret the Constitution before taking contemplated actions and is presumed to have discharged that obligation.

Put another way, we should revive, but reconstruct and prune, an element in Thayer's classic argument for judicial deference to the national legislature and executive.[159] Thayer presumed that Congress and the president, not courts, had primary authority to interpret the Constitution. For him, the question of judicial review was not a question of what the Constitution means, but a question of whether the judgment of Congress or the president about what the Constitution means was itself reasonable, or at any rate not clearly unreasonable.[160] The part of Thayer's argument that I would reconstruct is the idea that legislatures and executives have the authority and the obligation independently to interpret the Constitution. The part that I would prune is the idea that courts are to be concerned solely with the question of reasonableness, not with the question of what the Constitution means. Furthermore, I would reject his stance of judicial deference to the national political processes across the board; instead, I propose such deference only outside the situations in which we have good reason to distrust those processes.

We must recognize, as Tushnet argues and Sunstein acknowledges, that the Constitution is self-enforcing through the political processes, without judicial review, in large areas in which the Supreme Court is quite aggressive today, including most importantly the areas of federalism, states' rights, and separation of powers along with property rights and economic liberties. We must also recognize that the Constitution is not self-enforcing through the political processes in general or in certain other areas. In particular, it is not self-enforcing with respect to individual rights that are preconditions for the trustworthiness of the outcomes of the political processes. Thus, a Constitution-perfecting approach to judicial review is warranted in these areas.

Finally, we must appreciate, with Tushnet and Sunstein, that the contrast between courts as "the forum of principle" and legislatures as the "battleground of power politics"[161] is overstated. In constitutional theory, there are several familiar responses to this contrast. One approach is to obliterate it, saying that neither institution is a forum of principle and that not only legislatures but also courts are battlegrounds of power politics. This approach is common in both political science literature about courts and in public choice literature in legal scholarship.[162]

A second approach, epitomized by Sunstein, is to say that, historically, legislatures and executives have been the true forums of principle, or at least better forums of principle than courts.[163] Proponents of this approach typically charge that the contrast rests on a historically myopic idolization of the Warren Court. The typical view is that courts "follow the election returns" rather than being an independent bulwark of rights or forum of principle. Another variation posits that when courts do not follow the election returns, they usually lag behind rather than forge ahead and therefore, historically, have largely been conservative rather than liberal or progressive. Thus, this approach leads to the claim that legislatures and executives, historically, have been more reliable and more effective forces for liberal or progressive change—and for the fuller realization of constitutional principles of freedom, equality, and justice— than have courts.

A third approach, which I take, is to argue that taking the Constitution seriously outside the courts requires that legislatures and executives, along with courts, be forums of principle in certain respects. This approach is implicit in Rawls's statement, quoted in chapter 4: "[W]hile the Court is special in this respect [as an "exemplar of public reason" in a "forum of principle"], the other branches of government can certainly, if they would but do so, be forums of principle along with it in debating constitutional questions."[164] Such an approach grows out of a Rawlsian conception of constitutional democracy like that I develop in this book. This approach might seem to reflect a view that legislatures and executives are no different from courts in this respect, but it need not. The point is that the contrast is overdrawn and that legislatures and executives, like courts, have obligations conscientiously to engage in constitutional interpretation and to vindicate constitutional norms.[165]

## Conclusion

In conclusion, for constitutional interpretation in circumstances of moral disagreement and political conflict, Sandel's civic republican constitutional theory is too thick and Sunstein's minimalist republican theory too thin. The two in combination, however, confirm that my liberal republican theory of constitutional constructivism is just right.

# PART III

# Adjusting, Preserving, and Perfecting the Scheme of Constitutional Democracy

## CHAPTER EIGHT

# Securing the Family of Basic Liberties as a Whole

W hat is to be done when basic liberties conflict with one another? How should we to address clashes of rights, or more precisely, clashes of higher order values or interests that underlie rights?[1] Constitutional constructivism, like John Rawls's political constructivism, accords priority to the family of equal basic liberties as a whole over the pursuit of conceptions of the public good or the imposition of perfectionist values.[2] This understanding of priority entails that it may be permissible to regulate certain basic liberties for the sake of securing others or the whole family of such liberties. No single basic liberty by itself is absolute. There may be clashes between them or the interests or values underlying them, for example, between concern for protecting freedom of expression and concern for securing equal citizenship for all. In this chapter, I illustrate how a constructivist guiding framework might help us frame and ultimately resolve such clashes in order to secure the family of basic liberties as a whole.

I explore what the structure of First Amendment law would look like if we were committed, not to protecting an absolutist First Amendment in isolation from the rest of the Constitution, but to securing a fully adequate scheme of the basic liberties as a whole. I focus on four important U.S. Supreme Court cases that involve clashes between the First Amendment's protection of freedom of expression and the Equal Protection Clause's concern for equal citizenship. In three of these cases, the Court protected freedom of expression to the exclusion (or indeed erasure) of equal citizenship. First, I present Rawls's own critique of *Buckley v. Valeo*[3] (striking down certain campaign finance regulations limiting expenditures) as an exemplar of how to secure equal protection or equal participation together with freedom of expression. Second, I sketch an analogous critique of *R.A.V. v. City of St. Paul*[4] (invalidating an ordinance prohibiting "bias-motivated crimes" including hateful racist expression) for privileging freedom of expression over equal protection. Third, I analyze *Roberts v. United States Jaycees*[5] (forbidding the Jaycees to exclude women) as a model of how the Supreme Court itself on occasion has taken equal citizenship seriously in the context of freedom of expression and association. Finally, with this example on hand, I criticize *Boy Scouts of America v. Dale*[6] (permitting the Boy Scouts to exclude homosexuals) for privileging freedom of association over equal protection.

My aim is not to offer new interpretations of these cases, or even to resolve them. Rather, it is to suggest that a constructivist guiding framework of basic liberties might help frame our judgments concerning what to do when confronting clashes between freedom of expression and equal protection. Those judgments would be guided by the aspiration to accord priority to the family of basic liberties as a whole, not to give priority to freedom of expression over equal protection.

## Securing Deliberative Democracy

Constitutional constructivism views the Constitution as incorporating the equal political liberties and seeking to guarantee their fair value in order that the processes of political decision will be open to all on a roughly equal basis. The Constitution also protects freedom of thought (including freedom of speech and press, freedom of assembly, and the like) so that the exercise of those liberties in those processes will be free and informed.[7] Constructivism treats the equal political liberties in a special way as expressed by the guarantee of their fair value because of their role and significance in relation to the political processes and hence to the exercise of the first moral power in the first fundamental case, that of securing deliberative democracy.[8] The equal political liberties are in this sense *primus inter pares*, first among the equal basic liberties that as a family have priority over the pursuit of utilitarian public good and the imposition of perfectionist values. The constructivist framework in this respect parallels the theory of "preferred freedoms" outlined in footnote four of *United States v. Carolene Products Co.*[9] and elaborated in John

Hart Ely's *Democracy and Distrust*.[10] (That theory, as discussed in chapter 2, is especially concerned to secure the basic liberties that are preconditions for the trustworthiness of the outcomes of the political processes by keeping the political processes open and protecting them from the corruption of prejudice against discrete and insular minorities.)

## The Priority of the Basic Liberties, or Taking Rights Seriously

Let us recall two familiar refrains within liberal political philosophy and constitutional theory about the status of basic liberties or rights. One, associated with Rawls, is about the "priority of the basic liberties."[11] The other, associated with Ronald Dworkin, is about "taking rights seriously."[12] These two formulations arose in part in response to concerns that utilitarians, pragmatists, and balancers of all stripes do not appreciate or honor the nerve or force of claims of basic liberties or rights. To generalize, there is a twofold worry: (1) that these balancers reduce stringent claims of basic liberties or rights of individuals to mere claims of interests and (2) that they elevate mere claims of interests of the government into stringent claims of rights.

Justice Felix Frankfurter—balancer *par excellence* and *bête noire* of any serious proponent of "taking rights seriously"—famously illustrated both moves. In concurrence in *Dennis v. United States*,[13] which upheld convictions of leaders of the Communist Party under the Smith Act during the Cold War, he reduced the First Amendment freedom of expression of individuals to a mere interest that Congress may balance against the claims of the whole nation to national security. And in the two cases involving compulsory flag salutes, *Minersville School District v. Gobitis* (for the majority upholding such salutes)[14] and *West Virginia Board of Education v. Barnette* (in dissent from the majority opinion invalidating such salutes),[15] he illustrated the second move by framing the clash between Jehovah's Witnesses' freedom of religion and freedom of expression and association, on the one hand, and the government's interest in inculcating patriotism through compelling students to salute the flag, on the other, as a "clash of rights."[16]

Frankfurter was criticized in both instances. In *Dennis*, Justice Hugo Black did so in dissent, powerfully arguing that the First Amendment is an absolute right that is not simply to be balanced away out of concern for national security. Black lamented that the Court's (and Frankfurter's) approach "waters down the First Amendment so that it amounts to little more than an admonition to Congress" that is likely to protect only "'safe' or orthodox views." He further expressed the "hope" that "in calmer times" the Court would "restore the First Amendment liberties to the high preferred place where they belong in a free society."[17]

In *Barnette,* Justice Robert Jackson for the majority (over Frankfurter's dissent) pointedly argued that there was no clash of rights at issue. Instead, the "sole conflict" was between the individual rights of the Jehovah's Witnesses to "self-determination" and the claims of governmental authority to inculcate orthodoxy.[18] Jackson famously added: "If there is any fixed star in our constitutional constellation, it is that no official, high or petty, can prescribe what shall be orthodox in politics, nationalism, religion, or other matters of opinion or force citizens to confess by word or act their faith therein."[19]

Both of these cases involved the First Amendment, and constitutional and political theorists who give "priority" to basic liberties or who "take rights seriously" are rightly proud to take their stand with Black and Jackson and against Frankfurter in these battles.[20] Moreover, many of the issues of the 1940s through the 1970s that gave rise to the refrains about the priority of basic liberties and taking rights seriously involved clashes between individual rights against the government and claims of governmental authority to restrict or regulate those rights to pursue the national security or the good of all.[21] And those clashes arose in situations where liberals rightly feared that the government was overestimating the threats posed by respect for individual rights and also exaggerating the fragility of our institutions and our way of life in the face of such threats.

But all this should not blind us to the possibility of there being genuine clashes of rights, or more precisely, clashes of higher order values or interests that underlie rights—unlike Frankfurter's wrongheaded conception of a clash of rights—in which giving priority to the family of basic liberties as a whole may preclude according "absolutist" protection to First Amendment freedoms. Put another way, in rightly being "anti-balancing," we may have overlooked the possibility of genuine clashes of rights or values or interests, and failed to provide a framework for thinking about how to address them. The general type of clash I discuss below is between the concern to protect freedom of expression, on the one hand, and the concern to secure equal citizenship for all, including racial minorities (*R.A.V.*), women (*Roberts*), and homosexuals (*Dale*), on the other.

*Mutual Adjustment of Basic Liberties to Secure the Family of Basic Liberties as a Whole*

What is Rawls's conception of the priority of the basic liberties? And how would a Rawlsian constructivism accord such priority while also addressing conflicts among basic liberties? Rawls acknowledges that his conception of the priority of the basic liberties, when applied to constitutional doctrine, bears a certain similarity to the well-known view of Alexander Meiklejohn.[22] Meiklejohn is well known for emphasizing the role of free speech in relation to self-government[23] and for arguing that the First Amendment is an absolute so far as political speech is concerned.[24] Rawls, however, distinguishes his account from Meiklejohn's view along three lines:

> First, the kind of primacy Meiklejohn gives to the political liberties and to free speech is here given to the family of basic liberties as a whole; second, the value of self-government, which for Meiklejohn often seems overriding, is counted as but one important value among others; and finally, the philosophical background of the basic liberties is very different.[25]

Like Rawls and unlike Meiklejohn, constitutional constructivism gives priority to the family of basic liberties as a whole and thus stringently protects not only the political liberties associated with deliberative democracy but also the personal liberties associated with deliberative autonomy. Likewise, constructivism conceives the important value of self-government to include personal self-government together with political self-government. Finally, constructivism's broader protection of basic liberties leads to a broader conception of the regulation of particular basic liberties (including political liberties and freedom of speech) in order to secure the family of basic liberties as a whole.

Meiklejohn famously argues that freedom of speech is absolute but may be regulated, by analogy to rules of order in a town meeting, to protect the system of self-government.[26] In similar fashion, Rawls argues that it is appropriate to engage in mutual adjustment of basic liberties to secure a fully adequate scheme of the whole family of basic liberties. As Rawls puts it, because "the various basic liberties are bound to conflict with one another, the institutional rules which define these liberties must be adjusted so that they fit into a coherent scheme of liberties." Thus, he concedes that "[t]he public use of our reason must be regulated" as distinguished from restricted. But he explains that the priority of the basic liberties requires that such regulation be done, so far as possible, to preserve "the central range of application" of each basic liberty. And he contends that "[t]he priority of these liberties is not infringed when they are merely regulated, as they must be, in order to be combined into one scheme."[27]

Notwithstanding such regulation or mutual adjustment of the basic liberties, Rawls's framework entails a form of absolutism. For "the priority of liberty means that the first principle of justice assigns the basic liberties, as given by a list, a special status": "They have an absolute weight (1) with respect to reasons of [utilitarian] public good and of perfectionist values" and (2) over the second principle of justice (concerning social and economic inequalities, including the difference principle). Hence, the priority of the basic liberties implies in practice that "a basic liberty can be limited or denied solely for the sake of one or more other basic liberties, and never . . . for reasons of [utilitarian] public good or of perfectionist values."[28] That is, utilitarian pursuits of the greatest happiness of the greatest number and perfectionist aspirations to inculcate a comprehensive conception of the good life do not justify overriding or limiting basic liberties. Nor do governmental efforts to satisfy the difference principle.

Rawls urges that the "mutual adjustment" of the basic liberties is justified on grounds allowed by the priority of these liberties as a family, no one of which is in itself absolute. This kind of adjustment, he contends, "is markedly different from a general balancing of interests which permits considerations of all kinds—political, economic, and social—to restrict these liberties, even regarding their content, when the advantages gained or injuries avoided are thought to be great enough." He explains: "[T]he adjustment of the basic liberties is grounded solely on their significance as specified by their role in the two fundamental cases." Furthermore, this adjustment is guided by the aim of specifying a fully adequate scheme of these liberties.[29]

The notion of balancing may be weak and truistic, as a metaphor for judgment, which in any event is necessary and so makes the notion trivial.[30] Or it may be strong and corrosive, such that it does not take rights seriously. Examples include utilitarian cost-benefit calculations reflected in Judge Learned Hand's "gravity of the evil" test as a formulation of the clear and present danger test[31] and Justice Frankfurter's ad hoc evaluations of specific threats[32] in the context of freedom of expression.

By contrast, Rawls's notion of the priority of the basic liberties precludes such balancing and does take these liberties seriously.

Constitutional constructivism shares First Amendment absolutists' aversion to balancing. But the notion of mutual adjustment within the family of basic liberties—in terms of the role and significance of a particular liberty for the free public use of our reason in the two fundamental cases of deliberative democracy and autonomy—may seem anathema to First Amendment absolutists. For example, for Ely, the problem with cases striking down regulations of the financing of electoral campaigns such as *Buckley* is that the Court strayed off an absolutist, categorical track of First Amendment analysis onto the slippery slope of a test that is merely "a more demanding sort of balancing or specific harm test."[33] For constitutional constructivism, though, the problem with cases like *Buckley* is that the Court failed to see the Constitution as a whole, and therefore failed to see that freedom of political expression may be regulated (though not restricted) in order to guarantee equal participation and the fair value of the equal political liberties.[34]

In assessing absolutist frameworks for First Amendment analysis, we should bear in mind Rawls's suggestion concerning the priority of the basic liberties:

> Whenever we enlarge the list of basic liberties we risk weakening the protection of the most essential ones and recreating within the scheme of liberties the indeterminate and unguided balancing problems we had hoped to avoid by a suitably circumscribed notion of priority.[35]

Similarly, whenever we enlarge or overextend the protection of one basic liberty such as freedom of expression, we risk weakening the protection of other basic liberties such as equal protection and recreating within the scheme of liberties the balancing problems we had hoped to avoid by the notion of priority.


## Guaranteeing the Fair Value of the Equal Political Liberties

Like Rawls's political liberalism, constitutional constructivism incorporates a guarantee of the fair value of the equal political liberties. This guarantee, Rawls argues, is "a natural focal point" between merely formal liberty, on the one hand, and a guarantee of the fair value for all basic liberties, on the other.[36] He distinguishes between merely formal basic liberties and the fair value of these liberties—or between *liberty* and *the worth of liberty*—as follows:

> The basic liberties are a framework of legally protected paths and opportunities. Of course, ignorance and poverty, and the lack of material means generally, prevent people from exercising their rights and from taking advantage of these openings. But rather than counting these and similar obstacles as restricting a person's liberty, we count them as affecting the worth of liberty, that is, the usefulness to persons of their liberties.[37]

He treats the equal political liberties in a special way, by "the guarantee that the political liberties, and only these liberties, are secured by [affording] their 'fair value.'"[38]

Rawls explains that this guarantee means that "the worth of the political liberties to all citizens, whatever their social or economic position, must be approximately equal, or at least sufficiently equal, in the sense that everyone has a fair opportunity to hold public office and to influence the outcome of political decisions." The guarantee has two noteworthy features:

> First, it secures for each citizen a fair and roughly equal access to the use of . . . the public facility specified by the constitutional rules and procedures which govern the political process and control the entry to positions of political authority. . . . [T]hese rules and procedures are to be a fair process, designed to yield just and effective legislation.

Rawls continues:

> Second, this public facility has limited space, so to speak. Hence, those with relatively greater means can combine together and exclude those who have less in the absence of the guarantee of fair value of the political liberties. . . . [T]he usefulness of our political liberties is far more subject to our social position and our place in the distribution of income and wealth than the usefulness of our other basic liberties.[39]

Guaranteeing the fair value of the equal political liberties entails that it may be permissible to regulate political liberties in order to ensure "a fair and equal access to the political process as a public facility."[40] This guarantee is thus analogous to Meiklejohn's notion of applying rules of order to regulate free discussion in a system of self-government.

Rawls admits that "[i]t is beyond the scope of a philosophical doctrine to consider in any detail the kinds of arrangements required to insure the fair value of the equal political liberties."[41] Nonetheless, he illustrates the problem of maintaining that fair value by considering measures that regulate the financing of electoral campaigns and referendums of the sort struck down in *Buckley v. Valeo* (limiting campaign expenditures)[42] and *First National Bank v. Bellotti* (prohibiting certain kinds of corporations, including banks, from making contributions for or against public referendums).[43] He argues that these regulations "were admissible attempts to achieve the aim of a fair scheme of representation in which all citizens could have a more full and effective voice."[44] From *Wesberry v. Sanders*[45] and *Reynolds v. Sims*,[46] which had affirmed the principle of "one person, one vote," Rawls infers that the right to vote that is protected under the U.S. Constitution involves more than the right simply to cast a vote that is counted equally: "[W]hat is fundamental is a political procedure which secures for all citizens a full and equally effective voice in a fair scheme of representation. Such a scheme is fundamental because the adequate protection of other basic rights depends on it. Formal equality is not enough."[47] Accordingly, he argues:

> If the Court means what it says in *Wesberry* and *Reynolds*, *Buckley* must sooner or later give way. The First Amendment no more enjoins a system of representation according to influence effectively exerted in free political rivalry between unequals than the Fourteenth Amendment enjoins a system of liberty of contract and free competition between unequals in the economy, as the Court thought in the *Lochner* era.[48]

As against Rawls's understanding of the principle of equal participation, the Court in *Buckley* thus seemed to embrace a notion of the veritable marketplace of ideas: a marketplace in which ideas and candidates, like commodities, are bought and sold.

Furthermore, in saying that "the concept that government may restrict the speech of some elements of our society in order to enhance the relative voice of others is wholly foreign to the First Amendment,"[49] the Court in *Buckley* seemed to reject the idea that Congress may try to guarantee the fair value of the equal political liberties. In doing so, Rawls argues, the Court failed to see the Constitution as a whole.[50] It did not recognize that freedom of political speech and the equal political liberties, as members of the family of equal basic liberties, may be adjusted to one another in order to guarantee the central range of application of these liberties in the first fundamental case of deliberative democracy. Neither did the Court see that securing the fair value of the equal political liberties is arguably justifiable on the basis of the Equal Protection Clause together with the Republican Form of Government Clause.[51] (Justice Byron R. White, dissenting in both *Buckley* and *First National Bank,* recognized that freedom of political expression was being regulated for the sake of protecting a system of freedom of expression, and that in this sense there were compelling governmental interests in regulation rooted in the First Amendment itself.)[52] Rawls's critique of *Buckley* (and *First National Bank*) illustrates how to secure equal protection or equal participation together with freedom of expression rather than privileging the latter to the exclusion of the former.[53]

More recent cases in which the Court has upheld campaign finance regulations—for example, *McConnell v. Federal Election Commission*,[54] upholding limitations on contributions to the political parties (or soft money)—have done so in the name of curbing corruption and the appearance of corruption, not in the name of adjusting freedom of expression and equal protection or securing the fair value of the equal political liberties. My aim here is not to weigh in on, much less resolve, campaign finance issues as such; the point is to model the mutual adjustment of basic liberties and the idea of guaranteeing the fair value of the equal political liberties.

### The Priority of the Family of Basic Liberties as a Whole: Taking Both Equal Citizenship and Freedom of Expression Seriously

Liberal theorists of freedom of expression and the Supreme Court alike have gotten on the bandwagon of First Amendment absolutism and taking freedom of expression seriously. In doing so, many have ignored or erased concern for securing equal citizenship for all. We need to reflect more on not only taking freedom of expression seriously, but also taking equality seriously. Put another way, (1) some may have taken the First Amendment too seriously (to the exclusion of concern for equal protection); (2) others may have taken the Equal Protection Clause too seriously (to the exclusion of concern for freedom of expression); and (3) we need a framework that does not take either too seriously to the exclusion of the other, but takes each seriously enough and in the right way. Constitutional constructivism provides such a guiding framework.

It should come as no surprise that in a world where First Amendment absolutism is familiar and established (and with it, taking freedom of expression seriously), yet where equal protection absolutism is not (and with it, taking equal citizenship seriously), we should have decisions privileging freedom of expression and association over equal protection like *Buckley, R.A.V.,* and *Boy Scouts.* The problem with each of these cases is similar: (1) failing (or refusing) to see the Constitution as a whole, and thus overemphasizing the commitment to freedom of expression or association; and (2) failing (or refusing) to honor the commitment to securing equal citizenship for all. We need to figure out ways to take freedom of expression and association together with equal protection seriously at once, at least to the extent of securing the core or central range of application of each. Yet we also need to rethink how to do this in order to avoid absolutism of one or the other as well as to avoid sliding into the morass of balancing generally. We need an architecture or structure of basic liberties that promises to secure the central range of application of both and also to avert such a slide.

The constructivist guiding framework sketched in the preceding chapters provides such an architecture or structure, and helps frame our judgments regarding what to do when confronting clashes between protecting freedom of expression and securing equal citizenship. Within this framework, we give priority to the whole family of basic liberties over utilitarian and perfectionist conceptions of general welfare or common good—not priority to any particular basic liberty over others. Furthermore, according priority to the whole family of basic liberties does not preclude regulating or adjusting one basic liberty to secure the central range of application of another. This adjustment may be acceptable so long as we secure the central range of application of the former basic liberty, for again, we are seeking to give priority to the whole family of basic liberties, not to pursue an absolutism of particular liberties. But note that this idea does not open the door generally to balancing rights against governmental interests: the only permissible type of regulating or adjusting of one basic liberty is to secure another basic liberty, not to pursue utilitarian or perfectionist conceptions of the general interest, the common good, or other ends.

Using as a point of departure Rawls's analysis of *Buckley,* I sketch how such a guiding framework might apply to *Roberts, R.A.V.,* and *Boy Scouts.*

Again, my aim is not to offer new interpretations of these cases nor to resolve them. Rather, it is architectural: to illustrate how we might use the guiding framework to structure the inquiry in such cases. I should make clear that my aim is to apply a Rawlsian view, not to explicate Rawls's own views.[55]

## R.A.V. v. City of St. Paul

*Buckley* was wrongly decided with respect to limitations on campaign expenditures, among other reasons, because the Court failed to see the Constitution as a whole. Therefore, it failed to see that freedom of political expression may be regulated (though not restricted) through campaign finance laws in order to try to ensure political equality, or the fair value of the equal political liberties, for equal citizens in a fair scheme of representation. The Court's single-minded focus on the First Amendment without regard to such preconditions for deliberative democracy blinded it to that compelling governmental objective.

A similar blindness may have been at work in Justice Scalia's opinion for the Court in *R.A.V.*,[56] which struck down a "Bias-Motivated Crime Ordinance"—punishing expression that "arouses anger, alarm or resentment in others on the basis of race, color, creed, religion, or gender"—as an impermissible content-based discrimination. The opinion declaimed: "The First Amendment does not permit St. Paul to impose special prohibitions on those speakers who express views on disfavored subjects."[57] Scalia and the Court resolutely refused to see the Constitution as a whole and therefore failed to see that freedom of hateful racist expression quite possibly may be regulated (though not restricted) in order to attempt to secure equal citizenship for members of groups who are subject to racial, religious, gender, or sexual orientation hostility. (This equality, too, is a precondition for deliberative democracy).[58]

T. M. Scanlon writes of ordinances like that at issue in *R.A.V.:* "But the proposed restrictions would restrict speech on the basis of its content, in violation of one of the limitations that Rawls placed on the regulation of campaign finances. This quandary raises the question of whether Rawls should regard this kind of regulation as an impermissible restriction."[59] Scanlon's formulation here implies that he accepts Scalia's view that the ordinance was discriminatory, whereas I accept Justice Stevens's view that it was evenhanded. In arguing that the ordinance imposed a "viewpoint discrimination" in favor of proponents of racial tolerance and equality, Scalia wrote: "St. Paul has no such authority to license one side of a debate to fight freestyle, while requiring the other to follow Marquis of Queensbury rules."[60] Stevens retorted:

> The St. Paul ordinance is evenhanded. In a battle between advocates of tolerance and advocates of intolerance, the ordinance does not prevent either side from hurling fighting words at the other on the basis of their conflicting ideas, but it does bar both sides from hurling such words on the basis of the target's "race, color, creed, religion or gender." To extend the Court's pugilistic metaphor, the St. Paul ordinance simply bans punches "below the belt"—by either party. It does not, therefore, favor one side of any debate.[61]

Even if Scanlon is right that Rawls might view this kind of regulation as an impermissible restriction, I noted above that my aim is to apply a Rawlsian framework, not to explicate Rawls's own views.[62]

My suggestion regarding what is wrong with Scalia's opinion accords with that of Stevens in his concurring opinion in *R.A.V.* Stevens argued that the First Amendment—in isolation from the whole scheme—is not an absolute.[63] Justice White made a similar argument in *R.A.V.*, mentioning the Equal Protection Clause and stating that "[i]n light of our Nation's long and painful experience with discrimination," the ordinance was plainly reasonable and the interest compelling.[64]

I suspect that even if the Court had seen the Constitution as a whole—looking at the Equal Protection Clause as well as the First Amendment—it still would have reached the same result in *R.A.V.* Indeed, Scalia officially credited (or paid lip service to) protecting racial minorities as a "compelling governmental interest."[65] He then proceeded to give short shrift to this point, though, concluding that the ordinance proscribing expression that "arouses anger, alarm or resentment in others on the basis of race" is not "necessary" to serve that interest, for there are less restrictive alternatives available, such as prosecution under trespass, arson, and similar statutes. Therefore, he concluded, the ordinance cannot survive strict scrutiny.[66] Justice White objected that Scalia gave new meaning to strict scrutiny.[67] More importantly, trespass, arson, and the like—the less restrictive alternatives Scalia vaunts—are not less restrictive means to the same end. The end is not merely to protect the private property of African American families. It is publicly to affirm their status as equal citizens. Trespass, arson, and similar statutes simply are not means to furthering that end; the Bias-Motivated Crime Ordinance is.

Scalia might object that for the government to affirm the equal citizenship of African Americans over racists' views of their inferiority is "thought control" and places us on the slippery slope toward totalitarianism—just as Judge Frank Easterbrook, in *American Booksellers Association v. Hudnut,* objected in the context of the government's affirming the equal citizenship of women in regulating pornography.[68] Such arguments are terribly overblown. Consider Canada's approaches to hate speech[69] and to pornography,[70] which are at odds with those in *R.A.V.* and *Hudnut.* And yet Canada has not fallen down the slippery slope into totalitarianism. (It is another matter whether Canada's approaches have been effective at moderating hate speech or pornography.)[71] Such comparative constitutional law inquiries might help deflate overblown slippery-slope arguments, whether made by conservative judges like Easterbrook and Scalia or liberal organizations like the American Civil Liberties Union. At the same time, we should acknowledge the risks involved in regulating or restricting such expression.

There may be, to be sure, pragmatic arguments against adopting ordinances or statutes like those at issue in *R.A.V.* Thus, in dissent in *Beauharnais v. Illinois,* an earlier decision upholding a conviction for hateful racist expression, Justice Black cautioned about the Pyrrhic victory—"Another such victory and I am undone"—of racial minorities in winning a decision protecting them against hate speech.[72] What losses might Black have believed offset the victory? It may be better not to make martyrs of racists, but to have their views out in the open to be combated. Such concerns are generally put forward in safety-valve arguments for protecting their freedom of speech: let them blow off steam. More generally, perhaps it is better not to fan the flames of worries about "political correctness" (whether conservative or liberal), worries that Justice Blackmun suggested animated Scalia's opinion for the Court in *R.A.V.*[73] Still, it is good to answer and combat the *R.A.V.* conception of the First Amendment itself on principle.[74]

## Roberts v. United States Jaycees

In the Supreme Court's decision in *Roberts,* unlike its decision in *Buckley,* the Court did not view it as "wholly foreign to the First Amendment" to regulate freedom of association on the basis of concern for equal protection. *Roberts* held that men's rights to associate with one another (and not to associate with women) in the United States Jaycees or Junior Chamber of Commerce, a commercial and civic organization, were overridden by women's rights not to be discriminated against in places of public accommodation.[75] (In the case, two local chapters of the Jaycees in Minnesota had begun admitting women and had been sanctioned by the national organization and threatened with expulsion.) The Court held that the state of Minnesota had a compelling governmental interest in eliminating gender discrimination in public accommodations.

Constitutional constructivism embraces such a holding as necessary to secure for women and men alike the common and guaranteed status of equal citizenship (also a precondition for deliberative democracy). It bears noting that the case distinguished between freedom of expressive association (which I would link to deliberative democracy)—"a right to associate for the purpose of engaging in those activities protected by the First Amendment"—and freedom of intimate association (which I would connect with deliberative autonomy)—"to secure individual liberty" and "the ability independently to define one's identity," the Constitution protects "choices to enter into and maintain certain intimate human relationships . . . against undue intrusion by the State."[76] Thus, *Roberts* suggested that freedom of association comes into play with respect to both moral powers in the fundamental cases of deliberative democracy and deliberative autonomy.

What might account for the difference between the Court's decisions in *Roberts* and *Buckley?* For one thing, freedom of association in particular just may not be as strong a right as freedom of expression in general—just not as sheltered from governmental regulation. For another, freedom of association in the commercial context is not as strong a right as freedom of expression in the political context. Justice O'Connor, concurring in *Roberts,* argued that commercial association does not warrant the stringent protection given to "expressive association"; the former is subject to reasonable regulations.[77] Another reason for the difference between the holdings may be that the concern for equal protection in *Roberts* was better defined or more bounded than that in *Buckley:* the state of Minnesota was simply trying to afford to women what was already available to men, namely, membership in a commercial and civic organization. Therefore, there were no potentially complicated questions of institutional design like those involved in a campaign finance scheme, such as how much expression is essential to secure equal participation or a fully effective voice in the political process.

*Roberts* illustrates how the constructivist guiding framework might apply in a situation involving a clash between freedom of expressive association and equal protection for women. Notably, the Court did not simply say that freedom of association is well-nigh absolute, and that it is "wholly foreign to the First Amendment"[78] or "thought control"[79] for government to take measures that express the view that women are equal citizens. Nor did Justice Brennan's opinion for the Court in *Roberts* do what Chief Justice Rehnquist's opinion for the Court subsequently did in *Boy Scouts:* simply defer to the Jaycees' claims that being forced to admit women would impair their expression or impede their ability to disseminate their views or message.[80] Instead, the Court recognized that the state was furthering a compelling governmental interest and that it was doing so through "the least restrictive means of achieving its ends."[81]

At the same time, the Court gave due regard to the Jaycees' claims to freedom of association. It concluded that "the Jaycees has failed to demonstrate that the Act imposes any serious burdens on the male members' freedom of expressive association." In particular, the Court, observing that the Jaycees already admitted women as junior members and invited them to participate in their training and community activities, held that there was "no basis in the record for concluding that admission of women as full voting members will impede the organization's ability to engage in these protected activities or to disseminate its preferred views."[82] We should treat *Roberts* as an archetype of how the Court might frame clashes between freedom of association and equal protection, and of how it might secure the core or central range of application of both freedoms, rather than privileging the former to the exclusion of the latter.

Not all liberals agree with this approach to mutual adjustment of freedom of association and equal protection. Some see *Roberts* as undermining pluralism. For example, Nancy Rosenblum and William Galston see it as enforcing "congruence" between the democratic values that should be affirmed in public life and the diverse values that may be pursued by associations in civil society.[83] They argue against the appropriateness of governmental intervention to enforce the democratic value of gender equality throughout civil society. (And Rosenblum is skeptical concerning whether second-class membership in an association like the Jaycees is tantamount to second-class citizenship in the polity.) But it is certainly possible to believe that *Roberts* was rightly decided as a matter of constitutional law, on the ground that prohibiting gender discrimination in "places of public accommodation" like the Jaycees is a compelling governmental interest, without thinking that it is appropriate for the government to intervene to enforce gender equality throughout civil society. For one thing, most institutions in civil society are not "public accommodations" as a matter of constitutional law and therefore are beyond the reach of the *Roberts* decision. For another, it is appropriate and justifiable in some circumstances for the government to regulate freedom of association in order to attempt to secure equal citizenship for all, including women and racial minorities. Rosenblum herself has acknowledged that the workplace is an important exception to the autonomy of group life and has fully endorsed, for example, Title VII (which prohibits employment discrimination on the basis of race, color, religion, sex, or national origin).[84] And so, to reject Rosenblum's conclusion regarding *Roberts* is not necessarily to reject her overall position against enforcing "congruence" between democratic values in public life and the values pursued by associations in civil society.[85]

## Boy Scouts of America v. Dale

The Boy Scouts of America, asserting that homosexual sexual conduct was inconsistent with the values they seek to instill, revoked the adult membership of James Dale, an Eagle Scout who was an avowed homosexual. The Supreme Court's decision in *Boy Scouts* held that it would violate the Boy Scouts' freedom of expressive association to require them to admit homosexuals because doing so would "materially interfere with the ideas that the organization sought to express."[86] *Boy Scouts* did not follow the example of *Roberts* by upholding New Jersey's attempt to regulate freedom of association in order to further the compelling governmental interest of prohibiting discrimination in public accommodations on the basis of sexual orientation. (The New Jersey law lists sexual orientation along with race and gender as prohibited bases of discrimination.)[87]

What could account for the different outcomes in *Roberts* and *Boy Scouts?* First, one might argue that there is a difference in the character of the freedom of association: that the Jaycees were engaged in commercial association, while the Boy Scouts were involved in civic association.

Second, one might argue that the Boy Scouts really were trying to communicate a message about moral straightness that required exclusion of homosexuals—Rehnquist's opinion in *Boy Scouts* granted that the

Scout Oath and Scout Law did not expressly mention sexual orientation, but emphasized that they did use the terms "morally straight" and
"clean"—whereas the Jaycees had no such message that required exclusion of women. But what if in *Roberts* the male Jaycees had said that their
message was not simply that "commerce is good," but that "commerce
by men is good, and commerce by women is bad, because men by
nature belong in the marketplace, and women by nature belong in the
home"? The Court's reasoning in *Boy Scouts* suggested that the male
Jaycees should have prevailed in that case on the ground that forcing
them to admit women would "materially interfere with the ideas that the
organization sought to express."[88]

Third, one might argue that there is a difference in the governmental
interests that could be invoked to justify the regulation of freedom of
association in the two cases. The majority opinion in *Boy Scouts* stated
that "[w]e recognized in cases such as *Roberts* . . . that States have a
compelling interest in eliminating discrimination against women in public
accommodations."[89] But in *Boy Scouts,* the legislature and Supreme
Court of New Jersey implicitly had adopted the view that the state has a
compelling interest in eliminating discrimination on the basis of sexual
orientation in public accommodations. The U.S. Supreme Court's
decision either failed to recognize that view or conclusorily dismissed it.
Even if the Court were not ready to go all the way with *Roberts* and
hold that a compelling governmental interest was present in *Boy Scouts*,
it should have taken at least a few steps in that direction, given its
decisions in *Romer v. Evans*[90] (invalidating a state constitutional amendment "bar[ring] homosexuals from securing protection" against discrimination) and *Lawrence v. Texas*[91] (striking down a state statute making it a
crime for two persons of the same sex to engage in certain intimate sexual
conduct not forbidden to two persons of the opposite sex). These two
cases held that governmental aims reflecting "animus" against or a "bare
desire to harm" a politically unpopular group like homosexuals do not
constitute legitimate governmental interests.[92] And they also suggested
that government may not take measures that "demean" the lives of
homosexual persons.[93] Together, *Romer* and *Lawrence* manifested some
concern for government's securing the status of gays and lesbians as free
and equal citizens.[94] Therefore, in adjusting the clash between the concerns for freedom of association of the Boy Scouts and for equal citizenship of homosexuals, the Court should have recognized the latter as a
more substantial concern than it did.

The Court might say that *Lawrence* and *Romer* are different because *Boy Scouts* involved diversity within civil society, and freedom not to associate has greater force there than when government has passed laws relating to homosexual sexual conduct or to homosexuals' status in the community (as was the case in *Lawrence* and *Romer*). Fair enough. But under New Jersey law, the Boy Scouts constitute a "public accommodation," just as under Minnesota law the Jaycees do (though the Court in *Boy Scouts* questioned the expansive reach of New Jersey's definition of "public accommodation"). So the difference between *Roberts* and *Boy Scouts* could come down to the difference between the Court's view of the interests in eradicating gender discrimination and sexual orientation discrimination.

We should acknowledge that, had it been the Jaycees rather than the Boy Scouts excluding homosexuals, the case *conceivably* might have come out differently. I allude to the bugaboo of the worry about homosexual scout leaders seducing boys or inspiring them—through their positive role models—to become more tolerant of homosexuals or indeed to become homosexuals (if one becomes a homosexual as distinguished from being one). Presumably there would be no analogous fear about adult Jaycees.

Finally, the majority opinion in *Boy Scouts* stated that "we must . . . give deference to an association's view of what would impair its expression" and that "Dale's presence in the Boy Scouts would, at the very least, force the organization to send a message, both to the youth members and the world, that the Boy Scouts accepts homosexual conduct as a legitimate form of behavior."[95] What if a white supremacist/separatist group objected to admitting blacks on the ground that doing so would impair its expression of its separatist view and would force it to send a message that association between whites and blacks is a legitimate form of behavior? The Court in *Roberts* was not bowled over by analogous arguments of the Jaycees, for it held: "[A]ny claim that admission of women as full voting members will impair a symbolic message conveyed by the very fact that women are not permitted to vote is attenuated at best."[96]

In dissent in *Boy Scouts,* Justice Stevens insightfully included concerns for equal citizenship in the analysis. He argued that "[u]nder the majority's reasoning, an openly gay male is irreversibly affixed with the label 'homosexual.' That label, even though unseen, communicates a message that permits his exclusion wherever he goes. . . . [R]eliance on such a justification is tantamount to a constitutionally prescribed symbol of inferiority."[97] Rehnquist's majority opinion did not even attempt to answer Stevens's powerful critique. Furthermore, Stevens saw the analogy between this symbol of inferiority and that involved in *Loving v. Virginia*[98] and racial prejudices more generally.[99] An anticaste principle of equal citizenship would condemn both alike. It is well to recall that the whites in *Brown v. Board of Education*[100] asserted a freedom of association claim: freedom not to associate with blacks.[101] Rehnquist may have failed to see the analogy or may have rejected it.[102] In any case, his opinion did not face up to it or otherwise acknowledge concerns for securing equal citizenship together with freedom not to associate.

## Conclusion

In this chapter, I have explored what the structure of the First Amendment would look like if we were committed, not to protecting an absolutist First Amendment in isolation from the rest of the Constitution, but to securing a fully adequate scheme of the basic liberties as a whole. My aim has been to suggest that a constructivist guiding framework of basic liberties might help frame our judgments concerning what to do when confronting clashes between freedom of expression and equal protection. Those judgments would be guided by the aspiration to accord priority to the family of basic liberties as a whole, not to give priority to freedom of expression over equal protection.

# Securing Constitutional Democracy in War and Crisis

I now turn to a fundamentally different aspect of securing constitutional democracy: preserving the constitutional order itself in circumstances of war and crisis. I consider whether it is justifiable, in such circumstances, to violate the Constitution in order to save it. Using as an example Abraham Lincoln's justification for suspending the writ of habeas corpus during the Civil War, I acknowledge the possibility that actions like Lincoln's may be *constitutionalist*—justifiable on the ground that they are necessary to preserve or restore the conditions for the constitutional order itself—though not strictly *constitutional*—justifiable in terms of fidelity to particular constitutional norms themselves. I consider whether *Bush v. Gore*, which resolved the 2000 presidential election controversy, might be justifiable along similar lines, as necessary to avert a constitutional crisis. I conclude that it is not. Beyond that, I argue that a Lincolnian constitutionalist jurisprudence opens the window to a positive benefits conception of the Constitution, as contrasted with the negative liberties conception that the Rehnquist Court embraced in cases like *DeShaney v. Winnebago County Department of Social Services*.[1] From the standpoint of such a jurisprudence, we would see securing constitutional democracy—together with its scheme of basic liberties—in terms of positive benefits that the government is obligated to afford. We would not conceive either the constitutional order itself or its basic liberties merely in terms of freedoms from government.

In this chapter, unlike previous chapters, I do not elaborate or apply constitutional constructivism's guiding framework to secure the basic liberties associated with constitutional democracy. Rather, as mentioned above, I reflect on whether there are circumstances in which, to preserve or restore the conditions of constitutional democracy itself, it may be justifiable to violate the Constitution. In that sense, the analysis may seem to proceed outside the guiding framework. Nonetheless, the inquiry is guided by the constitutionalist aspiration to secure the conditions in which these basic liberties can be respected and, one hopes, constitutional democracy can flourish.

## The "Supreme Object" of Securing Constitutional Democracy

War has unique implications for citizens of a constitutional democracy. It repels us in a way that helps define us. Reflection on our experience with war exposes our view of the nature of the Constitution and of constitutional obligation, the nature of constitutional maintenance, and the fundamental aims of constitutional reform.

Like most animal life, we fear life-threatening physical violence. Yet with us, unlike with some other members of the kingdom and even the species, fear of such violence tends to be our greatest fear, or so certain of our philosophical forebears believed. Hobbes invited us to join his reflections on the fear of violent death as epistemic of our true sociopolitical selves.[2] These reflections gave birth to our Lockean[3] or constitutional democratic way of life, our "constitution" in the cultural sense.[4] The legal part of America's constitution, accordingly, tries to do things that would have amazed an ancient Greek or Roman and that outrage some of today's true religious believers. The Constitution subordinates military to civilian authority (implicitly valuing peace over war and comfort over glory); it forbids establishment of religion and religious tests for office (implicitly trusting those who pursue earthly goods over clergy, as such); and it lets our governments hang horse thieves while forbidding any punishment whatever for those who turn our youth toward false gods and destroy their otherwise immortal souls.

In the same way that Hobbes and Locke presented the social contract as merely the means to peace and security, the Constitution was originally presented as a means to the ends of our constitutional democracy proclaimed in the Preamble: the union of the many, as distinguished from—better, as opposed to—the distinction of the few; domestic tranquility and the blessings of liberty, as opposed to the honor of disciplined self-sacrifice and the glory of imperial power. Add the amending provisions of Article V to the ends of the Preamble—and view both through the window to a constitution-making past (and to a constitution-making future?) that Article VII provides—and you can see the Constitution's instrumentalist dimension. That is, the Constitution is a means to the ends of our constitutional democracy prescribed in the Preamble.

Reflect further and you can see that this instrumentalist dimension dominates the Constitution's legal dimension, especially when the chips are down, as during times of war and crisis. Hobbes knew no logic that could convert an instrumental norm to a moral norm—because we consent to save ourselves, we owe nothing to the sovereign who turns on us to destroy us.[5] Jefferson wrote in the Declaration of Independence that a people has the right to abolish and reconstitute any government "as to them shall seem most likely to effect their Safety and Happiness." Madison wrote in *The Federalist* No. 45 that "the real welfare of the great body of the people, is the supreme object to be pursued," and that "no form of government whatever has any other value than as it may be fitted for the attainment of this object."[6] For Madison this included more than fidelity to the Articles of Confederation and "perpetual Union" to which the states had once consented; it included rejecting the Articles in favor of the Union and the plan of the Philadelphia Constitutional Convention.[7] Thus, constitution-making, not fidelity to any existing form of government, is at the heart of the constitutionalist persuasion and enterprise.

Pursuit of the "supreme object[s]" of the Constitution as more compelling than fidelity to supreme laws under the existing form of government (whether the Articles or the Constitution)? Madison cited the people's welfare to disestablish the old articles of union. The people's safety in time of war rationalized the unconstitutional Sedition Act. In time of civil war Lincoln cited the people's welfare to justify overriding constitutional rights, forms, and limits. The people's safety, as perceived, trumped the constitutional rights of Japanese Americans during World War II. George Bush, Donald Rumsfeld, John Ashcroft, and Alberto Gonzales also cited the people's safety in time of war—the "war on terrorism"—to justify overriding constitutional forms, rights, and limits after September 11, 2001. And, as in candor it would have admitted, the Rehnquist Court sacrificed its own constitutional principles to political and social order in the election of 2000, an episode of the present "Kulturkampf" or "culture war" to which Justice Scalia referred in dissent in *Romer v. Evans*[8] and *Lawrence v. Texas*.[9] Indeed,

*Bush v. Gore*[10] has proved to be something of an augur of what was to come. Bush, Florida Republicans, and the Rehnquist Court fabricated a constitutional crisis that the Rehnquist Court averted by securing Bush's victory. Then war and crisis without end became Bush's chief justifications for overriding constitutional limits in waging permanent war and indeed in governing domestically.[11]

These conceptions and events suggest the following mix of normative and behavioral propositions concerning the preservation and maintenance of a constitutional democracy such as our own:

1. Constitutional forms, rights, and limits tend to obtain only under more or less ideal conditions, and war (including culture war) and crisis are not such conditions.

2. Constitutional forms, rights, and limits give way (and sometimes ought to give way) to substantive constitutional ends, unless they can be conceived as aspects of substantive constitutional ends (free inquiry, reasonable diversity, and broadly representative legislative assemblies as aspects of the pursuit of the common good, for example, or freedom from religious establishment and free exercise as aspects of the moderate religiosity associated with constitutional democracy).

3. Respect for constitutional forms, rights, and limits entails a substantive policy agenda, an agenda informed by the social conditions under which honoring limits, rights, and forms makes sense or would make sense to reasonable actors. These conditions include peace or reasonable prospects for peace, international security, a generally secular reasonableness and commitment to honoring the limits of public reason in domestic politics, racial and ethnic integration, progress in the arts and sciences, and a general economic well-being.

4. Because there are different kinds of war, because both the presence and the imminence of war can be controversial, because what holds for war can reasonably hold for impending war, because war can be used as an excuse to achieve ends not otherwise achievable both internationally and domestically—for these reasons at least, constitutional forms are no substitute for a population that generally holds a political liberal conception of justice and exhibits and respects the civic virtues and attitudes necessary to sustain constitutional democracy and support constitutional forms.

5. The field of constitutional theory needs theories of constitutional ends, conditions, and civic virtues necessary to sustain constitutional democracy, together with theories of how to promote the requisite ends, conditions, and virtues.

## *Bush v. Gore:* **Constitutionalist Though Not Constitutional?**

In light of these propositions concerning what is necessary to secure constitutional democracy, let us revisit the Supreme Court's action in *Bush v. Gore.* James Bradley Thayer and Learned Hand warned that courts cannot save a people from ruin.[12] Many have doubted that courts can avert or resolve constitutional crises. But others have disagreed, contending that courts sometimes can resolve divisive national controversies.[13] Justice Scalia, joined by Chief Justice Rehnquist and Justice Thomas, derided this idea in 1992 in *Planned Parenthood v. Casey,* when the subject was abortion.[14] They had a change of heart in *Bush v. Gore.*

Conservatives generally had a change of heart about judicial statesmanship in the final days of election 2000. They looked to the Court to avert or resolve what they viewed as the constitutional crisis thrown up by the controversy surrounding the presidential election. Professor John Yoo proposed that the Court should take a page from *Casey* and resolve the controversy.[15] In a similar vein, the columnist William Safire would later urge that the Court "did itself proud" and "saved the Republic" from "much tension."[16] In this section I explore whether conservatives can justify *Bush* as an act of judicial statesmanship to avert a constitutional crisis.[17]

Make no mistake: I think the 5-4 decision in *Bush* is both unprincipled and bad.[18] Nevertheless, I do want to distinguish these attributes— *unprincipled* and *bad*—and to show how *Bush* might be thought good (or at least not irredeemably bad) while being unprincipled. I will leave it as a possibility, moreover, without argument here, that being good and unprincipled is better than being bad and principled. I thus leave it as a possibility that *Bush* was a good decision notwithstanding its unprincipled character. This will be small comfort to most of the conservative scholars who have tried in vain to defend the decision. For they cannot defend *Bush* as I am suggesting without forfeiting their basic view of both the nature of the Constitution (as a charter of negative liberties rather than positive benefits) and the judiciary's proper role.

Forget any and all attempts to square *Bush* with the provisions of Article II; the text, history, and conventional understanding of the Equal Protection Clause; the familiar normative relationships between legislatures, courts, and constitutions; and second-order rules like deference to state courts on matters of state law.[19] These attempts simply do not work, as indeed some conservatives have admitted. Conservatives have tried and failed to square *Bush* with rules and principles of the Constitution and constitutional law. Others will follow, and they too will fail, or so I believe and assume for purposes of this book. But if such rules and more general norms like maxims and principles cannot justify *Bush,* maybe constitutional ends, aspirations, or *goods* can. Maybe the Bush Five (Chief Justice Rehnquist and Justices O'Connor, Scalia, Kennedy, and Thomas) thought that the Court had to ignore the rules, even its own rules, to spare the country and the Constitution harm greater than the harm that comes from a decision exposing both the impotence and the mythical side of "the rule of law."

As we all know, the rule of law is contingent on circumstances that the law cannot guarantee. *Korematsu v. United States,* which sustained the exclusion and detention of Japanese Americans in "relocation centers" during World War II,[20] demonstrated that. So did the Great Depression, some say. And so, I add, did the actions of the founder of the Old Republican Party. Lincoln violated the Constitution to save the Union and the Constitution.[21]

Violate the Constitution to save it? There is no paradox once you realize that, as a practical matter at least (and as a theoretical matter too), fidelity to the Constitution always presupposes material conditions that the Constitution cannot guarantee. Lincoln felt that the war might be lost unless he displaced Congress's powers to raise armies and navies and to authorize spending, and suspended the writ of habeas corpus. Honoring the Constitution to a "T" and losing the war made no sense because losing the war would have destroyed all of the Constitution, and permanently. Conditions had either redefined fidelity to the Constitution or put it on the side of those who sought the Constitution's violent destruction. Conditions had installed the imperative of prudential statesmanship for the Constitution's sake over that of conformity to the Constitution's terms.

Honoring the Constitution to lose the Constitution made no constitutional sense to Lincoln for another reason: he saw the Constitution as the means to ends bigger than itself. In his special message to Congress on July 4, 1861, Lincoln described the struggle for the Union:

> [It] is a struggle for maintaining in the world that form and substance of government whose leading object is to elevate the condition of men; to lift artificial weights from all shoulders; to clear the paths of laudable pursuit for

all; to afford all an unfettered start and a fair chance in the race of life. Yielding to partial and temporary departures, from necessity, this is the leading object of the Government for whose existence we contend.[22]

Madison made the same kind of point in *The Federalist* No. 45 when he accused proponents of states' rights of forgetting that the "real welfare of the great body of the people, is the supreme object to be pursued; and that no form of government whatever has any other value than as it may be fitted for the attainment of this object."[23] Madison said more of the same when justifying the unconstitutional provisions for constitutional change that the Philadelphia Convention had proposed in 1787. "Let [the Convention's critics] declare," wrote Madison,

> whether it was of most importance to the happiness of the people of America that the Articles of Confederation should be disregarded, and an adequate government be provided, and the Union preserved; or that an adequate government should be omitted, and the Articles of Confederation preserved. Let them declare whether the preservation of these articles was the end for securing which a reform of the government was to be introduced as the means; or whether the establishment of a government adequate to the national happiness was the end at which these articles themselves originally aimed, and to which they ought, as insufficient means, to have been sacrificed.[24]

Formally, these statements by Lincoln and Madison are but instances of a more abstract proposition: our basic law is an instrument for pursuing the ends set forth in the Preamble. Our best statesmen disregard it when they have to because the constitutional norms are means to ends that are attractive independently of the means, and it is irrational, as Madison said, to sacrifice ends to means. The circumstances that Lincoln and Madison faced featured a conflict between ends and means such that following the prescribed means would have defeated the very ends for which the means were ordained as law. Following the basic law in these circumstances (either the Articles or the Constitution) would have been anticonstitutional if not unconstitutional. On these occasions constitutions are silent; fully constitutional conduct is impossible. All one can hope for are proconstitutional actions or, as I prefer, *constitutionalist* actions[25]—actions that either (as in Lincoln's case) restore the conditions for honoring old means or (as in Madison's case) replace means that cannot be fixed with better means to the same old *constitutional* ends.[26]

To save *Bush* from rank partisanship one must see the case in this instrumentalist light: as an unavoidable resort to unauthorized means to secure authorized ends. That is, one must see it as aspiring to be *constitutionalist* though not *constitutional*.

I must add, however, that a constitutionalist justification for *Bush* is ludicrous if a situation approximating Lincoln's is taken as a precondition for such arguments. After the Court's intervention in *Bush,* Adam Nagourney and David Barstow detailed in the *New York Times* what many commentators believed during the election controversy: the Republicans would do what they had to do to win Florida—whatever they had to do.[27] That included a resumption of the state legislature's power to name the electors should a count of the ballots have put Gore ahead. The Bush Five made clear in their "per curium" opinion that they read the Constitution as permitting a legislature to reclaim the electoral power at any time.[28] Two competing sets of electors would have left the election to the conscience of the Republicans in Congress, and on any plausible scenario that guaranteed a victory by Bush. The problem with this strategy was, of course, less legal than political: A party fully prepared to reject the voters' voice for the sake of partisan success would expose itself as being driven by more than mere partisanship—like an antidemocratic religiosity,[29] an antidemocratic racism,[30] an antidemocratic Social Darwinism,[31] or all three combined. The Republicans' thirst for victory thus threatened to destroy the very image of reasonable, moderate conservatism so skillfully and assiduously cultivated by their presidential candidate. No one can say what the public's reaction would have been, but action by Republican legislators that would have removed all doubt about their party's extremism could have destroyed or at least weakened the GOP nationally and endangered its allies. These allies included not only the Rehnquist Court, which would have been called on to approve the actions of the Florida Republicans, but also the Constitution, which can be interpreted to sanction what the Florida Republicans seemed determined to do.[32]

It is far from clear that the Bush Five could have saved the Republicans from themselves and the Constitution from the Republicans by any action other than the one taken: stopping the count. This did more than ensure Bush's presidency, though the Five doubtlessly saw that as a plus. It also spared the nation a constitutional crisis that the Republicans seemed determined to risk. A victim of that crisis might well have been the public's understanding of itself as part of an entity that can establish, structure, staff, orient, and limit a government by rules instrumental to its well-being. Because that understanding is inseparable from the Court's own reputation as a principled institution, as the joint opinion of Justices O'Connor, Kennedy, and Souter observed in *Casey*,[33] the Bush Five hurt the country to some extent by their unprincipled decision. But the damage to Court and country could have been much greater. The Court as an institution is bigger than any five or any nine, and its legitimacy can survive their mistakes, to some extent. But the Court's legitimacy is less able to survive clear *constitutional* mistakes of any consequence because the Court's legitimacy is predicated on the Constitution's legitimacy. A constitution that would have permitted a group of state legislators to overrule both the voters of Florida and the nation's electorate would doubtlessly have forfeited much of the community's esteem. And the public's inability to correct that constitutional mistake (the right wing of the Republican Party is more than strong enough nationally to block a constitutional amendment to change the system for electing the president) would surely have damaged the public's own constitutionalist pretensions even more than the decision in *Bush*.

So here we are: Constitution betrayed, but betrayed ostensibly for its own good and not in a way that most Americans could not help noticing. "[T]he prejudices of the community [are still] on [the Constitution's] side," a good thing, said Madison.[34] The Court did take what Yoo called an affordable "short-term hit to [its] legitimacy"[35] among the cognoscenti, who had little regard for this Court anyway. But the nation is okay—happy or at least content with its formal constitution. And that has to count for something, does it not? Who is willing to defend fidelity to the Constitution at the price of chaos? Al Gore was not; he went away quietly enough, as everyone expected him to, despite Bush's charge during the controversy that it was Gore who would do anything to win.

Professor Gerard V. Bradley shares this kind of theory of how to justify the actions of the Bush Five. He says that even if the Five were wrong about the "bloodletting" to come after the count, they acted rightly in trying to stop it before it began.[36] Why not credit them with "an act of political courage[?]" he asks. "[T]hey consciously redirected incoming fire towards the one institution that *everyone* said could take the heat[.] The Court threw itself on Florida's grenade." Heroism enough, to be sure, yet heroism made even *greater* because a unanimous court was "unavailable" to the Five.[37] Bradley does not mention Lincoln, but he might have cited him as another Republican who violated the Constitution to save it and the country. If Lincoln's actions were *constitutionalist,* though not strictly *constitutional,* can the same be said for our Heroic Five?

Maybe, but not just yet. Consider one more complication. Lincoln violated the Constitution (1) in the attempt to destroy its enemies and (2) in the service of its ends.[38] For Lincoln, securing the conditions of constitutional government meant securing the conditions for the rule of the Constitution's friends, not for the rule of those willing to put the Constitution at risk. On my theory of *Bush,* the Bush Five violated the Constitution to save it from harm if not simply to save it from destruction, as Lincoln did. But Lincoln defeated the grenade throwers while the Five did not even try. (Indeed, Scalia strained, both in his concurring opinion concerning the stay[39] and in the subsequent oral argument,[40] to make sure that the grenades thrown by Bush's lawyer Theodore Olson did not miss their mark.) They avoided what Bradley calls "bleeding" and "institutional meltdown"[41] by giving the grenade throwers what they would not be denied. The party that threatened institutional meltdown won *because* it threatened institutional meltdown. It held the Constitution hostage to its ambitions for the country, and the Five paid the ransom. By contrast, Lincoln's actions were constitutionalist, if not constitutional, because he sought to restore the conditions of constitutional democracy, conditions favorable to rule by those who would be the last to throw grenades.

Lincoln's actions were constitutionalist also because he acted in the service of constitutional ends, like union and equal opportunity. The Bush Five can claim to have acted for a constitutional end: domestic tranquility. Had Bush been elected by Congress after Gore prevailed in the Florida count, that would surely have jeopardized domestic tranquility, or so one could reasonably have believed, rendering constitutional means inadequate to constitutional ends and justifying a constitutionalist act to secure a constitutional end. Safire could have had this in mind in arguing that the Court "did itself proud" and "saved the Republic" from "much tension" instead of allowing the constitutionally prescribed procedures to take their course at great harm to the country, with the result that "we would have ended up exactly where we are today: with President-elect Bush."[42]

One problem for constitutional conservatives will be how to abandon a jurisprudence that until now has emphasized institutional norms (like states' rights, deference to the political process, and judicial restraint, to say nothing of separation of powers) and "negative liberties," *not* substantive ends and goods or positive benefits. *Bush* made sensible as a constitutionalist decision is wholly at odds with the negative liberties model of the Constitution long favored by libertarians and formally adopted by the Rehnquist Court in *DeShaney*.[43] For a constitutionalist justification presupposes that the Constitution promotes substantive goods or positive benefits in addition to protecting negative liberties. Constitutional conservatives will have problems justifying a jurisprudence that recognizes one or two constitutional ends—adding domestic tranquility to their negative liberty, in lieu of the framers' positive liberty and the Preamble's promise of liberty's "blessings"[44]—but not other positive goods, like a more perfect union and the general welfare. If theoretical consistency were a force in political events, defending *Bush* would require movement away from the negative liberties constitutionalism of the Rehnquist Court and back to the positive benefits constitutionalism of Lincoln.

## War, Crisis, and the Positive Benefits of Constitutional Democracy

Though I have few illusions about the political influence of intellectual goods like theoretical consistency, I note (albeit with mixed feelings) the somewhat Lincolnesque opinion of the U.S. Court of Appeals for the Fourth Circuit in *Hamdi v. Rumsfeld*.[45] (The Supreme Court subsequently vacated the judgment of the Fourth Circuit. I am citing the Fourth Circuit opinion not as authority but for its Lincolnesque conception.) In the week following the events of September 11, 2001, Congress authorized the president "to use all necessary and appropriate force" against nations, organizations, and persons that planned or aided terrorist acts, *as the president determines*.[46] Pursuant to this act, the United States declared two American citizens "enemy combatants" to be held and interrogated indefinitely without formal charges, legal counsel, or visitors. One such enemy combatant, Yaser Esam Hamdi, was, in the court's words, "seized in Afghanistan during . . . active military hostilities" that followed the American invasion in early October 2001. Hamdi was brought to the United States, declared an enemy combatant, and held without formal charges, counsel, or visitors in the Navy brig at Norfolk, Virginia.

In affirming the government's power to hold Hamdi in isolation and without formal charges, a unanimous three-judge panel of the Fourth Circuit led by Chief Judge J. Harvie Wilkinson III emphasized the practical difficulties that courts face in trying to second guess the decisions of field commanders on distant battlefields. But Wilkinson and his colleagues were not saying that constitutional rights must sometimes yield to the demands of war. They offered "a more profound understanding of our rights" than that implicit in the conventional dichotomy between individual rights and governmental powers. "For the judicial branch to trespass upon the exercise of the warmaking powers," they said, "would be an infringement of the right to self-determination and self-governance at a time when the care of the common defense is most critical. This right of the people is no less a right because it is possessed collectively."[47]

Here the court recognized a right of the people to act through their government in pursuit of a good, national security, that helps them make sense of the original act of establishing that government and vesting it with warmaking powers. By deferring to those charged with using those powers, the court presents itself as letting the Constitution speak, not as silencing it. Thus conceived, the Constitution is first and foremost a charter of ends, goods, or benefits like national security. It is more than a charter of negative rights against government. And, if the Constitution is a charter of the ends that help make sense of some of its granted powers, why not also a charter of the ends that help make sense of the rest of its powers, ends like the general welfare of the people and justice?[48]

Whether the Fourth Circuit's conception in *Hamdi* is a straw in the wind remains to be seen. (The Supreme Court decision vacating the Fourth Circuit's ruling did not directly engage that conception.) In the meantime, however, we see no movement from the negative constitutionalism of *DeShaney* in the writings of Chief Justice Rehnquist. In his book *All the Laws But One: Civil Liberties in Wartime*,[49] Rehnquist approves Lincoln's famous formulation: that if he had not suspended the writ of habeas corpus during the Civil War, that would have meant allowing "all the laws, but one, to go unexecuted, and the government itself to go to pieces, lest that one be violated." More generally, Rehnquist practically embraces the idea—*inter arma silent leges*—that during war the laws (and the Constitution) are silent.

In an essay in the *New York Times,* Adam Cohen ponders the implications of Rehnquist's book for the Bush administration's restrictions on civil liberties in the current "war on terrorism."[50] He bemoans that Rehnquist quotes, with approval, not only Lincoln but also Francis Biddle, President Franklin Roosevelt's attorney general, who said: "The Constitution has not greatly bothered any wartime president." Cohen continues,

"[T]he most disturbing aspect of Rehnquist's book is the lack of outrage, or even disappointment, he evinces when rights are sacrificed."

Rehnquist lacks outrage because although he gets the title of his book from Lincoln, he does not get his jurisprudence or attitudes from Lincoln. For Rehnquist, when constitutional forms, rights, and limits are suspended, indeed the laws are silent and everything is permitted to the executive. Rehnquist fails to see or to subscribe to Lincoln's positive constitutionalism: He fails to see, as Lincoln saw, that when the Constitution is suspended, the executive has restorative obligations, affirmative obligations to work actively toward restoring conditions in which the Constitution can function as law. These affirmative obligations include the pursuit of domestic policies that would restore respect for constitutional forms, rights, and limits. As argued above, Lincoln violated the Constitution to save the Union and the Constitution, and he did so without paradox because fidelity to the Constitution always presupposes material conditions that the Constitution cannot guarantee. Again, honoring the Constitution to lose the Constitution made no constitutional sense to Lincoln for another reason: with Madison, he saw the Constitution as means to ends bigger than itself. His special message to Congress on July 4, 1861, quoted above, bears quoting again: the struggle for the Union

> is a struggle for maintaining in the world that form and substance of government whose leading object is to elevate the condition of men; to lift artificial weights from all shoulders; to clear the paths of laudable pursuit for all; to afford all an unfettered start and a fair chance in the race of life. Yielding to partial and temporary departures, from necessity, this is the leading object of the Government for whose existence we contend.

## War, Crisis, and Affirmative Obligations to Secure the Preconditions for Constitutional Democracy

In sum, war is epistemic. It revealed to Hobbes and Locke the nature of humans and the purpose of political life. It reveals to us the nature of the Constitution and what it means to maintain it. War is conventionally seen as testing the limits of constitutionalism, the point at which we compromise or even abandon constitutional forms and rights. But war reminds us of the Preamble's promise of a good thing—the common defense—which is good because it anticipates the peaceful state where we enjoy other preambulary goods like domestic tranquility and the blessings of liberty, justly distributed and justly secured. Instead of saying victory in war competes with constitutional forms and rights, we might consider peace a prerequisite of honoring forms and enjoying rights.

Peace is a provision of power. It is adumbrated by authorizations or "powers" to declare war, raise armies and navies, and so forth. Power and its positive provisions are thus prerequisite to following institutional norms and honoring negative liberties. And the relationship holds for other institutional norms and negative liberties: no market or property, for example, without governmental provisions like a monetary system, laws defining and securing property, civil and criminal courts whose judgments are executed by force if need be and, in the end, the active cultivation of the skills and values on which a culture of property depends. The general point is made in *The Federalist* No. 1: no government, no liberty; they are on the same side.[51] Lincoln repeats the message three score and fourteen years later. See peace (a provision of power like the power to wage war) as prerequisite to constitutional forms and liberties and you

- restore the Constitution to coherence;
- preserve the positive Constitution of the Preamble and the ratification campaign;
- carry forward to the present the root idea of the Declaration of Independence and *The Federalist* No. 1 that constitution-making, not fidelity to any existing form of government, is at the heart of the constitutionalist persuasion and enterprise; and
- expose the positive side of the oath to preserve and defend the Constitution, for one can do neither without securing peace and what *The Federalist* No. 45 calls the "welfare of the great body of the people."

War thus reveals the essentially *positive* nature of the Constitution and the overriding *positive duty* of those who take the oath to preserve and defend it. Lincoln is the exemplar of this view: His duty was to restore the conditions for honoring constitutional forms and constitutional rights. Though he sacrificed both to the war effort, they remained normative for him because the war sought to restore the conditions for honoring them. Lincoln also saw the need not just to perpetuate the institutions of our constitutional democracy but also to cultivate the virtues on which they depend—including the virtues of leadership and citizenship on those occasions when fidelity to institutions defeats the very purposes for which they were instituted. Thus, he stands as the exemplar of the constitutionalist view of securing constitutional democracy in war and crisis.

# Constitutional Imperfections and the Pursuit of Happy Endings: Perfecting Our Imperfect Constitution

It is in the nature of legal interpretation—not just but particularly constitutional interpretation—to aim at happy endings. — Ronald Dworkin

In concluding this book, I discuss constitutional imperfections and the pursuit of what Sanford Levinson has called "happy endings" in constitutional interpretation.[1] Levinson and others have expressed skepticism about constitutional theories like mine on the ground that they always seem to lead to happy endings: that the Constitution, properly interpreted, requires the result that my normative political theory recommends. Henry Monaghan famously ridicules such theories as conceptions of "our perfect Constitution."[2] Christopher Eisgruber helpfully frames this type of criticism in terms of a "no pain, no claim" test.[3] The basic idea is that a constitutional theory has no serious claim on our attention unless the theorist putting it forward suffers some pain by acknowledging that the Constitution does not secure everything that she or he would protect in a perfect Constitution. In response to this challenge, many constitutional theorists have been at pains to demonstrate that their theories sanction all manner of imperfections, tragedies and stupidities, and unhappy endings.

My theory—which I present without apology as a Constitution-perfecting theory—invites perfect Constitution challenges more straightforwardly than perhaps any other theory. At very least, it shares that distinction with Ronald Dworkin's moral reading of the Constitution,[4] Lawrence G. Sager's justice-seeking account of our Constitution and constitutional practice,[5] and Sotirios A. Barber's moral realist reading of the Constitution.[6] In this chapter, I respond to such challenges. In doing so, I resist the peculiar trend in constitutional theory to prove my positivist mettle by making a virtue of all the constitutional imperfections, tragedies and stupidities, and unhappy endings that my theory sanctions. Put another way, I question the wisdom of submitting constitutional theories to perfect Constitution challenges or a "no pain, no claim" test. Our Constitution is indeed imperfect in many ways. But we should strive to interpret it so as to mitigate its imperfections and to avoid interpretive tragedies or stupidities. We should aspire to interpret the Constitution so as to make it the best it can be.[7] That is, we should embrace a Constitution-perfecting theory of interpretation, which proudly aims at happy endings rather than reveling in the imperfections that the Constitution might be interpreted to embody. Instead of a "no pain, no claim" test, I embrace what Eisgruber has called a "no gain, no claim" test.[8] From this standpoint, a constitutional theory has no serious claim on our attention unless it promises some gain, in the sense that adhering to it might help us realize our constitutional aspirations. By now it should be clear that my Constitution-perfecting theory promises considerable gain and thus abundantly satisfies the latter test.

## Three Perfect Constitution Challenges

My response to perfect Constitution or happy endings challenges proceeds in three parts, corresponding to three versions of such challenges. First, I take up the classic perfect Constitution challenge as formulated by Monaghan and Levinson. I respond by acknowledging what Sager has called the "thinness" or "moral shortfall" of our judicially enforced Constitution and constitutional law—even in my Constitution-perfecting theory and his justice-seeking account—as compared with our "thicker" or richer commitments to constitutional and political justice. I show how both Sager's thesis of judicial underenforcement of constitutional norms and his account of the domain of constitutional justice help rebut the classic perfect Constitution challenge that Constitution-perfecters like me and justice-seekers like Sager interpret the Constitution to incorporate every result that our normative political theories recommend.

Second, I turn to a more complex version of the challenge formulated by Bruce Ackerman, which I call the "entrenchment challenge." Ackerman proclaims that, as a normative political theorist, he is a "rights foundationalist" who would entrench certain fundamental rights in the Constitution against amendment or repeal in the manner of the German Basic Law.[9] But he claims that, as a positivist constitutional theorist, he is a "dualist" who must admit the imperfection of the American scheme, which does not entrench unalienable rights and indeed is open to repealing our fundamental rights, including freedom of religion and freedom of speech. Ackerman submits that the very imperfection of our constitutional scheme proves the superiority of his account of it, "dualist democracy," over theories like mine, which he interprets as "rights foundationalist." I respond by critiquing his account of the purposes of entrenchment and arguing that the absence of provisions in our Constitution explicitly entrenching fundamental rights is not an "embarrassment" for theories like mine.

Third, I grapple with the most dramatic version of the perfect Constitution challenge, which I call the "tragedies challenge." As the book *Constitutional Stupidities, Constitutional Tragedies* explains: "A constitutional 'tragedy' is a decision that is required by a proper interpretation of the Constitution but that is otherwise much to be regretted and therefore tragic in its combination of inevitability and ill consequences."[10] The challenge taken up by the contributors to the book is to "set forth the most tragic result their constitutional methodology would yield." I resist the tragedies challenge in analyzing constitutional tragedy in dying. I argue against making a virtue of the tragedies my theory would yield. And I argue for avoiding interpretive tragedies with bad endings. Instead, I embrace a "no gain, no claim" approach that aspires to perfect our imperfect Constitution by interpreting it in a manner that might deserve our fidelity.


## Our Perfect Constitution? Reflections on the Thinness of Constitutional Law

Dworkin's moral reading, Sager's justice-seeking account, and my own Constitution-perfecting theory straightforwardly invite Monaghan's classic perfect Constitution challenge. According to Dworkin, the Constitution embodies abstract moral principles rather than lays down particular historical conceptions, and interpreting and applying those principles require fresh judgments of political theory about how they are best understood. On Sager's justice-seeking account, the Constitution embodies general moral concepts and judges exercise independent normative judgment in interpreting it; indeed, judges are partners with, rather than merely agents of, the constitutional founders and amenders, and their joint project is to bring our political community into greater conformity with justice. My Constitution-perfecting theory developed in this book is unmistakably a moral reading and a justice-seeking account. I sketch how Sager's account helps rebut the first challenge as applied to theories like Dworkin's, Sager's, and my own.

Some critics charge that Dworkin's moral reading is utopian in two senses. One, it is a moral reading for a perfect liberal utopia: Dworkin would interpret the Constitution to protect every right and produce every outcome that his liberal political philosophy would entail. Two, it is literally a theory for no particular place: he would give the same moral reading irrespective of the actual history and practice of the constitutional scheme, for example, the same for Britain as for the United States. Hence, these critics contend that Dworkin's theory fails to fit our actual imperfect Constitution and doctrine and that it is not adequately grounded in an account of our constitutional practice and scheme of institutions. To be fair to Dworkin, he contends that the moral reading is constrained by the requirements of fit, justification, and integrity. Thus it is bound to account for—to fit and justify—the legal materials of our existing constitutional order and practice. And so, even if Dworkin's theory of constitutional interpretation aims to provide the best interpretation of these legal materials—to make the Constitution the best it can be—it is not unbounded and therefore is not a conception of a perfect Constitution as Monaghan imagines it to be.

In response to Levinson's happy endings challenge to Dworkin and to his book *Freedom's Law*,[11] Dworkin gives what are basically three responses. First, he concedes that the Constitution is not perfect, for it does not protect "all the important principles of political liberalism."[12] Second, to illustrate that he does not believe our Constitution is perfect, he asserts that while justice requires welfare rights, they are not constitutionally protected. Such a stance, he claims, distinguishes his approach from that of Frank Michelman, who believes that our Constitution does protect welfare rights[13] (thus implying that theorists like Michelman are more vulnerable to the perfect Constitution challenge than he is). Third, Dworkin nonetheless argues that "[i]t is in the nature of legal interpretation—not just but particularly constitutional interpretation—

to aim at happy endings."[14] The implication here is that those who think the perfect Constitution challenge is dispositive of aspirational constitutional theories like Dworkin's simply do not understand the nature of our Constitution as a scheme of abstract moral principles and the nature of interpretation of such a scheme. I concur with Dworkin's view that constitutional interpretation in our scheme aims at happy endings.

If Dworkin's moral reading of the Constitution, though it embodies abstract moral principles, does not incorporate all the important principles of justice, we need an account of the difference between the two. Dworkin's highly general formulation of the moral reading may seem to blur the distinction between constitutional law and justice, as well as that between constitutional law and morality generally. To be sure, the constraints of fit, justification, and integrity entail gaps between the Constitution, on the one hand, and justice and morality generally, on the other. But Dworkin says little about any such gaps, and what he does say implies that the gaps may be narrow. For example, he says that the Constitution is abstract, and therefore that it should come as no surprise that any right we can argue for as a matter of political morality we can also argue for as a matter of constitutional law.[15] And where he does acknowledge a significant gap between the Constitution and justice, for example, with welfare rights, he does not provide a general account of why the Constitution as he conceives it does not incorporate elements of justice like welfare rights. Thus, Dworkin may leave his readers wondering whether his theory practically entails that the U.S. Constitution is a perfect liberal Constitution.

A helpful orienting idea concerning how moral readers like Dworkin and Constitution perfecters like me should respond to the classic perfect Constitution challenge is what Sager calls the "thinness" of constitutional law and, more particularly, the moral shortfall of the judicially enforced Constitution.[16] According to Sager's "underenforcement thesis," certain constitutional principles required by justice are judicially underenforced, yet nonetheless may impose affirmative obligations outside the courts on legislatures, executives, and citizens generally to realize them more fully. This view is an important component of a full moral reading, a justice-seeking account, or a Constitution-perfecting theory of the Constitution. For it helps make sense of the evident thinness or moral shortfall of constitutional law as compared with our thicker or richer commitments to justice. For example, instead of saying that the Constitution does not secure welfare rights—the move that Dworkin makes—we can say, with

Sager (and Michelman), that the Constitution *does* secure rights to minimum welfare, but it leaves enforcement of those rights in the first instance to legislatures and executives. Once a scheme of welfare rights and benefits is in place, courts have a secondary role in enforcing it equally and fairly.[17] Sager also analyzes the constitutional obligation to repair the harms of historic injustice, including entrenched racial and gender disadvantage, in terms of the underenforcement thesis.[18]

Sager's account of the domain of constitutional justice also helps meet the perfect Constitution challenge. He distinguishes (1) judicially enforceable constitutional law (or the judicially enforced Constitution) from (2) the domain of constitutional justice, which he in turn distinguishes from (3) that of political justice and (4) that of morality generally.[19] Imagine a series of progressively thicker concentric circles representing these four domains. And note that the latter three domains are not judicially enforceable but are left to enforcement in the Constitution outside the courts, by legislatures, executives, and citizens generally. The classic perfect Constitution challenge casually charges moral readers with believing that the judicially enforced Constitution is perfect, ignoring these distinctions. Sager's justice-seeking account underscores just how thin a moral reading of the judicially enforced Constitution has to be—as compared with our thicker conceptions of constitutional justice, political justice, and morality—in order to be credible as an account of our constitutional practice. By doing so, it provides a nuanced and powerful response to the classic perfect Constitution challenge, which glosses over these refined distinctions.

Truth be told, that challenge is overblown and directed at moral readers, justice seekers, and Constitution perfecters who themselves, if they exist at all, gloss over Sager's refined distinctions. My Constitution-perfecting theory embraces Sager's account of the thinness of constitutional law and the moral shortfall of the judicially enforced Constitution. It accordingly recognizes many imperfections in our judicially enforced Constitution as compared with normative liberal political theory.


## Responding to Imperfection through Entrenchment

[The People of America] reared the fabrics of governments which have no model on the face of the globe. — *The Federalist* No. 14[20]

*Our Alienable, Imperfect Dualist Constitution?*

Ackerman's complex version of the perfect Constitution challenge—the entrenchment challenge—grows out of the tradition of "American exceptionalism," which insists on the distinctiveness of our "fabrics of government" from European models. Ackerman argues that the American Constitution is dualist rather than rights foundationalist. Dualists conceive the Constitution as "democratic first, rights-protecting second" in the sense that judicial protection of constitutional rights against encroachments by the ordinary law of legislation "depend[s] on a prior democratic affirmation on the higher lawmaking track" of the Constitution. Rights foundationalists "reverse this priority," for they hold that "the Constitution is first concerned with protecting rights; only then does it authorize the People to work their will on other matters."[21] Theories like John Rawls's, Ronald Dworkin's, and mine, Ackerman contends, are rights foundationalist rather than dualist in his specific sense.[22] (As stated above, my theory is dualist in the general sense—that it distinguishes between the constituent power of We the People, expressed in the higher law of the Constitution, and the ordinary power of officers of government, expressed in the ordinary law of legislative bodies—without being committed to dualism in Ackerman's specific sense.)[23] I put to one side that I reject his characterization of such theories as rights foundationalist; my aim here is to respond to his entrenchment challenge.

Ackerman's argument for dualism over rights foundationalism emphasizes a contrast between the American Constitution and the German Basic Law concerning entrenchment. Our Constitution, he observes, "has never (with two exceptions . . .) explicitly entrenched existing higher law against subsequent amendment by the People."[24] The two exceptions are Article V's prohibition of amendments affecting the African slave trade until 1808 and depriving a state of equal representation in the Senate without its consent. The Basic Law, by contrast, "explicitly declare[s] that a long list of fundamental human rights *cannot* constitutionally be revised, regardless of the extent to which a majority of Germans support repeal."[25] Article 79(3) entrenches unalienable human rights to dignity, the fundamental principles of free democratic basic order, and the basic structure of federalism.[26]

Ackerman submits that practices regarding entrenchment provide an important crucible for testing whether a constitutional order is dualist or rights foundationalist[27] and thus whether his theory or theories like mine provide a better account of the American constitutional scheme. He contends that the absence of "German-style entrenchment" of fundamental rights in the American Constitution—and thus the repealability or alienability of such rights—is an "embarrassment" for rights foundationalists but not for dualists.[28] He also states that our constitutional experience with entrenchment, through the two exceptions involving slavery and federalism, has been "very negative" and has not served the cause of human freedom.[29] From these aspects of our constitutional document and history, he concludes that rights foundationalism "is inconsistent with the existing premises of the American higher lawmaking system."[30] For in America "it is the People who are the source of rights,"[31] and We the People are not bound by a higher law than the higher law of the Constitution.[32] In the crucible of entrenchment, Ackerman argues, ours proves to be an alienable, imperfect dualist Constitution, unlike the unalienable rights foundationalist Basic Law.

Ackerman thus contends that our Constitution, unlike the German Basic Law, is open to "morally disastrous" amendments repealing fundamental rights.[33] To test this contention, he conjures up two hypothetical amendments. The first establishes Christianity as the state religion of the American people, thereby repealing the fundamental right to liberty of conscience. The second forbids repeal of the first, thereby entrenching it and in effect repealing freedom of speech and dualist democracy itself.[34] Ackerman states that dualists would accept these amendments as valid while rights foundationalists would reject them as unconstitutional. Asserting that in America, unlike Germany, "almost all lawyers" would consider "absurd" or "preposterous" the idea that an amendment to the Constitution might be unconstitutional, Ackerman claims that dualism better fits our constitutional order than does rights foundationalism.[35]

Ackerman goes on to confess that, as a citizen and a political philosopher, he is a rights foundationalist who would be proud to be a member of the generation that "finally redeem[ed] the promise of the Declaration of Independence by entrenching *inalienable* rights into our Constitution," including liberty of conscience and freedom of speech.[36] We should recall that his earlier writings include *Social Justice in the Liberal State*,[37] a work of rights foundationalist political philosophy that bears affinities to the liberal political philosophies of Rawls and Dworkin, from whom he now wishes to distance himself as a dualist constitutional theorist.[38] Michael Klarman has suggested that Ackerman's confession that he yearns to move "beyond dualism" to a rights foundationalist constitutional order evinces a "glaring contradiction" that undermines his commitment to popular sovereignty and raises the question "why one should take seriously Ackerman's detailed exegesis of dualist democracy."[39]

Whether or not he falls into contradiction, Ackerman is straining mightily to prove his democratic and positivist mettle by proclaiming that he would uphold the validity of the above hypothetical amendments as a dualist constitutional theorist, though he would consider them "morally disastrous" as a rights foundationalist political philosopher. With all the zeal of a born-again positivist who has seen the errors of his rights foundationalist past, Ackerman kneels before the altar of Monaghan's imperfect Constitution, striving to show that his constitutional theory passes the "no pain, no claim" test. Indeed, Ackerman does more than confess his past as a rights foundationalist, for he also admits his present temptation to move beyond dualism to rights foundationalism and to entrench a new Bill of Rights against subsequent amendment.[40] Yet he maintains that he does not succumb, proving his democratic and positivist virtue by unveiling his imperfect dualist Constitution.[41] Ackerman's entrenchment challenge basically charges theorists like me of succumbing to the temptation to interpret the American Constitution as if it were a more perfect rights foundationalist scheme like that of the German Basic Law.

### The Purposes of Entrenchment: To Express Constitutive Principles or to Reflect Compromises with Such Principles?

Should we be persuaded by Ackerman's argument against rights foundationalism through the entrenchment challenge and his contrast between the U.S. Constitution and the German Basic Law? Are practices of entrenchment a good crucible for testing the basic commitments of a constitutional order? What are the purposes of entrenchment? Perhaps entrenchment clauses express constitutive principles. Let us posit a positivist who believes that if you want to know the constitutive principles on which a constitutional order is founded, you should examine what provisions are explicitly entrenched in the constitutional document against subsequent amendment. Applying this test, the positivist would conclude from Article 79(3) of the German Basic Law that the constitutive principles of the German scheme of government were unalienable human rights to dignity, the fundamental principles of free democratic basic order, and the basic structure of federalism. But such a positivist would find Article V of the U.S. Constitution cryptic (or deeply unjust) on first sight: for entrenchment of protection of the African slave trade until 1808 and equal representation of the states in the Senate hardly look like constitutive principles of a constitutional order.[42] This discovery might lead to either of two conclusions: that the Constitution simply recognizes no fundamental rights as constitutive principles, or that in our constitutional document entrenchment performs a role other than that of expressing constitutive principles. Ackerman basically draws the former conclusion; I pursue the latter.

What alternative role might Article V entrenchment play in our Constitution? Perhaps Article V entrenches provisions that reflect deep compromises with the Constitution's constitutive principles: the protection of the African slave trade with the principle that all persons are created equal, and the equal representation of the states in the Senate with the principle of the equal representation of citizens. The founders concluded that both compromises were necessary to "the forging of the Union": the slave states insisted on the former, the small states on the latter.[43] Thus, both imperfections were considered necessary "to form a more perfect Union" than the Articles of Confederation. From this standpoint, contra Ackerman, we can see that Article V entrenched features of the Constitution that were vulnerable to being repealed through democratic procedures, precisely because they manifested such deep compromises with our constitutive principles and ordained such an imperfect Constitution.

With this idea of the purpose of entrenchment on hand, we should reassess Ackerman's contrast between American and German practices. Ackerman may make such haste to disparage the American experience with "German-style entrenchment," and to taint it by association with slavery, that he overlooks this alternative purpose of bolstering vulnerable features of a scheme of government. Moreover, his discussion obscures a deeper similarity: both the American and German founders expressly entrenched provisions of their new constitutional orders that they considered necessary to secure the transition to a more perfect union. Again, in making the transition from the Articles of Confederation to the Constitution, the small states insisted on equal representation in the Senate, and the slave states on protection of the African slave trade. In the aftermath of the failures of the Weimar Constitution and the atrocities of Nazism, the founders of the Federal Republic of Germany insisted on entrenching certain unalienable human rights and structural principles that had been outrageously disregarded during the Nazi regime.[44]

Both countries expressly entrenched the features of their new constitutional orders that were feared to be in greatest need of bolstering, and at greatest risk of repeal through democratic procedures, given their historical circumstances. As it happens, the U.S. Constitution explicitly entrenched provisions that deeply *compromised* its founding principles, while the German Basic Law explicitly entrenched provisions that profoundly *expressed* its reconstruction principles. But both schemes responded to imperfection by entrenchment.[45]

Therefore, the fact that our Constitution, unlike the German Basic Law, does not explicitly entrench unalienable rights or constitutive principles is not an "embarrassment" for theories like mine. Ackerman's entrenchment version of the perfect Constitution challenge does not establish that his theory of dualism provides a better account of the American scheme of government than does my theory. Nor does it prove that our "American exceptionalism"—the distinctiveness of our "fabrics of government" from European models—consists in the fact that we have an alienable, imperfect dualist Constitution.

## Resisting Rather Than Reveling in Constitutional Tragedies

A constitutional "tragedy" is a decision that is required by a proper interpretation of the Constitution but that is otherwise much to be regretted and therefore tragic in its combination of inevitability and ill consequences. A dozen eminent scholars of constitutional law will set forth the most tragic result their constitutional methodology would yield. — AALS Panel on Constitutional Tragedies

[W]e are ourselves authors of a tragedy, and that the finest and best we know how to make. [O]ur whole polity has been constructed as a dramatization of a noble and perfect life; that is what we hold to be in truth the most real of tragedies. — Plato, *Laws*

### *Constitutional Imperfections, Tragedies, and Other Misfortunes*

Finally, I respond to the tragedies version of the perfect Constitution challenge as framed in the first epigraph to this section.[46] What is a constitutional tragedy? How does it differ from or relate to an imperfection in the constitutional document (for example, the imperfect provision for affirmative liberties, which has led to decisions like *Dandridge v.*

*Williams, San Antonio v. Rodriguez, Harris v. McRae,* and *DeShaney v. Winnebago County*)?[47] A failure of the constitutional order (for example, the failure to generate the civic virtue necessary for citizens to affirm basic liberties, which might lead to a breakdown of the wall of separation between church and state or more generally to a culture war that imperils basic liberties)?[48] A decision in constitutional law that has horrible consequences for the lives of particular citizens or groups and for the way of life of the polity (for example, *Dred Scott v. Sandford, Plessy v. Ferguson,* and *Korematsu v. United States*)?[49] A decision that has disastrous consequences for interpretive method and for the development of doctrine in important areas (for example, *Slaughter-House Cases* and *Bowers v. Hardwick*)?[50] A decision that makes a travesty of our constitutional order (for example, *Buckley v. Valeo,* which reduces our political system from a fair scheme of equal participation to a veritable marketplace of ideas)?[51] Finally, how does a constitutional tragedy differ from or relate to a constitutional stupidity (for example, the fact that the entire Bill of Rights did not apply to the states from the beginning)?[52] However we answer these questions, it is clear that we have no dearth of constitutional misfortunes.[53]

I conceive constitutional tragedy in three senses. First, it would be tragic if the Constitution were to allow or require terrible evil or grave injustice, and if fidelity to the Constitution were to mandate complicity in such evil or injustice. The most glaring example would be the original Constitution's protection of slavery, and the complicity exacted from judges and other officials who enforced the fugitive slave laws.[54] Second, it would be tragic if the Constitution were wrongly interpreted to sanction a terrible evil or grave injustice, when in fact the Constitution, rightly interpreted, allows or requires a good outcome or happy ending.[55] For example, we might speak of *Plessy v. Ferguson* and *Bowers v. Hardwick* as constitutional tragedies in this sense (and, happily, both were overruled). Finally, some cases present "tragic issues" or necessitate "tragic choices." Justice Frankfurter characterized the first flag-salute case as "an illustration of what the Greeks thousands of years ago recognized as a tragic issue, namely, the clash of rights, not the clash of wrongs," and he conceived the Supreme Court's responsibility as being "to reconcile two rights in order to prevent either from destroying the other."[56]

Applying these three senses of tragedy, I argue—in response to the tragedies challenge—that it was a constitutional tragedy for the Supreme Court to hold in *Washington v. Glucksberg* that the Constitution does not protect the right to die, including the right of terminally ill persons to physician-assisted suicide, thereby overruling the Ninth Circuit decision in *Compassion in Dying v. Washington*[57] (and the Second Circuit decision in *Quill v. Vacco*).[58] First, such a holding entails that the Constitution sanctions a grievous wrong, a horrible form of tyranny: allowing the state to impose on its citizens, against the grain of their conscientious, considered convictions about dying with dignity, what they regard as a ruinous, tragic ending of their lives.[59] Second, such a decision represents an awful interpretive tragedy, for the Constitution, rightly interpreted, does not permit this dreadful evil but, to the contrary, requires the happy ending of allowing citizens to author their own tragic endings. Third, and last, the question of whether the Constitution protects the right to die evidently presents a tragic issue as Frankfurter conceived it, for it involves a clash between two fundamental values: persons' right to autonomy in making certain important decisions for themselves and the state's authority to promote respect for the sanctity of life. The character of our polity will be defined by how we reconcile or destroy those values. Both proponents and opponents of protecting the right to die believe that it would be a tragedy if the other side were to prevail. Thus, no matter which way the Court had resolved this clash, its decision would be bewailed as a tragedy. This fact confirms that the right to die is the stuff of which constitutional tragedy is made.

## Tragedy in Dying

It was tragic for the Supreme Court to hold that the Constitution does not protect the right to die, including the right of terminally ill persons to physician-assisted suicide. First, the state's proscription of physician-assisted suicide is tantamount to conscription of terminally ill persons into involuntary servitude.[60] The state commandeers those persons' bodies, lives, and deaths into service in fostering its conception of how to honor the sanctity of life. It exposes its dangerous presupposition that ultimately persons do not own themselves but are "mere creatures of the state" or of God.[61] What is more, the state exacts such service in the face of those persons' conscientious, considered convictions about how to lead their own lives and deaths, and indeed about how to respect the sanctity of life.[62] Thus, the state attempts to use terminally ill persons' bodies, lives, and deaths as pulpits for preaching a message or viewpoint about sanctity that they conscientiously reject.

In effect, the state tries to impose a sentence of life imprisonment, or imprisonment in life, on terminally ill persons who wish to end their own lives. To be sure, the state seeks to justify this evil, requiring this undignified sacrifice and unspeakable suffering, in the name of a supreme good or ultimate value, promoting respect for the sanctity of life. That effort does not redeem the evil but, to the contrary, makes it more terrible and tyrannical. It shows that the state's asserted power to promote respect for the sanctity of life by prohibiting physician-assisted suicide is "an injury got up as a gift," an intolerable evil disguised and imposed as a supreme good.[63]

Second, the state's prohibition of physician-assisted suicide usurps citizens' power to make certain important decisions for themselves. I have argued that the right to die is among the basic liberties that are essential to deliberative autonomy: such rights reserve to persons the power to deliberate about and decide how to live their own lives, with respect to certain matters unusually important for personal self-government, over a complete life, from cradle to grave.[64] Put another way, these basic liberties are significant preconditions for persons' development and exercise of deliberative autonomy in making certain fundamental decisions affecting their destiny, identity, or way of life, and they span a complete lifetime. Decisions concerning the timing and manner of a person's death are among the most significant decisions for deliberative autonomy that a person may make in a lifetime. If the Constitution does not reserve such decisions to persons, it betrays its "promise" of a "rational continuum" of liberty.[65] A Constitution that does not protect the right to die, paradoxically, is not worth living under and not worth dying for.

These claims about conscription and usurpation suggest that the Constitution, now interpreted not to protect the right to die, is woefully imperfect from the standpoint of a vigorous conception of deliberative autonomy.[66] Does this amount to a constitutional tragedy? It is tragic because it entails that the Constitution sanctions a terrible evil, a horrible form of tyranny: allowing the state to impose on some citizens, against the grain of their conscientious, considered convictions about dying with dignity, what they regard as a ruinous, tragic ending of their lives. The Constitution permits the state to do this at the crucial moment when terminally ill persons are seeking to author the final chapters of their own personal tragedies.

The noble protagonists in this constitutional tragedy are citizens who have the courage to use their own deliberative reason and to take

responsibility for their own lives and for their own judgments about how
to respect the sanctity of life. The tragic flaw of these protagonists—the
characteristic that is both their greatness and their downfall—is their
autonomy, their daring to live autonomously rather than as mere creatures of the state or of God. They seek to exercise their deliberative
autonomy to give their tragedies a good, dignified, and noble ending, to
write their own final chapters in character with, or so as to maintain
integrity with, their conceptions of a good life—to die, as to live, with
dignity.[67] The state, however, wishes to usurp their authorship of their
own tragedies, to conscript them as mere players in its own tragedy about
the sanctity of life. Thus, the state refuses to "[v]ex not [their] ghost[s]"
as they lie terminally ill, at death's door.[68] Instead, it prolongs their pain
and exacerbates their anguish, in effect maintaining wards of would-be
cadavers as monuments to its view of the sanctity of life.

Most problematically, the state asserts, at terminally ill persons' ultimate moment of self-authorship, that they are not in fact the authors of
their own lives and tragedies. The state proclaims that it is the author of
their lives, at least of their tragedies. It basically says to them what the
Athenian Stranger (on behalf of the state) says to the tragedians in
Plato's *Laws:* "[W]e are ourselves authors of a tragedy, and that the finest
and best we know how to make. [O]ur whole polity has been constructed
as a dramatization of a noble and perfect life; that is what we hold to be in
truth the most real of tragedies."[69] But in our constitutional democracy,
citizens are not mere creatures of the state or of God, nor are we mere
players in the state's tragedy, its "dramatization of a noble and perfect
life." Rather, we citizens are the authors of our own tragedies, "the finest
and best *we* know how to make." The state is not authorized to act as the
master tragedian.[70] We must ask: "Whose tragedy is it, anyway?"[71] In our
constitutional democracy, the answer is: "It is each citizen's, not the
state's."


*Interpretive Tragedies with Bad Endings*


The holding by the Supreme Court that the Constitution does not protect
the right to die represents a further interpretive tragedy, for the Constitution, rightly interpreted, does not permit this dreadful evil but, to the
contrary, requires the happy ending of allowing citizens to author their
own tragic endings. Have I resisted the tragedies challenge—the question
framed in the first epigraph to this section—which is whether the Consti-

tution, rightly interpreted, is woefully imperfect in the sense that it permits terrible evil or requires a tragic ending? Have I succumbed to the temptation of interpreting the Constitution as if it were a perfect rather than a tragic Constitution? More generally, do I aspire to interpret the Constitution so as to give every potential tragedy a happy ending? Raising these questions leads to another aspect of constitutional tragedy, one that I call "interpretive tragedies with bad endings."

First, it is an interpretive tragedy if the Constitution is wrongly interpreted to sanction a terrible evil or grave injustice, when in fact the Constitution, rightly interpreted, allows or requires a good outcome or happy ending. It is notable that when constitutional scholars and jurists lament dreadful cases that have sanctioned grave injustice, such as *Dred Scott, Plessy, Korematsu,* and *Bowers*, they ordinarily do not say that those cases were rightly decided and that the Constitution requires such injustice. Instead, they typically argue that the cases were wrongly decided, and that the injustice could have been averted if only the Court had rightly interpreted the Constitution (for example, if only the dissenters' interpretations had prevailed). Indeed, a dreadful outcome is, if anything, more tragic if the wrong could have been avoided and a good outcome was available. In short, when the Constitution is interpreted to allow or require evil or injustice, the tragedy is often that the Constitution was wrongly, not rightly, interpreted.

Second, it would be a shame if constitutional scholars were to say that such interpretive tragedies could not have been avoided, or even to revel in the evil or injustice that the Constitution might be interpreted to allow, in order to avoid being charged with believing that we have a perfect Constitution that always provides a happy ending. (Indeed, it is unfortunate that the perfect Constitution challenge uses our willingness to profess that the Constitution is imperfect and sanctions terrible evil as a measure of our fidelity to the Constitution.) Our Constitution is indeed imperfect in many ways. But we should strive to interpret it so as to mitigate its imperfections, and to avoid interpretive tragedies with bad endings. We should aspire to interpret the Constitution so as to make it the best it can be.[72] That is, we should embrace a Constitution-perfecting theory of interpretation, which proudly aims at happy endings rather than reveling in the Constitution's imperfections or in the evil that it might be interpreted to permit.[73]

Finally, interpretive tragedies with bad endings, such as the holding that the Constitution does not protect the right to die, dramatically highlight that the Constitution is imperfect to the extent that it leaves such significant basic liberties hanging so precariously, twisting in the political winds, so vulnerable to becoming the latest casualty in the constitutional culture war (as witnessed by the Terri Schiavo case). We have a constitution of principle rather than a constitution of detail.[74] Our Constitution does not specifically enumerate all the basic liberties that are necessary to secure the preconditions for social cooperation on the basis of mutual respect and trust among free and equal citizens in our constitutional democracy, such as the right to die. Yet if those basic liberties are not honored, the outcomes of the political processes are not trustworthy. Under our Constitution, the protection of those basic liberties ultimately depends on the civic virtue, reasonableness, and civility of the citizenry. It would be a tragedy for our constitutional order if the citizens were to prove too corrupt, unreasonable, and uncivil—too untrustworthy—to live up to its commitments and aspirations by honoring basic liberties necessary to securing constitutional democracy, including the right to die.

## No Gain, No Claim: Perfecting Our Imperfect Constitution

The Constitution will endure as a vital charter of human liberty as long as there are those with the courage to defend it, the vision to interpret it, and the fidelity to live by it. — Justice William J. Brennan Jr.

Rather than submitting to versions of the perfect Constitution challenge or "no pain, no claim" test, we should embrace the "no gain, no claim" test. From this standpoint, a constitutional theory has no serious claim on our attention unless it promises some gain, in the sense that adhering to it might help us realize our constitutional aspirations as expressed in the best accounts of our Constitution and constitutional practice. My Constitution-perfecting theory abundantly satisfies the latter test, for it promises the considerable gain of securing the basic liberties associated with deliberative democracy and deliberative autonomy that are preconditions for the trustworthiness of our constitutional democracy.

I close this book with three reasons for embracing a no gain, no claim approach and a Constitution-perfecting theory that aspires to interpret our imperfect Constitution in a manner that might deserve our fidelity.[75] The first reason is hortatory: my Constitution-perfecting theory exhorts judges, elected officials, and citizens to reflect on and deliberate about our deepest principles and highest aspirations as a people. It does not conceive the commitment to fidelity to the Constitution as commanding us to follow the authority of the past. It exhorts us to conceive fidelity in terms of *honoring* our aspirational principles rather than merely *following* our historical practices and concrete original understanding, which no doubt have fallen short of those principles.

The second, related reason is critical: my Constitution-perfecting theory encourages, indeed requires, a reflective, critical attitude toward our history and practices rather than enshrining them. It recognizes that our principles may fit and justify most of our practices or precedents but that they will criticize some of them for failing to live up to our constitutional commitments to principles such as liberty and equality. Put another way, my theory does not confuse or conflate our principles and traditions with our history, or our aspirational principles with our historical practices. Again, it recognizes that fidelity to the Constitution requires honoring our aspirational principles, not following our historical practices and concrete original understanding. That is, fidelity to the Constitution requires that we disregard or criticize certain aspects of our history and practices in order to be faithful to the principles embodied in the Constitution.

The final reason is justificatory: my Constitution-perfecting theory, because it understands that the quest for fidelity in interpreting our imperfect Constitution exhorts us to interpret it so as to make it the best it can be, gives us hope of interpreting our imperfect Constitution in a manner that may deserve our fidelity, or at least may be able to earn it. It does not enshrine an imperfect Constitution that does not deserve our fidelity. No gain, no claim if we are to secure constitutional democracy.

# Notes

## Chapter One

1. Olmstead v. United States, 277 U.S. 438, 478 (1928) (Brandeis, J., dissenting); see also Whitney v. California, 274 U.S. 357, 375 (1927) (Brandeis, J., concurring) ("Those who won our independence believed that the final end of the State was to make men free to develop their faculties; and that in its government the *deliberative forces* should prevail over the arbitrary. They valued liberty both as an end and as a means. They believed liberty to be the secret of happiness and courage to be the secret of liberty") (emphasis added).

2. ROBERT H. BORK, THE TEMPTING OF AMERICA: THE POLITICAL SEDUCTION OF THE LAW 95, 97 (1990) (criticizing Griswold v. Connecticut, 381 U.S. 479 [1965]).

3. CATHARINE A. MACKINNON, *Privacy v. Equality: Beyond* Roe v. Wade, in FEMINISM UNMODIFIED: DISCOURSES ON LIFE AND LAW 93, 102 (1987) (citations omitted).

4. MICHAEL J. SANDEL, LIBERALISM AND THE LIMITS OF JUSTICE 182 (1982); MARY ANN GLENDON, RIGHTS TALK: THE IMPOVERISHMENT OF POLITICAL DISCOURSE 47–48 (1991).

5. John Hart Ely, *Democracy and the Right to be Different*, 56 N.Y.U. L. REV. 397, 405 (1981).

6. 539 U.S. 558 (2003).

7. Id. at 574.

8. Planned Parenthood v. Casey, 505 U.S. 833, 851 (1992); Roe v. Wade, 410 U.S. 113 (1973).

9. *Lawrence*, 539 U.S. at 575.

10. Id. at 588, 590, 599, 590, 602 (Scalia, J., dissenting).

11. JOHN RAWLS, POLITICAL LIBERALISM (1993) [hereinafter RAWLS, PL]. In *Political Liberalism*, Rawls significantly reformulates his well-known theory of justice as fairness. See JOHN RAWLS, A THEORY OF JUSTICE (1971). He also addresses "the problem of political liberalism": "How is it possible that there

may exist over time a stable and just society of free and equal citizens profoundly divided by reasonable though incompatible religious, philosophical, and moral doctrines?" RAWLS, PL, supra, at xviii. Put another way, he asks: "How is it possible that deeply opposed though reasonable comprehensive doctrines may live together and all affirm the political conception [of justice] of a constitutional regime?" Id. The major change from *A Theory of Justice* is that the earlier work had treated his conception of justice as fairness not as a political conception but as a comprehensive philosophical doctrine that all citizens would endorse in a well-ordered society. See id. at xv–xvii.

Much work in constitutional theory has been inspired by Rawls's *A Theory of Justice*, most notably that of David A. J. Richards, Frank I. Michelman, and Samuel Freeman. See, e.g., DAVID A. J. RICHARDS, THE MORAL CRITICISM OF LAW (1977); DAVID A. J. RICHARDS, TOLERATION AND THE CONSTITUTION (1986); DAVID A. J. RICHARDS, FOUNDATIONS OF AMERICAN CONSTITUTIONALISM (1989); DAVID A. J. RICHARDS, CONSCIENCE AND THE CONSTITUTION (1993); Frank I. Michelman, *Foreword: On Protecting the Poor Through the Fourteenth Amendment*, 83 HARV. L. REV. 7 (1969); Frank I. Michelman, *In Pursuit of Constitutional Welfare Rights: One View of Rawls' Theory of Justice*, 121 U. PA. L. REV. 962 (1973); Frank I. Michelman, *Welfare Rights in a Constitutional Democracy*, 1979 WASH. U. L.Q. 659. For applications of Rawls's work since *A Theory of Justice* to constitutional theory, see, e.g., Frank I. Michelman, *Rawls on Constitutionalism and Constitutional Law*, in THE CAMBRIDGE COMPANION TO JOHN RAWLS 394 (Samuel Freeman ed., 2003); Samuel Freeman, *Constitutional Democracy and the Legitimacy of Judicial Review*, 9 LAW & PHIL. 327 (1990–91); Samuel Freeman, *Original Meaning, Democratic Interpretation, and the Constitution*, 21 PHIL. & PUB. AFF. 3 (1992).

12. JOHN HART ELY, DEMOCRACY AND DISTRUST (1980).

13. CASS R. SUNSTEIN, THE PARTIAL CONSTITUTION (1993) [hereinafter SUNSTEIN, PC].

14. See Laurence H. Tribe, *The Puzzling Persistence of Process-Based Constitutional Theories*, 89 YALE L.J. 1063 (1980) [hereinafter Tribe, *Puzzling Persistence*] (expressing puzzlement at the "persistence of process-based constitutional theories"). For a retort, see Michael J. Klarman, *The Puzzling Resistance to Political Process Theory*, 77 VA. L. REV. 747, 772–82 (1991) (providing a partial defense of Ely's theory against various critiques).

15. I mean "perfecting" in the sense of interpreting the Constitution with integrity so as to render it a coherent whole, not in Henry Monaghan's caricatured sense of "Our Perfect Constitution" as a perfect liberal utopia or an "ideal object" of political morality. See Henry P. Monaghan, *Our Perfect Constitution*, 56 N.Y.U. L. REV. 353, 356 (1981); cf. Frank I. Michelman, *Constancy to an Ideal Object*, 56 N.Y.U. L. REV. 406, 407 (1981) (distinguishing "weak-sense perfectionism" or "constitutional rationalism" from "strong-sense perfectionism"). For the notion

of law as integrity, see RONALD DWORKIN, LAW'S EMPIRE 176–224 (1986) [hereinafter DWORKIN, LE].

16. By "elegance," I mean to suggest the notion of elegance in the construction of scientific theories. An important reason for the attractiveness of Ely's theory is its elegance. For an assessment of Ely's book that stresses this aspect, see Harry H. Wellington, *The Importance of Being Elegant*, 42 OHIO ST. L.J. 427 (1981).

17. I have coauthored a work organizing constitutional interpretation on the basis of these three fundamental interrogatives. See WALTER F. MURPHY, JAMES E. FLEMING, SOTIRIOS A. BARBER & STEPHEN MACEDO, AMERICAN CONSTITUTIONAL INTERPRETATION (3d ed. 2003).

18. See RONALD DWORKIN, LIFE'S DOMINION 119, 126–29 (1993) (contrasting a "constitution of principle" [a scheme of abstract, normative principles] with a "constitution of detail" [a list of particular, antique rules] [emphasis omitted]); see also *Lawrence*, 539 U.S. at 578–79 ("Had those who drew and ratified the Due Process Clauses of the Fifth Amendment or the Fourteenth Amendment known the components of liberty in its manifold possibilities, they might have been more specific. They did not presume to have this insight. . . . As the Constitution endures, persons in every generation can invoke its principles in their own search for greater freedom."); *Casey*, 505 U.S. at 901 (joint opinion of O'Connor, Kennedy, and Souter, JJ.) (conceiving the Constitution as a "covenant" or "coherent succession" embodying "ideas and aspirations that must survive more ages than one").

19. For the notion of "reasoned judgment" in the specific context of substantive due process, see the joint opinion in *Casey*, 505 U.S. at 849 ("The inescapable fact is that adjudication of substantive due process claims may call upon the Court in interpreting the Constitution to exercise that same capacity which by tradition courts always have exercised: reasoned judgment"). The joint opinion was echoing Justice Harlan's famous conception of judgment, not as a formula or bright-line rule, but as a "rational process." See Poe v. Ullman, 367 U.S. 497, 542 (1961) (Harlan, J., dissenting); cf. RAWLS, PL, supra note 11, at 222 ("[W]e may over the course of life come freely to accept, as the outcome of reflective thought and *reasoned judgment*, the ideals, principles, and standards that specify our basic rights and liberties, and effectively guide and moderate the political power to which we are subject" [emphasis added]).

20. See RAWLS, PL, supra note 11, at 236 & n.23. For the two dimensions of best interpretation, fit and justification, see chapter 2.

21. See RAWLS, PL, supra note 11, at 240. Others have expressed similar views concerning the gap between the judicially enforceable Constitution and the Constitution that is binding outside the courts. See, e.g., SUNSTEIN, PC, supra note 13, at 9–10, 138–40, 145–61, 350; LAWRENCE G. SAGER, JUSTICE IN PLAINCLOTHES: A THEORY OF AMERICAN CONSTITUTIONAL PRACTICE 84–128 (2004); Lawrence G. Sager, *The Why of Constitutional Essentials*, 72 FORDHAM L. REV. 1421 (2004);

Frank I. Michelman, *Justice as Fairness, Legitimacy, and the Question of Judicial Review: A Comment*, 72 FORDHAM L. REV. 1407 (2004).

22. RAWLS, PL, supra note 11, at 90–99.

23. For the constructivist aspiration to interpret the Constitution so as to make it the best it can be, see DWORKIN, LE, supra note 15, at 176–275; RONALD DWORKIN, A MATTER OF PRINCIPLE 146–66 (1985) [hereinafter DWORKIN, AMOP].

24. See Frank I. Michelman, *On Regulating Practices with Theories Drawn from Them: A Case of Justice as Fairness*, in NOMOS: THEORY AND PRACTICE 309 (Ian Shapiro & Judith Wagner DeCew eds., 1995).

25. See chapter 4.

26. For the formulation "fits most and criticizes some," I am indebted to Lewis D. Sargentich. See Gregory C. Keating, *Fidelity to Pre-existing Law and the Legitimacy of Legal Decision*, 69 NOTRE DAME L. REV. 1, 38 (1993) (using this formulation in developing a general conception of legal justification).

27. 198 U.S. 45 (1905). See Cass R. Sunstein, Lochner's *Legacy*, 87 COLUM. L. REV. 873, 873 (1987) (characterizing *Lochner* as an infamous "defining case" in constitutional law, and a "spectre" that "has loomed over most important constitutional decisions"); cf. KARL MARX & FRIEDRICH ENGELS, MANIFESTO OF THE COMMUNIST PARTY (1848), *reprinted in* THE MARX-ENGELS READER 469, 473 (Robert C. Tucker ed., 2d ed. 1978) ("A spectre is haunting Europe—the spectre of Communism").

28. See, e.g., Adkins v. Children's Hosp., 261 U.S. 525 (1923) (striking down a federal minimum-wage law for women and minors as in violation of the Due Process Clause of the Fifth Amendment); *Lochner*, 198 U.S. at 61 (invalidating, under the Due Process Clause of the Fourteenth Amendment, a state maximum-hours law that the Court described as "mere meddlesome interference[ ] with the rights of the individual" to liberty of contract).

29. 300 U.S. 379 (1937) (upholding a state minimum-wage law and signaling the demise of the *Lochner* era by overruling *Adkins*).

30. For accounts of the official demise of *Lochner*, see, e.g., LAURENCE H. TRIBE, AMERICAN CONSTITUTIONAL LAW §§ 8-6 to 8-7 (2d ed. 1988); Robert G. McCloskey, *Economic Due Process and the Supreme Court: An Exhumation and Reburial*, 1962 SUP. CT. REV. 34, 36–38; Sunstein, supra note 27, at 873–83.

31. See, e.g., BORK, supra note 2; John Hart Ely, *The Wages of Crying Wolf: A Comment on* Roe v. Wade, 82 YALE L.J. 920 (1973). Ely apparently coined the term "Lochnering" or "to *Lochner*." Id. at 944.

32. 410 U.S. 113 (1973).

33. Ely, supra note 31, at 933–45.

34. 304 U.S. 144, 152 n.4 (1938).

35. 505 U.S. at 846 (joint opinion of O'Connor, Kennedy & Souter, JJ.). Justices Stevens and Blackmun, who would have reaffirmed *Roe* in its entirety, joined parts 1–3, 5-a, 5-c, and 6 of the joint opinion, supplying the fourth and fifth votes necessary

to make those parts the opinion of the Court, thus reaffirming *Roe*. The remaining four Justices would have overruled *Roe*. Prior to the decision in *Casey*, some scholars believed that the Court's decision in Bowers v. Hardwick, 478 U.S. 186 (1986), was evidence of "the second death of substantive due process." See Daniel O. Conkle, *The Second Death of Substantive Due Process*, 62 IND. L.J. 215 (1987).

36. *Casey*, 505 U.S. at 998 (Scalia, J., concurring in the judgment in part and dissenting in part) (analogizing *Roe* and *Casey* to *Lochner* and Dred Scott v. Sandford, 60 U.S. [19 How.] 393 [1857]); see also Antonin Scalia, *Originalism: The Lesser Evil*, 57 U. CIN. L. REV. 849, 862–65 (1989).

37. 539 U.S. at 586 (Scalia, J., dissenting).

38. See, e.g., Tribe, *Puzzling Persistence*, supra note 14, *reprinted in* LAURENCE H. TRIBE, CONSTITUTIONAL CHOICES 9 (1985) (retitled *The Pointless Flight from Substance*) (arguing that Ely's theory takes a pointless flight from making substantive constitutional choices to perfecting processes); Ronald Dworkin, *The Forum of Principle*, 56 N.Y.U. L. REV. 469, 470 (1981) (originally entitled *The Flight from Substance*, see *Commentary*, 56 N.Y.U. L. REV. 525, 539 n.* [1981]), *reprinted in* DWORKIN, AMOP, supra note 23, at 33, 34 (arguing that the flights from substance to process and original understanding "end in failure" because "[j]udges cannot decide what the pertinent intention of the Framers was, or which political process is really fair or democratic, unless they make substantive political decisions of just the sort the proponents of intention or process think judges should not make").

39. In *Casey*, the joint opinion resisted the temptations, in interpreting the Due Process Clause of the Fourteenth Amendment, to take a flight from substantive liberties to procedural liberties or to original understanding. See *Casey*, 505 U.S. at 847–49 (acknowledging that it was "tempting" to abdicate the responsibility of exercising reasoned judgment). The joint opinion discussed the infamous era of *Lochner*, id. at 861–62, but it reiterated that the Due Process Clause protects substantive liberties, "a realm of personal liberty which the government may not enter." Id. at 847. Justice Scalia angrily replied that the Court's "temptation" is not to abdicate responsibility but rather "in the quite opposite and more natural direction—towards systematically eliminating checks upon its own power; and it succumbs." Id. at 981 (Scalia, J., concurring in the judgment in part and dissenting in part). For similar notions of "temptation" and "seduction," see BORK, supra note 2, passim.

40. See SUNSTEIN, PC, supra note 13, at 104–5, 142–45.

41. The allusion is to G. W. F. HEGEL, PHILOSOPHY OF RIGHT 13 (T. M. Knox trans., 1942) ("When philosophy paints its grey in grey, then has a shape of life grown old. By philosophy's grey in grey it cannot be rejuvenated but only understood. The owl of Minerva spreads its wings only with the falling of the dusk"). The pertinence of the Hegelian death knell is that Ely, by giving the *Carolene Products* paradigm its fullest development, or its most expansive elaboration, revealed the process-perfecting tradition's ultimate incompleteness, if not rendered it anachro-

nistic. Many scholars have suggested that Ely perfected the *Carolene Products* tradition. See Paul Brest, *The Substance of Process*, 42 OHIO ST. L.J. 131, 131–32 (1981); Richard D. Parker, *The Past of Constitutional Theory—And Its Future*, 42 OHIO ST. L.J. 223, 240–45 (1981).

42. See SUNSTEIN, PC, supra note 13, at 144, 142–44 (arguing that none of the criticisms of Ely's theory "fundamentally damages the view that interpretive principles should be based first and foremost on considerations of democracy" and acknowledging parallels between the two themes of Ely's theory of judicial review and his own theory).

43. These terms are for the most part consistent with Rawls's, Ely's, and Sunstein's usages. On occasion, however, Sunstein refers to his own theory of deliberative democracy as a theory of "constitutional democracy." See, e.g., SUNSTEIN, PC, supra note 13, at 14, 193.

There is a long-standing conflict between the political and constitutional theories of constitutionalism and democracy. In their purest forms, constitution-alism is concerned with limited government and democracy with unfettered majority rule. See MURPHY, FLEMING, BARBER & MACEDO, supra note 17, at 43–59. The political system of the United States is a complex hybrid of constitu-tionalism and democracy, or a constitutional democracy, rather than a representa-tive democracy. See id. A constitutional democracy is a system in which a constitution imposes limits on the content of legislation: to be valid, a law must be consistent with fundamental rights and liberties embodied in the constitution. A representative democracy, by contrast, is a system in which there are no constitu-tional limits on the content of legislation: whatever a majority enacts is law, provided the appropriate procedural preconditions are met. See JOHN RAWLS, JUSTICE AS FAIRNESS: A RESTATEMENT § 44 (2001). Constitutional constructivism is a theory of constitutional democracy, whereas Ely's theory, with certain qualifica-tions, is a theory of representative democracy. Sunstein claims to resolve "the much-vaunted opposition between constitutionalism and democracy" through his theory of deliberative democracy. SUNSTEIN, PC, supra note 13, at 142. I argue that the model of constitutional democracy better fits and justifies our constitutional document and underlying constitutional order than does Ely's model of represen-tative democracy or Sunstein's model of deliberative democracy.

44. For Rawls's reference to trustworthiness, see RAWLS, PL, supra note 11, at 319; see also chapter 4.

45. As for the notion of giving both substance and process their due, contrast Monaghan, supra note 15, at 355 (referring, disparagingly, to "the 'due substance clauses': substantive due process and substantive equal protection").

46. MICHAEL J. SANDEL, DEMOCRACY'S DISCONTENT: AMERICA IN SEARCH OF A PUBLIC PHILOSOPHY (1996).

47. CASS R. SUNSTEIN, LEGAL REASONING AND POLITICAL CONFLICT (1996); CASS R. SUNSTEIN, ONE CASE AT A TIME: JUDICIAL MINIMALISM ON THE SUPREME COURT (1999).

48. Cass R. Sunstein, *What Did* Lawrence *Hold? Of Autonomy, Desuetude, Sexuality, and Marriage*, 2003 Sup. Ct. Rev. 27, 30.

49. 424 U.S. 1 (1976).

50. 505 U.S. 377 (1992).

51. 468 U.S. 609 (1984).

52. 530 U.S. 640 (2000).

53. 531 U.S. 98 (2000).

54. 489 U.S. 189 (1989).

55. See *Colloquy, Fidelity as Integrity*, 65 Fordham L. Rev. 1357, 1358 (1997) (statement of Sanford Levinson).

56. See Monaghan, supra note 15.

57. See Christopher L. Eisgruber, *Justice and the Text: Rethinking the Constitutional Relation between Principle and Prudence*, 43 Duke L.J. 1, 7 (1993) (referring to Monaghan, supra note 15).

58. Id.

## Chapter Two

1. John Hart Ely, Democracy and Distrust 75–77 (1980) [hereinafter Ely, DD] (characterizing his own theory as filling in the outlines of United States v. Carolene Products Co., 304 U.S. 144, 152 n.4 [1938]); see Paul Brest, *The Substance of Process*, 42 Ohio St. L.J. 131, 131 (1981) (stating that Ely's book "culminates" the *Carolene Products* tradition); Richard D. Parker, *The Past of Constitutional Theory—And Its Future*, 42 Ohio St. L.J. 223, 223 (1981) (claiming that Ely's book "perfect[s]" the tradition).

2. Ely, DD, supra note 1, at 75–88.

3. Id. at 73–75, 87.

4. John Hart Ely, *The Wages of Crying Wolf: A Comment on* Roe v. Wade, 82 Yale L.J. 920, 943–45 (1973) [hereinafter Ely, *Wages*].

5. See Ely, DD, supra note 1, at 82, 88; James E. Fleming, *A Critique of John Hart Ely's Quest for the Ultimate Constitutional Interpretivism of Representative Democracy*, 80 Mich. L. Rev. 634 (1982).

6. Ely, DD, supra note 1, at vii. Some constitutional theorists who popularized the terms"interpretivism" and "noninterpretivism" subsequently repudiated that dichotomy. Compare Thomas C. Grey, *Do We Have an Unwritten Constitution?* 27 Stan. L. Rev. 703, 714–18 (1975) (proposing a "noninterpretive" theory as an alternative to the "pure interpretive model") with Thomas C. Grey, *The Constitution as Scripture*, 37 Stan. L. Rev. 1, 1 (1984) (recanting the dichotomy, stating that "[w]e are all interpretivists; the real arguments are not over whether judges should stick to interpreting, but over what they should interpret and what interpretive attitudes they should adopt"). I, like others, reject the distinction between interpretivism and noninterpretivism. See, e.g., William F. Harris II,

THE INTERPRETABLE CONSTITUTION 127–28 (1993). Ronald Dworkin rejected the dichotomy from the beginning in *The Forum of Principle*, 56 N.Y.U. L. REV. 469, 471–76 (1981) [hereinafter Dworkin, *Forum*], *reprinted in* RONALD DWORKIN, A MATTER OF PRINCIPLE 33, 34–38 (1985) [hereinafter DWORKIN, AMOP], and also rejected the dichotomy between originalism and nonoriginalism, id. at 471 n.7. That dichotomy is similar to the one between interpretivism and noninterpretivism. If there is a difference between interpretivism and originalism, it seems to be that the former places greater emphasis on constitutional text (or language) and the latter on intention or understanding of the framers and ratifiers (or history).

7. ELY, DD, supra note 1, at 1.

8. See Planned Parenthood v. Casey, 505 U.S. 833, 979–1002 (1992) (Scalia, J., concurring in the judgment in part and dissenting in part); Griswold v. Connecticut, 381 U.S. 479, 507–27 (1965) (Black, J., dissenting); HUGO L. BLACK, A CONSTITUTIONAL FAITH (1969); ROBERT H. BORK, THE TEMPTING OF AMERICA (1990); ANTONIN SCALIA, A MATTER OF INTERPRETATION (1997); Antonin Scalia, *Originalism: The Lesser Evil*, 57 U. CIN. L. REV. 849 (1989) [hereinafter Scalia, *Originalism*]. Needless to say, there are great variations among the advocates of this approach.

9. ELY, DD, supra note 1, at 1.

10. 410 U.S. 113, 152–53 (1973) (holding that the right to privacy, although "not explicitly mention[ed] in the Constitution," encompasses a woman's decision whether or not to terminate a pregnancy).

11. 539 U.S. 558, 562, 578 (2003) (observing that "those who drew and ratified the Due Process Clauses" did not "presume to have [the] insight" to be "more specific" in enumerating "the components of liberty in its manifold possibilities," and holding that "liberty presumes an autonomy of self that includes freedom of thought, belief, expression, and certain intimate conduct").

12. See, e.g., ALEXANDER M. BICKEL, THE LEAST DANGEROUS BRANCH (1962); RONALD DWORKIN, TAKING RIGHTS SERIOUSLY (1977) [hereinafter DWORKIN, TRS]; RONALD DWORKIN, FREEDOM'S LAW: THE MORAL READING OF THE AMERICAN CONSTITUTION (1996); RONALD DWORKIN, LIFE'S DOMINION (1993) [hereinafter DWORKIN, LD]; LAURENCE H. TRIBE, ABORTION: THE CLASH OF ABSOLUTES (1990). There are, of course, considerable differences among the proponents of this approach. I, like Dworkin, reject the terms "noninterpretivism" and "nonoriginalism" for such theories. See supra note 6.

13. THE FEDERALIST No. 78, at 467, 469 (Alexander Hamilton) (Clinton Rossiter ed., 1961); Marbury v. Madison, 5 U.S. (1 Cranch) 137, 177–78 (1803). Numerous scholars, however, have disputed the clause-bound interpretivists' (or originalists') pretension to a monopoly on the classical justification. See, e.g., BRUCE ACKERMAN, WE THE PEOPLE: FOUNDATIONS 60–61, 72 (1991); SOTIRIOS A. BARBER, THE CONSTITUTION OF JUDICIAL POWER 157–58 (1993); DWORKIN, TRS, supra note 12, at 131–49; DWORKIN, LD, supra note 12, at 118–47.

14. See, e.g., BORK, supra note 8, at 143–60; Scalia, *Originalism*, supra note 8, at 862–64.

15. See, e.g., DWORKIN, TRS, supra note 12, at 278 (arguing that it is not inconsistent to recognize fundamental rights grounded in equal concern and respect while criticizing *Lochner* for protecting a right that is not so grounded); LAURENCE H. TRIBE & MICHAEL C. DORF, ON READING THE CONSTITUTION 65–66 (1991) (arguing that the Constitution protects certain individual rights but not laissez-faire capitalism as presumed in *Lochner*).

16. See, e.g., Dworkin, *Forum*, supra note 6, at 469–500, 516 (arguing that the flight from substance to original intention—or from making substantive choices to enforcing choices made long ago by the framers and ratifiers—fails because judges cannot decide what the pertinent original intention was without making substantive political decisions of the sort that the proponents of original intention are at pains to insist that judges avoid). Cass Sunstein argues that Bork's originalism is "formalist" in insisting that "the meaning of texts is usually or always a simple matter of fact"—"the neutral, apolitical invocation of the original understanding of the founders"—and "authoritarian" in that it "ultimately traces legal legitimacy to an exercise of power, to the view that might makes right." CASS R. SUNSTEIN, THE PARTIAL CONSTITUTION 94–95, 94–104, 107–10 (1993) [hereinafter SUNSTEIN, PC].

17. ELY, DD, supra note 1, at vii.

18. See id. at 1–9, 11–41; John Hart Ely, *Constitutional Interpretivism: Its Allure and Impossibility*, 53 IND. L.J. 399 (1978) [hereinafter Ely, *Impossibility*].

19. See ELY, DD, supra note 1, at 3–5. For the "counter-majoritarian difficulty," see BICKEL, supra note 12, at 16. Of course, Ely's approach to "our usual conceptions" of the Constitution is not necessarily the only way of framing the issue. It reflects a particular conception of what the Constitution is and how it ought to be interpreted.

20. ELY, DD, supra note 1, at 13.

21. The Ninth Amendment provides: "The enumeration in the Constitution, of certain rights, shall not be construed to deny or disparage others retained by the people." U.S. CONST. amend. IX.

22. ELY, DD, supra note 1, at 14–38. The Fourteenth Amendment contains the three clauses in one sentence: "No State shall make or enforce any law which shall abridge the *privileges or immunities* of citizens of the United States; nor shall any State deprive any person of life, liberty, or property, without *due process* of law; nor deny to any person within its jurisdiction the *equal protection* of the laws." U.S. CONST. amend. XIV (emphases added). The Fifth Amendment's Due Process Clause provides: "[No person shall be] deprived of life, liberty, or property, without due process of law." U.S. CONST. amend. V. Ely rejects the common view that the Due Process Clauses are similarly open-ended and justify recognition of "unenumerated" substantive rights, arguing that "'substantive due process' is a

contradiction" and, by the same token, "'procedural due process' is redundant."
ELY, DD, supra note 1, at 18 & n.*.

23. ELY, DD, supra note 1, at 28. Ely wrote these particular words with
reference to the Privileges or Immunities Clause, but uses similar formulations
in interpreting the Equal Protection Clause. See id. at 32 (stating that "the Equal
Protection Clause has to amount to what I claimed the Privileges or Immunities
Clause amounts to, a rather sweeping mandate to judge of the validity of governmental choices"). He also writes that "the conclusion that the Ninth Amendment
was intended to signal the existence of federal constitutional rights beyond those
specifically enumerated in the Constitution is the only conclusion its language
seems comfortably able to support." Id. at 38.

24. Id. at 38–41. The most transparent attempt to read such clauses out of the
Constitution is Robert Bork's. Bork has advanced an "ink blot" thesis with regard
to both the Ninth Amendment and the Privileges or Immunities Clause. See BORK,
supra note 8, at 166 (likening the Privileges or Immunitites Clause to a provision
that has been "obliterated past deciphering by an ink blot"); Nomination of
Robert H. Bork to be Associate Justice of the Supreme Court of the United States:
Hearings before the Senate Comm. on the Judiciary, 100th Cong., 1st Sess. 249
(1987) (testimony of Judge Robert H. Bork) [hereinafter Nomination Hearings]
(analogizing the Ninth Amendment to a text whose meaning cannot be known
because it is covered by an "ink blot").

25. ELY, DD, supra note 1, at 3–5, 43–72.

26. United States v. Carolene Products Co., 304 U.S. 144, 152–53 n.4 (1938)
(citations omitted).

27. ELY, DD, supra note 1, at 73–77, 103.

28. Id. at 88.

29. See id. at 73–101.

30. See id. at 12.

31. See id. at 88, 101–2.

32. See, e.g., Brest, supra note 1, at 137; Dworkin, Forum, supra note 6, at 470;
Laurence H. Tribe, The Puzzling Persistence of Process-Based Constitutional
Theories, 89 YALE L.J. 1063, 1064 (1980) [hereinafter Tribe, Puzzling Persistence].
For a recent exception, which emphasizes Ely's coherentism, see Michael C. Dorf,
The Coherentism of Democracy and Distrust, 114 YALE L.J. 1237 (2005).

33. See, e.g., Bruce A. Ackerman, Discovering the Constitution, 93 YALE L.J.
1013, 1047–48 (1984). But see Fleming, supra note 5, at 638–46 (critiquing Ely's
project as a failed quest for an ultimate interpretivism); Douglas Laycock, Taking
Constitutions Seriously: A Theory of Judicial Review, 59 TEX. L. REV. 343, 360
(1981) (taking Ely's claim seriously but concluding that Ely is not ultimately an
interpretivist).

34. Some scholars, however, have noted similarities between Ely's and Dworkin's theories. See, e.g., James O'Fallon, Book Review, 68 CAL. L. REV. 1070, 1091

(1980) (reviewing ELY, DD, supra note 1); Lawrence G. Sager, *Rights Skepticism and Process-Based Responses*, 56 N.Y.U. L. REV. 417, 426 (1981).

35. See RONALD DWORKIN, LAW'S EMPIRE 238–75, 379–402 (1985) [hereinafter DWORKIN, LE]; DWORKIN, TRS, supra note 12, at 105–30.

36. See LEARNED HAND, THE BILL OF RIGHTS 73–74 (1958) (stating that rule by "Platonic Guardians" would deny citizens the satisfaction of participation in a common venture); BORK, supra note 8, at 355, 210–14, 252–54, 351–55 (criticizing constitutional theorists who "would remake our constitution out of moral philosophy" for engaging in political judging and for succumbing to the "temptations of utopia").

37. For Dworkin's formulations of the two dimensions of best interpretation, fit and justification, see DWORKIN, LE, supra note 35, at 239; DWORKIN, AMOP, supra note 6, at 119, 143–45.

38. See ELY, DD, supra note 1, at 75–101; see also *Commentary*, 56 N.Y.U. L. REV. 525, 527–28 (1981) (statement of Ely) (characterizing interpretation as "striving for 'reflective equilibrium'"); John Hart Ely, *Democracy and the Right to Be Different*, 56 N.Y.U. L. REV. 397, 398 n.4 (1981) [hereinafter Ely, *Different*] (describing interpretation as a quest for reflective equilibrium).

39. Dworkin initially put forth a constructivist method of legal interpretation by analogy to Rawls's conception of justification in political philosophy as a quest for reflective equilibrium between our considered judgments and underlying principles of justice. See DWORKIN, TRS, supra note 12, at 159–68. Dworkin argues, by analogy, that legal interpretation proceeds back and forth between extant legal materials and underlying principles toward reflective equilibrium between them. In chapter 4 I distinguish between constructivism in Dworkin's general methodological sense and constructivism in Rawls's specific substantive sense.

40. See ELY, DD, supra note 1, at 82–87, 219 n.119; see also Dworkin, *Forum*, supra note 6, at 512 & n.101 (arguing that Dworkin's theory is "the theory on which Ely himself actually relies [in spite of much that (Ely) says]").

41. ELY, DD, supra note 1, at 101.

42. Id. at 86, 82–87.

43. Id. at 82 (quoting DWORKIN, TRS, supra note 12, at 180) (emphasis in original).

44. Id. at 237 n.54; JOHN HART ELY, ON CONSTITUTIONAL GROUND 6, 14 (1996) [hereinafter ELY, OCG]. Ely states the substantive basis for his theory of representative democracy in qualified utilitarianism most clearly in Ely, *Impossibility*, supra note 18, at 405–8. See also John Hart Ely, *Professor Dworkin's External/ Personal Preference Distinction*, 1983 DUKE L.J. 959, 979–80; *Commentary*, supra note 38, at 540–41 (statements of Ely and Dworkin discussing a utilitarian conception of democracy). Despite similarities between their substantive political theories, Ely's theory is more utilitarian than Dworkin's. Indeed, Dworkin is well

known for his critiques of utilitarianism, though he has engaged in internal critiques concerning the rights that utilitarianism itself presupposes if it is to honor its egalitarian promise that "each is to count for one and no one for more than one." See DWORKIN, TRS, supra note 12, at 275–77.

45. See Ely, *Impossibility*, supra note 18, at 406 & n.29.

46. ELY, DD, supra note 1, at 79, 82; see also John Hart Ely, *Another Such Victory: Constitutional Theory and Practice in a World Where Courts Are No Different from Legislatures*, 77 VA. L. REV. 833, 840 n.15 (1991) [hereinafter Ely, *Another*] (explaining that his theory is intended to be as compatible with a "republican" model as with a "pluralist" model).

47. Tribe, *Puzzling Persistence*, supra note 32, at 1063.

48. Id. at 1064. Tribe makes this argument with respect to both themes of Ely's *Carolene Products* theory. Id. at 1067–79.

49. Id. at 1068.

50. See Dworkin, *Forum*, supra note 6, at 470, 500–16.

51. SUNSTEIN, PC, supra note 16, at 104–5, 143–44, 369 n.17 (acknowledging that Dworkin and Tribe have made similar arguments).

52. See, e.g., Dworkin, *Forum*, supra note 6, at 513–16; Owen M. Fiss, *Foreword: The Forms of Justice*, 93 HARV. L. REV. 1, 9–10, 16–17 (1979); Tribe, *Puzzling Persistence*, supra note 32, at 1064, 1076.

53. See, e.g., Parker, supra note 1, at 239–57.

54. See SUNSTEIN, PC, supra note 16, at 143–44.

55. For my use of the terms "representative democracy," "deliberative democracy," and "constitutional democracy," see chapter 1.

56. Ely, *Wages*, supra note 4, at 943–45.

57. Id. at 933–45.

58. See ELY, DD, supra note 1, at 43–72.

59. Id. at 71.

60. Tribe, *Puzzling Persistence*, supra note 32, at 1065–67. Dworkin and Ackerman make similar arguments, as does Sunstein. See SUNSTEIN, PC, supra note 16, at 104; Ackerman, supra note 33, at 1047–48; Ronald Dworkin, *Equality, Democracy, and Constitution: We the People in Court*, 28 ALBERTA L. REV. 324, 328, 343–44 (1990).

61. See ELY, DD, supra note 1, at 88, 87–101. But see id. at 101 (conceding that "the argument from the general contours of the Constitution is necessarily a qualified one"). Ely also makes two other arguments for his theory. See infra text accompanying note 89.

62. ELY, DD, supra note 1, at 87, 92.

63. Id. at 93–94.

64. Id. at 95–97.

65. See id. at 98–100.

66. Ely, *Impossibility*, supra note 18, at 400; see ELY, DD, supra note 1, at 193 n.45.

67. ELY, DD, supra note 1, at 87.

68. But see Ely, *Different*, supra note 38, at 400 (responding to Fleming, supra note 5, and maintaining that "it does no violence to these provisions to read them as I believe they ultimately must be read, as protecting rights of participation in the processes and outputs of representative government").

69. In speaking of "anomalies," I mean to echo THOMAS S. KUHN, THE STRUCTURE OF SCIENTIFIC REVOLUTIONS 52–53 (enlarged 2d ed. 1970) (defining "anomalies" as violations of "paradigm-induced expectations that govern normal science"). On "mistakes," see DWORKIN, TRS, supra note 12, at 118–23 (conceiving "mistakes" as legal materials that are inconsistent with the theory that provides the best scheme of justification for a body of law and therefore lack generative force).

70. ELY, DD, supra note 1, at 76.

71. U.S. CONST. amend. IX.

72. ELY, DD, supra note 1, at 33, 34.

73. Id. at 34.

74. Id. at 38; see also CHARLES L. BLACK JR., DECISION ACCORDING TO LAW 43, 43–44 (1981) (suggesting that Ely and he had moved and seconded that "the Ninth Amendment . . . at long last be adopted"); Charles L. Black Jr., *The Unfinished Business of the Warren Court*, 46 WASH. L. REV. 3, 44 (1970) ("The stone the builders rejected may yet be the cornerstone of the temple").

75. *See* ELY, DD, supra note 1, at 34–41. For critical responses, see BORK, supra note 8, at 166, 183–85; Russell L. Caplan, *The History and Meaning of the Ninth Amendment*, 69 VA. L. REV. 223, 259–64 (1983); Thomas B. McAffee, *The Original Meaning of the Ninth Amendment*, 90 COLUM. L. REV. 1215, 1220–22 (1990). Bork has tried to read the Ninth Amendment (along with the Privileges or Immunities Clause) out of the Constitution with his "ink blot" thesis. See supra note 24.

76. Laurence H. Tribe, *Contrasting Constitutional Visions: Of Real and Unreal Differences*, 22 HARV. C.R.-C.L. L. REV. 95, 100 (1987); see also TRIBE & DORF, supra note 15, at 54–55, 110–11 (treating the Ninth Amendment as a rule of interpretation that expresses a presumption in favor of generalizing from specific, enumerated rights to others retained by the people).

77. See, e.g., Griswold v. Connecticut, 381 U.S. 479, 485, 484–85 (1965) (citing the Ninth Amendment in discussing the "zone of privacy created by several fundamental constitutional guarantees"); id. at 486–93 (Goldberg, J., concurring) (emphasizing the role of the Ninth Amendment in supporting the Court's protection of fundamental personal rights not specifically mentioned in the Constitution); Roe v. Wade, 410 U.S. 113, 153 (1973) (citing the Ninth Amendment in support of the right of a woman to decide whether to terminate a pregnancy); Richmond Newspapers v. Virginia, 448 U.S. 555, 579 n.15 (1980) (citing the Ninth Amendment in upholding the right of the public to attend criminal trials); Bowers v. Hardwick, 478 U.S. 186, 201–3 (1986) (Blackmun, J., dissenting) (objecting to the Court's holding that the right to privacy did not extend to protect homosexual

intimate association and the Court's refusal to consider whether Georgia's sodomy law ran afoul of the Ninth Amendment); Planned Parenthood v. Casey, 505 U.S. 833, 847–48 (1992) (joint opinion) (citing the Ninth Amendment to support its rejection of the views that the Due Process Clause of the Fourteenth Amendment protects only those rights specifically enumerated in the first eight amendments [Justice Black's view] or "only those practices, defined at the most specific level, that were protected . . . by other rules of law when [it] was ratified" [Justice Scalia's view]). But see *Griswold*, 381 U.S. at 520 (Black, J., dissenting) (protesting that " [u]se of any such broad, unbounded judicial authority [as the Ninth Amendment or Fourteenth Amendment as construed by Justice Douglas's opinion of the Court and Justice Goldberg's concurring opinion] would make of this Court's members a day-to-day constitutional convention"); *Casey*, 505 U.S. at 1000 (Scalia, J., concurring in the judgment in part and dissenting in part) (claiming angrily that the joint opinion treats the Ninth Amendment as "a literally boundless source of additional, unnamed, unhinted-at 'rights'").

Entire scholarly symposiums and books have been devoted to interpreting the Ninth Amendment. See, e.g., 1 THE RIGHTS RETAINED BY THE PEOPLE (Randy Barnett ed., 1989); 2 THE RIGHTS RETAINED BY THE PEOPLE (Randy Barnett ed., 1993). For critical responses, see supra note 75.

78. For reservations about the distinction between enumerated and "unenumerated" rights, see, e.g., DWORKIN, LD, supra note 12, at 129–31.

79. See *Griswold*, 381 U.S. at 492 (Goldberg, J., concurring) (arguing that the Ninth Amendment is a rule of construction for the Constitution as a whole, not an independent source of constitutional rights).

80. Id. at 491 (citations omitted).

81. Id. at 490–91 (citing Marbury v. Madison, 5 U.S. [1 Cranch] 137, 174 [1803]).

82. 17 U.S. (4 Wheat.) 316, 406, 407 (1819) (emphasis in original).

83. See *Griswold*, 381 U.S. at 490 n.6 (Goldberg, J., concurring) (citing BENNETT B. PATTERSON, THE FORGOTTEN NINTH AMENDMENT [1955]).

84. See WILLIAM SHAKESPEARE, THE TRAGEDY OF KING LEAR act 1, sc. 4.

85. See *Griswold*, 381 U.S. at 519, 518–20 (Black, J., dissenting) (arguing that the Ninth Amendment does not give the Court authority to invalidate laws that it thinks violate "fundamental principles of liberty and justice" [quoting *Griswold*, 381 U.S. at 491 (Goldberg, J., concurring)]); BORK, supra note 8, at 166, 183–85 (outlining the "ink blot" thesis of the Privileges or Immunities Clause and the Ninth Amendment); *Nomination Hearings*, supra note 24, at 249 (affirming Bork's ink blot theory as applied to the Ninth Amendment); Henry P. Monaghan, *Our Perfect Constitution*, 56 N.Y.U. L. REV. 353, 365–67 (1981) (describing the Ninth Amendment as "entirely empty" and the "schedule of rights" in the Constitution as "a list closed as of 1791"); see also *Casey*, 505 U.S. at 1000 (Scalia, J., concurring in the judgment in part and dissenting in part) (construing the Ninth Amendment in terms of a closed list plus narrowly conceived traditions).

86. Ely, *Impossibility*, supra note 18, at 445. By implication, Ely's analysis also applies to Bork's originalism. Bork certainly treats Ely's critique of clause-bound interpretivism as being aimed at theories like his own. See BORK, supra note 8, at 178–85, 194–99.

87. For an analysis suggesting parallels between Justice Black's and Ely's predicaments and their responses to them, see Fleming, supra note 5, at 646–48.

88. See ELY, DD, supra note 1, at 100 (stating that the right of individuals to bear arms and liberty of contract have been "'repealed' by judicial construction").

89. See id. at 87–103.

90. For an analysis of constitutional interpretation on the basis of these interrogatives, along with the interrogative *how* ought the Constitution to be interpreted, see WALTER F. MURPHY, JAMES E. FLEMING, SOTIRIOS A. BARBER & STEPHEN MACEDO, AMERICAN CONSTITUTIONAL INTERPRETATION (3d ed. 2003).

91. See chapter 4.

92. ELY, DD, supra note 1, at 73–75 (arguing that the "deep structure" of the Warren Court's jurisprudence was that of footnote four of *Carolene Products*, not discovering substantive fundamental values).

93. See James Bradley Thayer, *The Origin and Scope of the American Doctrine of Constitutional Law*, 7 HARV. L. REV. 129 (1893) (arguing for judicial deference to Congress and the president, absent a clear mistake, on the ground that politically elected officials are the primary makers of policy as well as the primary interpreters of the Constitution in our scheme of government). It is important to bear in mind, however, that footnote four of *Carolene Products*, which Ely elaborates in *Democracy and Distrust*, defines itself in opposition to Thayer's doctrine of the clear mistake by setting forth three exceptions to the general presumption of constitutionality and deferential scrutiny of legislative (and executive) actions.

During 1993, a symposium was held at Northwestern University School of Law to mark the centennial of the publication of Thayer's essay. See *One Hundred Years of Judicial Review: The Thayer Centennial Symposium*, 88 Nw. U. L. REV. 1 (1993). None other than Ely gave the keynote address. See id. at vi. It is published in ELY, OCG, supra note 44, at 25–30.

94. See James Bradley Thayer, *John Marshall*, in JAMES BRADLEY THAYER, OLIVER WENDELL HOLMES & FELIX FRANKFURTER ON JOHN MARSHALL 1, 86 (Philip B. Kurland ed., 1967) ("The tendency of a common and easy resort to [judicial review] . . . is to dwarf the political capacity of the people, and to deaden its sense of moral responsibility").

95. Lochner v. New York, 198 U.S. 45, 65 (1905) (Harlan, J., dissenting); id. at 74 (Holmes, J., dissenting).

96. See G. Edward White, *Revisiting James Bradley Thayer*, 88 Nw. U. L. REV. 48, 48–49 (1993).

97. Ely, *Another*, supra note 46.

98. Ely's article, however, does not constitute a "surrender." Id. at 854 n.57; see also JOHN HART ELY, WAR AND RESPONSIBILITY 54 (1993) (applying the theory of *Democracy and Distrust* to justify judicial review as a corrective for Congress's evasion of its constitutional responsibilities in deciding what wars we should and should not fight).

99. See SUNSTEIN, PC, supra note 16.

## Chapter Three

1. JOHN HART ELY, DEMOCRACY AND DISTRUST (1980) [hereinafter ELY, DD].

2. CASS R. SUNSTEIN, THE PARTIAL CONSTITUTION 1–2, 6 (1993) [hereinafter SUNSTEIN, PC]. In this chapter, I focus on *The Partial Constitution*, Sunstein's first and best book in constitutional theory, because it provides his fullest exposition of a substantive vision of the Constitution as embodying a deliberative democracy. Much of his subsequent work has focused more on the role of courts than on the commitments of the Constitution itself. In chapter 7, I examine Sunstein's work in developing the idea of judicial "minimalism."

3. John Hart Ely, *The Wages of Crying Wolf: A Comment on* Roe v. Wade, 82 YALE L.J. 920 (1973) [hereinafter Ely, *Wages*].

4. See SUNSTEIN, PC, supra note 2, at 45–62, 259–61; Cass R. Sunstein, Lochner's Legacy, 87 COLUM. L. REV. 873, 874–75, 882–83 (1987) [hereinafter Sunstein, *Legacy*].

5. See SUNSTEIN, PC, supra note 2, at 68–92, 130–31; Sunstein, *Legacy*, supra note 4, at 874–75, 883–902.

6. See SUNSTEIN, PC, supra note 2, at 104–5, 142–44.

7. See id. at 142–44.

8. 478 U.S. 186 (1986).

9. 539 U.S. 558 (2003).

10. See SUNSTEIN, PC, supra note 2, at 17–39, 123–61 (setting out the core commitments of deliberative democracy and arguing that this substantive political theory better fits and justifies the text, history, and structure of the Constitution than do alternative theories).

11. Id. at 51–62, 123, 133–34.

12. Id. at 133–41.

13. Id. at 133–34. For Sunstein's critique of status quo neutrality, see id. at 3–7, 40–67, 68–92, 134. For his critique of analogies between politics and economics, and citizens and consumers, see id. at 164, 134–35, 162–94.

14. See id. at 135–36.

15. Id. at 139; see also id. at 60. For a fuller development of this idea, see CASS R. SUNSTEIN, THE SECOND BILL OF RIGHTS: FDR's UNFINISHED REVOLUTION AND WHY WE NEED IT MORE THAN EVER (2004).

16. See Sunstein, PC, supra note 2, at 136, 259–61, 402 n.17. For Sunstein's fuller treatment of sexual orientation, see, e.g., Cass R. Sunstein, One Case at a Time: Judicial Minimalism on the Supreme Court 137–71 (1999); Cass R. Sunstein, *What Did* Lawrence *Hold? Of Autonomy, Desuetude, Sexuality, and Marriage*, 2003 Sup. Ct. Rev. 27, 30, 48–52, 53–60 [hereinafter Sunstein, *What Did* Lawrence *Hold?*].

17. Sunstein, PC, supra note 2, at 137.

18. Cf. Christopher L. Eisgruber, *Disagreeable People*, 43 Stan. L. Rev. 275, 297–98 (1990) (reviewing Robert F. Nagel, Constitutional Cultures: The Mentality and Consequences of Judicial Review [1989]) (contending that American culture inevitably will breed disagreement over the meaning of constitutional principles).

19. Sunstein, PC, supra note 2, at 137–40, 402 n.17.

20. Id. at 142–44.

21. See id. at v–vi, 9–10, 138–40, 145–61, 350; see also Paul Brest, *The Conscientious Legislator's Guide to Constitutional Interpretation*, 27 Stan. L. Rev. 585, 586 (1975) (arguing that legislators have a duty to interpret the Constitution conscientiously and that the deferential rationality standards applied by courts—for example, to the Due Process and Equal Protection Clauses—do not comprehend all that is demanded of legislators who fulfill that duty); Lawrence G. Sager, Justice in Plainclothes 84–92 (2004); Lawrence G. Sager, *Fair Measure: The Legal Status of Underenforced Constitutional Norms*, 91 Harv. L. Rev. 1212, 1213 (1978) (rejecting the modern view that confines constitutional norms to the scope of federal judicial enforcement and distinguishing between the judicially enforced Constitution and the Constitution itself that is binding outside the courts).

22. See Sunstein, PC, supra note 2, at 145–53.

23. See id. at 138–40, 148–49.

24. See James Bradley Thayer, *The Origin and Scope of the American Doctrine of Constitutional Law*, 7 Harv. L. Rev. 129 (1893) [hereinafter Thayer, *Origin*]; chapter 2; see also James Bradley Thayer, *John Marshall*, in James Bradley Thayer, Oliver Wendell Holmes & Felix Frankfurter on John Marshall 1, 86 (Philip B. Kurland ed., 1967) ("The tendency of a common and easy resort to [judicial review] . . . is to dwarf the political capacity of the people, and to deaden its sense of moral responsibility").

25. See Sunstein, PC, supra note 2, at 142.

26. Id. at 143.

27. See id. at 143–44.

28. Id.

29. Ely, DD, supra note 1, at 82; see chapter 2.

30. 424 U.S. 1 (1976).

31. 410 U.S. 113 (1973).

32. *Buckley*, 424 U.S. at 48–49.

33. See SUNSTEIN, PC, supra note 2, at 84–85, 223–24; Cass R. Sunstein, *Beyond the Republican Revival*, 97 YALE L.J. 1539, 1576–78 (1988) [hereinafter Sunstein, *Beyond*]; Sunstein, *Legacy*, supra note 4, at 883–84.

34. See SUNSTEIN, PC, supra note 2, at 387 n.45 (quoting John Rawls, *The Basic Liberties and Their Priority*, in 3 THE TANNER LECTURES ON HUMAN VALUES 1, 76 (Sterling M. McMurrin ed., 1982), *reprinted in* JOHN RAWLS, POLITICAL LIBERALISM 289, 360–61 (1993) [hereinafter RAWLS, PL]).

35. RAWLS, PL, supra note 34, at 362.

36. See SUNSTEIN, PC, supra note 2, at 137–40, 223–24.

37. See RAWLS, PL, supra note 34, at 5–6, 356–63 (explaining the guarantee of the fair value of the equal political liberties and distinguishing it from formal equality).

38. 377 U.S. 533 (1964).

39. 376 U.S. 1 (1964).

40. RAWLS, PL, supra note 34, at 361, 360–63.

41. JOHN HART ELY, ON CONSTITUTIONAL GROUND 6, 13–14 (1996) [hereinafter ELY, OCG].

42. Id. at 14 (quoting Mill's analysis of Bentham). For discussion of Ely's qualified utilitarianism, see chapter 2.

43. See ELY, DD, supra note 1, at 82–87 (explaining the commitment to equal concern and respect in the design and administration of the political institutions that govern majorities and minorities alike). As H. L. A. Hart pointed out, Bentham's utilitarian principle of the equal weighting of preferences is "no respecter of persons." H. L. A. HART, *Natural Rights: Bentham and John Stuart Mill*, in ESSAYS ON BENTHAM 79, 97, 97–99 (1982) (citation omitted). That apparent egalitarianism and impartiality is a principal source of the appeal that utilitarianism has had. See id. at 97–98; RONALD DWORKIN, TAKING RIGHTS SERIOUSLY 275 (1977); RONALD DWORKIN, A MATTER OF PRINCIPLE 360 (1985) [hereinafter DWORKIN, AMOP].

44. See Ely, *Wages*, supra note 3, at 933–45. For an account of critiques (such as Ely's) of the right to privacy and abortion that emphasizes the ghost of *Lochner*, see Helen Garfield, *Privacy, Abortion, and Judicial Review: Haunted by the Ghost of* Lochner, 61 WASH. L. REV. 293 (1986).

45. See Ely, *Wages*, supra note 3, at 933–35; see also ELY, DD, supra note 1, at 164–70, 247–49 n.52 (arguing that women are not insular, nor are they a minority). Ely's famous critiques of *Roe* in *The Wages of Crying Wolf* and *Democracy and Distrust* were not his final words on the legitimacy of *Roe*, however. After the Supreme Court reaffirmed *Roe* in Planned Parenthood v. Casey, 505 U.S. 833 (1992), Ely wrote what he described as a "fan letter" to the three justices who authored the joint opinion in that case. Ely praised their opinion as "excellent": "not only reaching what seem to me entirely sensible results, but defending the

refusal to overrule *Roe v. Wade* splendidly." ELY, OCG, supra note 41, at 305. Ely added in commentary on the letter: "*Roe* has contributed greatly to the more general move toward equality for women, which seems to me not only good but also in line with the central themes of our Constitution." Id.

46. See SUNSTEIN, PC, supra note 2, at 259–61.

47. See id. at 259–61, 270–85. Decisional autonomy and bodily integrity are the two doctrinal strands on which the joint opinion in *Casey* relied in officially reaffirming the central holding of *Roe*. See *Casey*, 505 U.S. at 851–53, 857. The joint opinion notably does not use the word "privacy" to refer to the substantive liberty that is protected by the Due Process Clause, though it does speak of precedents that have "'respected the private realm of family life which the state cannot enter.'" Id. at 851 (citation omitted); see Linda C. McClain, *The Poverty of Privacy?* 3 COLUM. J. GENDER & L. 119, 127–33 (1992) (discussing the virtual disappearance of "privacy" in the joint opinion in *Casey* in favor of a conception of autonomy that does not "insulate" persons from governmental persuasion).

48. SUNSTEIN, PC, supra note 2, at 259, 272. Sunstein rightly notes that the joint opinion in *Casey* emphasized issues of sexual equality. Id. at 284. And he correctly stresses that Justices Blackmun and Stevens in their separate opinions also emphasized equality. Id. His quotation from Justice Stevens, however, omits the crucial passage that shows that Stevens regards liberty and equality as intertwined. Stevens wrote: "*Roe* is an integral part of a correct understanding of *both the concept of liberty and* the basic equality of men and women." *Casey*, 505 U.S. at 912 (Stevens, J., concurring in part and dissenting in part) (emphasis added). Sunstein omits the italicized passage regarding liberty.

49. 347 U.S. 483 (1954).

50. 60 U.S. (19 How.) 393 (1857). Compare SUNSTEIN, PC, supra note 2, at 260–61 (analogizing *Roe* and *Casey* to *Brown*), with *Casey*, 505 U.S. at 995, 998 (Scalia, J., concurring in the judgment in part and dissenting in part) (asserting that the joint opinion's "description of the place of *Roe* in the social history of the United States is unrecognizable" and drawing analogies between *Roe*, on the one hand, and *Lochner* and *Dred Scott*, on the other).

51. RAWLS, PL, supra note 34, at 4–5, 299 (referring to Benjamin Constant, Liberty of the Ancients Compared with That of the Moderns, Address before the Athénée Royal in Paris [1819], *reprinted in* BENJAMIN CONSTANT, POLITICAL WRITINGS 307 [Biancamaria Fontana ed. & trans., 1988]); see JOHN RAWLS, A THEORY OF JUSTICE 201 (1971) [hereinafter RAWLS, TJ]. Locke's most significant work in this respect is JOHN LOCKE, TWO TREATISES OF GOVERNMENT (Peter Lasletted., 2d ed. 1967) (3d ed. 1698); Rousseau's is JEAN-JACQUES ROUSSEAU, THE SOCIAL CONTRACT (Roger D. Masters ed. & Judith R. Masters trans., 1978) (1762).

52. See, e.g., LOUIS HARTZ, THE LIBERAL TRADITION IN AMERICA (1955); HERBERT J. STORING, WHAT THE ANTI-FEDERALISTS WERE FOR (1981).

53. See, e.g., J. G. A. POCOCK, THE MACHIAVELLIAN MOMENT (1975); GORDON S. WOOD, THE CREATION OF THE AMERICAN REPUBLIC, 1776–1787 (1969); GORDON S. WOOD, THE RADICALISM OF THE AMERICAN REVOLUTION (1992); Symposium, *The Republican Civic Tradition*, 97 YALE L.J. 1493 (1988).

54. Roberto Unger has described this conflict, encapsulated in Constant's famous contrast, as "the stranglehold of a false antithesis." ROBERTO M. UNGER, THE CRITICAL LEGAL STUDIES MOVEMENT 41 (1986). For Rawls's attempt to move beyond this impasse, see RAWLS, PL, supra note 34, at 5. For Michelman's efforts, see Frank I. Michelman, *Law's Republic*, 97 YALE L.J. 1493, 1524–32 (1988) [hereinafter Michelman, *Law's Republic*]; Frank I. Michelman, *Foreword: Traces of Self-Government*, 100 HARV. L. REV. 4, 36–47 (1986).

55. See SUNSTEIN, PC, supra note 2, at 373 n.18, 133–41 (stating that "it appears that the often-drawn opposition between liberalism and republicanism is, in the American tradition, a large mistake" and outlining the principles of a synthesis, liberal republicanism or deliberative democracy); Sunstein, *Beyond*, supra note 33, at 1567, 1566–71 (criticizing scholars who have posited an "opposition between liberal and republican thought" as stemming from a "caricature" of the liberal tradition).

56. SUNSTEIN, PC, supra note 2, at 142.

57. See Richard A. Epstein, *Modern Republicanism—Or the Flight from Substance*, 97 YALE L.J. 1633 (1988) [hereinafter Epstein, *Flight*] (critiquing both Sunstein, *Beyond*, supra note 33, and Michelman, *Law's Republic*, supra note 54).

58. Id. at 1633.

59. See chapter 2.

60. Epstein, *Flight*, supra note 57, at 1634–36.

61. See, e.g., BRUCE ACKERMAN, WE THE PEOPLE: FOUNDATIONS 303, 302–3 (1991) (stating that the "Founders' genius" resided in the way that they artfully recombined received ideas and practices into new constitutional patterns); SHELDON S. WOLIN, POLITICS AND VISION: CONTINUITY AND INNOVATION IN WESTERN POLITICAL THOUGHT (rev. ed. 2004).

62. Epstein, *Flight*, supra note 57, at 1634.

63. Id. at 1635, 1649–50; see also RICHARD A. EPSTEIN, TAKINGS 11–18 (1985) [hereinafter EPSTEIN, TAKINGS] (advancing a putatively Lockean theory in the context of the Takings Clause).

64. See SUNSTEIN, PC, supra note 2, at 143; chapter 6.

65. 300 U.S. 379 (1937). See EPSTEIN, TAKINGS, supra note 63, at 306–30 (arguing that much of the New Deal and the modern welfare state is unconstitutional).

66. See chapter 4. Rawls contends that his political liberalism or political constructivism is compatible with "classical republicanism" or "civic republicanism." See RAWLS, PL, supra note 34, at 205–6. He maintains, however, that it is not compatible with "civic humanism" as a form of Aristotelianism that sees taking part in democratic politics "as the privileged locus of the good life." Id. at 206.

Such a strong form of republicanism gives primacy to the liberties of the ancients rather than resolving the impasse between those liberties and the liberties of the moderns. See id. at 5, 206.

67. For a fuller statement of these two themes, see chapter 4.

68. By putting these two themes so schematically, I do not mean to imply that the realms of political self-government and personal self-government (or self-determination) are entirely distinct. To the contrary, for active, responsible citizens, deliberation concerning the common good in the political realm may be an important aspect of their pursuit of their conception of the good or of how to lead their own lives. See RAWLS, PL, supra note 34, at 206.

69. 539 U.S. at 562, 574.

70. 505 U.S. at 851 (joint opinion).

71. 478 U.S. at 217 (1986) (Stevens, J., dissenting) (quoting Fitzgerald v. Porter Mem. Hosp., 523 F.2d 716, 719–20 [7th Cir. 1975] [Stevens, J.] [footnotes omitted], *cert. denied*, 425 U.S. 916 [1976]).

72. *Casey*, 505 U.S. at 916 (Stevens, J., concurring in part and dissenting in part) (emphasis added).

73. See SUNSTEIN, PC, supra note 2, at 141, 373 n.18; Sunstein, *Beyond*, supra note 33, at 1566–71.

74. See SUNSTEIN, PC, supra note 2, at 141, 175, 186; see also Sunstein, *Beyond*, supra note 33, at 1567 (noting affinities between his synthesis, liberal republicanism, and Rawls's integration of the liberal tradition and republican thought).

75. See JOHN RAWLS, JUSTICE AS FAIRNESS: A RESTATEMENT 146 n.16, 148 (2001) (discussing deliberative democracy as an aspect of constitutional democracy and referring favorably to Sunstein's treatment of deliberative political discussion in Sunstein, *Beyond*, supra note 33).

76. See SUNSTEIN, PC, supra note 2, at 133–41. Sunstein acknowledges that his failure to say more about the "constitutionally central issue of religion" is a "significant gap" in *The Partial Constitution*. Cass R. Sunstein, *Liberal Constitutionalism and Liberal Justice*, 72 TEX. L. REV. 305, 311 n.29 (1993) (replying to James E. Fleming, *Constructing the Substantive Constitution*, 72 TEX. L. REV. 211 [1993]).

77. Sunstein, *Beyond*, supra note 33, at 1551 (citing RAWLS, TJ, supra note 51, at 205–21).

78. Id. at 1555 n.85. Sunstein further states that this exclusion of religion from politics has also been based "on the notion that religious conviction is a matter of private right." Id.

79. Id. (citing Stephen Holmes, *Gag Rules or the Politics of Omission*, in CONSTITUTIONALISM AND DEMOCRACY 19 [Jon Elster & Rune Slagstad eds., 1988]).

80. See West Virginia State Bd. of Educ. v. Barnette, 319 U.S. 624, 640–42 (1943) (recognizing the potential for oppression through any coercion of belief). Rawls recognizes both aspects of religious liberty. See RAWLS, PL, supra note 34, at 36–38, 134–40, 151–54; RAWLS, TJ, supra note 51, at 205–21.

81. 262 U.S. 390, 401–2 (1923).

82. 268 U.S. 510, 535 (1925).

83. 381 U.S. 479 (1965) (holding that a Connecticut statute that criminalized the use of contraceptives by married persons violated the right to privacy created by several fundamental constitutional guarantees).

84. 388 U.S. 1 (1967) (holding that a Virginia statute preventing interracial marriage violated both the Equal Protection and Due Process Clauses). The casebook Sunstein coauthored reprints, in the section on equal protection, the portion of Chief Justice Warren's opinion that holds that the miscegenation statute denied the Lovings equal protection but omits the portion that holds that the statute also deprived them of liberty without due process of law. Id. at 12; see GEOFFREY R. STONE, LOUIS M. SEIDMAN, CASS R. SUNSTEIN, MARK V. TUSHNET & PAMELA S. KARLAN, CONSTITUTIONAL LAW 529–31 (5th ed. 2005).

85. 410 U.S. 113 (1973) (holding that a Texas statute criminalizing abortions except those performed "for the purpose of saving the life of the mother" violated the right to privacy protected by the Due Process Clause).

86. 431 U.S. 494 (1977) (Powell, J., plurality opinion) (holding that a city ordinance limiting occupancy of a dwelling unit to members of a single family, and narrowly defining "family" to exclude certain extended family arrangements, violated the Due Process Clause).

87. 505 U.S. 833 (1992) (reaffirming the "central holding" of *Roe*, that the Due Process Clause protects the right of a woman to decide whether to terminate a pregnancy, but upholding certain aspects of Pennsylvania's abortion law while invalidating the spousal notification provision).

88. 539 U.S. 558 (2003) (overruling *Bowers* and holding that a law making it a crime for two persons of the same sex to engage in certain intimate sexual conduct violated homosexuals' right to privacy or autonomy protected by the Due Process Clause).

89. But see Cass R. Sunstein, *Sexual Orientation and the Constitution: A Note on the Relationship between Due Process and Equal Protection*, 55 U. CHI. L. REV. 1161, 1172, 1173 (1988) [hereinafter Sunstein, *Relationship*] (acknowledging that "tradition is sometimes treated as aspirational" and discussing the "references to tradition" in *Griswold*).

90. Jed Rubenfeld, *The Right of Privacy*, 102 HARV. L. REV. 737, 784 (1989) (emphasis in original). Rubenfeld emphasizes, for example, the profound sense in which laws restricting abortion reduce women to "mere instrumentalities of the state," and "take diverse women with every variety of career, life-plan, and so on, and make mothers of them all." Id. at 790, 788. I refer to the right to privacy or autonomy as an "antitotalitarian principle of liberty" to suggest a parallel with Sunstein's anticaste principle of equality. (I use the term "totalitarian" in Rubenfeld's sense, not the stronger sense applied to Nazi Germany or the Communist Soviet Union.)

91. See Cass R. Sunstein, Legal Reasoning and Political Conflict 155–56 (justifying *Griswold* on the basis of desuetude); Sunstein, *What Did* Lawrence *Hold?*, supra note 16, at 30, 48–52, 53–60 (justifying *Lawrence* on the ground of desuetude).

92. Sunstein, PC, supra note 2, at 136.

93. 539 U.S. at 562.

94. Sunstein, PC, supra note 2, at 257–61, 270–85.

95. Id. at 185–86.

96. Id. at 184.

97. Id. at 186. For a discussion of Rawls's conception of citizens as free and equal persons, see chapter 4.

98. 478 U.S. 186 (1986). I put to one side the question of whether the Privileges or Immunities Clause provides a firmer ground for protecting substantive liberties than the Due Process Clause. See, e.g., David A. J. Richards, Conscience and the Constitution 199–232 (1993) (arguing that the Privileges or Immunities Clause, not the Due Process Clause, expresses the nationalization of human rights); Laurence H. Tribe, American Constitutional Law § 7-4 (2d ed. 1988) (acknowledging that the Privileges or Immunities Clause has been historically eclipsed by the Due Process and Equal Protection Clauses, but suggesting that it is potentially robust as a basis for vindicating personal rights); see also Robert J. Kaczorowski, *Revolutionary Constitutionalism in the Era of the Civil War and Reconstruction*, 61 N.Y.U. L. Rev. 863, 925–28 (1986) (arguing that the privileges and immunities of citizenship comprehended by the Fourteenth Amendment provide a principled basis for protecting rights that are essential to the enjoyment of life, liberty, and property).

99. 539 U.S. 558 (2003).

100. 478 U.S. at 186. Accordingly, the Court upheld Georgia's statute that prohibited sodomy, as applied to consensual homosexual sodomy. The decision was by a narrow 5-4 majority. Subsequently, the Georgia Supreme Court invalidated, on state constitutional grounds, the very Georgia law upheld in *Bowers: Powell v. State*, 510 S.E.2d 18 (Ga. 1998). It ruled that private consensual sodomy is protected within the right to privacy guaranteed by the Georgia Constitution's due process clause. Ultimately, the U.S. Supreme Court overruled *Bowers* in *Lawrence*.

101. *Bowers*, 478 U.S. at 191.

102. See id. at 194–95.

103. Id. at 191 (quoting Palko v. Connecticut, 302 U.S. 319, 325 [1937] [Cardozo, J.]).

104. Id. at 192 (quoting Moore v. City of E. Cleveland, 431 U.S. 494, 503 [1977] [Powell, J., plurality opinion]).

105. Id. at 194.

106. Cf. Sunstein, *Legacy*, supra note 4, at 873 (discussing *Lochner* and *Brown* as examples of "defining cases").

107. See, e.g., Daniel O. Conkle, *The Second Death of Substantive Due Process*, 62 IND. L.J. 215, 242 (1987); cf. LAURENCE H. TRIBE & MICHAEL C. DORF, ON READING THE CONSTITUTION 55–60, 74–79, 116–17 (1991) (reading *Bowers* as a retreat from the right to privacy).

108. See Michael H. v. Gerald D., 491 U.S. 110, 127 n.6 (1989) (Scalia, J., plurality opinion); ROBERT H. BORK, THE TEMPTING OF AMERICA 116–26 (1990).

109. 300 U.S. 379 (1937).

110. Perhaps a more apt analogy is between *Bowers* and San Antonio Indep. Sch. Dist. v. Rodriguez, 411 U.S. 1 (1973). The latter case, without explicitly overruling any precedents, curbed the expansion of both the fundamental rights and the suspect classification branches of equal protection analysis, proclaiming that "[i]t is not the province of this Court to create substantive constitutional rights in the name of guaranteeing equal protection of the laws." Id. at 33. Just as *Rodriguez* took a "this far and no further" approach to "substantive equal protection," so too *Bowers* took a similar approach to substantive due process.

111. For the analogy between *Bowers* and Plessy v. Ferguson, 163 U.S. 537 (1896), see Sunstein, *Relationship*, supra note 89, at 1162 (quoting Watkins v. United States Army, 847 F.2d 1329, 1358 [9th Cir. 1988] [Reinhardt, J., dissenting], *withdrawn but aff'd*, 875 F.2d 699 [9th Cir. 1989] [*en banc*], *cert. denied*, 498 U.S. 957 [1990]). The analogy between *Bowers* and *Lochner* is suggested by Sunstein's analysis of *Bowers* in relation to status quo neutrality, epitomized in *Lochner*. See Sunstein, *Relationship*, supra note 89, at 1168–74. Before *Bowers* was decided, Ely argued that sexual orientation should be recognized as a suspect classification under the Equal Protection Clause, and he anticipated the analogy to *Plessy*. See ELY, DD, supra note 1, at 163.

112. 478 U.S. at 192–94. As Justice Stevens pointed out in dissent in *Bowers*, the historical "condemnation was equally damning for heterosexual and homosexual sodomy." Id. at 215 (Stevens, J., dissenting). And as Justice Blackmun retorted in dissent, quoting Holmes's dissent in *Lochner:* "[T]he fact that [such] moral judgment . . . may be 'natural and familiar . . . ought not to conclude our judgment upon the question whether statutes embodying them conflict with the Constitution of the United States.'" Id. at 199 (Blackmun, J., dissenting) (quoting Lochner v. New York, 198 U.S. 45, 76 [1905] [Holmes, J., dissenting]).

113. 163 U.S. at 550.

114. See SUNSTEIN, PC, supra note 2, at 131–32, 402 n.17; Sunstein, *Relationship*, supra note 89, at 1163, 1170–74, 1179. Sunstein concedes that due process and tradition are sometimes treated as "aspirational" rather than backward-looking and rooted in status quo neutrality. See Sunstein, *Relationship*, supra note 89, at 1173.

115. Sunstein, *Relationship*, supra note 89, at 1173–74.

116. See SUNSTEIN, PC, supra note 2, at 131–32, 136, 259–61, 402 n.17; Sunstein, *Relationship*, supra note 89, at 1163, 1174–75, 1179.

117. See Sunstein, *Relationship*, supra note 89, at 1162–70, 1175–79.

118. See TRIBE & DORF, supra note 107, at 115–16 (criticizing Sunstein's argument concerning the relationship between due process and equal protection "[a]s a matter of constitutional theory," but conceding that it might be a good proposal "as a matter of advocacy and legal strategy").

119. See ELY, DD, supra note 1, at 14–21, 82–87, 135–79; Ely, *Wages*, supra note 3, at 933–45.

120. RONALD DWORKIN, FREEDOM'S LAW: THE MORAL READING OF THE AMERICAN CONSTITUTION 73 (1996) [hereinafter DWORKIN, FL].

121. Id. (quoting *Palko*, 302 U.S. at 325). Dworkin himself, based on his earlier work elaborating equal concern and respect as a ground for rights, has been charged with trying to derive too much from equality and too little from liberty. See H. L. A. HART, *Between Utility and Rights*, in ESSAYS IN JURISPRUDENCE AND PHILOSOPHY 198, 214, 217, 221 (1983) (arguing that Dworkin has "sought to derive too much from the idea of equal concern and respect"; that "[w]hat is fundamentally wrong is the suggested interpretation of denials of freedom as denials of equal concern or respect"; and that as to certain denials of freedom, equality plays an "empty but misleading role" better performed by liberty or respect).

122. DWORKIN, FL, supra note 120, at 73.

123. 347 U.S. 497, 499 (1954) (emphasis added). (*Bolling* was the District of Columbia companion case to Brown v. Board of Education, 347 U.S. 483 [1954].) The Court continued: "[W]e do not imply that the two are always interchangeable phrases." Id. Hence, the Court held that although the Equal Protection Clause does not apply to the federal government, racially segregated public schools in the District of Columbia are unconstitutional under the Due Process Clause of the Fifth Amendment, which does apply.

124. See DWORKIN, FL, supra note 120, at 104–12; RONALD DWORKIN, LIFE'S DOMINION 16–72 (1993); *Casey*, 505 U.S. at 912, 915–20 (Stevens, J., concurring in part and dissenting in part).

125. See RONALD DWORKIN, SOVEREIGN VIRTUE: THE THEORY AND PRACTICE OF EQUALITY 453–65 (2000).

126. Cruzan v. Director, Mo. Dep't of Health, 497 U.S. 261, 294 (1990) (Scalia, J., concurring).

127. *Michael H.*, 491 U.S. at 123–27 & n.6 (Scalia, J., plurality opinion) (arguing in general that we should conceive constitutional rights at a highly specific level of generality and holding in particular that the Fourteenth Amendment does not protect a relationship between a biological father and a child whose mother was married to and cohabiting with another man at the time of the child's conception

and birth on the ground that such relationships have not been historically protected).

128. *Cruzan*, 497 U.S. at 301.

129. Id. at 300.

130. *Casey*, 505 U.S. at 998 (Scalia, J., concurring in the judgment in part and dissenting in part). For a critique of conservative or originalist invocation of the ghost of *Dred Scott* in criticizing *Roe* and *Casey*, see Christopher L. Eisgruber, Dred *Again: Originalism's Forgotten Past*, 10 CONST. COMMENT. 37, 46–50 (1993) (arguing that Chief Justice Taney's opinion of the Court in *Dred Scott* embraced a version of originalism).

131. See *Michael H.*, 491 U.S. at 127 n.6 (Scalia, J., plurality opinion); *Cruzan*, 497 U.S. at 294 (Scalia, J., concurring).

132. See SUNSTEIN, PC, supra note 2, at 130 (interpreting Scalia as a Burkean defender of status quo neutrality as a baseline and referring to EDMUND BURKE, REFLECTIONS ON THE REVOLUTION IN FRANCE [1790]).

133. See Thayer, *Origin*, supra note 24, at 156 ("[U]nder no system can the power of courts go far to save a people from ruin; our chief protection lies elsewhere").

134. See Sanford Levinson, *The Democratic Faith of Felix Frankfurter*, 25 STAN. L. REV. 430, 439 (1973) (interpreting Frankfurter's theory of "judicial restraint" as rooted in a "democratic faith" and a conviction that "the Court had abused beyond salvation" its limited mandate through its interpretation of the Due Process Clauses during the era of *Lochner*); see also SANFORD LEVINSON, CONSTITUTIONAL FAITH 3–4 (1988) (discussing Frankfurter's constitutional faith).

135. See Grutter v. Bollinger, 539 U.S. 306, 346 (2003) (Scalia, J., concurring in part and dissenting in part); City of Richmond v. J. A. Croson Co., 488 U.S. 469, 528 (1989) (Scalia, J., concurring); see also Antonin Scalia, *The Disease as Cure*, 1979 WASH. U. L.Q. 147.

136. See Sunstein, *What Did* Lawrence *Hold?*, supra note 16; chapter 7.

137. See Laurence H. Tribe, *The Puzzling Persistence of Process-Based Constitutional Theories*, 89 YALE L.J. 1063, 1072–77 (1980) (arguing that Ely's theory should be complemented with rights derived from a conception of the person, intimate association, and what is needed to realize one's humanity); Ronald Dworkin, *The Forum of Principle*, 56 N.Y.U. L. REV. 469, 510–16 (1981), *reprinted in* DWORKIN, AMOP, supra note 43, at 33, 65–69 (contending that Ely's theory presupposes a conception of moral independence).

138. See SUNSTEIN, PC, supra note 2, at 270–85. Sunstein's analysis of a woman's right to abortion, although it emphasizes equality rather than liberty, and indeed unnecessarily puts in doubt the due process justification for such a right, see id. at 285, appears to resort to notions like autonomy and independence, not just an anticaste principle of equality. In this respect, it is telling that Sunstein acknowledges his debt to two classic articles—involving samaritanism and antisubordination—that intertwine privacy and equality, although he criticizes

them for not sufficiently emphasizing issues of equality. See id. at 396 n.21 (citing Judith J. Thomson, *A Defense of Abortion*, 1 PHIL. & PUB. AFF. 47 [1971]; Donald Regan, *Rewriting* Roe v. Wade, 77 MICH. L. REV. 1569 [1979]).

139. 539 U.S. at 562.

140. Id. at 575; see chapter 7. Sunstein's analysis of the holding in *Lawrence* acknowledges both the autonomy strand and the equality strand of the decision, though he argues for interpreting the decision as justifiable on the ground of desuetude. See Sunstein, *What Did* Lawrence *Hold?*, supra note 16, at 29–30.

141. See Adarand Constructors v. Pena, 515 U.S. 200 (1995) (applying strict scrutiny "consistently" to racial classifications, whether they disadvantage racial minorities or benefit them, for example, through affirmative action programs). The majority, however, stopped short of embracing the strong conception of racial neutrality or color-blindness advocated by Justices Scalia and Thomas. Id. at 237 (acknowledging that affirmative action programs may be justifiable to eliminate the "lingering effects of racial discrimination against minority groups"). Justice Stevens's dissent argued for an anticaste conception of equal protection. Id. at 243 (arguing that "[t]here is no moral or constitutional equivalence between a policy that is designed to perpetuate a caste system and one that seeks to eradicate racial subordination") (Stevens, J., dissenting).

142. See Sunstein, *Relationship*, supra note 89, at 1170, 1173.

143. *Bolling*, 347 U.S. at 499 (emphasis added).

144. DWORKIN, FL, supra note 120, at 73.

145. *Lawrence*, 539 U.S. at 562.

146. See Olmstead v. United States, 277 U.S. 438, 478 (1928) (Brandeis, J., dissenting). In his dissent in *Bowers*, Justice Blackmun quotes Brandeis's famous formulation of the right to privacy as "the right to be let alone." *Bowers*, 478 U.S. at 199 (Blackmun, J., dissenting); cf. ELY, DD, supra note 1, at 178–79 (analogizing the tradition of the frontier, and the right of "dissenting or 'different' individuals" to relocate, to the "exit" option as distinguished from the "voice" option). For discussion of the idea of an "exit" option or the "frontier" in constitutional law, see chapter 5.

147. But see SUNSTEIN, PC, supra note 2, at v–vi (distinguishing "partial" in the sense of biased and "partial" in the sense of not whole).

## Chapter Four

1. JOHN RAWLS, POLITICAL LIBERALISM (1993) [hereinafter RAWLS, PL].

2. See chapter 1 (discussing JOHN HART ELY, DEMOCRACY AND DISTRUST [1980] [hereinafter ELY, DD], and CASS R. SUNSTEIN, THE PARTIAL CONSTITUTION [1993]) [hereinafter SUNSTEIN, PC]).

3. See RAWLS, PL, supra note 1, at xiv–xxi, xxvii–xxx, 89–129. See generally id. at 89–129 (developing the notion of political constructivism). Rawls initially put

forward his theory, justice as fairness, in fully elaborated form in *A Theory of Justice*. JOHN RAWLS, A THEORY OF JUSTICE (1971) [hereinafter RAWLS, TJ]. For a brief account of the major changes between *A Theory of Justice* and *Political Liberalism*, see RAWLS, PL, supra note 1, at xv–xvii. To the degree that the latter book makes Rawls's political conception of justice appear less universal, and so perhaps less interesting to some political philosophers, it may make his conception more immediately applicable to American constitutional theory and hence more interesting to constitutional theorists. That is, the more limited or parochial Rawls's aim, as a matter of political philosophy, the more directly he speaks to constitutional theorists and citizens in our constitutional democracy.

4. See RAWLS, PL, supra note 1, at 3–22.

5. See id. at 90–99.

6. See id. at 28, 93–99, 107–10.

7. Id. at 3.

8. See id., passim.

9. For Dworkin's formulations of the two dimensions of best interpretation, fit and justification, see, e.g., RONALD DWORKIN, LAW'S EMPIRE 239 (1986); RONALD DWORKIN, A MATTER OF PRINCIPLE 119, 143–45 (1986) [hereinafter DWORKIN, AMOP]. For another development of a constructivism in a general methodological sense, see Richard H. Fallon Jr., *A Constructivist Coherence Theory of Constitutional Interpretation*, 100 HARV. L. REV. 1189 (1987).

10. See RONALD DWORKIN, TAKING RIGHTS SERIOUSLY 159–68 (1977) [hereinafter DWORKIN, TRS]. In developing a constitutional constructivism, I am not engaged in quests for certainty and for deep foundations for constitutional law. For an insightful critique of grand constitutional theories as being engaged in such quests, see DANIEL A. FARBER & SUZANNA SHERRY, DESPERATELY SEEKING CERTAINTY: THE MISGUIDED QUEST FOR CONSTITUTIONAL FOUNDATIONS (2002).

11. Dworkin has formulated the two dimensions of best interpretation, fit and justification, in several ways. See supra note 9. In some formulations, he speaks of a dimension of fit and a dimension of political morality. Rawls expresses reservations about "political morality" as a formulation of the second dimension, for it may appear too broad. RAWLS, PL, supra note 1, at 236 n.23. He instead formulates "best interpretation" as "the one that best fits the relevant body of [constitutional] materials, and justifies it in terms of the public conception of justice or a reasonable variant thereof." Id. at 236. He concludes, however: "I doubt that this view differs in substance from Dworkin's." Id. at 237 n.23.

12. ARISTOTLE, THE POLITICS OF ARISTOTLE bk. I, ch. II, §§ 15–16, at 1253a (Ernest Barker trans. & ed., 1948).

13. RAWLS, TJ, supra note 3, at 243.

14. See ARISTOTLE, supra note 12, at 1253a; see also RAWLS, PL, supra note 1, at 134; RAWLS, TJ, supra note 3, at 25, 325 (both interpreting Aristotle's theories).

15. See RAWLS, PL, supra note 1, at xxiii–xxx, 3–11, 134–37, 303–4.

16. For a brief discussion of the difference between justice as fairness as a political liberalism and justice as fairness as a comprehensive liberalism, see id. at xv–xviii.

17. See id. at 37, 144.

18. Id. at 37.

19. See id. at 9–10, 154.

20. See id., passim.

21. See id. at 6, 223, 295.

22. See id. at 174–76, 190–95, 203–9.

23. Id. at 5–6.

24. Id. at 291.

25. Id. at 292–93, 325.

26. Id. at 28; see id. at 66–71; John Rawls, *Kantian Constructivism in Moral Theory* (1980) [hereinafter Rawls, *Kantian Constructivism*], *reprinted in* JOHN RAWLS, COLLECTED PAPERS 303, 340–58 (Samuel Freeman ed., 1999) [hereinafter RAWLS, COLLECTED PAPERS].

27. See RAWLS, PL, supra note 1, at 13–14, 78.

28. Id. at 28, 66–71; see also Rawls, *Kantian Constructivism*, supra note 26, at 340–58; John Rawls, *Reply to Habermas*, 92 J. PHIL. 132, 156–70 (1995) [hereinafter Rawls, *Reply*] (responding to the charge that his political liberalism is such a theory advanced in Jürgen Habermas, *Reconciliation through the Public Use of Reason: Remarks on John Rawls'* Political Liberalism, 92 J. PHIL. 109, 128–31 [1995]).

29. See Frank I. Michelman, *On Regulating Practices with Theories Drawn from Them: A Case of Justice as Fairness*, in NOMOS: THEORY AND PRACTICE 309 (Ian Shapiro & Judith Wagner DeCew eds., 1995).

30. See RAWLS, PL, supra note 1, at 336–40; RAWLS, TJ, supra note 3, at 194–201. For Rawls's account of the original position, see RAWLS, PL, supra note 1, at 22–28, 304–10.

31. See RAWLS, PL, supra note 1, at 227.

32. Id. at 228–29, 232, 298; see also id. at 164–68, 236 n.23 (explaining that the overlapping consensus concerning the political conception of justice encompasses such rights and liberties). Notably, the constitutional essentials do not include Rawls's famous "difference principle," that "[s]ocial and economic inequalities . . . are to be to the greatest benefit of the least advantaged members of society." Id. at 6–7, 228–30, 337. Moreover, the right to basic necessities may not be judicially enforceable in the absence of legislative or executive measures. Similarly, the right to personal property may be judicially underenforced. See chapter 6.

In *The Law of Peoples*, Rawls argues that a liberal political conception of justice and a reasonably just constitutional democracy must ensure "sufficient all-purpose means to enable all citizens to make intelligent and effective use of their freedoms." JOHN RAWLS, THE LAW OF PEOPLES 49 (1999). He mentions five kinds of institutions or arrangements that are necessary to prevent "social and economic inequalities from becoming excessive" and to achieve stability: (1) "[a] certain fair equality of opportunity"; (2) "[a] decent distribution of income and wealth"; (3) "[s]ociety as employer of last resort"; (4) "[b]asic health care assured for all citizens"; and (5) "[p]ublic financing of elections and ways of assuring the availability of public information on matters of policy." Id. at 49, 50.

33. RAWLS, PL, supra note 1, at 228–30, 337.

34. Id. at 337.

35. See id. at 233 n.18, 362–63.

36. Id. at 231–34 (referring to BRUCE ACKERMAN, WE THE PEOPLE: FOUNDATIONS [1991]). But see infra note 86 (distinguishing between a commitment to dualism in a general sense and a commitment to dualism in Ackerman's specific sense).

37. See RAWLS, PL, supra note 1, at 233, 240. I put to one side the question of whether judicial review is a necessary requirement in a constitutional democracy; suffice it to say that judicial review exists as an institutional device for preserving the higher law of the constitution in some existing constitutional democracies, such as our own.

38. See id. at 15–20, 29–35, 299–304.

39. See id. at 19, 302, 332.

40. See id. at 19, 302, 332, 335.

41. See id. at 19, 29–35, 79, 109; RAWLS, TJ, supra note 3, at 504–12.

42. See RAWLS, PL, supra note 1, at 332.

43. Id. at 18 n.20, 86–88. At the same time, Rawls does posit a "reasonable moral psychology" whereby citizens "want to be, and to be recognized as, . . . members" of society. Id. at 81, 86.

44. See id. at 332–35. I use Sunstein's term, "deliberative democracy," to refer to this first fundamental case or theme in order to emphasize its similarity to Sunstein's principal theme. Rawls also speaks of "deliberative democracy" as an aspect of constitutional democracy. See JOHN RAWLS, JUSTICE AS FAIRNESS: A RESTATEMENT 148 (2001) [hereinafter RAWLS, JF]; see also RAWLS, PL, supra note 1, at 214 n.3 (speaking of "deliberative democracy" as an aspect of political liberalism).

45. See RAWLS, PL, supra note 1, at 337.

46. Id. Rawls treats the equal political liberties in a special way: "by including in the first principle of justice the guarantee that the political liberties, and only these liberties, are secured by [guaranteeing] their 'fair value.'" Id. at 327. Rawls explains that "this guarantee means that the worth of the political liberties to all citizens, whatever their social or economic position, must be approximately equal, or at least sufficiently equal, in the sense that everyone has a fair opportunity to hold public office and to influence the outcome of political decisions." Id. "Formal equality is not enough" where the equal political liberties are concerned. Id. at 361.

47. Id. at 335, 337.

48. See id. at 332–35. I use the term "deliberative autonomy" to refer to this second fundamental case or theme for four reasons: first, to emphasize that the idea builds on Rawls's idea of persons' second moral power, the capacity for a conception of the good, as the power of "deliberative reason," see supra text accompanying note 40; second, to recognize its similarity to Justice Stevens's analysis of "decisional autonomy" in terms of "deliberation" about important decisions concerning how to live one's own life, see chapter 5; third, to suggest parallels between the structure of "deliberative" autonomy and that of "deliberative" democracy; and fourth, to acknowledge affinities between constitutional constructivism and other theories that conceive our Constitution as a scheme of deliberative or reflective self-government, see chapter 5.

Deliberative autonomy includes not only deliberation but also decisionmaking. For the sake of simplicity, I intend to encompass the concepts of "deliberating about and deciding how to live their own lives" within the expressions "deliberative autonomy" or "deliberating about their conception of the good."

49. See RAWLS, PL, supra note 1, at 337–38.

50. See id. at 335–38.

51. Id. at 335. The rights and liberties covered by the rule of law include, for example, procedural due process, habeas corpus, freedom from unreasonable searches and seizures, and freedom from self-incrimination. See RAWLS, TJ, supra note 3, at 235–43; Samuel Freeman, *Original Meaning, Democratic Interpretation, and the Constitution*, 21 PHIL. & PUB. AFF. 3, 26, 31 (1992).

52. See RAWLS, PL, supra note 1, at 335.

53. See Freeman, supra note 51, at 30–33 (arguing that equal political rights and other basic liberties such as liberty of conscience and freedom of association are essential to democratic sovereignty).

54. RAWLS, PL, supra note 1, at 368.

55. Id. at 156, 368. On the idea of a guiding framework for deliberation, reflection, and judgment, see RAWLS, TJ, supra note 3, at 53; Rawls, *Kantian Constructivism*, supra note 26, at 346–51.

56. See RAWLS, PL, supra note 1, at 156, 368 (arguing that the proper role of his conception of justice is as a framework that may help others in their deliberations on constitutional essentials).

57. See infra text accompanying notes 106–14 (arguing that constitutional constructivism better satisfies Ely's three criteria for an acceptable theory than does his own theory).

58. For a work organizing constitutional interpretation on the basis of these three fundamental interrogatives, see WALTER F. MURPHY, JAMES E. FLEMING, SOTIRIOS A. BARBER & STEPHEN MACEDO, AMERICAN CONSTITUTIONAL INTERPRETATION (3d ed. 2003).

59. See RONALD DWORKIN, LIFE'S DOMINION 119, 126–29 (1993) (contrasting a "constitution of principle" [a scheme of abstract, normative principles] with a "constitution of detail" [a list of specific, antique rules] [emphasis omitted]); see

also Lawrence v. Texas, 539 U.S. 558, 578–79 (2003) ("Had those who drew and ratified the Due Process Clauses of the Fifth Amendment or the Fourteenth Amendment known the components of liberty in its manifold possibilities, they might have been more specific. They did not presume to have this insight. . . . As the Constitution endures, persons in every generation can invoke its principles in their own search for greater freedom"); Planned Parenthood v. Casey, 505 U.S. 833, 901 (1992) (joint opinion) (conceiving the Constitution as a "covenant" or "coherent succession" embodying "ideas and aspirations that must survive more ages than one").

60. See *Casey*, 505 U.S. at 849 (joint opinion); see also Poe v. Ullman, 367 U.S. 497, 542 (1961) (Harlan, J., dissenting) (conceiving judgment as a "rational process"); cf. RAWLS, PL, supra note 1, at 222 (discussing "reasoned judgment").

61. See RAWLS, PL, supra note 1, at 236 & n.23. For the two dimensions of best interpretation, fit and justification, see supra note 9.

62. See id. at 232–33, 237. Constitutional constructivism entails a "protestant" conception of *who* may interpret the Constitution. See SANFORD LEVINSON, CONSTITUTIONAL FAITH 29, 9–53 (1988) ("As to the ultimate authority to interpret the source of doctrine, the protestant position is based on the legitimacy of individualized [or at least nonhierarchical communal] interpretation"); see also Michelman, supra note 29, at 325–36 (arguing that Rawls's political liberalism rejects "judicial supremacy"); Frank I. Michelman, *Justice as Fairness, Legitimacy, and the Question of Judicial Review: A Comment*, 72 FORDHAM L. REV. 1407 (2004) (analyzing what Rawls wrote about the question of judicial review). For more radical "protestant" conceptions insisting that the people themselves, not courts, are the ultimate interpreters of the Constitution, see, e.g., MARK TUSHNET, TAKING THE CONSTITUTION AWAY FROM THE COURTS (1999); LARRY D. KRAMER, THE PEOPLE THEMSELVES: POPULAR CONSTITUTIONALISM AND JUDICIAL REVIEW (2004). I have constructively engaged with the arguments of these two books in James E. Fleming, *The Constitution Outside the Courts*, 86 CORNELL L. REV. 215 (2000) (reviewing TUSHNET, supra) [hereinafter Fleming, *Outside*], and James E. Fleming, *Judicial Review without Judicial Supremacy: Taking the Constitution Seriously Outside the Courts*, 73 FORDHAM L. REV. 1377 (2005) (analyzing KRAMER, supra) [hereinafter Fleming, *Judicial Supremacy*].

63. See RAWLS, PL, supra note 1, at 240. Others have expressed similar views concerning the gap between the judicially enforceable Constitution and the Constitution that is binding outside the courts. See, e.g., SUNSTEIN, PC, supra note 2, at 9–10, 138–40, 145–61, 350; LAWRENCE G. SAGER, JUSTICE IN PLAINCLOTHES: A THEORY OF AMERICAN CONSTITUTIONAL PRACTICE 84–128 (2004) [hereinafter SAGER, PLAINCLOTHES]; Lawrence G. Sager, *The Why of Constitutional Essentials*, 72 FORDHAM L. REV. 1421 (2004); Frank I. Michelman, *Rawls on Constitutionalism and Constitutional Law*, in THE CAMBRIDGE COMPANION TO RAWLS 394 (Samuel Freeman ed., 2003).

64. RAWLS, PL, supra note 1, at 231, 235–37, 240 (referring to Dworkin's notion of courts as a "forum of principle," in Ronald Dworkin, *The Forum of Principle*, 56 N.Y.U. L. REV. 469, 516–18 [1981] [hereinafter Dworkin, *Forum*], *reprinted in* DWORKIN, AMOP, supra note 9, at 33, 69–71 [1985]).

65. See, e.g., SUNSTEIN, PC, supra note 2, at 145–53. It is not the role of courts to say in the first instance what arrangements are necessary to secure the preconditions for deliberative democracy and deliberative autonomy, but to ensure that the arrangements enacted by legislatures do not flout these preconditions. See RAWLS, PL, supra note 1, at 362.

66. See RAWLS, PL, supra note 1, at 219–20, 359–63; RAWLS, TJ, supra note 3, at 221–28, 356–62.

67. See RAWLS, PL, supra note 1, at 79–81, 335. Rawls himself does not provide any systematic discussion of homosexuality or sexual orientation. In discussing the idea of public reason, he gives examples of arguments concerning same-sex marriage. See John Rawls, *The Idea of Public Reason Revisited* (1997) [hereinafter Rawls, *Revisited*], *reprinted in* RAWLS, COLLECTED PAPERS, supra note 26, at 573, 587, 588, 596 n.60.

68. 304 U.S. 144, 152–53 n.4 (1938).

69. See RAWLS, PL, supra note 1, at 213–20, 223–30; Freeman, supra note 51, at 17, 20–29.

70. Rawls speaks of the limits of public reason as imposing "a moral, not a legal, duty—the duty of civility." RAWLS, PL, supra note 1, at 217. He subsequently added: "I emphasize that [the moral duty of civility] is not a legal duty, for in that case it would be incompatible with freedom of speech." Rawls, *Revisited*, supra note 67, at 577. Rawls suggests that the idea of public reason does not forbid citizens to rely on their religious beliefs in public discussions of political matters, provided that they also in due course support their political proposals in terms of the values of public reason. See id. at 584, 591–94 (discussing "wide" view of public reason); RAWLS, PL, supra note 1, at 247–54 (adopting an "inclusive" view of public reason). For valuable discussions and applications of Rawls's idea of public reason to constitutional theory, see Samuel Freeman, *Political Liberalism and the Possibility of a Just Democratic Constitution*, 69 CHI.-KENT L. REV. 619 (1994); Lawrence B. Solum, *Inclusive Public Reason*, 75 PAC. PHIL. Q. 217 (1994); Edward B. Foley, *Political Liberalism and Establishment Clause Jurisprudence*, 43 CASE W. RES. L. REV. 963 (1993); see also Samuel Freeman, *Public Reason and Political Justifications*, 72 FORDHAM L. REV. 2021 (2004).

71. Securing deliberative autonomy would not involve Lochnering in Sunstein's sense, for these constraints on deliberative democracy are not reflections of status quo neutrality. Instead, they are rooted in a conception of citizens as free and equal and of what is necessary for the development and exercise of their two moral powers.

72. See RAWLS, PL, supra note 1, at 6, 223, 295.

73. Id. at 294–99.

74. See id. at 359–63 (critiquing Buckley v. Valeo, 424 U.S. 1 [1976]). For fuller discussion of Rawls's critique of *Buckley* and his idea of guaranteeing the fair value of the equal political liberties, see chapter 8.

75. ALEXANDER MEIKLEJOHN, FREE SPEECH AND ITS RELATION TO SELF-GOVERNMENT, in POLITICAL FREEDOM: THE CONSTITUTIONAL POWERS OF THE PEOPLE 3 (1965).

76. See RAWLS, PL, supra note 1, at 290 n.1.

77. Id. at 319; see ELY, DD, supra note 2, at 101–4.

78. Fleming, *Outside*, supra note 62. I also have taken up the arguments against judicial supremacy in KRAMER, supra note 62, and the arguments for judicial underenforcement of certain constitutional norms in SAGER, PLAIN-CLOTHES, supra note 63. See Fleming, *Judicial Supremacy*, supra note 62.

79. Cf. Richmond Newspapers, Inc. v. Virginia, 448 U.S. 555, 587 (1980) (Brennan, J., concurring in the judgment) ("[T]he First Amendment . . . has a structural role to play in securing and fostering our republican system of self-government").

80. Contra ROBERT H. BORK, THE TEMPTING OF AMERICA 120, 351–55, passim (1990) (asserting that protection of substantive rights such as privacy ignores original understanding and illegitimately imposes on democracy rights derived from abstract moral philosophy); ELY, DD, supra note 2, at 56–60 (suggesting that protection of substantive fundamental values like autonomy illegitimately superimposes on democracy the "reason" of moral philosophers or philosopher-kings).

81. Cf. THE REPUBLIC OF PLATO bk. II, at 368e, bk. VIII, at 543c–545c (Francis MacDonald Cornford trans., 1941).

82. See Gibbons v. Ogden, 22 U.S. (9 Wheat.) 1, 220 (1824) (Marshall, C.J.) (criticizing antifederalists, who argued for a narrow construction of the Constitution in general and the commerce power in particular, contending that they would "explain away the constitution of our country, and leave it, a magnificent structure, indeed, to look at, but totally unfit for use"). On narrow conceptions of originalism as forms of "ancestor worship," see Freeman, supra note 51, at 16.

83. By "homology" or "homologous," I mean "having the same relation to an original or fundamental type; corresponding in type of structure." 5 The Oxford English Dictionary 359 (1933). The term "homology" also connotes "symmetry in organization." Id. For a sophisticated analysis of homologies in constitutional interpretation, see WILLIAM F. HARRIS II, THE INTERPRETABLE CONSTITUTION (1993).

84. Cf. Charles L. Black Jr., *On Reading and Using the Ninth Amendment*, in 1 THE RIGHTS RETAINED BY THE PEOPLE: THE HISTORY AND MEANING OF THE NINTH AMENDMENT 337, 349 (Randy Barnett ed., 1989) ("This process of combination has naturally engendered some new ideas; even two musical tones, sounded together, produce a third").

85. In speaking of "anomalies," I echo THOMAS S. KUHN, THE STRUCTURE OF SCIENTIFIC REVOLUTIONS 52–53 (enlarged 2d ed. 1970). In referring to "add-ons," I am following Freeman, supra note 51, at 41.

86. Constitutional constructivism is dualist in a general sense without being committed to dualism in the specific sense of Bruce Ackerman's theory of dualist democracy. See ACKERMAN, supra note 36, at 3–33. That is, it accepts the idea of two tracks of lawmaking without endorsing his complex apparatus of higher lawmaking through "structural amendments" to the Constitution outside the formal Article V amending procedures.

87. See Marbury v. Madison, 5 U.S. (1 Cranch) 137, 177–78 (1803); THE FEDERALIST No. 78, at 467, 469 (Alexander Hamilton) (Clinton Rossiter ed., 1961).

88. See ACKERMAN, supra note 36, at 7–10, 35 (coining the term "monism").

89. See chapter 3.

90. For formulations of the tension between the competing traditions of constitutionalism and democracy along these lines, and of constitutional democracy as a hybrid form of government, see, e.g., MURPHY, FLEMING, BARBER & MACEDO, supra note 58, at 43–59; Walter F. Murphy, *An Ordering of Constitutional Values*, 53 S. CAL. L. REV. 703, 707–8 (1980); see also HARRIS, supra note 83, at 162 (speaking of the "tense juncture of liberalism and democracy which, as substantive political models oriented alternatively to individual- and collective-oriented rights, underlie the American constitutional enterprise"); CHARLES H. MCILWAIN, CONSTITUTIONALISM: ANCIENT AND MODERN 129–46 (rev. ed. 1947) (tension between *jurisdictio*, the restriction of power by judicial proclamation of rights, and *gubernaculum*, the concentrated exercise of power for the common good); GIOVANNI SARTORI, DEMOCRATIC THEORY 353–83 (2d ed. 1962) (tension between *liberalism*, concerned with limited government, freedom, the rights of the individual, and the rule of law, and *democracy*, concerned with unfettered majority rule, equality, general welfare, and the rule of legislators). Sunstein claims to dissolve "the much-vaunted opposition between constitutionalism and democracy" through his theory of deliberative democracy. *See* SUNSTEIN, PC, supra note 2, at 142. But he does so by either recasting constitutionalist rights as preconditions for democracy or leaving them out altogether.

For powerful recent formulations of constitutional self-government that seek to reconcile the tensions between constitutionalism and democracy, see CHRISTOPHER L. EISGRUBER, CONSTITUTIONAL SELF-GOVERNMENT (2001); JED RUBENFELD, FREEDOM AND TIME: A THEORY OF CONSTITUTIONAL SELF-GOVERNMENT (2001); and the symposium critiquing these books, SYMPOSIUM: THEORIES OF CONSTITUTIONAL SELF-GOVERNMENT, 71 FORDHAM L. REV. 1721 (2003). For my critique, see James E. Fleming, *The Missing Selves in Constitutional Self-Government*, 71 FORDHAM L. REV. 1789 (2003).

91. 3 U.S. (3 Dall.) 386, 388 (1798). One scholar, reflecting on the bicentennial of *Calder*—and its classic debate between Justices Chase as constitutional idealist and Iredell as constitutional skeptic—characterizes my theory as that of

a latter-day Justice Chase (and Jeremy Waldron's theory, e.g., in his LAW AND DISAGREEMENT [1999], as that of a latter-day Justice Iredell). See Edward B. Foley, *The Bicentennial of* Calder v. Bull: *In Defense of a Democratic Middle Ground*, 59 OHIO ST. L.J. 1599 (1998).

92. 6 F. Cas. 546, 551 (C.C.E.D. Pa. 1823) (No. 3,230) (Washington, J., riding circuit).

93. See RAWLS, JF, supra note 44, at § 44; RAWLS, PL, supra note 1, at 233–34.

94. MURPHY, FLEMING, BARBER & MACEDO, supra note 58, at 43.

95. See RAWLS, PL, supra note 1, at 233–34. By using "counter-majoritarian" and "deviant," I am echoing Bickel's famous formulation of the idea that judicial review poses a "counter-majoritarian difficulty" or is a "deviant institution" in a representative democracy. ALEXANDER M. BICKEL, THE LEAST DANGEROUS BRANCH: THE SUPREME COURT AT THE BAR OF POLITICS 16, 18 (1962).

96. To the contrary, for active, responsible citizens, deliberation concerning the common good in the political realm may be an important aspect of their pursuit of their conception of the good or of how to lead their own lives. See RAWLS, PL, supra note 1, at 206.

97. See Frank I. Michelman, *Law's Republic*, 97 YALE L.J. 1493, 1524–37 (1988).

98. Compare Sunstein's critique of Ely for apparently assuming that democracy is a relatively uncontroversial notion. SUNSTEIN, PC, supra note 2, at 104–5 (criticizing ELY, DD, supra note 2). Yet Sunstein himself is vulnerable to a similar critique regarding autonomy, for he asserts, without justification, that protecting certain rights in the name of reinforcing democracy is "less adventurous" than protecting the very same rights in the name of securing autonomy. See Cass R. Sunstein, *Liberal Constitutionalism and Liberal Justice*, 72 TEX. L. REV. 305, 312 (1993) (replying to James E. Fleming, *Constructing the Substantive Constitution*, 72 TEX. L. REV. 211, 260–75 [1993]).

99. My argument here parallels that of Rawls in replying to Habermas's charge that Rawls's political liberalism treats the "modern liberties" or "private autonomy" as "prepolitical" or "prior to all political will formation." See Rawls, *Reply*, supra note 28, at 156–70 (replying to Habermas, supra note 28, at 128–31). Rawls argues that the "liberties of the moderns" (which I relate to deliberative autonomy) and the "liberties of the ancients" (which I associate with deliberative democracy) are "co-original and of equal weight." Id. at 163.

100. For examples of such critiques, see, e.g., BENJAMIN R. BARBER, STRONG DEMOCRACY: PARTICIPATORY POLITICS FOR A NEW AGE 30–32, 43–44, 142–43 (1984) (from standpoint of civic republicanism); Habermas, supra note 28 (from standpoint of discourse ethics). For Rawls's reply to Habermas's critique, see Rawls, *Reply*, supra note 28, at 156–70.

101. For critiques along these lines, see, e.g., BORK, supra note 80, at 139; ELY, DD, supra note 2, at 100–1.

102. See RONALD DWORKIN, FREEDOM'S LAW: THE MORAL READING OF THE AMERICAN CONSTITUTION (1996) [hereinafter DWORKIN, FL] (criticizing "majoritarian" conceptions of democracy that accept "the majoritarian premise," or the principle that when a group or polity must make a collective decision, fairness requires the decision favored by a majority of its members; arguing for a "constitutional" conception of democracy that defines democracy as requiring that certain preconditions of democratic legitimacy be satisfied [which for Dworkin include rights of moral independence or autonomy]); Lawrence G. Sager, *The Incorrigible Constitution*, 65 N.Y.U. L. REV. 893, 897–909 (1990) (criticizing majoritarian theories of popular sovereignty on the ground that they are beset by the "majoritarian difficulty" and are irreconcilable with the Constitution, which places limits on majoritarianism).

103. Cf. CATHARINE A. MACKINNON, TOWARD A FEMINIST THEORY OF THE STATE 3 (1989) ("Marxism and feminism are one and that one is Marxism") (citation omitted).

104. By "elegant," I mean to suggest the notion of elegance in the construction of scientific theories. Ely emphasizes that the value of *Democracy and Distrust*, which elaborates the *Carolene Products* framework, is that it (elegantly) frames the appropriate set of questions for constitutional interpretation. See *Commentary*, 56 N.Y.U. L. REV. 525, 528 (1981) (statement of Ely). I contend that my guiding framework has a similar value, although of course it frames the appropriate questions differently.

105. ELY, supra note 2, at 75–88.

106. See id. at 88, 87–101 (arguing from "the nature of the United States Constitution" for a "representation-reinforcing approach to judicial review" rather than a substantive value-protecting approach).

107. Id. at 102; see id. at 88.

108. See DWORKIN, FL, supra note 102, at 75 (characterizing Ely's theory as adopting an "'external' revisionist strategy" that "plainly begs the question" what conception of democracy the Constitution establishes and that "rewrites [the Constitution] to make it more congenial to what the revisionists consider the best theory of democracy").

109. ELY, supra note 2, at 102; see id. at 88, 103.

110. See Dworkin, *Forum*, supra note 64, at 516–18.

111. See RAWLS, PL, supra note 1, at 240.

112. See DWORKIN, TRS, supra note 10, at 14–45, 46–80, 87–88, 104–5, 126, 160–62 (contrasting the constructivist model of principles with the positivist model of rules as different conceptions of the rule of law and arguing for the former as superior to the latter). Contrast Scalia's positivist understanding of the rule of law as a law of rules (or, as I like to put it, the rule of rules). See Antonin Scalia, *The Rule of Law as a Law of Rules*, 56 U. CHI. L. REV. 1175 (1989). For a valuable analysis of the model of principles and the model of rules as competing understandings of the

ideal of the rule of law, see Gregory C. Keating, *Fidelity to Pre-existing Law and the Legitimacy of Legal Decision*, 69 NOTRE DAME L. REV. 1 (1993).

113. West Virginia State Bd. of Educ. v. Barnette, 319 U.S. 624, 638, 640 (1943), *overruling* Minersville Sch. Dist. v. Gobitis, 310 U.S. 586 (1940). In *Gobitis*, Justice Frankfurter's opinion of the Court emphasized that courts "possess no marked and certainly no controlling competence" as compared with state legislatures and school boards in deciding whether compelling a salute to the flag inculcates patriotism. *Gobitis*, 310 U.S. at 597–98.

114. See chapter 2.

115. See BORK, supra note 80, at 210–14, 351–55; Henry P. Monaghan, *Our Perfect Constitution*, 56 N.Y.U. L. REV. 353, 356 (1981).

116. See John Hart Ely, *Democracy and the Right to Be Different*, 56 N.Y.U. L. REV. 397, 401 (1981) (quoting paraphrase of Lochner v. New York, 198 U.S. 45, 75 [1905] [Holmes, J., dissenting] with respect to John Stuart Mill's *On Liberty*). But see Commonwealth v. Wasson, 842 S.W.2d 487, 496–98 (Ky. 1992) (implying that the Kentucky Constitution *does* enact Mill's *On Liberty*).

117. *Casey*, 505 U.S. at 940 (Blackmun, J., concurring in part, concurring in the judgment in part, and dissenting in part).

118. But see BORK, supra note 80, at 211 (ridiculing efforts to apply Rawls's *A Theory of Justice* to interpreting our Constitution).

119. See supra text accompanying notes 33–35.

120. RAWLS, PL, supra note 1, at 337.

121. Lochner v. New York, 198 U.S. 45 (1905).

122. See RICHARD A. EPSTEIN, TAKINGS (1985) (advocating stringent judicial protection of economic liberties, though under the Takings Clause and the Contracts Clause rather than the Due Process Clauses); RANDY E. BARNETT, RESTORING THE LOST CONSTITUTION: THE PRESUMPTION OF LIBERTY (2004) (arguing for stringent judicial protection of liberties, including economic liberties, against the baseline of a presumption of liberty and against governmental regulation).

123. See RAWLS, PL, supra note 1, at 8, 124, 342–43; RAWLS, TJ, supra note 3, at 19–20, 579–81 (both discussing certain "fixed points," or moral convictions about which people generally agree and for which any theory of justice must account); see also DWORKIN, TRS, supra note 10, at 159–68 (describing Rawls's theory of reflective equilibrium between the "fixed points" of considered judgments and underlying principles in which people adjust between principles and judgments until a fit or equilibrium is reached).

124. See James E. Fleming, *Fidelity to Our Imperfect Constitution*, 65 FORDHAM L. REV. 1335 (1997).

125. For the idea of courts as exemplars of public reason in a forum of principle, see supra text accompanying note 64. By "seminar," I mean to echo BICKEL, supra note 95, at 26 (quoting Eugene V. Rostow, *The Democratic Character of Judicial Review*, 66 HARV. L. REV. 193, 208 [1952]).

126. See supra notes 59–60 and accompanying text.

127. See THE FEDERALIST No. 78, supra note 87, at 465 (Hamilton) ("The judiciary . . . may truly be said to have neither force nor will but merely judgment"). For the phrase "reasoned judgment," see *Casey*, 505 U.S. at 849 (joint opinion). For Scalia's angry reply, invoking *The Federalist* No. 78, see id. at 996 (Scalia, J., concurring in the judgment in part and dissenting in part). For Rawls's (presumably coincidental) usage of the phrase "reasoned judgment," see RAWLS, PL, supra note 1, at 222.

128. Michael H. v. Gerald D., 491 U.S. 110, 127 n.6 (Scalia, J., plurality opinion).

129. BORK, supra note 80.

130. ANTONIN SCALIA, A MATTER OF INTERPRETATION (1997).


## Chapter Five

1. Olmstead v. United States, 277 U.S. 438, 478 (1928) (Brandeis, J., dissenting); see also Whitney v. California, 274 U.S. 357, 375 (1927) (Brandeis, J., concurring) ("Those who won our independence believed that the final end of the State was to make men free to develop their faculties; and that in its government the *deliberative forces* should prevail over the arbitrary. They valued liberty both as an end and as a means. They believed liberty to be the secret of happiness and courage to be the secret of liberty") (emphasis added). In this book, I do not claim to be elaborating Brandeis's vision of "the right to be let alone." I quote his famous passage because I wish to echo his idea that the Constitution "secure[s] conditions favorable to the pursuit of happiness" and because many critics of the right to privacy or autonomy quote Brandeis in caricaturing this idea.

2. I list many of these "unenumerated" rights below. See infra text accompanying note 17.

3. For analysis of the "flights from substance" to process and narrowly conceived original understanding, see chapter 1.

4. 478 U.S. 186, 194–95 (1986) (rejecting the argument that the Due Process Clause of the Fourteenth Amendment protects a right to homosexual sodomy on the ground that such a right has "little or no cognizable roots in the language or design of the Constitution").

5. 505 U.S. 833, 979 (1992) (Scalia, J., concurring in the judgment in part and dissenting in part). Scalia bitterly protested the official reaffirmation of the "central holding" of Roe v. Wade, 410 U.S. 113 (1973), that the Due Process Clause of the Fourteenth Amendment protects the right of a woman to decide whether to terminate a pregnancy, and confidently declaimed that he is sure that it does not "because of two simple facts: (1) the Constitution says absolutely nothing about

[a right to abortion], and (2) the longstanding traditions of American society have permitted [abortion] to be legally proscribed." 505 U.S. at 980.

6. 539 U.S. 558, 586 (2003) (Scalia, J., dissenting). Scalia angrily criticized the majority opinion for overruling *Bowers* and for holding that the Due Process Clause protects the right of homosexuals to liberty or autonomy to engage in certain intimate sexual conduct. He despaired that the Court's ruling "effectively decrees the end of all morals legislation." Id. at 599.

7. See generally CHARLES L. BLACK JR., STRUCTURE AND RELATIONSHIP IN CONSTITUTIONAL LAW (1969).

8. Charles L. Black Jr., *The Unfinished Business of the Warren Court*, 46 WASH. L. REV. 3, 31–45 (1970) [hereinafter Black, *Unfinished Business*].

9. See, e.g., CHARLES L. BLACK JR., A NEW BIRTH OF FREEDOM: HUMAN RIGHTS, NAMED AND UNNAMED (1997); CHARLES L. BLACK JR., THE HUMANE IMAGI- NATION (1986); CHARLES L. BLACK JR., DECISION ACCORDING TO LAW 43–54 (1981) [hereinafter BLACK, DECISION]; Charles L. Black Jr., *Further Reflections on the Constitutional Justice of Livelihood*, 86 COLUM. L. REV. 1103, 1104 (1986) [herein- after Black, *Livelihood*]; Charles L. Black Jr., *On Reading and Using the Ninth Amendment*, in 1 THE RIGHTS RETAINED BY THE PEOPLE: THE HISTORY AND MEAN- ING OF THE NINTH AMENDMENT 337, 337–49 (Randy Barnett ed., 1989) [hereinafter Black, *Ninth*]. The allusion to "stones" is to Black, *Unfinished Business*, supra note 8, at 44 ("The stone the builders rejected [the Ninth Amendment] may yet be the cornerstone of the temple"). Black largely rejects the distinction between "enumerated" and "unenumerated" rights. See infra text accompanying note 106.

10. See, e.g., *Casey*, 505 U.S. at 998 (Scalia, J., concurring in the judgment in part and dissenting in part); Michael H. v. Gerald D., 491 U.S. 110, 123–27, 127 n.6 (1989) (Scalia, J., plurality opinion); Morrison v. Olson, 487 U.S. 654, 715 (1988) (Scalia, J., dissenting); ROBERT H. BORK, THE TEMPTING OF AMERICA 85–87, 95–100, 110–26, 150, 162–63, 351–55 (1990); ANTONIN SCALIA, A MATTER OF IN- TERPRETATION (1997) [hereinafter SCALIA, INTERPRETATION]; Antonin Scalia, *Orig- inalism: The Lesser Evil*, 57 U. CIN. L. REV. 849, 853–54, 862–65 (1989) [herein- after Scalia, *Originalism*].

11. See JOHN HART ELY, DEMOCRACY AND DISTRUST 73–104 (1980) [hereinafter ELY, DD]; John Hart Ely, *The Wages of Crying Wolf: A Comment on* Roe v. Wade, 82 YALE L.J. 920, 935–36 (1973) [hereinafter Ely, *Wages*].

12. See CASS R. SUNSTEIN, THE PARTIAL CONSTITUTION 119–22, 259–61 (1993) [hereinafter SUNSTEIN, PC].

13. BORK, supra note 10, at 120 n.*.

14. Black, *Ninth*, supra note 9, at 343. For reasoning by analogy, see, e.g., id. at 342–44; Black, *Unfinished Business*, supra note 8, at 37–45. For reflective equilib- rium, see, e.g., JOHN RAWLS, POLITICAL LIBERALISM 8 (1993) [hereinafter RAWLS, PL]; JOHN RAWLS, A THEORY OF JUSTICE 20–21, 48–51 (1971) [hereinafter RAWLS, TJ]; RONALD DWORKIN, TAKING RIGHTS SERIOUSLY 159–68 (1977) [hereinafter DWORKIN, TRS].

15. BORK, supra note 10, at 95.

16. BLACK, DECISION, supra note 9.

17. See, e.g., West Virginia State Bd. of Educ. v. Barnette, 319 U.S. 624, 630, 642 (1943) (liberty of conscience, freedom of thought, and right to self-determination); Roberts v. United States Jaycees, 468 U.S. 609, 617–18 (1984) (freedom of association, including both expressive association and intimate association); Lawrence v. Texas, 539 U.S. 558, 574–75 (2003) (right to privacy or autonomy to engage in homosexual intimate association); Moore v. City of E. Cleveland, 431 U.S. 494, 503–4 (1977) (right to live with one's family, whether nuclear or extended); Crandall v. Nevada, 73 U.S. (6 Wall.) 35 (1868) (right to travel); Shapiro v. Thompson, 394 U.S. 618, 629–30 (1969) (right to travel or relocate); Saenz v. Roe, 526 U.S. 489 (1999) (right to travel); Turner v. Safley, 482 U.S. 78, 95–96 (1987) (right to marry); Loving v. Virginia, 388 U.S. 1, 12 (1967) (right to marry); Skinner v. Oklahoma, 316 U.S. 535, 541 (1942) (right to procreate); Griswold v. Connecticut, 381 U.S. 479, 485–86 (1965) (right within marital association to use contraceptives); Eisenstadt v. Baird, 405 U.S. 438, 453 (1972) (right of individual, married or single, to use contraceptives); Carey v. Population Servs. Int'l, 431 U.S. 678, 694 (1977) (right to distribute contraceptives); Roe v. Wade, 410 U.S. 113, 153 (1973) (right of a woman to decide whether to terminate a pregnancy); Planned Parenthood v. Casey, 505 U.S. 833, 860 (1992) (reaffirming "central holding" of *Roe* and emphasizing decisional autonomy and bodily integrity); Meyer v. Nebraska, 262 U.S. 390, 400 (1923) (right to direct the education of children); Pierce v. Society of Sisters, 268 U.S. 510, 534–35 (1925) (right to direct the upbringing and education of children); Washington v. Harper, 494 U.S. 210, 221–22 (1990) (right to bodily integrity, in particular, to avoid unwanted administration of antipsychotic drugs); Rochin v. California, 342 U.S. 165, 172–73 (1952) (right to bodily integrity, in particular, to be protected against the extraction of evidence obtained by "breaking into the privacy" of a person's mouth or stomach); Cruzan v. Director, Mo. Dep't of Health, 497 U.S. 261, 279 (1990) (assuming for purposes of the case a "right to die" that includes the "right to refuse lifesaving hydration and nutrition"); id. at 339–45 (Stevens, J., dissenting) (arguing that decisions about death are a matter of individual conscience); see also Whalen v. Roe, 429 U.S. 589, 599–600 (1977) (right to privacy includes both an "individual interest in avoiding disclosure of personal matters" and an "interest in independence in making certain kinds of important decisions"); Stanley v. Georgia, 394 U.S. 557, 564 (1969) (right to receive ideas and to be free from unwanted governmental intrusions into the privacy of one's home).

18. But see Washington v. Glucksberg, 521 U.S. 702 (1997) (declining the extend the right to die assumed in *Cruzan*—the right to refuse unwanted lifesaving hydration and nutrition—to include the right to physician-assisted suicide). For a critique of *Glucksberg*'s approach to the due process inquiry, see chapter 6. For a critique of its holding regarding the right to die, see chapter 10.

19. In speaking of the bones and shards as fitting into, and being justifiable within, a coherent structure, I refer to Dworkin's formulation of the two dimensions of best interpretation: fit and justification. See RONALD DWORKIN, LAW'S EMPIRE 239 (1986).

20. I draw this account of a narrow originalist archaeologist from several sources. See, e.g., *Lawrence*, 539 U.S. at 586 (Scalia, J., dissenting); *Casey*, 505 U.S. at 980, 999–1000 (Scalia, J., concurring in the judgment in part and dissenting in part); *Cruzan*, 497 U.S. at 300 (Scalia, J., concurring); *Michael H.*, 491 U.S. at 123–27 & n.6 (Scalia, J., plurality opinion); *Bowers*, 478 U.S. at 194–95; BORK, supra note 10; SCALIA, INTERPRETATION, supra note 10; Scalia, *Originalism*, supra note 10.

21. I base this account of a process-perfecting archaeologist on ELY, DD, supra note 11, at 73–104, and, to a lesser extent, on SUNSTEIN, PC, supra note 12, at 133–41. For an account of Procrustes and Hercules, see chapter 2.

22. RONALD DWORKIN, FREEDOM'S LAW: THE MORAL READING OF THE AMERICAN CONSTITUTION 73 (1996) [hereinafter DWORKIN, FL]; see also RAWLS, PL, supra note 14, at 15–20, 29–35, 299–304 (grounding equal basic liberties on a conception of citizens as free and equal persons, together with a conception of society as a fair system of social cooperation). This account of a constructivist archaeologist is based on DWORKIN, TRS, supra note 14, at 159–68; RAWLS, TJ, supra note 14, at 46–53, 577–87; RAWLS, PL, supra note 14, at 89–129.

23. 478 U.S. at 199–214 (Blackmun, J., dissenting); id. at 214–20 (Stevens, J., dissenting).

24. Id. at 217 (Stevens, J., dissenting) (quoting Fitzgerald v. Porter Memorial Hosp., 523 F.2d 716, 719–20 [7th Cir. 1975] [Stevens, J.] [footnotes omitted], *cert. denied*, 425 U.S. 916 [1976]).

25. 429 U.S. at 599–600 (writing for a unanimous Court, Justice Stevens stated that the right to privacy includes both decisional and informational dimensions).

26. 478 U.S. at 202, 204 (Blackmun, J., dissenting).

27. 468 U.S. at 618.

28. Id. at 619.

29. *Casey*, 505 U.S. at 915 (Stevens, J., concurring in part and dissenting in part) (emphasis added); see also *Cruzan*, 497 U.S. at 339–45 (Stevens, J., dissenting) (arguing that choices about death are a matter of individual conscience).

30. *Casey*, 505 U.S. at 915, 919–20 (Stevens, J., concurring in part and dissenting in part). Jane Cohen analyzes Stevens's idea of decisional autonomy in terms of "deliberative autonomy." See Jane Maslow Cohen, *A Jurisprudence of Doubt: Deliberative Autonomy and Abortion*, 3 COLUM. J. GENDER & L. 175 (1992).

31. 505 U.S. at 927 (Blackmun, J., concurring in part, concurring in the judgment in part, and dissenting in part).

32. Id. at 927–28.

33. Id. at 851; Cf. Lee v. Weisman, 505 U.S. 577, 592 (1992) (affirming that the First Amendment protects freedom of conscience).

34. See *Casey*, 505 U.S. at 851, 856, 857, 897–98.

35. *Lawrence*, 539 U.S. at 562, 574.

36. Id. at 567, 575, 578.

37. Meyer v. Nebraska, 262 U.S. 390, 402 (1923) ("[The] ideas touching the relation between individual and state [in ancient Sparta and Plato's ideal commonwealth, which 'submerge the individual and develop ideal citizens'] were wholly different from those upon which our institutions rest").

38. Pierce v. Society of Sisters, 268 U.S. 510, 535 (1925) ("The fundamental theory of liberty upon which all governments in this Union repose excludes any general power of the state to standardize its children by forcing them to accept instruction from public teachers only. The child is not the mere creature of the state").

39. Griswold v. Connecticut, 381 U.S. 479, 486 (1965) ("We deal with a right of privacy older than the Bill of Rights. . . . Marriage is . . . intimate to the degree of being sacred. It is an association that promotes a way of life").

40. Loving v. Virginia, 388 U.S. 1, 12 (1967) ("The freedom to marry has long been recognized as one of the vital personal rights essential to the orderly pursuit of happiness by free men").

41. Eisenstadt v. Baird, 405 U.S. 438, 453 (1972) ("If the right of privacy means anything, it is the right of the individual, married or single, to be free from unwarranted governmental intrusion into matters so fundamentally affecting a person as the decision whether to bear or beget a child"). As Laurence Tribe notes, "the effect of *Eisenstadt* was to single out as decisive in *Griswold* the element of reproductive autonomy," not just the protection of the heterosexual marital relationship. LAURENCE H. TRIBE, AMERICAN CONSTITUTIONAL LAW 1339 (2d ed. 1988) (footnotes omitted).

42. Moore v. City of E. Cleveland, 431 U.S. 494, 506 (1977) ("[T]he Constitution prevents [the city] from standardizing its children—and its adults—by forcing all to live in certain narrowly defined family patterns").

43. Carey v. Population Servs. Int'l, 431 U.S. 678, 687–88 (1977) (stressing that prior decisions such as *Griswold*, *Eisenstadt*, and *Roe* protected the right to "[i]ndividual autonomy in matters of childbearing" and the individual's "right of decision" about procreation from unjustified intrusion by the government).

44. Roe v. Wade, 410 U.S. 113, 153 (1973) ("Th[e] right of privacy, whether it be founded in the Fourteenth Amendment's concept of personal liberty and restrictions upon state action, as we feel it is, or, as the District Court determined, in the Ninth Amendment's reservation of rights to the people, is broad enough to encompass a woman's decision whether or not to terminate her pregnancy").

45. West Virginia State Bd. of Educ. v. Barnette, 319 U.S. 624, 641–42 (1943). In *Barnette*, the Court invalidated a state board of education's requirement that students salute the flag as a violation both of "a right of self-determination in matters that touch individual opinion and personal attitude" and of the First Amendment. Id. at 630, 641.

46. Jed Rubenfeld, *The Right of Privacy*, 102 HARV. L. REV. 737, 784 (1989). For example, Rubenfeld emphasizes the profound sense in which laws restricting abortion reduce women to "mere instrumentalities of the state," and "take diverse women with every variety of career, life-plan, and so on, and make mothers of them all." Id. at 788, 790; see JED RUBENFELD, FREEDOM AND TIME: A THEORY OF CONSTITUTIONAL SELF-GOVERNMENT 221–55 (2001). See also LAURENCE H. TRIBE, ABORTION: THE CLASH OF ABSOLUTES 92–93 (1990) (characterizing *Meyer* and *Pierce* as "bulwarks in our legal system" and as ancestors of the right of women "not to be made mothers against their will"). I refer to the right to privacy or autonomy as an "antitotalitarian principle of liberty" to suggest a parallel with Sunstein's anticaste principle of equality. See SUNSTEIN, PC, supra note 12, at 137–41.

47. *Casey*, 505 U.S. at 848–49, 901 (joint opinion).

48. Id. at 847.

49. BORK, supra note 10, at 95–100. We still do not know the full extent of the right to privacy forty years later (and it's a good thing, too). For that matter, we never know the full extent of any constitutional principle, least of all any important one.

50. See DWORKIN, FL, supra note 22, at 276–87 (arguing that Bork was not confirmed largely because of his rejection of a constitutional right to privacy).

51. Cf. *Barnette*, 319 U.S. at 642 ("If there is any fixed star in our constitutional constellation, it is that no official, high or petty, can prescribe what shall be orthodox in politics, nationalism, religion, or other matters of opinion or force citizens to confess by word or act their faith therein").

52. 347 U.S. 483 (1954) (holding that racial segregation of public schools violated the Equal Protection Clause).

53. Charles Black offered sensible resolutions for the methodological crises that *Brown* and *Griswold* provoked in constitutional law. See Charles L. Black Jr., *The Lawfulness of the Segregation Decisions*, 69 YALE L.J. 421 (1960) (defending *Brown*); Black, *Unfinished Business*, supra note 8, at 31–45 (defending *Griswold*).

54. See Nomination of Anthony M. Kennedy to Be Associate Justice of the Supreme Court of the United States: Hearings before the Senate Comm. on the Judiciary, 100th Cong., 2d Sess. 135–36, 164–65 (1988); Nomination of David H. Souter to Be Associate Justice of the Supreme Court of the United States: Hearings before the Senate Comm. on the Judiciary, 101st Cong., 2d Sess. 172–76 (1990); 1 Nomination of Judge Clarence Thomas to Be Associate Justice of the Supreme Court of the United States: Hearings before the Senate Comm. on the Judiciary, 102d Cong., 1st Sess. 225, 364 (1991); Nomination of Judge John G. Roberts to Be Chief Justice of the Supreme Court of the United States: Hearings before the Senate Comm. on the Judiciary, 109th Cong., 1st Sess. (2005). For Scalia's assertion that *Griswold* was rightly decided according to his conception of the due process inquiry, see *Michael H.*, 491 U.S. 110, 128 n.6 (Scalia, J., plurality opinion). For his argument that *Roe* was wrongly decided, see *Casey*, 505 U.S. at 979 (Scalia, J., concurring in the judgment in part and dissenting in part).

55. See Nomination of Ruth Bader Ginsburg to Be Associate Justice of the Supreme Court of the United States: Hearings before the Senate Comm. on the Judiciary, 103d Cong., 1st Sess. 207, 282 (1993); Nomination of Stephen G. Breyer to Be Associate Justice of the Supreme Court of the United States: Hearings before the Senate Comm. on the Judiciary, 103d Cong., 2d Sess. 138 (1994). Breyer, while a law clerk, wrote the first draft of Justice Goldberg's concurrence in *Griswold*. See David J. Garrow, Liberty and Sexuality: The Right to Privacy and the Making of *Roe v. Wade* 250 (1994).

56. *Casey*, 505 U.S. at 857 (joint opinion) (referring to the line of decisions exemplified by *Griswold*, which protect "liberty relating to intimate relationships, the family, and decisions about whether or not to beget or bear a child").

57. Ely, DD, supra note 11, at 87, 92.

58. Id. at 87–101.

59. Id. at 93–100. Ely also acknowledges that the Constitution protects the substantive values of private property and the obligation of contracts. Id. at 91–92, 97–98.

60. Id. at 101.

61. Black, *Unfinished Business*, supra note 8, at 44 (referring to the Ninth Amendment).

62. See chapter 1.

63. See Rawls, PL, supra note 14, at 89–99 (contrasting political constructivism with theories of moral realism [including natural law and natural rights] along these lines).

64. See Frank I. Michelman, *On Regulating Practices with Theories Drawn from Them: A Case of Justice as Fairness*, in Nomos: Theory and Practice 309 (Ian Shapiro & Judith Wagner DeCew eds., 1995).

65. See chapter 4 (observing that within Rawls's political constructivism, equal basic liberties are conceived, not as "true," but as "most reasonable for us," and are worked up from the way citizens are regarded in the public political culture of our constitutional democracy, in the basic political texts [for example, the Constitution and the Declaration of Independence], and in the tradition and practice of the interpretation of those texts).

66. For discussion of aspirational principles, see chapter 6.

67. For the formulation "fits most and criticizes some," I am indebted to Lewis D. Sargentich. See Gregory C. Keating, *Fidelity to Pre-existing Law and the Legitimacy of Legal Decision*, 69 Notre Dame L. Rev. 1, 38 (1993) (using this formulation in developing a general conception of legal justification).

68. Gerald Dworkin, The Theory and Practice of Autonomy 6 (1988); see also John Christman, *Introduction*, in The Inner Citadel: Essays on Individual Autonomy 3 (John Christman ed., 1989) (analyzing many different conceptions of autonomy in contemporary discourse).

69. See Dworkin, supra note 68, at 12; Joel Feinberg, Harm to Self 27 (1986).

70. FEINBERG, supra note 69, at 27–28.

71. See, e.g., id. at 27–28, 49–51 (distinguishing between national sovereignty and personal sovereignty and referring to personal autonomy as "the realm of inviolable sanctuary most of us sense in our own beings"); Frank I. Michelman, *Foreword: Traces of Self-Government*, 100 HARV. L. REV. 4, 55–56 (1986) (stating that the conflict between "two principles—of 'individual' and 'community' self-determination—reflects a characteristic tension in the general concept of self-government"); see also RONALD DWORKIN, LIFE'S DOMINION 53 (1993) [hereinafter DWORKIN, LD] (referring to privacy or autonomy as a matter of "sovereignty over personal decisions").

72. See chapter 4; see also DWORKIN, LD, supra note 71 (referring to exercise of autonomy as involving deliberation).

73. See supra text accompanying note 29.

74. See, e.g., STEPHEN MACEDO, LIBERAL VIRTUES 163–202 (1990) (analyzing the Constitution as reflecting a liberal scheme of "reflective self-governance"); ROGERS M. SMITH, LIBERALISM AND AMERICAN CONSTITUTIONAL LAW 198–259 (1985) (analyzing the Constitution as embodying a liberal scheme of "rational liberty," "deliberative self-direction," or "reflective self-governance").

75. There is a rich, sophisticated, and powerful literature discussing substantive liberties embraced by deliberative autonomy in terms of privacy, autonomy, or liberty. There is a similarly rich literature analyzing deliberation about and pursuit of conceptions of the good. See, e.g., DWORKIN, LD, supra note 71; MACEDO, supra note 74; DAVID A. J. RICHARDS, CONSCIENCE AND THE CONSTITUTION: HISTORY, THEORY, AND LAW OF THE RECONSTRUCTION AMENDMENTS (1993) [hereinafter RICHARDS, CONSCIENCE]; DAVID A. J. RICHARDS, TOLERATION AND THE CONSTITUTION (1986) [hereinafter RICHARDS, TOLERATION]; SMITH, supra note 74; see also WILL KYMLICKA, LIBERALISM, COMMUNITY AND CULTURE (1989); JOSEPH RAZ, THE MORALITY OF FREEDOM (1986); Martha C. Nussbaum, *Human Functioning and Social Justice: In Defense of Aristotelian Essentialism*, 20 POL. THEORY 202 (1992).

76. Liberal theorists rarely hold as self-determining or "unencumbered" a view of the self as communitarians, civic republicans, and deconstructionists assign to them, but usually recognize the important shaping role of society. See, e.g., STEPHEN HOLMES, THE ANATOMY OF ANTILIBERALISM 176–79, 190–97 (1993); RAWLS, PL, supra note 14, at 27. They typically, however, reject strong social constructionist models of the self because such models undermine the possibility of a commitment to agency and autonomy. Cf. SEYLA BENHABIB, SITUATING THE SELF 228–29 (1992) (arguing that a strong version of postmodernism would undermine "feminist commitment to women's agency and sense of selfhood").

77. See DWORKIN, LD, supra note 71, at 148–68. Many communitarians, civic republicans, and perfectionists dispute the idea of the individual as the site of moral agency, responsibility, and independence. See, e.g., ROBERT P. GEORGE, MAKING MEN MORAL: CIVIL LIBERTIES AND PUBLIC MORALITY 83–109, 129–60

(1993); MICHAEL J. SANDEL, DEMOCRACY'S DISCONTENT: AMERICA IN SEARCH OF A PUBLIC PHILOSOPHY 91–119, 350 (1996); MICHAEL J. SANDEL, LIBERALISM AND THE LIMITS OF JUSTICE 15–65 (1982) [hereinafter SANDEL, LLJ].

78. Rubenfeld, supra note 46, at 784.

79. See *Casey*, 505 U.S. at 851 (joint opinion); DWORKIN, LD, supra note 71, at 150–59.

80. *Casey*, 505 U.S. at 851 (joint opinion).

81. *Loving*, 388 U.S. at 12.

82. *Lawrence*, 539 U.S. at 571 (quoting *Casey*, 505 U.S. at 850 [joint opinion]).

83. See MACEDO, supra note 74, at 214–27; Linda C. McClain, *Rights and Irresponsibility*, 43 DUKE L.J. 989, 1070–75 (1994).

84. See, e.g., Gillette v. United States, 401 U.S. 437, 441 (1971) (upholding, against a challenge under the Free Exercise Clause, a statute exempting from military conscription any person who "is conscientiously opposed to participation in war in any form" and requiring a showing that the objection must have a grounding in "religious training and belief").

85. Nonetheless, Robin West has suggested that support for reproductive freedom "should rest upon the demonstrated capacity of pregnant women to decide whether to carry a fetus to term or to abort responsibly." Robin West, *Foreword: Taking Freedom Seriously*, 104 HARV. L. REV. 43, 82–83 (1990). But see Linda C. McClain, *"Atomistic Man" Revisited: Liberalism, Connection, and Feminist Jurisprudence*, 65 S. CAL. L. REV. 1171, 1252–53 (1992) (expressing concern that West's approach might open the door to requiring individual women to demonstrate that they have exercised their reproductive freedom responsibly).

86. *Casey*, 505 U.S. at 872, 877 (joint opinion) (stating that the government "may enact rules and regulations designed to encourage [a pregnant woman] to know that there are philosophic and social arguments of great weight . . . in favor of continuing the pregnancy to full term," for "[w]hat is at stake is the woman's right to make the ultimate decision, not a right to be insulated from all others in doing so"). But see id. at 916 (Stevens, J., concurring in part and dissenting in part) (agreeing with the joint opinion that the government "may take steps to ensure that a woman's choice 'is thoughtful and informed,'" but insisting that "[d]ecisional autonomy must limit the State's power to inject into a woman's most personal *deliberations* its own views of what is best") (emphasis added).

87. See DWORKIN, LD, supra note 71, at 150–59 (distinguishing between encouraging responsibility and compelling or coercing conformity). I nonetheless believe that *Casey* was wrong in upholding the twenty-four-hour waiting period and certain aspects of the informed consent requirements as constitutional.

88. Reynolds v. Sims, 377 U.S. 533, 555 (1964); Harper v. Virginia State Bd. of Elections, 383 U.S. 663, 670 (1966). It may be long since forgotten that the right to vote (at least in state elections) is an "unenumerated" fundamental right, and that

cases such as *Reynolds* and *Harper*, like *Griswold* and *Roe*, met with charges by commentators and judges that the Court was engaging in "Lochnering." See, e.g., Ely, *Wages*, supra note 11, at 935–37, 943–45 (criticizing such pre-*Roe* charges by analogy to the fable of the boy who cried "wolf"). Technically, *Harper* did not decide whether the Constitution protects a right to vote in state elections, for the Court stated: "[I]t is enough to say that once the franchise is granted to the electorate, lines may not be drawn which are inconsistent with the Equal Protection Clause." 383 U.S. at 665.

89. One could press the analogy between voting and abortion further. Literacy tests for voting can be seen as analogous to informed consent requirements for abortion. Many measures that were once defended as safeguarding deliberative or responsible voting, such as literacy tests, poll taxes, and property requirements, have been invalidated. See, e.g., U.S. CONST. amend. XXIV (prohibiting poll tax for federal elections); Voting Rights Act of 1965, 42 U.S.C. § 1973b (1988) (banning states from requiring certain literacy tests); *Harper*, 383 U.S. at 666 (invalidating poll tax for state elections).

90. See RAWLS, PL, supra note 14, at 18 n.20, 86–88.

91. See id. at 13, 175.

92. Id. at 206 (mentioning, as an example, HANNAH ARENDT, THE HUMAN CONDITION [1958]).

93. Id. at 37, 78, 145, 199–200 (discussing the comprehensive liberalisms of Kant and Mill).

94. See LINDA C. MCCLAIN, THE PLACE OF FAMILIES: FOSTERING CAPACITY, EQUALITY, AND RESPONSIBILITY (2006).

95. *Barnette*, 319 U.S. at 642.

96. *Casey*, 505 U.S. at 851 (joint opinion).

97. See RAWLS, PL, supra note 14, at 9–10, 154. Ronald Dworkin and David Richards have compellingly generalized liberty of conscience beyond narrow, traditional religious liberty. See, e.g., DWORKIN, LD, supra note 71, at 160–68; RICHARDS, CONSCIENCE, supra note 75; RICHARDS, TOLERATION, supra note 75.

98. For a valuable discussion of the difference between privileging and protecting religious conceptions of the good, see Christopher L. Eisgruber and Lawrence G. Sager, *The Vulnerability of Conscience: The Constitutional Basis for Protecting Religious Conduct*, 61 U. CHI. L. REV. 1245, 1250–54 (1994).

99. For contrary views that liberty of conscience should be interpreted narrowly to protect only religious liberty, rather than broadly to protect autonomy, see Michael W. McConnell, *The Origins and Historical Understanding of Free Exercise of Religion*, 103 HARV. L. REV. 1410, 1488–1500 (1990) [hereinafter McConnell, *Historical Understanding*]; Michael W. McConnell, *Religious Freedom at a Crossroads*, 59 U. CHI. L. REV. 115, 172–75 (1992) [hereinafter McConnell, *Crossroads*]; Michael J. Sandel, *Freedom of Conscience or Freedom of Choice?* in ARTICLES OF FAITH, ARTICLES OF PEACE 74, 87–92 (James Davison Hunter & Os Guinness eds., 1990).

100. See SANDEL, LLJ, supra note 77, at 182; MARY ANN GLENDON, RIGHTS TALK: THE IMPOVERISHMENT OF POLITICAL DISCOURSE 47–61 (1991).

101. See *Roberts*, 468 U.S. at 617–22 (distinguishing "expressive association" from "intimate association"); Kenneth L. Karst, *The Freedom of Intimate Association*, 89 YALE L.J. 624 (1980).

102. See chapter 7 (responding to Sandel's critique of the right to autonomy).

103. See DWORKIN, LD, supra note 71, at 160–68 (suggesting that there is no dearth of "textual homes" for such rights, including the Due Process Clauses, the Equal Protection Clause, and the First Amendment, to say nothing of the Privileges or Immunities Clause).

104. *Loving*, 388 U.S. at 12.

105. Nonetheless, narrow originalists resist generalizing liberty of conscience (or freedom of association) to embrace ideas like deliberative autonomy. See McConnell, *Crossroads*, supra note 99, at 172–75; McConnell, *Historical Understanding*, supra note 99, at 1488–1500.

106. DWORKIN, LD, supra note 71, at 129–31, 143–44 ("spurious"); DWORKIN, FL, supra note 22, at 72, 76–81 ("bogus"); BLACK, DECISION, supra note 9, at 41–54; Black, *Livelihood*, supra note 9, at 1108–11; Black, *Ninth*, supra note 9, at 342–49.

107. Palko v. Connecticut, 302 U.S. 319, 325 (1937) (citations omitted).

108. *Griswold*, 381 U.S. at 482–83.

109. Poe v. Ullman, 367 U.S. 497, 544 (1961) (Harlan, J., dissenting) ("[T]oday those decisions would probably have gone by reference to the concepts of freedom of expression and conscience").

110. BORK, supra note 10, at 48–49.

111. GARROW, supra note 55, at 245–56.

112. I do not concede that there is anything spooky or scary about penumbras and emanations, whether from particular provisions, *Griswold*, 381 U.S. at 483–85, or from the "totality of the constitutional scheme under which we live," *Poe*, 367 U.S. at 521 (Douglas, J., dissenting). I simply observe that in our constitutional culture many people are frightened by such talk.

113. 302 U.S. at 327 ("Of that freedom [of thought and speech] one may say that it is the matrix, the indispensable condition, of nearly every other form of freedom"). My discussion of "matrix values" benefits from, though is not the same as, the analysis in WILLIAM F. HARRIS II, THE INTERPRETABLE CONSTITUTION 97 (1993).

114. *Reynolds*, 377 U.S. at 562 (quoting Yick Wo v. Hopkins, 118 U.S. 356, 370 [1886]).

115. *Palko*, 319 U.S. at 325, 328 (citation omitted).

116. See DWORKIN, LD, supra note 71, at 160–68 (arguing that the First Amendment, along with the Due Process Clause and the Equal Protection Clause, provides a "textual home" for the right to procreative autonomy).

117. *Palko*, 319 U.S. at 325.

118. See DWORKIN, LD, supra note 71, at 166 (criticizing the "odd taste for neatness" of proponents of a "constitution of detail" who "want rights mapped uniquely onto constitutional clauses with no overlap").

119. Id.

120. *Poe*, 367 U.S. at 521 (Douglas, J., dissenting).

121. For a sophisticated development of the idea of "transcendent structuralism," see HARRIS, supra note 113, at 144–58. Harris explains: "Transcendent structuralism looks for structures and coherent wholes outside the Constitution which are signaled by the document." Id. at 152. He continues: "This style of interpretation calls for a nondocumentary but still bounded theorizing about the fundamental principles that justify the nature and composition of a set of given political institutions." Id. at 152–53. Cf. BLACK, DECISION, supra note 9, at 53 ("[T]he Ninth Amendment . . . makes possible fully rational discourse in the formation of personal rights law, toward the construction of a coherent system. . . . In this transcendent sense, the Ninth Amendment could be the gate to the best kind we can attain of decision according to law").

122. For discussions of the idea of the "frontier" or an "exit" option in constitutional law, see ELY, DD, supra note 11, at 178–79; H. N. HIRSCH, A THEORY OF LIBERTY: THE CONSTITUTION AND MINORITIES 243 (1992); Abner S. Greene, Kiryas Joel *and Two Mistakes about Equality*, 96 COLUM. L. REV. 1, 8–16, 17–18, 39–57 (1996); see also THE FRONTIER IN AMERICAN CULTURE: ESSAYS BY RICHARD WHITE AND PATRICIA NELSON LIMERICK (James R. Grossman ed., 1994).

123. See John Hart Ely, *Democracy and the Right to Be Different*, 56 N.Y.U. L. REV. 397, 405 (1981).

124. See ELY, DD, supra note 11, at 178.

125. See id. (discussing Crandall v. Nevada, 73 U.S. [6 Wall.] 35 [1868]); id. at 179 (referring to the notion of the "voice" option in ALBERT O. HIRSCHMAN, EXIT, VOICE, AND LOYALTY [1970]).

126. Id. at 179 (referring to the notion of the "exit" option in HIRSCHMAN, supra note 125).

127. Id. at 172, 179.

128. See id. at 99, 123.

129. In elaborating the idea of a political conception of justice, Rawls assumes a "closed society" that members enter only by birth and exit only by death. RAWLS, PL, supra note 14, at 12. In that sense, he assumes for the sake of simplicity that there is no "exit" option.

130. For the idea of religious exemptions from general laws as a "partial" exit option, see Greene, supra note 122.

131. See Robert F. Copple, *Privacy and the Frontier Thesis: An American Intersection of Self and Society*, 34 AM. J. JURIS. 87 (1989).

132. Cf. Ronald Dworkin, *Soulcraft*, N.Y. REV. BOOKS, Oct. 12, 1978, at 18 (reviewing GEORGE F. WILL, THE PURSUIT OF HAPPINESS AND OTHER SOBERING THOUGHTS (1978) (criticizing Will's idea that "statecraft is, inevitably, soulcraft").

133. RAWLS, PL, supra note 14, at 335.

134. The Supreme Court has rejected the "importance" of an asserted right as the criterion for deciding whether the Constitution protects it in the context of the Equal Protection Clause. See San Antonio Indep. Sch. Dist. v. Rodriguez, 411 U.S. 1, 30 (1973). I have several responses. First, the Court rejected a criterion of significance *simpliciter*. Second, the early Burger Court was at pains to cabin equality, especially where the expenditure of money was involved. For institutional reasons, it is understandable that the Court would shy away from ordering exact equality in education and the restructuring of school financing schemes. But *Rodriguez*, even while it rejected the importance of an asserted right as the criterion for deciding whether "to create substantive constitutional rights in the name of guaranteeing equal protection of the laws," id. at 33, did seem practically to assume that education was so significant or important for democracy that there might be a constitutional right to a minimally adequate education (even if not to an exactly equal education). Id. at 36–37. Third, constitutional constructivism acknowledges that certain basic liberties that are significant for deliberative autonomy or deliberative democracy nonetheless may be judicially unenforceable or underenforced norms, especially if they implicate institutional limits of courts.

Likewise, the Supreme Court has rejected the "importance" of an asserted right as the criterion for deciding whether the Constitution protects it in the context of the Due Process Clause. See Washington v. Glucksberg, 521 U.S. 702, 727–28 (1997) ("That many of the rights and liberties protected by the Due Process Clause sound in personal autonomy does not warrant the sweeping conclusion that any and all important, intimate, and personal decisions are so protected, *Rodriguez*, and *Casey* did not suggest otherwise"). In chapter 6 I criticize *Glucksberg*'s formulation of the due process inquiry, and in chapter 10 I argue that it was wrongly decided.

135. See RAWLS, PL, supra note 14, at 178–79.

136. See generally GLENDON, supra note 100 (popularizing the term "rights talk"). For a critique of Glendon's analysis of "rights talk" and of the assertion of frivolous rights in contemporary American society, see McClain, supra note 83, at 1001–8, 1046–54.

137. RAWLS, PL, supra note 14, at 292.

138. See id. at 294–99. For further discussion, see chapter 8.

139. DWORKIN, TRS, supra note 14.

140. RAWLS, PL, supra note 14, at 296.

141. Id.; Cf. R.A.V. v. City of St. Paul, 505 U.S. 377, 415 (1992) (Blackmun, J., concurring) (arguing that "[i]f all expressive activity must be accorded the same protection, that protection will be scant" and thus that decisions purporting to expand First Amendment protection may actually weaken it).

142. Black, *Ninth*, supra note 9, at 343.

143. See chapter 6 (discussing flights from autonomy by conservative justices as well as by progressive and feminist scholars).

144. See, e.g., GLENDON, supra note 100.

## Chapter Six

1. See chapter 5, note 17 and accompanying text.

2. 302 U.S. 319, 325 (1937).

3. 491 U.S. 110, 141 (1989) (Brennan, J., dissenting). For insightful analysis of Brennan's conception of tradition, see Frank I. Michelman, BRENNAN AND DEMOCRACY 99–112 (1999); Frank I. Michelman, *Super Liberal: Romance, Community, and Tradition in William J. Brennan, Jr.'s Constitutional Thought*, 77 VA. L. REV. 1261, 1312–20 (1991) [hereinafter Michelman, *Super Liberal*].

4. 491 U.S. at 127 n.6 (Scalia, J., plurality opinion).

5. 367 U.S. 497, 542–43 (1961) (Harlan, J., dissenting).

6. *Palko*, 302 U.S. at 325; see Griswold v. Connecticut, 381 U.S. 479, 484–85 (1965) (officially avoiding substantive due process but still protecting an "unenumerated" right to privacy because several "specific" constitutional guarantees "have penumbras, formed by emanations from those guarantees that help give them life and substance," that "create zones of privacy"); Roe v. Wade, 410 U.S. 113, 152–53 (1973) (applying Cardozo's formulation in *Palko* in protecting an "unenumerated" right of a woman to decide whether to terminate a pregnancy).

7. *Palko*, 302 U.S. at 325 (citations omitted).

8. See Bowers v. Hardwick, 478 U.S. 186, 192–94 (1986).

9. I do not claim that the Due Process Clause incorporates all of justice, or that due process is purely aspirational principles as opposed to historical practices, or indeed that the Court ever has fulfilled the promise of the *Palko* formulation.

10. *Poe*, 367 U.S. at 543 (Harlan, J., dissenting).

11. Planned Parenthood v. Casey, 505 U.S. 833 (1992); Lawrence v. Texas, 539 U.S. 558 (2003).

12. See SOTIRIOS A. BARBER, ON WHAT THE CONSTITUTION MEANS 84–85 (1984) (drawing a similar distinction between history and tradition); id. at 33–37, 54–62 (making a similar analysis of constitutional aspirations); see also Michelman, *Super Liberal*, supra note 3, at 1312–20 (distinguishing between tradition as historical practice and tradition as abstract norms in analyzing tradition in Justice Brennan's constitutional jurisprudence).

13. See supra note 6 (discussing *Griswold* and *Roe*). To be sure, *Bolling* and *Loving* involved equal protection as well as due process, but that supports my thesis that the two clauses overlap and are intertwined. See chapter 3.

14. Bolling v. Sharpe, 347 U.S. 497, 499 (1954) (companion case to Brown v. Board of Education, 347 U.S. 483 [1954]).

15. Loving v. Virginia, 388 U.S. 1, 12 (1967).

16. *Bowers*, 478 U.S. at 192–94. In dissent, Justice Blackmun criticized Justice White's formulation of the right at issue, arguing that the case instead was about

"'the most comprehensive of rights and the right most valued by civilized men,' namely, 'the right to be let alone.'" Id. at 199 (quoting Olmstead v. United States, 277 U.S. 438, 478 [1928] [Brandeis, J., dissenting]). For a critique of *Bowers*'s conception of the due process inquiry as "authoritarian" as distinguished from "self-revisionary" (which parallels my distinction between "historical practices" and "aspirational principles"), see Frank I. Michelman, *Law's Republic*, 97 YALE L.J. 1493, 1496, 1514 (1988); see also James E. Fleming, Lawrence's *Republic*, 39 TULSA L. REV. 563 (2004).

17. *Bowers*, 478 U.S. at 214–16 (Stevens, J., dissenting).

18. 491 U.S. at 123–27 & 127 n.6 (Scalia, J., plurality opinion); see also Cruzan v. Director, Mo. Dep't of Health, 497 U.S. 261, 294 (1990) (Scalia, J., concurring) ("[N]o 'substantive due process' claim can be maintained unless the claimant demonstrates that the State has deprived him of a right historically and traditionally protected against state interference").

19. *Michael H.*, 491 U.S. at 127–28 n.6 (Scalia, J., plurality opinion).

20. Id. at 125, 127.

21. *Cruzan*, 497 U.S. at 300–1 (Scalia, J., concurring).

22. Id. at 300.

23. *Michael H.*, 491 U.S. at 141 (Brennan, J., dissenting).

24. *Casey*, 505 U.S. at 847–48.

25. Id. at 848–50. Thus, *Casey* to some extent replays the great debate concerning constitutional interpretation from *Griswold*, with the joint opinion playing Harlan to Scalia's Black. See *Griswold*, 381 U.S. at 499 (1965) (Harlan, J., concurring); id. at 507 (Black, J., dissenting).

26. *Poe*, 367 U.S. at 542–43 (Harlan, J., dissenting).

27. *Casey*, 505 U.S. at 849, 901; see also id. at 847–48 (resisting the "temptation" to abdicate the responsibility to engage in "reasoned judgment" in the due process inquiry).

28. See CHARLES FRIED, ORDER AND LAW 72 (1991); LAURENCE H. TRIBE & MICHAEL C. DORF, ON READING THE CONSTITUTION 76–79, 116–17 (1991).

29. For Scalia's attack on "reasoned judgment," see *Casey*, 505 U.S. at 982–84, 1000 (Scalia, J., concurring in the judgment in part and dissenting in part).

30. RONALD DWORKIN, LIFE'S DOMINION 119–22, 126–29 (1993); see *Poe*, 367 U.S. at 542 (Harlan, J., dissenting).

31. For a characterization and critique of Harlan's conception of the Constitution as a "common law constitution," see Bruce Ackerman, *The Common Law Constitution of John Marshall Harlan*, 36 N.Y.L. SCH. L. REV. 5 (1991).

32. Henry M. Hart Jr., *Foreword: The Time Chart of the Justices*, 73 HARV. L. REV. 84, 101 (1959) ("first-rate lawyers"). See *Poe*, 367 U.S. at 542 (Harlan, J., dissenting) ("The best that can be said is that through the course of this Court's decisions [due process] has represented the balance which our Nation, built upon postulates of respect for the liberty of the individual, has struck between that liberty and the demands of organized society").

33. ALEXANDER M. BICKEL, THE LEAST DANGEROUS BRANCH 55 (1962).

34. See JOHN HART ELY, DEMOCRACY AND DISTRUST 43–72 (1980) [hereinafter ELY, DD].

35. See chapter 3 (criticizing Sunstein's argument that the Equal Protection Clause is forward-looking and critical of existing practices, and that the Due Process Clause is largely backward-looking and supportive of long-standing practices).

36. As stated in the text, we should distinguish between Harlan's due process methodology and his own application of it. For example, Fried as well as Tribe and Dorf claim to apply Harlan-like methodologies to conclude that *Bowers* was wrongly decided, despite the fact that Harlan, in his dissent in *Poe*, 367 U.S. at 546, specifically contemplated that states had the power to outlaw homosexual conduct. See FRIED, supra note 28, at 81–85; TRIBE & DORF, supra note 28, at 76–79, 116–17. White's opinion for the Court in *Bowers* observed that whereas in 1961 all fifty states outlawed sodomy, by 1986 only twenty-four states continued to provide criminal penalties for sodomy performed in private and between consenting adults. 478 U.S. at 193–94. That legal transformation from 1961 to 1986 suggests a tradition from which we are breaking, to paraphrase Harlan's dissent in *Poe*, 367 U.S. at 542 (Harlan, J., dissenting). Harlan wrote in 1961, before the tradition that by his account is a "living thing" began to evolve.

Thus, Fried as well as Tribe and Dorf have sought to save Harlan's formulation from how he himself would have applied it. While I applaud their effort and accept its soundness and prudence, I would supplement it by putting forward the criterion of significance for deliberative autonomy. That criterion, though not hostile toward Harlan's formulation, suggests a more focused inquiry and one that is more critical of our historical practices on the basis of our aspirational principles.

37. 521 U.S. 702, 720 (1997).

38. Id. at 720–21.

39. Id. at 721, 722 n.17.

40. *Michael H.*, 491 U.S. at 127–28 n.6 (Scalia, J., plurality opinion).

41. *Cruzan*, 497 U.S. at 294 (Scalia, J., concurring).

42. *Michael H.*, 491 U.S. at 132 (O'Connor, J., concurring).

43. See id.

44. *Casey*, 505 U.S. at 848–50. This is notwithstanding Rehnquist's suggestion to the contrary in *Glucksberg*. See supra text accompanying note 39.

45. See *Cruzan*, 497 U.S. at 279.

46. See id. at 293–300 (Scalia, J., concurring).

47. *Glucksberg*, 521 U.S. at 723.

48. See Compassion in Dying v. Washington, 79 F.3d 790 (9th Cir. 1996) (*en banc*), rev'd sub nom. Washington v. Glucksberg, 521 U.S. 702 (1997).

49. *Glucksberg*, 521 U.S. at 790 (Breyer, J., concurring).

50. Id. at 740, 743 (Stevens, J., concurring).

51. *Michael H.*, 491 U.S. at 125, 127 (Scalia, J., plurality opinion).

52. 262 U.S. 390 (1923).

53. 268 U.S. 510 (1925).

54. 381 U.S. 479 (1965).

55. 388 U.S. 1 (1967).

56. 410 U.S. 113 (1973).

57. 431 U.S. 494 (1977).

58. See, e.g., *Casey*, 505 U.S. at 922 (Rehnquist, C.J., concurring in part and dissenting in part); *Roe*, 410 U.S. at 171 (Rehnquist, J., dissenting); *Casey*, 505 U.S. at 979 (Scalia, J., concurring in part and dissenting in part).

59. Lawrence v. Texas, 539 U.S. 558 (2003).

60. Id. at 588 (Scalia, J., dissenting).

61. Id. at 578.

62. 405 U.S. 438 (1972).

63. 431 U.S. 678 (1977).

64. 505 U.S. 833 (1992).

65. 517 U.S. 620 (1996).

66. *Lawrence*, 539 U.S. at 564–66, 573–76.

67. *Bowers*, 478 U.S. at 197 (Burger, C.J., concurring). Burger also specifically characterized that moral teaching in terms of "Judeao-Christian moral and ethical standards." Id. at 196.

68. *Lawrence*, 539 U.S. at 571–77; id. at 573 (citing Dudgeon v. United Kingdom, 3 Eur. Ct. H. R. 40 [1981]) .

69. 125 S. Ct. 1183, 1198–1200 (2005).

70. See, e.g., David Fontana, *Refined Comparativism in Constitutional Law*, 49 UCLA L. REV. 539 (2001); Sarah K. Harding, *Comparative Reasoning and Judicial Review*, 28 YALE J. INT'L L. 409 (2003); Matthew S. Raalf, Note, *A Sheep in Wolf's Clothing: Why the Debate Surrounding Comparative Constitutional Law Is Spectacularly Ordinary*, 73 FORDHAM L. REV. 1239 (2005); Mark Tushnet, *The Possibilities of Comparative Constitutional Law*, 108 YALE L.J. 1225 (1999).

71. 302 U.S. at 325.

72. 125 S. Ct. at 1190 (quoting Trop v. Dulles, 356 U.S. 86, 100–1 [1958] [plurality opinion]).

73. *Lawrence*, 539 U.S. at 567–72.

74. See 478 U.S. at 214–16 (Stevens, J., dissenting).

75. See *Lawrence*, 539 U.S. at 568.

76. See id. at 572.

77. Id. Others have made this argument before. See supra note 36.

78. I assume (or concede) that Harlan and the joint opinion in *Casey* also chart a middle course. But I contend that constitutional constructivism's guiding framework charts a superior middle course.

79. See supra text accompanying notes 21–22 and chapter 3.

80. *Palko*, 302 U.S. at 325.

81. *Loving*, 388 U.S. at 12.

82. See chapter 5, note 17 and accompanying text. The criterion of significance also can account for why certain other asserted rights are not on the list. See infra text accompanying notes 110–28.

83. 505 U.S. at 901.

84. 539 U.S. at 578.

85. *Casey*, 505 U.S. at 998, 1000 (Scalia, J., concurring in the judgment in part and dissenting in part).

86. By "homology," I simply mean symmetry in the structures of these two bodies of constitutional law. Homology or homologous means "having the same relation to an original or fundamental type; corresponding in type of structure." 5 THE OXFORD ENGLISH DICTIONARY 359 (1933). Homology also connotes "symmetry in organization." Id. For a sophisticated analysis of homologies in constitutional interpretation, see WILLIAM F. HARRIS II, THE INTERPRETABLE CONSTITUTION (1993).

For a somewhat analogous attempt to apply doctrinal structures of the First Amendment to the Takings Clause, see Richard A. Epstein, *Property, Speech, and the Politics of Distrust*, 59 U. CHI. L. REV. 41, 47–59 (1992). I do not adopt the view that the First Amendment is solely concerned with process to the exclusion of substance, or with deliberative democracy to the exclusion of deliberative autonomy. Freedom of thought and expression are important for deliberative autonomy as well as for deliberative democracy. I simply am making observations about the structure of First Amendment jurisprudence in relation to that of substantive due process jurisprudence.

87. See, e.g., LAURENCE H. TRIBE, AMERICAN CONSTITUTIONAL LAW 832–944 (2d ed. 1988) (discussing "two-level" theory of freedom of speech based on the Court's assessment of its relative value); see also Harry Kalven Jr., *The Metaphysics of the Law of Obscenity*, 1960 SUP. CT. REV. 1, 10. More than anyone else on the Court in recent years, Justice Stevens has appreciated the centrality of judgments of significance in First Amendment jurisprudence. See, e.g., R.A.V. v. City of St. Paul, 505 U.S. 377, 421 (1992) (Stevens, J., concurring) ("Speech about public officials or matters of public concern receives greater protection than speech about other topics. It can, therefore, scarcely be said that the regulation of expressive activity cannot be predicated on its content: Much of our First Amendment jurisprudence is premised on the assumption that content makes a difference").

88. See, e.g., ELY, DD, supra note 34, at 105–16; CASS R. SUNSTEIN, DEMOCRACY AND THE PROBLEM OF FREE SPEECH 8–11, 121–29 (1993) [hereinafter SUNSTEIN, DPFS].

89. See Miller v. California, 413 U.S. 15 (1973) (obscenity); Brandenburg v. Ohio, 395 U.S. 444 (1969) (incitement to imminent lawless action); New York

Times v. Sullivan, 376 U.S. 254 (1964) (libel); Beauharnais v. Illinois, 343 U.S. 250 (1952) (group libel); Chaplinsky v. New Hampshire, 315 U.S. 568 (1942) (fighting words). Admittedly, these categories have eroded over time, partly due to the pressure of autonomy and neutrality theories. See SUNSTEIN, DPFS, supra note 88, at 137–44, 167–208 (defending a two-tier conception of the First Amendment and criticizing autonomy-based conceptions and some neutrality conceptions); TRIBE, supra note 87, at 832–944.

90. See, e.g., ELY, DD, supra note 34, at 109–11.

91. But see *R.A.V.*, 505 U.S. at 391–92 (extending prohibition on content discrimination and more stringent scrutiny to apply within traditionally unprotected category of fighting words). Content-neutral time, place, and manner regulations, erosion of the categories of unprotected expression, and the development of an intermediate level of protection for commercial speech add complications to this scheme. See TRIBE, supra note 87, at 789–94, 890–904.

92. See ELY, DD, supra note 34, at 105–16; CASS R. SUNSTEIN, THE PARTIAL CONSTITUTION 232–56 (1993) [hereinafter SUNSTEIN, PC]; SUNSTEIN, DPFS, supra note 88, at 121–29.

93. See, e.g., *Casey*, 505 U.S. at 847 (joint opinion); id. at 927 (Blackmun, J., concurring in part, concurring in the judgment in part, and dissenting in part).

94. I put to one side the complications introduced by the Court's development of intermediate levels of scrutiny, undue burden tests, and the like.

95. Nor are these judgments readily made by studying historical facts in the narrow, neutral way that Scalia and Bork assert. See *Casey*, 505 U.S. at 1000 (Scalia, J., concurring in the judgment in part and dissenting in part); ROBERT H. BORK, THE TEMPTING OF AMERICA 139–60, 176–78, 213–14 (1990). They can be made only through elaborating a substantive political theory of the Constitution.

96. Remarkably, the theorists who have the most difficulty with the idea of making judgments about the significance of certain types of decisions in the substantive due process area are not uncommonly the ones who have the least difficulty with the idea of making judgments about the significance of certain types of expression in the First Amendment area. Ely and Bork come to mind as leading examples. Bork argued for limiting the language of the "enumerated" First Amendment to protecting political speech on the basis of inferences from the structure of a republican form of government, from which he would also derive the "unenumerated" right to vote, notwithstanding his attacks (a mere ten pages later) on the right to privacy for being "unenumerated." See BORK, supra note 95, at 85–87, 95–100; Robert H. Bork, *Neutral Principles and Some First Amendment Problems*, 47 IND. L.J. 1, 19–35 (1971). But see BORK, supra note 95, at 333 (stating that he "later abandoned" the position that the Constitution protects only political speech, not because it "was not true, but because it results in an unworkable rule"). Similarly, Ely construes the language of the First Amendment principally to protect political expression because it is "critical to the functioning of an open

and effective democratic process," despite his critique of theories of protecting "unenumerated" substantive fundamental rights on the ground that they require judgments concerning what rights are fundamental or important. See ELY, DD, supra note 34, at 43–72, 87–88, 93–94, 105.

97. *Bowers*, 478 U.S. at 194.

98. But see SUNSTEIN, PC, supra note 92, at 84–85, 223–24 (arguing that the legacy of *Lochner* includes First Amendment decisions such as Buckley v. Valeo, 424 U.S. 1 [1976]); see also Mark Tushnet, *An Essay on Rights*, 62 TEX. L. REV. 1363, 1387 (1984) ("The first amendment has replaced the due process clause as the primary guarantor of the privileged"). In *Buckley*, 424 U.S. at 48–49, the Court struck down certain campaign finance restrictions on the ground that "the concept that government may restrict the speech of some elements of our society in order to enhance the relative voice of others is wholly foreign to the First Amendment." According to Sunstein, *Buckley* is part of the legacy of *Lochner* because it evinces status quo neutrality in the sense that the Court treats the status quo of existing distributions of wealth and political power as a neutral, prepolitical state of nature or baseline and therefore holds that interfering with it is an impermissible, partisan objective. SUNSTEIN, PC, supra note 92, at 84–85, 223–24.

99. See chapter 3. Scalia embraced *Buckley*'s invalidation of expenditure limitations (though he rejected its upholding of contribution limitations) in Austin v. Michigan Chamber of Commerce, 494 U.S. 652, 683 (1990) (Scalia, J., dissenting). See also McConnell v. Federal Election Comm'n, 540 U.S. 93, 248 (2003) (Scalia, J., concurring in part and dissenting in part) (stating that he continued to believe that *Buckley* was wrongly decided with respect to its upholding of contribution limitations).

100. See chapter 3 (contrasting Ely's and Sunstein's understandings of what was wrong with *Lochner*).

101. For the idea of carrying forward "the unfinished business of Charles Black," see chapter 5. Black and Dworkin have argued persuasively that the First Amendment is not as different from other constitutional provisions (such as the Due Process and Equal Protection Clauses) with respect to the largely "spurious" or "bogus" distinction between "enumerated" and "unenumerated" rights as narrow originalists are at pains to maintain. See chapter 5.

102. See, e.g., Richard H. Fallon Jr., *Two Senses of Autonomy*, 46 STAN. L. REV. 875, 875–76 (1994).

103. Indeed, we sometimes hear calls for a comprehensive autonomy approach to the First Amendment: to cease allowing regulation of some or all categories of currently unprotected expression, such as fighting words, obscenity, incitement to imminent lawless action, libel, or group libel. See, e.g., Eric M. Freedman, *A Lot More Comes Into Focus When You Remove the Lens Cap: Why Proliferating New Communications Technologies Make It Particularly Urgent for the Supreme Court to Abandon Its Inside-Out Approach to Freedom of Speech and Bring Obscenity,*

*Fighting Words, and Group Libel within the First Amendment*, 81 IOWA L. REV. 883 (1996).

In referring to "a comprehensive Millian principle of the autonomy or individuality of citizens," I mean to evoke but not to offer an interpretation of T. M. Scanlon's well-known autonomy theory and "Millian principle" of freedom of expression. There are differences between these two sorts of Millian principle. Scanlon generalized Meiklejohn's famous theory of the absolute First Amendment beyond political speech to virtually all speech. See Thomas M. Scanlon, *A Theory of Freedom of Expression*, 1 PHIL. & PUB. AFF. 204 (1972). For Meiklejohn's theory, see ALEXANDER MEIKLEJOHN, FREE SPEECH AND ITS RELATION TO SELF-GOVERNMENT, in POLITICAL FREEDOM: THE CONSTITUTIONAL POWERS OF THE PEOPLE 3 (1965); Alexander Meiklejohn, *The First Amendment Is an Absolute*, 1961 SUP. CT. REV. 245. He subsequently reconstructed his theory, allowing greater room for continuing to recognize categories of unprotected expression. See T. M. Scanlon Jr., *Freedom of Expression and Categories of Expression*, 40 U. PITT. L. REV. 519 (1979); see also T. M. Scanlon Jr., *Content Regulation Reconsidered,* in DEMOCRACY AND THE MASS MEDIA 331 (Judith Lichtenberg ed., 1990). For other leading autonomy theories of the First Amendment, see, e.g., C. EDWIN BAKER, HUMAN LIBERTY AND FREEDOM OF SPEECH (1989); DAVID A. J. RICHARDS, TOLERATION AND THE CONSTITUTION (1986); SUSAN H. WILLIAMS, TRUTH, AUTONOMY, AND SPEECH (2004).

104. By "Millian harm principle," I refer to Mill's idea that the only justification for government's interfering with a person's liberty is to prevent harm to others, not harm to self. In other words, government may regulate only "other-regarding," not merely "self-regarding" action. See JOHN STUART MILL, ON LIBERTY 10–11 (David Spitz ed., 1975) (1859).

105. See, e.g., JOEL FEINBERG, HARM TO SELF 56 (1986) (arguing that autonomy implies a right to personal sovereignty that embraces "all those decisions that are 'self-regarding,' that is, which primarily and directly affect only the interests of the decision-maker").

106. Cf. chapter 3 (discussing the Janus-faced Fourteenth Amendment in criticizing Sunstein's analysis of the relationship between due process and equal protection).

107. John Hart Ely, *Democracy and the Right to be Different*, 56 N.Y.U. L. REV. 397, 405 (1981) [hereinafter Ely, *Different*].

108. See ELY, DD, supra note 34, at 59 n.**, 94.

109. Ely, *Different*, supra note 107, at 401 (quotation omitted); see chapter 4 (responding to a similar paraphrase of Justice Holmes's *Lochner* dissent with respect to Rawls's *A Theory of Justice* and *Political Liberalism*).

110. Rawls distinguishes political liberalism from the comprehensive liberalisms of Mill and Kant. JOHN RAWLS, POLITICAL LIBERALISM 98–100, 154–58, 199–200 (1993) [hereinafter RAWLS, PL]. A comprehensive liberalism is itself a

comprehensive philosophical conception of the good, from which Rawls distinguishes his own political conception of justice. Id. at 154–58.

111. See ELY, DD, supra note 34, at 178; chapter 5.

112. Kelley v. Johnson, 425 U.S. 238, 249–53 (1976) (Marshall, J., dissenting) (hair length); Doe v. Bolton, 410 U.S. 179, 213 (1973) (Douglas, J., concurring) (loafing).

113. See ROGERS M. SMITH, LIBERALISM AND AMERICAN CONSTITUTIONAL LAW 234–35 (1985) (critiquing the "romantic liberalism" associated with Justices Douglas and Marshall); Rogers M. Smith, *The Constitution and Autonomy*, 60 TEX. L. REV. 175, 189–90 (1982) (noting the broad range of freedoms protected under the "privacy as autonomy" view of Justices Douglas and Marshall).

114. Especially, for example, if hair length is related to religious or cultural practices. Anti-loafing ordinances might also pose problems if aimed against homeless persons.

115. JOHN RAWLS, A THEORY OF JUSTICE (1971).

116. See RAWLS, PL, supra note 110, at 98–100, 199–200.

117. See id. at xvi–xvii.

118. See RANDY E. BARNETT, RESTORING THE LOST CONSTITUTION: THE PRESUMPTION OF LIBERTY (2004).

119. See RAWLS, PL, supra note 110, at 291–92, 294–98.

120. See James E. Fleming, *Fidelity, Basic Liberties, and the Specter of* Lochner, 41 WM. & MARY L. REV. 147, 147, 165–73 (1999); William Michael Treanor, *The Original Understanding of the Takings Clause and the Political Process*, 95 COLUM. L. REV. 782, 855–87 (1995). Contra Epstein, supra note 86, at 47–59.

121. See, e.g., RICHARD A. EPSTEIN, TAKINGS (1985); RICHARD A. EPSTEIN, SKEPTICISM AND FREEDOM (2003); BARNETT, supra note 118. But see ROBERT NOZICK, ANARCHY, STATE, AND UTOPIA 163 (1974) (stating that a hypothetical "socialist society would have to forbid capitalist[ic] acts between consenting adults").

122. Lochner v. New York, 198 U.S. 45, 61 (1905).

123. See STEPHEN MACEDO, LIBERAL VIRTUES 209 (1990) (arguing that liberalism does not rule out certain mild forms of paternalism).

124. Id.; see also SMITH, supra note 113, at 213 (arguing that liberalism allows prohibition of actions that "endanger[] persons' continuing capacities for rational deliberation").

125. Admittedly, some forms of paternalism (or other laws) may drive some people who feel that "they've had enough" to exercise their "exit" option, pull up stakes, and seek a "frontier." To do precisely that is itself one of such persons' "unenumerated" fundamental rights encompassed by the foregoing list. For analyses of the "exit" option or the "frontier" in constitutional law, see chapter 5.

126. *Lawrence*, 539 U.S. at 599 (Scalia, J., dissenting).

127. Id. at 590.

128. Thus, the idea of deliberative autonomy is not nearly as broad as the general libertarian slogan "Don't tread on me." In a free society, we should be grateful to the libertarians, for they serve as a salutary reminder that the exercise of coercive political power always requires a justification and entails some loss of liberty; but we should not confuse their slogan and beliefs with constitutional essentials such as deliberative autonomy.

129. CATHARINE A. MACKINNON, *Privacy v. Equality: Beyond* Roe v. Wade, in FEMINISM UNMODIFIED: DISCOURSES ON LIFE AND LAW 100 (1987).

130. Id. at 102.

131. See id. at 100–2; Mary E. Becker, *The Politics of Women's Wrongs and the Bill of "Rights": A Bicentennial Perspective*, 59 U. CHI. L. REV. 453, 453–55 (1992); Mary E. Becker, *Towards a Progressive Politics and a Progressive Constitution*, 69 FORDHAM L. REV. 2007 (2001); Robin West, *Reconstructing Liberty*, 59 TENN. L. REV. 441, 454–61 (1992).

132. See CATHARINE A. MACKINNON, ONLY WORDS 71–110 (1993); Elizabeth M. Schneider, *The Violence of Privacy*, 23 CONN. L. REV. 973 (1991); West, supra note 131, at 454–61.

133. For works defending privacy from feminist viewpoints, see ANITA L. ALLEN, UNEASY ACCESS: PRIVACY FOR WOMEN IN A FREE SOCIETY (1988); Linda C. McClain, *"Atomistic Man" Revisited: Liberalism, Connection, and Feminist Juris-prudence*, 65 S. CAL. L. REV. 1171 (1992); Linda C. McClain, *Inviolability and Privacy: The Castle, the Sanctuary, and the Body*, 7 YALE J.L. & HUMAN. 195 (1995) [hereinafter McClain, *Inviolability*]; Linda C. McClain, *The Poverty of Privacy?* 3 COLUM. J. GENDER & L. 119, 124–50 (1992); Schneider, supra note 132, at 975.

134. See Catharine A. MacKinnon, *Reflections on Sex Equality under Law*, 100 YALE L.J. 1281, 1311 (1991).

135. See DWORKIN, supra note 30, at 53–54.

136. MACKINNON, supra note 129, at 100–2.

137. See, e.g., McClain, *Inviolability*, supra note 133, at 207–20. McClain observes that neither MacKinnon nor Robin West offers any examples of courts using these privacy precedents to justify marital rape exemptions, and states that she has found no such examples. Id. at 217.

138. See id. at 216–20.

139. The distinction, though, is problematic. See SOTIRIOS A. BARBER, WELFARE AND THE CONSTITUTION (2003); Susan Bandes, *The Negative Constitution: A Cri-tique*, 88 MICH. L. REV. 2271 (1990). For further discussion, see chapter 9.

140. 448 U.S. 297 (1980); see MACKINNON, supra note 129, at 96–102.

141. 489 U.S. 189 (1989).

142. See *Harris*, 448 U.S. at 329 (Brennan, J., dissenting, joined by Justices Marshall and Blackmun); id. at 337 (Marshall, J., dissenting); id. at 348 (Blackmun, J., dissenting); *DeShaney*, 489 U.S. at 203 (Brennan, J., dissenting, joined by Justices Marshall and Blackmun); id. at 212 (Blackmun, J., dissenting).

143. See, e.g., *Casey*, 505 U.S. at 944 (Rehnquist, C.J., concurring in the judgment in part and dissenting in part); id. at 979 (Scalia, J., concurring in the judgment in part and dissenting in part); *DeShaney*, 489 U.S. at 191 (Rehnquist, C.J., and Scalia, J., joining majority); *Michael H.*, 491 U.S. at 113 (Scalia, J., plurality opinion, in which Rehnquist, C.J., joined); *Roe*, 410 U.S. at 171 (Rehnquist, J., dissenting).

144. See RAWLS, PL, supra note 110, at 221 n.8; accord Cass R. Sunstein, *Beyond the Republican Revival*, 97 YALE L.J. 1539, 1567 (1988) (stating that it is a "large mistake to suggest that liberal thinkers believed that threats lay only in government intrusions and that there was no right to protection from private power"). Mill, another important liberal thinker, criticized misplaced protection of liberty permitting the "almost despotic power of husbands over wives" and argued that "wives should have the same rights, and should receive the protection of the law in the same manner, as all other persons." MILL, supra note 104, at 97; see also SUSAN MOLLER OKIN, JUSTICE, GENDER, AND THE FAMILY 89–109 (1989); Susan Moller Okin, *Reason and Feeling in Thinking about Justice*, 99 ETHICS 229 (1989) (both setting forth a feminist argument that Rawls's liberal conceptions provide a basis for a critique of gender inequality). This is not to suggest that our Constitution in general requires protection from private power, but rather to observe that Rawls's political liberalism does.

145. LAWRENCE G. SAGER, JUSTICE IN PLAINCLOTHES: A THEORY OF AMERICAN CONSTITUTIONAL PRACTICE 84 (2004). Sager argues, rightly, that "the obligation to reform structurally entrenched social bias" is a precept of political justice that is "justifiably underenforced by the judiciary." Id. at 87. He argues that there are "complex choices of strategy and responsibility that are properly the responsibility of popular political institutions" in the first instance rather than courts. I largely agree with him in this respect. Sager has noted affinities between his view of the "thinness" of adjudicated constitutional law as compared with our richer conceptions of justice, on the one hand, and Rawls's view that constitutional essentials are thinner than the whole of justice, on the other. See Lawrence G. Sager, *The Why of Constitutional Essentials*, 72 FORDHAM L. REV. 1421 (2004).

146. *Olmstead*, 277 U.S. at 478 (Brandeis, J., dissenting). Again, I make no claim to be interpreting Brandeis's own conception of "the right to be let alone." See chapter 5.

147. Charles L. Black Jr., *Further Reflections on the Constitutional Justice of Livelihood*, 86 COLUM. L. REV. 1103, 1117 (1986).

148. Id.

## Chapter Seven

1. See JOHN RAWLS, POLITICAL LIBERALISM 3–22 (1993) [hereinafter RAWLS, PL]. I do not claim that the role of constitutional theory in general—or my theory

in particular—is to settle moral disagreement and political conflict. For a powerful and ingenious argument to the contrary, see LOUIS MICHAEL SEIDMAN, OUR UN-SETTLED CONSTITUTION (2001). Reasonable disagreement will persist, given what Rawls calls "the fact of reasonable pluralism." That fact about our constitutional order should be appreciated and cultivated rather than decried or overridden.

2. MICHAEL J. SANDEL, DEMOCRACY'S DISCONTENT: AMERICA IN SEARCH OF A PUBLIC PHILOSOPHY (1996) [hereinafter SANDEL, DD].

3. 539 U.S. 558 (2003).

4. CASS R. SUNSTEIN, LEGAL REASONING AND POLITICAL CONFLICT (1996) [hereinafter SUNSTEIN, LRPC]; CASS R. SUNSTEIN, ONE CASE AT A TIME: JUDICIAL MINIMALISM ON THE SUPREME COURT (1999) [hereinafter SUNSTEIN, OCAT].

5. Cass R. Sunstein, *What Did* Lawrence *Hold? Of Autonomy, Desuetude, Sexuality, and Marriage*, 2003 SUP. CT. REV. 27, 30 [hereinafter Sunstein, *What Did* Lawrence *Hold?*].

6. *Lawrence*, 539 U.S. at 562, 574.

7. See RAWLS, PL, supra note 1, at 37 (arguing that a single, comprehensive doctrine can be maintained only through the use of oppressive state power).

8. SANDEL, DD, supra note 2, at 4.

9. Id. at 5.

10. Id. at 4.

11. Id. at 5.

12. See Michael J. Sandel, *The Constitution of the Procedural Republic: Liberal Rights and Civic Virtues*, 66 FORDHAM L. REV. 1, 2 (1997); see also SANDEL, DD, supra note 2, at 6.

13. CASS R. SUNSTEIN, THE PARTIAL CONSTITUTION 133–41, 373 n.18 (1993) [hereinafter SUNSTEIN, PC].

14. SUNSTEIN, LRPC, supra note 4, at 7 (criticizing Ronald Dworkin, *The Forum of Principle*, 56 N.Y.U. L. REV. 469 (1981) [hereinafter Dworkin, *Forum*], *reprinted in* RONALD DWORKIN, A MATTER OF PRINCIPLE 33 (1985) [hereinafter DWORKIN, AMOP]).

15. Id. at 4, 37.

16. SUNSTEIN, OCAT, supra note 4.

17. 381 U.S. 479 (1965).

18. 505 U.S. 833 (1992).

19. See RONALD DWORKIN, LIFE'S DOMINION 157–68 (1993) [hereinafter DWORKIN, LD].

20. SANDEL, DD, supra note 2, at 106.

21. Sunstein elaborates these notions of "shallow," "narrow," and "deep" in SUNSTEIN, OCAT, supra note 4, at 10–19.

22. See SANDEL, DD, supra note 2, at 94–100.

23. See id. at 95–100.

24. *Griswold*, 381 U.S. at 485.

25. See SANDEL, DD, supra note 2, at 96.

26. Id. (quoting *Griswold*, 381 U.S. at 486).

27. See id. at 97–98.

28. 405 U.S. 438, 453 (1972) (emphasis in original).

29. 410 U.S. 113, 154 (1973).

30. 431 U.S. 678, 687 (1977).

31. *Casey*, 505 U.S. at 860.

32. SANDEL, DD, supra note 2, at 99 (quoting *Casey*, 505 U.S. at 851).

33. *Casey*, 505 U.S. at 857, 851.

34. 478 U.S. 186 (1986). For critique, see SANDEL, DD, supra note 2, at 103–8.

35. 539 U.S. 558 (2003). See infra text accompanying notes 67–113.

36. See *Bowers*, 478 U.S. at 190–91, 195–96, 196.

37. See SANDEL, DD, supra note 2, at 99–100.

38. See id. at 104–6.

39. 394 U.S. 557, 559 (1969). Sandel gives the example of People v. Onofre, 415 N.E.2d 936 (N.Y. 1980), in which New York's highest court struck down that state's sodomy law on the ground that it violated the right to privacy. See SANDEL, DD, supra note 2, at 106 n.57.

40. SANDEL, DD, supra note 2, at 107.

41. Id. at 106, 107.

42. See id.

43. *Bowers*, 478 U.S. at 205 (Blackmun, J., dissenting) (citation omitted).

44. Id. at 217 (Stevens, J., dissenting) (quoting Fitzgerald v. Porter Memorial Hosp., 523 F.2d 716, 719 [7th Cir. 1975] [Stevens, J.]) (footnotes omitted), *cert. denied*, 425 U.S. 916 (1976).

45. For a helpful feminist analysis of the problem of the constraining effects of sex inequality on women's choices and capacity for self-government, see NANCY J. HIRSCHMANN, THE SUBJECT OF LIBERTY: TOWARD A FEMINIST THEORY OF FREEDOM (2003).

46. Historically, one justification for toleration was the conviction that coercion and compulsion corrupt belief. Translated to contemporary constitutional law, that conviction is present in the statement in *Casey* that beliefs about "one's own concept of existence, of meaning, of the universe, and of the mystery of human life . . . could not define the attributes of personhood were they formed under compulsion of the State." *Casey*, 505 U.S. at 851; see LINDA C. MCCLAIN, THE PLACE OF FAMILIES: FOSTERING CAPACITY, EQUALITY, AND RESPONSIBILITY (2006) (discussing the anticompulsion rationale for toleration).

47. *Bowers*, 478 U.S. at 205 (Blackmun, J., dissenting) (emphasis in original).

48. *Casey*, 505 U.S. at 852.

49. Id. at 851–52, 856.

50. See SUNSTEIN, PC, supra note 13, at 283–84.

51. *Casey*, 505 U.S. at 852.

52. Id. at 850.

53. Id. at 878.

54. See DWORKIN, LD, supra note 19, at 151–59. Elsewhere, I have assessed Dworkin's arguments, specifically presenting them as undercutting Sandel's critique of "minimalist liberalism." See James E. Fleming and Benjamin C. Zipursky, *Rights, Responsibilities, and Reflections upon the Sanctity of Life*, in RONALD DWORKIN (Arthur Ripstein ed., forthcoming).

55. See, e.g., CARLOS A. BALL, THE MORALITY OF GAY RIGHTS (2003); Chai R. Feldblum, *Sexual Orientation, Morality, and the Law: Devlin Revisited*, 57 U. PITT. L. REV. 237, 304–12 (1996).

56. 440 Mass. 309, 322, 798 N.E.2d 941, 954 (2003).

57. David Nather, "Social Conservatives Propel Bush, Republicans to Victory," *CQ Weekly*, Nov. 6, 2004, at 2586. However, subsequent analyses of initial findings that "moral values" were an animating issue for 22 percent of voters have identified flaws with polling questions and cautioned against overemphasizing the role of "moral values" in Bush's reelection. Jim Rutenberg, "Poll Question Stirs Debate on Meaning of 'Values,'" *New York Times*, Nov. 6, 2004, at A13. Eleven states passed constitutional amendments barring same-sex marriage. "State Constitutional Amendments Defining Marriage," washingtonpost.com, Nov. 24, 2004.

58. "Bush's Remarks on Marriage Amendment," *New York Times*, Feb. 25, 2004, at A18.

59. See, e.g., John M. Finnis, *Law, Morality, and "Sexual Orientation,"* 69 NOTRE DAME L. REV. 1049 (1994) (arguing that same-sex unions cannot realize the goods of marriage). For an argument that Finnis has too narrowly conceived the goods of marriage, see Paul J. Weithman, *Natural Law, Morality, and Sexual Complementarity*, in SEX, PREFERENCE, AND FAMILY: ESSAYS ON LAW AND NATURE 227 (David M. Estlund & Martha C. Nussbaum eds., 1997).

60. For Rawls's idea of public reason, see generally RAWLS, PL, supra note 1, at 212–54; John Rawls, *The Idea of Public Reason Revisited* (1997) [hereinafter Rawls, *Revisited*], *reprinted in* JOHN RAWLS, COLLECTED PAPERS 573 (Samuel Freeman ed., 1999). Sandel criticizes Rawls's idea of public reason in Michael J. Sandel, *Political Liberalism*, 107 HARV. L. REV. 1765, 1789–94 (1994) (reviewing RAWLS, PL, supra note 1) [hereinafter Sandel, *Political Liberalism*].

61. See Sandel, *Political Liberalism*, supra note 60, at 1794. By contrast, Rawls's idea of public reason allows citizens to make arguments in the public square based on their comprehensive moral doctrines, provided that in due course they give properly public reasons and appeal to political values to support those arguments. See Rawls, *Revisited*, supra note 60, at 584, 591–94.

62. In Baehr v. Lewin, 74 Haw. 530, 852 P.2d 44 (1993), a plurality of the Hawaii Supreme Court held that a law limiting marriage to opposite-sex couples discriminated against same-sex couples on the basis of sex in violation of the state constitution. Subsequently, an amendment to the state constitution, art. I, § 23, overturned the decision in *Baehr* by returning power to the legislature "to reserve

marriage to opposite-sex couples." Nonetheless, the Hawaii legislature passed a "reciprocal beneficiaries statute"—basically a civil union statute—to "extend certain rights and benefits which are presently available only to married couples to couples composed of two individuals who are legally prohibited from marrying under state law." Same-sex couples may enter into a reciprocal beneficiary relationship and become entitled to many, but not all, of the rights and benefits accorded to married couples. Haw. Rev. Stat. §§ 572C-1 et seq.

In Baker v. State, 170 Vt. 194, 744 A.2d 864 (1999), the Supreme Court of Vermont held that a state law limiting marriage to opposite-sex couples, and excluding same-sex couples, violated the Common Benefits Clause of the Vermont Constitution (its analogue to the Equal Protection Clause of the U.S. Constitution). Soon after the decision, the Vermont Legislature enacted a statute recognizing same-sex civil unions while not recognizing same-sex marriage. Nonetheless, it afforded all of the benefits of marriage (except the name "marriage") to such civil unions. An Act Relating to Civil Unions, 2000 Vt. ALS 91.

In Halpern v. Toronto (City), 172 O.A.C. 276 (2003), the highest court of the province of Ontario, Canada held that the statute limiting marriage to opposite-sex couples violated the equal protection provisions of Canada's Charter of Rights and Freedoms; see also Eagle Canada, Inc. v. Canada (Attorney Gen.), 13 B.C.L.R. (4th) 1 (2003) (same).

63. Both the joint opinion in *Casey* and the majority opinion in *Lawrence* reflect this idea. See infra text accompanying note 87.

64. Michael S. Moore refers to the "goodness of pluralism, tolerance, and autonomy" in formulating a liberal response to Sandel. Michael S. Moore, *Sandelian Antiliberalism*, 77 CAL. L. REV. 539, 550 (1989).

65. See Linda C. McClain, *Toleration, Autonomy, and Governmental Promotion of Good Lives: Beyond "Empty" Toleration to Toleration as Respect*, 59 OHIO ST. L.J. 19 (1998) [hereinafter McClain, *Beyond "Empty" Toleration to Toleration as Respect*] (arguing for a model of toleration as respect over a model of empty toleration).

66. 798 N.E.2d at 973.

67. Sunstein, *What Did* Lawrence *Hold?*, supra note 5, at 29–30.

68. See, e.g., SANDEL, DD, supra note 2, at 4–8, 91–119.

69. *Lawrence*, 539 U.S. at 562, 574.

70. JOHN STUART MILL, ON LIBERTY 10–11 (David Spitz ed., 1975) (1859).

71. *Lawrence*, 539 U.S. at 567.

72. Id. at 578.

73. See Randy E. Barnett, *Justice Kennedy's Libertarian Revolution:* Lawrence v. Texas, 2002–3 CATO SUPREME COURT REVIEW 21.

74. 539 U.S. at 574 (quoting *Casey*, 505 U.S. at 851).

75. Id. (quoting *Casey*, 505 U.S. at 851).

76. Id. at 588 (Scalia, J., dissenting).

77. Sandel cringed at these passages when the joint opinion in *Casey* initially uttered them. See SANDEL, DD, supra note 2, at 99.

78. Id.

79. *Lawrence*, 539 U.S. at 565–67.

80. Id. at 562, 574.

81. SANDEL, DD, supra note 2, at 94–98. For Glendon's similar analysis, see MARY ANN GLENDON, RIGHTS TALK: THE IMPOVERISHMENT OF POLITICAL DISCOURSE 57 (1991).

82. SANDEL, DD, supra note 2, at 97–99.

83. See 539 U.S. at 574, 578.

84. SANDEL, DD, supra note 2, at 106–7.

85. Id. at 107.

86. *Lawrence*, 539 U.S. at 571.

87. Id. (quoting *Casey*, 505 U.S. at 850).

88. Id. at 567, 575, 578.

89. See McClain, *Beyond "Empty" Toleration to Toleration as Respect*, supra note 65.

90. *Lawrence*, 539 U.S. at 574–75.

91. See Romer v. Evans, 517 U.S. 620, 634–36 (1996).

92. 539 U.S. at 579 (O'Connor, J., concurring in the judgment).

93. See Frank I. Michelman, *Law's Republic*, 97 YALE L.J.1493, 1532–37 (1988).

94. *Lawrence*, 539 U.S. at 575.

95. See id. at 567, 574, 578. Indeed, in a recent "epilogue" to his critique of *Bowers*, Sandel offers an analysis of *Lawrence* that is similar to mine: "But despite its rhetoric of autonomy and choice, Justice Kennedy's opinion also gestured toward a different, more substantive reason for striking down the Texas law— that it wrongly demeaned a morally legitimate mode of life." Sandel continues: "Privacy rights should protect the sexual intimacy of gays and straights alike, not because sex reflects autonomy and choice, but because it expresses an important human good." MICHAEL J. SANDEL, PUBLIC PHILOSOPHY: ESSAYS ON MORALITY IN POLITICS 142 (2005) [hereinafter SANDEL, PUBLIC PHILOSOPHY].

96. Id. at 590 (Scalia, J., dissenting).

97. Compare id. at 574 (majority) with id. at 590 (Scalia, J., dissenting).

98. 262 U.S. 390 (1923).

99. 478 U.S. at 190–91.

100. *Lawrence*, 539 U.S. at 599 (Scalia, J., dissenting).

101. Id. at 590.

102. Id. at 602.

103. Id. (quoting id. at 575 [majority]).

104. Id. at 602.

105. See *Romer*, 517 U.S. at 631.

106. *Bowers*, 478 U.S. at 196.

107. *Lawrence*, 539 U.S. at 568.

108. Id.; see Jonathan Ned Katz, The Invention of Heterosexuality 10 (1995).

109. Michelman, supra note 93, at 1493, 1502, 1513–14.

110. See *Lawrence*, 539 U.S. at 585.

111. See id. at 574; cf. Sandel, Public Philosophy, supra note 95, at 142 (discussed supra note 95) (analyzing Kennedy's opinion as recognizing important human goods, not simply celebrating autonomy and choice).

112. See id. at 567.

113. Id.

114. See, e.g., Cass R. Sunstein, *Liberal Constitutionalism and Liberal Justice*, 72 Tex. L. Rev. 305, 312 (1993) (suggesting that reliance on equal protection principles could provide a narrower and more secure basis for judicial decisions).

115. Sunstein, LRPC, supra note 4, at 156.

116. See id. at 155.

117. Id. at 156.

118. Id.

119. Sunstein, *What Did* Lawrence *Hold?*, supra note 5, at 30.

120. See Sunstein, LRPC, supra note 4, at 180–81; Sunstein, PC, supra note 13, at 270–75, 402 n.17.

121. Sunstein, LRPC, supra note 4, at 181.

122. See id. at 180.

123. Id.

124. Sunstein, PC, supra note 13, at 402 n.17.

125. See Sunstein, LRPC, supra note 4, at 180–81.

126. Id. at 181.

127. See Sunstein, OCAT, supra note 4, at 156 (contending that the opinion in Loving v. Virginia, 388 U.S. 1 [1967], which ruled that a ban on miscegenation was unconstitutional, was maximalist because it rested in part on a right to marry grounded in substantive due process, not simply on equal protection).

128. Cass R. Sunstein, *Massachusetts Gets It Right: Federal Appeal*, New Republic, Dec. 22, 2003, at 21, 22. In the same issue of the magazine, Jeffrey Rosen wrote the piece sounding in judicial minimalism that some might have expected Sunstein to write. See Jeffrey Rosen, *Massachusetts Gets It Wrong on Gay Marriage: Immodest Proposal*, New Republic, Dec. 22, 2003, at 19.

129. 517 U.S. at 635. Sunstein discusses *Romer* in Sunstein, OCAT, supra note 4, at 137–62.

130. *Romer*, 517 U.S. at 634, 635 (quoting USDA v. Moreno, 413 U.S. 528, 534 [1973]).

131. See Sunstein, OCAT, supra note 4, at 151, 156–67.

132. See supra text accompanying notes 5 & 119.

133. See Sunstein, PC, supra note 13, at 259.

134. See chapter 3.

135. 347 U.S. 483 (1954).

136. SUNSTEIN, PC, supra note 13, at 260.

137. 388 U.S. 1 (1967).

138. SUNSTEIN, LRPC, supra note 4, at 95; SUNSTEIN, PC, supra note 13, at 402 n.17.

139. SUNSTEIN, LRPC, supra note 4, at 180–81; SUNSTEIN, OCAT, supra note 4 at 159–61.

140. See SUNSTEIN, LRPC, supra note 4, at 180–81.

141. Compare MARY ANN GLENDON, ABORTION AND DIVORCE IN WESTERN LAW 47, 47–50 (1987) (arguing that a "decision leaving abortion regulation basically up to state legislatures would have encouraged constructive activity by partisans of both sides"), with LAURENCE H. TRIBE, ABORTION: THE CLASH OF ABSOLUTES 49–51 (1990) (stating that "the history of abortion law reform in the United States seriously undermines [Glendon's] claim").

142. See TRIBE, supra note 141, at 143–47.

143. 539 U.S. at 573–74.

144. *Romer*, 517 U.S. at 644.

145. See SUNSTEIN, OCAT, supra note 4, at 155–56. For a critique of Sunstein's distinction between due process and equal protection along these lines, see chapter 3.

146. See RONALD DWORKIN, SOVEREIGN VIRTUE: THE THEORY AND PRACTICE OF EQUALITY 49–50 (2000); see also Ronald Dworkin, *The Arduous Virtue of Fidelity: Originalism, Scalia, Tribe, and Nerve*, 65 FORDHAM L. REV. 1249, 1268 (1996) (criticizing *Romer* for not overruling *Bowers* and criticizing pragmatic approaches to distinguishing those cases: "Lives don't pause while the passive, pragmatic virtues drape themselves in epigrams and preen in law journal articles").

147. SUNSTEIN, LRPC, supra note 4, at 194.

148. Id. at 95.

149. See id. at 79–83.

150. Id. at 177 (pointing out that judges confront only small-scale pieces of systemic controversies, are drawn from relatively narrow segments of society, and generally lack any philosophical training or other unique bases for moral evaluation).

151. Id. at 176. Here Sunstein endorses the argument made in GERALD N. ROSENBERG, THE HOLLOW HOPE: CAN COURTS BRING ABOUT SOCIAL CHANGE? (1991).

152. See, e.g., RONALD DWORKIN, TAKING RIGHTS SERIOUSLY (1997); Dworkin, *Forum*, supra note 14.

153. West Virginia State Bd. of Educ. v. Barnette, 319 U.S. 624, 638, 640 (1943) (Jackson, J., for the majority), *overruling* Minersville Sch. Dist. v. Gobitis, 310 U.S. 586 (1940) (Frankfurter, J., for the majority).

154. See SUNSTEIN, PC, supra note 13, at 9–10 (suggesting that in constitutional theory too much emphasis has been put on the courts' role and that nonjudicial strategies of interpretation and enforcement should be considered).

155. James Bradley Thayer, *The Origin and Scope of the American Doctrine of Constitutional Law*, 7 HARV. L. REV. 129 (1893).

156. SUNSTEIN, PC, supra note 13, at 145–61.

157. See, e.g., id. at 9–10; ROBIN WEST, PROGRESSIVE CONSTITUTIONALISM (1994); LAWRENCE G. SAGER, JUSTICE IN PLAINCLOTHES: A THEORY OF AMERICAN CONSTITUTIONAL PRACTICE (2004); LARRY D. KRAMER, THE PEOPLE THEMSELVES: POPULAR CONSTITUTIONALISM AND JUDICIAL REVIEW (2004); *Symposium: Theories of Taking the Constitution Seriously Outside the Courts*, 73 FORDHAM L. REV. 1341 (2005). A notable earlier book challenged the view that the Constitution is solely what the courts say it is and analyzed the responsibility of members of Congress to deliberate on constitutional issues. See DONALD G. MORGAN, CONGRESS AND THE CONSTITUTION: A STUDY OF RESPONSIBILITY (1966). Other recent works taking the Constitution seriously outside the courts include STEPHEN M. GRIFFIN, AMERICAN CONSTITUTIONALISM (1996); SANFORD LEVINSON, CONSTITUTIONAL FAITH (1988); WAYNE D. MOORE, CONSTITUTIONAL RIGHTS AND POWERS OF THE PEOPLE (1996); KEITH E. WHITTINGTON, CONSTITUTIONAL CONSTRUCTION: DIVIDED POWERS AND CONSTITUTIONAL MEANING (1999). For assessments of "juristocracy" and the empowerment of judiciaries through constitutionalization to the detriment of democratic politics, see RAN HIRSCHL, TOWARDS JURISTOCRACY: THE ORIGINS AND CONSEQUENCES OF THE NEW CONSTITUTIONALISM (2004); Linda C. McClain & James E. Fleming, *Constitutionalism, Judicial Review, and Progressive Change*, 84 TEXAS LAW REVIEW 433 (2005).

158. MARK TUSHNET, TAKING THE CONSTITUTION AWAY FROM THE COURTS (1999). For a fuller critique, see James E. Fleming, *The Constitution Outside the Courts*, 86 CORNELL LAW REVIEW 215 (2000).

159. See Thayer, supra note 155, at 148–56.

160. See id. at 150.

161. This contrast is famously put in Dworkin, *Forum*, supra note 14, at 516–18.

162. See, e.g., JEFFREY SEGAL & HAROLD SPAETH, THE SUPREME COURT AND THE ATTITUDINAL MODEL (1993); Frank B. Cross, *The Judiciary and Public Choice*, 50 HASTINGS L.J. 355 (1999); Frank B. Cross, *Political Science and the New Legal Realism: A Case of Unfortunate Interdisciplinary Ignorance*, 92 NW. U. L. REV. 251 (1997).

163. See, e.g., SUNSTEIN, LRPC, supra note 4, at 7, 59–60.

164. See chapter 4 (quoting RAWLS, PL, supra note 1, at 240).

165. For the second or third approach to get off the ground, we need a fuller account of constitutional interpretation outside the courts than Tushnet and Sunstein have provided. That is, we need an account of what legislatures and executives are supposed to do when they engage in conscientious constitutional

interpretation. Besides Tushnet's and Sunstein's work, and the works cited supra note 157, the most promising work includes NEAL DEVINS & LOUIS FISHER, THE DEMOCRATIC CONSTITUTION (2004); LOUIS FISHER, CONSTITUTIONAL DIALOGUES: INTERPRETATION AS POLITICAL PROCESS (1988); LOUIS FISHER & NEAL DEVINS, POLITICAL DYNAMICS OF CONSTITUTIONAL LAW (3d ed. 2000); Louis Fisher, *Constitutional Interpretation by Members of Congress*, 63 N.C. L. REV. 707 (1985); Keith E. Whittington, *Extrajudicial Constitutional Interpretation: Three Objections and Responses*, 80 N.C. L. REV. 773 (2002). See also JEREMY WALDRON, THE DIGNITY OF LEGISLATION (1999); JEREMY WALDRON, LAW AND DISAGREEMENT (1999).

## Chapter Eight

1. T. M. Scanlon perceptively and rigorously argues that we should acknowledge clashes of such higher order interests or values, but not clashes of institutionally specified rights. See T. M. Scanlon, *Adjusting Rights and Balancing Values*, 72 FORDHAM L. REV. 1477, 1478–79 (2004) [hereinafter Scanlon, *Adjusting Rights*] (replying to James E. Fleming, *Securing Deliberative Democracy*, 72 FORDHAM L. REV. 1435 [2004], an article from which I draw in this chapter).

2. See JOHN RAWLS, POLITICAL LIBERALISM 223, 295 (1993) [hereinafter RAWLS, PL].

3. 424 U.S. 1 (1976).

4. 505 U.S. 377 (1992).

5. 468 U.S. 609 (1984).

6. 530 U.S. 640 (2000).

7. RAWLS, PL, supra note 2, at 6, 223, 295.

8. Id. at 330. Rawls argues that "[i]t is not because political life and the participation by everyone in democratic self-government is regarded as the preeminent good for fully autonomous citizens." Id. Even so, Rawls does not side with that strand of modern liberalism that regards the political liberties as having only instrumental value, and as lacking intrinsic value. See id. at 298–99. He is, after all, trying to dispel the conflict between the traditions of democratic thought associated with Constant's distinction between the liberties of the moderns and the liberties of the ancients. Id. at 299. See chapter 4.

9. 304 U.S. 144, 152–53 n.4 (1938).

10. See JOHN HART ELY, DEMOCRACY AND DISTRUST 75–77 (1980) [hereinafter ELY, DD].

11. JOHN RAWLS, A THEORY OF JUSTICE 541–48 (1971) [hereinafter RAWLS, TJ]; RAWLS, PL, supra note 2, at 294–99.

12. RONALD DWORKIN, TAKING RIGHTS SERIOUSLY (1977) [hereinafter DWORKIN, TRS].

13. 341 U.S. 494, 517–61 (1951) (Frankfurter, J., concurring).

14. 310 U.S. 586 (1940).

15. 319 U.S. 624, 646–71 (1943) (Frankfurter, J., dissenting).

16. WALTER F. MURPHY, JAMES E. FLEMING, SOTIRIOS A. BARBER & STEPHEN MACEDO, AMERICAN CONSTITUTIONAL INTERPRETATION 1267–69 (3d ed. 2003) (reprinting letter from Felix Frankfurter to Harlan Fiske Stone concerning *Minersville*).

17. *Dennis*, 341 U.S. at 579–81 (Black, J., dissenting).

18. *Barnette*, 319 U.S. at 630–31.

19. Id. at 642.

20. For examples of leading constitutional theorists who proudly took their stand in favor of absolutism (or stringent protection of fundamental rights of free expression) over and against balancing, see, e.g., C. EDWIN BAKER, HUMAN LIBERTY AND FREEDOM OF SPEECH (1989); DWORKIN, TRS, supra note 12; ELY, DD, supra note 10; THOMAS I. EMERSON, THE SYSTEM OF FREEDOM OF EXPRESSION (1970); Alexander Meiklejohn, *The First Amendment Is an Absolute*, 1961 SUP. CT. REV. 245 [hereinafter Meiklejohn, *Absolute*]. Leading political philosophers who take a similar stance include Rawls and Scanlon. See RAWLS, PL, supra note 2, at 344, 352–56; Thomas M. Scanlon, *A Theory of Freedom of Expression*, 1 PHIL. & PUB. AFF. 204 (1972); T. M. Scanlon Jr., *Freedom of Expression and Categories of Expression*, 40 U. PITT. L. REV. 519 (1979).

21. No one made this clearer than Ronald Dworkin in his famous call for taking rights seriously and in his arguments that individual rights are not simply to be balanced against governmental claims of authority. See DWORKIN, TRS, supra note 12, at 184–205.

22. RAWLS, PL, supra note 2, at 290 n.1.

23. ALEXANDER MEIKLEJOHN, FREE SPEECH AND ITS RELATION TO SELF-GOVERNMENT, in POLITICAL FREEDOM: THE CONSTITUTIONAL POWERS OF THE PEOPLE 3 (1965) [hereinafter MEIKLEJOHN, SELF-GOVERNMENT].

24. Meiklejohn, *Absolute*, supra note 20.

25. RAWLS, PL, supra note 2, at 290 n.1.

26. MEIKLEJOHN, SELF-GOVERNMENT, supra note 23, at 24–28.

27. RAWLS, PL, supra note 2, at 295, 296.

28. Id. at 294 & n.10, 295, 299.

29. Id. at 358–59.

30. See Louis Henkin, *Infallibility under Law: Constitutional Balancing*, 78 COLUM. L. REV. 1022 (1978) (distinguishing between "balancing as interpretation" and "balancing as doctrine").

31. See United States v. Dennis, 183 F.2d 201, 212 (2d Cir. 1950) (L. Hand, J.). In *Dennis v. United States*, 341 U.S. 494, 510 (1951), Chief Justice Fred M. Vinson, writing for a plurality of the Supreme Court, adopted Hand's formulation of the clear and present danger test as a gravity of the evil test, which itself is

an adaptation of Hand's balancing formula for negligence. This test in effect waters down the "clear and present danger" test (famously articulated in Justice Brandeis's concurrence in *Whitney v. California*, 274 U.S. 357, 375–78 [1927]) to the remote bad tendency test articulated in Justice Sanford's majority opinion in *Whitney*, see id. at 371, *overruled by* Brandenburg v. Ohio, 395 U.S. 444, 449 (1969); see also HARRY KALVEN JR., A WORTHY TRADITION: FREEDOM OF SPEECH IN AMERICA 198 (Jamie Kalven ed., 1988).

32. See ELY, DD, supra note 10, at 108–9 (criticizing Frankfurter's concurring opinion in *Dennis*, 341 U.S. at 517–61).

33. See id. at 115, 233–34 n.27.

34. See RAWLS, PL, supra note 2, at 362.

35. Id. at 296.

36. Id. at 329.

37. Id. at 325–26; see also RAWLS, TJ, supra note 11, at 204–5. In *The Law of Peoples*, Rawls argues that a liberal political conception of justice, and a reasonably just constitutional democracy, must ensure "sufficient all-purpose means to enable all citizens to make intelligent and effective use of their freedoms." He mentions five kinds of institutions or arrangements that are necessary to prevent "social and economic inequalities from becoming excessive" and to achieve stability: (1) "[a] certain fair equality of opportunity"; (2) "[a] decent distribution of income and wealth"; (3) "[s]ociety as employer of last resort"; (4) "[b]asic health care assured for all citizens"; and (5) "[p]ublic financing of elections and ways of assuring the availability of public information on matters of policy." JOHN RAWLS, THE LAW OF PEOPLES 49, 50 (1999) [hereinafter RAWLS, LP].

38. RAWLS, PL, supra note 2, at 327; see also RAWLS, TJ, supra note 11, at 224–28, 233–34, 277–79, 356.

39. RAWLS, PL, supra note 2, at 327, 328.

40. Id. at 328.

41. Id. at 327. Rawls acknowledges that "[h]ow best to proceed is a complex and difficult matter," but he suggests that "one guideline for guaranteeing fair value seems to be to keep political parties independent of large concentrations of private economic and social power in a private-property democracy, and of government control and bureaucratic power in a liberal socialist regime." Id. at 328.

42. 424 U.S. 1 (1976).

43. 435 U.S. 765 (1978).

44. RAWLS, PL, supra note 2, at 362.

45. 376 U.S. 1 (1964).

46. 377 U.S. 533 (1964).

47. RAWLS, PL, supra note 2, at 361.

48. Id. at 362.

49. *Buckley*, 424 U.S. at 48–49.

50. RAWLS, PL, supra note 2, at 362.

51. Cf. ELY, DD, supra note 10, at 122 (arguing that the principle of "one person, one vote" is best justified as "the joint product of the Equal Protection and Republican Form [of Government] Clauses").

52. See *First Nat'l Bank*, 435 U.S. at 803–4 (White, J., dissenting); see also *Buckley*, 424 U.S. at 257–66 (White, J., dissenting). Rawls indicates that his discussion is in sympathy with White's dissenting opinions in both of these cases. RAWLS, PL, supra note 2, at 359 n.72.

53. Rawls's criticism of *Buckley* included signing the 1999 "Statement in Support of Overturning *Buckley v. Valeo*," organized jointly by the Brennan Center for Justice, the National Voting Rights Institute, and the U.S. Public Interest Research Group. (I also signed that statement.) In *The Law of Peoples*, Rawls argued that in a deliberative democracy, public deliberation must be "set free from the curse of money." RAWLS, LP, supra note 37, at 139. There he argued for "[p]ublic financing of elections and ways of assuring the availability of public information on matters of policy." Id. at 50.

As stated above, my aim is not to propose a resolution of the problems raised by campaign finance regulation. There have been many thoughtful treatments of and proposals regarding such regulation. See, e.g., BRUCE ACKERMAN & IAN AYRES, VOTING WITH DOLLARS (2002); Ronald Dworkin, *The Curse of American Politics*, N.Y. REV. BOOKS, Oct. 17, 1996, at 23; Edward B. Foley, *Equal-Dollars-Per-Voter: A Constitutional Principle of Campaign Finance*, 94 COLUM. L. REV. 1204 (1994); Eric Freedman, *Campaign Finance and the First Amendment: A Rawlsian Analysis*, 85 IOWA L. REV. 1065 (2000); David Strauss, *Corruption, Equality, and Campaign Finance*, 94 COLUM. L. REV. 1369 (1994); Kathleen Sullivan, *Against Campaign Finance Reform*, 1998 UTAH L. REV. 311.

54. 540 U.S. 93 (2003). The Supreme Court recently granted certiorari to consider whether Vermont's mandatory limits on campaign expenditures by candidates for public office violate the First Amendment and the Court's decision in *Buckley*. Landell v. Sorrell, 381 F.3d 91 (2d Cir. 2004), *cert. granted sub nom.* Randall v. Sorrell, 73 U.S.L.W. 3686 (U.S. Sept. 27, 2005) (No. 04-1528).

55. Cf. John Rawls, *Kantian Constructivism in Moral Theory* (1980), *reprinted in* JOHN RAWLS: COLLECTED PAPERS 303–5 (Samuel Freeman ed., 1999) (distinguishing between his own "Kantian" view and "Kant's view").

56. 505 U.S. 377 (1992). Here I cannot do justice to the complex issues raised by *R.A.V.*, nor is that my aim. For discussion of such issues, see, e.g., CASS R. SUNSTEIN, DEMOCRACY AND THE PROBLEM OF FREE SPEECH 180–93 (1993); Akhil Reed Amar, *The Case of the Missing Amendments: R.A.V. v. City of St. Paul*, 106 HARV. L. REV. 124 (1992) [hereinafter Amar, *The Case of the Missing Amendments*]; Elena Kagan, *Regulation of Hate Speech and Pornography after R.A.V.*, 60 U. CHI. L. REV. 873 (1993); Steven H. Shiffrin, *Racist Speech, Outsider Jurisprudence, and the Meaning of America*, 80 CORNELL L. REV. 43 (1994); Symposium: *Hate Speech after R.A.V.: More Conflict between Free Speech and Equality?* 18

WM. MITCHELL L. REV. 889 (1992). On the problems of regulating hate speech more generally, see, e.g., Charles R. Lawrence III, *If He Hollers Let Him Go: Regulating Racist Speech on Campus*, 1990 DUKE L.J. 431; Mari J. Matsuda, *Public Response to Racist Speech: Considering the Victim's Story*, 87 MICH. L. REV. 2320 (1989); Nadine Strossen, *Regulating Racist Speech on Campus: A Modest Proposal?* 1990 DUKE L.J. 484.

57. 505 U.S. at 391.

58. Cf. Amar, *The Case of the Missing Amendments*, supra note 56, at 151–60 (criticizing the Court's opinion in *R.A.V.* for ignoring the Reconstruction Amendments). But see Alex Kozinski & Eugene Volokh, *A Penumbra Too Far*, 106 HARV. L. REV. 1639, 1657 (1993) (arguing, in response to Amar, supra note 56, that the Thirteenth and Fourteenth Amendments are "missing" from *R.A.V.* because "penumbras and emanations are dangerous business," and these provisions' "shadows" are "too tenuous" or "too far" from the First Amendment to be brought to bear on the case).

59. Scanlon, *Adjusting Rights*, supra note 1, at 1485.

60. *R.A.V.*, 505 U.S. at 392.

61. Id. at 435 (Stevens, J., concurring).

62. See supra text accompanying note 55.

63. *R.A.V.*, 505 U.S. at 421–23 (Stevens, J., concurring).

64. Id. at 407 (White, J., concurring). It is not clear to what extent Virginia v. Black, 538 U.S. 343 (2003), has narrowed *R.A.V.* There, the Court held 6-3 that states may make it a crime to burn a cross with an intent to intimidate, provided that the law clearly puts the burden on prosecutors to prove that the act was intended as a threat and not as a form of symbolic expression. Id. at 363–67. The Court, however, held that the Virginia statute at issue was unconstitutional. Id. at 367. In *Black*, Justice O'Connor's opinion for the Court said that "[a] ban on cross burning carried out with the intent to intimidate is fully consistent with our holding in *R.A.V.* and is proscribable under the First Amendment." Id. at 363. Notably, the arguments in support of the constitutionality of such laws in the case did not emphasize the concern for securing equal citizenship for African Americans so much as the idea that threats with intent to intimidate are not speech. For example, Justice Thomas argued that the statute addressed only conduct, not speech, and so "there is no need to analyze it under any of our First Amendment tests." Id. at 395 (Thomas, J., dissenting). He argued that the message of cross burning is terror and intimidation that does not qualify as protected expression. Id. at 390–94.

65. *R.A.V.*, 505 U.S. at 395.

66. Id. at 380 n.1, 395–96.

67. Id. at 403–4 (White, J., concurring).

68. See American Booksellers Ass'n v. Hudnut, 771 F.2d 323, 328 (7th Cir. 1985), *aff'd mem.*, 475 U.S. 1001 (1986).

69. The Queen v. Keegstra, [1990] 3 S.C.R. 697, sustained an anti-hate speech law very much like St. Paul's. Amendments to Canada's constitutional text adopted in 1982 included: "Everyone has the following fundamental freedoms . . . (b) freedom of thought, belief, opinion and expression, including freedom of the press and other media of communication." Can. Const. pt. I, § 2 (Constitution Act, 1982) (Canadian Charter of Rights and Freedoms). Still, a close 4-3 majority reasoned that the law was constitutional because it furthered democratic principles and because racial, ethnic, or religious slurs were not essential to the purposes of free expression. In stark contrast to Scalia's opinion, Chief Justice Dickson stated for the majority: "While we must guard carefully against judging expression according to its popularity, it is equally destructive of free expression values, as well as those other values which underlie a free and democratic society, to treat all expression as equally crucial to those principles at the core of § 2(b)." Id. at 760.

70. Butler v. The Queen, [1992] 1 S.C.R. 452, while acknowledging that Canada's criminal obscenity law restricted freedom of expression, upheld the law on the ground that it was justifiable to ban pornography that harms women. The decision redefined pornography as sexually explicit material that involves violence or degradation. Id. at 485. In explicitly accepting the argument that pornography harms women, the court stated: "[I]f true equality between male and female persons is to be achieved, we cannot ignore the threat to equality resulting from exposure to audiences of certain types of violent and degrading material." Id. at 497.

71. Scanlon expresses reservations on this score. Scanlon, *Adjusting Rights*, supra note 1, at 1485.

72. 343 U.S. 250, 275 (1952) (Black, J., dissenting).

73. 505 U.S. at 415–16 (Blackmun, J., concurring).

74. For thoughtful efforts to do so, see, e.g., Steven J. Heyman, *Righting the Balance: An Inquiry into the Foundations and Limits of Freedom of Expression*, 78 B.U. L. Rev. 1275 (1998); Steven J. Heyman, *Spheres of Autonomy: Reforming the Content Neutrality Doctrine in First Amendment Jurisprudence*, 10 Wm. & Mary Bill Rts. J. 647 (2002); Russell K. Robinson, Boy Scouts & Burning Crosses: Bringing Balance to the Court's Lopsided Approach to the Intersection of Equality and Speech (unpublished manuscript, on file with author).

75. 468 U.S. at 625–27. The many thoughtful analyses of the problems implicated by *Roberts* include the following: Amy Gutmann, Identity in Democracy 99–103 (2003) [hereinafter Gutmann, Identity in Democracy]; Nancy L. Rosenblum, Membership and Morals: The Personal Uses of Pluralism in America 158–76 (1998) [hereinafter Rosenblum, Membership and Morals]; George Kateb, *The Value of Association*, in Freedom of Association 35 (Amy Gutmann ed., 1998); Douglas O. Linder, *Freedom of Association after Roberts v. United States Jaycees*, 82 Mich. L. Rev. 1878 (1984); Nancy L. Rosenblum, *Compelled Associa-*

*tion: Public Standing, Self-Respect, and the Dynamic of Exclusion,* in FREEDOM OF ASSOCIATION, supra, at 75 [hereinafter Rosenblum, *Compelled Association*].

76. 468 U.S. at 617–22.

77. Id. at 634 (O'Connor, J., concurring in part and concurring in the judgment).

78. *Buckley,* 424 U.S. at 49.

79. *Hudnut,* 771 F.2d at 328.

80. 530 U.S. at 653.

81. *Roberts,* 468 U.S. at 626.

82. Id. at 627.

83. See ROSENBLUM, MEMBERSHIP AND MORALS, supra note 75, at 158–76; William A. Galston, *Civil Society, Civic Virtue, and Liberal Democracy,* 75 CHI.-KENT L. REV. 603, 604–5 (2000).

84. See ROSENBLUM, MEMBERSHIP AND MORALS, supra note 75, at 163–64; Rosenblum, *Compelled Association,* supra note 75, at 80, 85.

85. Linda McClain and I have pursued such issues. Linda C. McClain & James E. Fleming, *Some Questions for Civil Society-Revivalists,* 75 CHI.-KENT L. REV. 301 (2000).

86. 530 U.S. at 657. For fuller discussion of *Boy Scouts,* the issues it raises, and its implications for freedom of association, see, e.g., GUTMANN, IDENTITY IN DEMOCRACY, supra note 75, at 103–12; Dale Carpenter, *Expressive Association and Anti-Discrimination Law after* Dale: *A Tripartite Approach,* 85 MINN. L. REV. 1515 (2001); Richard A. Epstein, *The Constitutional Perils of Moderation: The Case of the Boy Scouts,* 74 S. CAL. L. REV. 119 (2000); Daniel Farber, *Speaking in the First Person Plural: Expressive Associations and the First Amendment,* 85 MINN. L. REV. 1483 (2001); Madhavi Sunder, *Cultural Dissent,* 54 STAN. L. REV. 495 (2001).

87. N.J. Stat. Ann. §§ 10:5-4, 10:5-5 (West 2002); see also *Boy Scouts,* 530 U.S. at 645, 661–62.

88. *Boy Scouts,* 530 U.S. at 657.

89. Id.

90. 517 U.S. 620 (1996).

91. 539 U.S. 558 (2003).

92. See *Romer,* 517 U.S. at 626–31; *Lawrence,* 539 U.S. at 574–75.

93. *Lawrence,* 539 U.S. at 578.

94. See chapter 7.

95. *Boy Scouts,* 530 U.S. at 653.

96. *Roberts,* 468 U.S. at 627.

97. *Boy Scouts,* 530 U.S. at 696 (Stevens, J., dissenting).

98. 388 U.S. 1 (1967).

99. *Boy Scouts,* 530 U.S. at 699–700 (Stevens, J., dissenting).

100. 347 U.S. 483 (1954).

101. See the much criticized analysis of whites' claim of freedom not to associate with blacks in Herbert Wechsler, *Toward Neutral Principles of Constitutional Law*, 73 Harv. L. Rev. 1, 34 (1959).

102. Rehnquist probably would have rejected any analogy between discrimination on the basis of race and discrimination on the basis of sexual orientation. Here it is well to recall that Scalia, in dissent in *Romer*, took umbrage at such analogies. See *Romer*, 517 U.S. at 636 (Scalia, J., dissenting).

## Chapter Nine

1. 489 U.S. 189 (1989).

2. Thomas Hobbes, Leviathan chap. 13 (C. B. MacPherson ed., 1968) (1651).

3. John Locke, Two Treatises of Government (Peter Laslett ed., 2d ed. 1967) (3d ed. 1698).

4. For the notion of a constitution as a way of life, as distinguished from a constitutional text, see Walter F. Murphy, James E. Fleming, Sotirios A. Barber & Stephen Macedo, American Constitutional Interpretation 1 (3d ed. 2003).

5. Hobbes, supra note 2, at chaps. 14, 21.

6. The Federalist No. 45, at 289 (James Madison) (Clinton Rossiter ed., 1961).

7. The Federalist Nos. 40, 45 (James Madison).

8. 517 U.S. 620, 636 (1996) (Scalia, J., dissenting).

9. 539 U.S. 558, 602 (2003) (Scalia, J., dissenting).

10. 531 U.S. 98 (2000).

11. See, e.g., Francis X. Clines, *Karl Rove's Campaign Strategy Seems Evident: It's the Terror, Stupid*, N.Y. Times, May 10, 2003, at A20; Todd S. Purdum, *Crises, Crises Everywhere, What Is a President to Do?* N.Y. Times, Feb. 9, 2003, § 4, at 1; Carl Hulse, *War Dividend: Looking for Domestic Gains from the Success Abroad*, N.Y. Times, Apr. 13, 2003, § 4, at 3; Paul Krugman, *Inventing a Crisis*, N.Y. Times, Dec. 7, 2004, at A27.

12. See, e.g., James Bradley Thayer, *The Origin and Scope of the American Doctrine of Constitutional Law*, 7 Harv. L. Rev. 129, 156 (1893) ("[U]nder no system can the power of courts go far to save a people from ruin; our chief protection lies elsewhere"); Learned Hand, *The Spirit of Liberty*, in The Spirit of Liberty 189, 190 (Irving Dilliard ed., 3d ed., 1960) ("Liberty lies in the hearts of men and women; when it dies there, no constitution, no law, no court can save it. . . . While it lies there it needs no constitution, no law, no court to save it").

13. In Planned Parenthood v. Casey, 505 U.S. 833, 865–69 (1992), the joint opinion of Justices O'Connor, Kennedy, and Souter made such claims for the Supreme Court.

14. Scalia, joined by Rehnquist and Thomas, partially dissented in *Casey*, 505 U.S. at 979, 998, invoking the specter of Dred Scott v. Sandford, 60 U.S. (19 How.) 393 (1857). He argued that the joint opinion in *Casey*, like Taney's majority opinion in *Dred Scott*, displayed the hubris of its authors' belief that the Supreme Court could resolve divisive national controversies with legitimacy. *Casey*, 505 U.S. at 995–1002.

15. John Yoo, *The Right Moment for Judicial Power*, N.Y. TIMES, Nov. 25, 2000, at A19; David G. Savage & Henry Weinstein, *Supreme Court Ruling: Right or Wrong?* L.A. TIMES, Dec. 21, 2000, at A24 (quoting John Yoo, who draws a parallel between *Bush v. Gore* and the abortion decisions of the Supreme Court).

16. William Safire, *The Coming Together*, N.Y. TIMES, Dec. 14, 2000, at A39.

17. I put aside the question of the legitimacy and appropriateness of such prudential judicial statesmanship in a constitutional democracy committed to a constitution of principle.

18. I agree with Ronald Dworkin's arguments that the decision is deeply troubling for those who are committed to a constitution of principle. See Ronald Dworkin, *A Badly Flawed Election*, N.Y. REV. BOOKS, Jan. 11, 2001, at 53. Furthermore, I want to make clear that I do not blush at the mention of arguments that Bush's ascension to power was a *coup d'etat*, see, e.g., Bruce Ackerman, *Anatomy of a Constitutional Coup*, LONDON REV. BOOKS, Feb. 8, 2001, at 3, and that the Bush Five are disgraceful partisans. In fact, I signed the Law Professors' Statement that "By Stopping the Vote Count in Florida, the U.S. Supreme Court Used Its Power to Act as Political Partisans, not Judges of a Court of Law," N.Y. TIMES, Jan. 13, 2001, at A7. For the stronger claim that the Bush Five "committed one of the biggest and most serious crimes this nation has ever seen—pure and simple, the theft of the presidency," see Vincent Bugliosi, *None Dare Call It Treason*, THE NATION, Feb. 5, 2001, at 11, 14.

19. The vast literature on the presidential election controversy includes HOWARD GILLMAN, THE VOTES THAT COUNTED: HOW THE COURT DECIDED THE 2000 PRESIDENTIAL ELECTION (2001); ABNER S. GREENE, UNDERSTANDING THE 2000 ELECTION: A GUIDE TO THE LEGAL BATTLE THAT DECIDED THE PRESIDENCY (2001); RICHARD A. POSNER, BREAKING THE DEADLOCK: THE 2000 ELECTION, THE CONSTITUTION, AND THE COURTS (2001); A BADLY FLAWED ELECTION: DEBATING BUSH V. GORE (Ronald Dworkin ed., 2002); BUSH V. GORE: THE QUESTION OF LEGITIMACY (Bruce Ackerman ed., 2002); THE VOTE: BUSH, GORE, AND THE SUPREME COURT (Cass R. Sunstein & Richard A. Epstein eds., 2001).

20. 323 U.S. 214 (1944).

21. For a recent historical examination of Lincoln's constitutional jurisprudence, see DANIEL FARBER, LINCOLN'S CONSTITUTION (2003).

22. ABRAHAM LINCOLN: HIS SPEECHES AND WRITINGS 607 (Roy P. Basler ed., 1946).

23. THE FEDERALIST NO. 45, at 289 (James Madison).

24. THE FEDERALIST NO. 40, at 249 (James Madison).

25. See SOTIRIOS A. BARBER, ON WHAT THE CONSTITUTION MEANS (1984); JOHN E. FINN, CONSTITUTIONS IN CRISIS: POLITICAL VIOLENCE AND THE RULE OF LAW (1991).

26. I venture a typological hypothesis or distinction here for purposes of discussion. Lincoln is a case of constitutional *maintenance:* restore conditions for honoring old means to old ends. Madison is a case of constitutional *reform:* replace failed means with effective means to old ends.

27. Adam Nagourney & David Barstow, *G.O.P.'s Depth Outdid Gore's Team in Florida*, N.Y. TIMES, Dec. 22, 2000, at A1. See also Bob Herbert, *To Any Lengths*, N.Y. TIMES, Dec. 11, 2000, at A31.

28. *Bush*, 531 U.S. at 102–4.

29. See, e.g., the symposium, *The End of Democracy? The Judicial Usurpation of Politics*, FIRST THINGS, Nov. 1996, at 18.

30. See, e.g., the complaint filed in NAACP v. Harris (Jan. 10, 2001), available at www.naacp.org.

31. See, e.g., STEPHEN E. GOTTLIEB, MORALITY IMPOSED: THE REHNQUIST COURT AND LIBERTY IN AMERICA (2000) (analyzing the jurisprudence of Rehnquist, Scalia, and Thomas in terms of Social Darwinism).

32. I do not believe that the Constitution *rightly* interpreted would sanction what the Florida Republicans seemed determined to do; I mean only that the Constitution *can* be so interpreted.

33. 505 U.S. at 841.

34. THE FEDERALIST NO. 49, at 315 (James Madison).

35. Savage & Weinstein, supra note 15, at A24 (quoting John Yoo).

36. Gerard V. Bradley, Bush v. Gore—*A Case in Conservative Judicial Activism?* 16 WORLD AND I, June 1, 2001, at 292.

37. Id. (italics in original).

38. Furthermore, we should bear in mind the distinction between, on the one hand, an executive like Lincoln acting outside the Constitution in order to save it and, on the other, a court doing so. Lincoln not only had broader authority to act but also faced greater democratic accountability for his actions.

39. I refer, in particular, to Scalia's statement concurring in the 5-4 decision to stay the Florida hand count: "The counting of votes that are of questionable legality does in my view threaten irreparable harm to [Bush], and to the country, by casting a cloud upon what he claims to be the legitimacy of his election." Bush v. Gore, 531 U.S. 1046, 1047 (2000) (Scalia, J., concurring).

40. See Maureen Dowd, *The Bloom Is Off the Robe*, N.Y. TIMES, Dec. 13, 2000, at A35 (mocking Scalia's questions of Theodore Olson in the oral argument by saying, "Come on, Ted, do I have to plead your case for Bush as well as hear it?").

41. Bradley, supra note 36.

42. Safire, supra note 16.

43. 489 U.S. 189 (1989).

44. See SOTIRIOS A. BARBER, WELFARE AND THE CONSTITUTION (2003).

45. 316 F.3d 450 (4th Cir. 2003), *judgment vacated*, 124 S. Ct. 2633 (2004).

46. Public Law No. 107–40, September 18, 2001.

47. *Hamdi*, 316 F.3d at 463.

48. For a positive benefits conception of the Constitution, see BARBER, supra note 44.

49. WILLIAM H. REHNQUIST, ALL THE LAWS BUT ONE: CIVIL LIBERTIES IN WARTIME (1998).

50. *Chief Justice Rehnquist's Ominous History of Wartime Freedom*, N.Y. TIMES, Sept. 22, 2002, § 4, at 12. Adam Cohen also published an insightful essay on Rehnquist's more recent book, CENTENNIAL CRISIS: THE DISPUTED ELECTION OF 1876 (2004). Adam Cohen, *Justice Rehnquist Writes on* Hayes v. Tilden, *with His Mind on* Bush v. Gore, N.Y. TIMES, March 21, 2004, § 4, at 10. Cohen writes: "[E]ven readers keenly interested in history may have trouble seeing [Rehnquist's book] as anything but an allegory, and apologia, for the Supreme Court's ruling in *Bush v. Gore.*" Id.

51. THE FEDERALIST NO. 1 (Alexander Hamilton).


## Chapter Ten

1. See Colloquy, *Fidelity as Integrity*, 65 FORDHAM L. REV. 1357, 1358 (1997) (statement of Sanford Levinson).

2. See Henry P. Monaghan, *Our Perfect Constitution*, 56 N.Y.U. L. REV. 353 (1981).

3. See Christopher L. Eisgruber, *Justice and the Text: Rethinking the Constitutional Relation between Principle and Prudence*, 43 DUKE L.J. 1, 7 (1993) (referring to Monaghan, supra note 2).

4. See RONALD DWORKIN, FREEDOM'S LAW: THE MORAL READING OF THE AMERICAN CONSTITUTION (1996) [hereinafter DWORKIN, FL].

5. LAWRENCE G. SAGER, JUSTICE IN PLAINCLOTHES: A THEORY OF AMERICAN CONSTITUTIONAL PRACTICE (2004).

6. See, e.g., SOTIRIOS A. BARBER, THE CONSTITUTION OF JUDICIAL POWER (1993).

7. See RONALD DWORKIN, LAW'S EMPIRE 176–275 (1986) [hereinafter DWORKIN, LE]; RONALD DWORKIN, A MATTER OF PRINCIPLE 146–66 (1985) [hereinafter DWORKIN, AMOP].

8. Eisgruber, supra note 3, at 7.

9. BRUCE ACKERMAN, WE THE PEOPLE: FOUNDATIONS 319–22 (1991).

10. CONSTITUTIONAL STUPIDITIES, CONSTITUTIONAL TRAGEDIES 170–71 n.25 (William N. Eskridge Jr. & Sanford Levinson eds., 1998). I contributed an essay to that book and in this chapter I draw from that essay.

11. See DWORKIN, FL, supra note 7, at 36. In colloquy with Dworkin at the Fordham conference on Fidelity in Constitutional Theory, Levinson revealed himself to be the reviewer who had raised this question or challenge of Dworkin's manuscript. *Colloquy*, supra note 1, at 1358.

12. DWORKIN, FL, supra note 7, at 36.

13. Id. (citing Frank I. Michelman, *Foreword: On Protecting the Poor Through the Fourteenth Amendment*, 83 HARV. L. REV. 7 [1969]).

14. Id. at 38.

15. Id. at 73.

16. SAGER, supra note 5, at 84–92.

17. Id. at 95–102.

18. Id. at 84–128.

19. Id. at 129–60. See Lawrence G. Sager, *The Why of Constitutional Essentials*, 72 FORDHAM L. REV. 1421, 1423–29 (2004) (using concentric circles to illustrate these four domains).

20. THE FEDERALIST No. 14, at 104 (James Madison) (Clinton Rossiter ed., 1961).

21. ACKERMAN, supra note 9, at 13. For an argument that Ackerman's formulation presents a "false dichotomy" because both democracy and rights, or popular sovereignty and unalienable rights, are constitutive principles of our constitutional democracy, see Samuel Freeman, *Original Meaning, Democratic Interpretation, and the Constitution*, 21 PHIL. & PUB. AFF. 3, 41–42 (1992). For a similar argument, though not directed specifically against Ackerman, that our constitutional order is a hybrid scheme of democracy (majority rule) and constitutionalism (limited government), or constitutional democracy, see chapter 4.

22. ACKERMAN, supra note 9, at 11 (referring to John Rawls, *Kantian Constructivism in Moral Theory*, 77 J. PHIL. 515 [1980]; RONALD DWORKIN, TAKING RIGHTS SERIOUSLY [1977] [hereinafter DWORKIN, TRS]; DWORKIN, LE, supra note 7).

23. See chapter 4. I have developed fuller critiques of Ackerman's dualist constitutional theory in other work. See James E. Fleming, *We the Exceptional American People*, 11 CONST. COMM. 355 (1994); James E. Fleming, *We the Unconventional American People*, 65 U. CHI. L. REV. 1513 (1998).

24. ACKERMAN, supra note 9, at 13.

25. Id. at 15 (emphasis in original).

26. Article 79(3) of the German Basic Law provides in relevant part: "Amendments of this Basic Law affecting the division of the Federation into Laender, the participation on principle of the Laender in legislation, or the basic principles laid down in Articles 1 and 20, shall be inadmissible." Articles 1 and 20 relate to the protection of unalienable human rights to dignity and the free democratic basic order, specifically, the right to resist any person or persons seeking to abolish the constitutional order, a democratic and social federal state. For a translation of portions of the Basic Law of the Federal Republic of Germany, see WALTER

F. MURPHY & JOSEPH TANENHAUS, COMPARATIVE CONSTITUTIONAL LAW: CASES AND COMMENTARIES (1977). For analyses of the constitutional theory of the Basic Law, and of its entrenchment of certain basic principles against subsequent amendment, see, e.g., JOHN E. FINN, CONSTITUTIONS IN CRISIS: POLITICAL VIOLENCE AND THE RULE OF LAW 185–91 (1991); DONALD P. KOMMERS, THE CONSTITUTIONAL JURISPRUDENCE OF THE FEDERAL REPUBLIC OF GERMANY 36–39, 52–55 (1989); Walter F. Murphy, *Excluding Political Parties: Problems for Democratic and Constitutional Theory*, in GERMANY AND ITS BASIC LAW 173, 173–78 (Paul Kirchhof & Donald P. Kommers eds., 1993).

27. ACKERMAN, supra note 9, at 13.

28. Id. at 14. See also Bruce Ackerman, *Constitutional Politics/Constitutional Law*, 99 YALE L.J. 453, 469 (1989) (using the stronger formulation "a very great embarrassment").

29. ACKERMAN, supra note 9, at 15 (referring to entrenchment of African slave trade until 1808). See also id. at 326 n.21 (referring to entrenchment of equal representation of each state in the Senate and claiming that "[t]his effort to entrench federalism caused all sorts of trouble in the aftermath of the Civil War").

30. Id. at 15.

31. Id.

32. In using formulations like that in the text ("We the People are not bound by a higher law"), I do not intend to personify the constituent power, that is, to conflate the citizenry (the people) with the constituent power (We the People). For a sophisticated treatment of the difference between the "Constitutional People" and the "sovereign constitution-making people," see WILLIAM F. HARRIS II, THE INTERPRETABLE CONSTITUTION 201–4 (1993).

33. ACKERMAN, supra note 9, at 14–15.

34. Id. at 14–15 & 15–16 n.

35. Id. at 15 & 15 n. Ackerman states: "I doubt, moreover, that one may find many American lawyers who seriously disagree—even among those who presently wrap themselves up in foundationalist rhetoric." Id. at 14–15.

36. Id. at 321. See also id. at 16.

37. BRUCE A. ACKERMAN, SOCIAL JUSTICE IN THE LIBERAL STATE (1980).

38. ACKERMAN, supra note 9, at 11 (referring to Rawls, supra note 22; DWORKIN, TRS, supra note 22; DWORKIN, LE, supra note 7). But see id. at 30, 327–28 n.49 (noting that his own work in political philosophy builds on the liberal tradition that includes Rawls); Bruce Ackerman, *Political Liberalisms*, 91 J. PHIL. 364 (1994) (criticizing JOHN RAWLS, POLITICAL LIBERALISM [1993], while also acknowledging similarities between Rawls's political philosophy and his own).

39. Michael J. Klarman, *Constitutional Fact/Constitutional Fiction: A Critique of Bruce Ackerman's Theory of Constitutional Moments*, 44 STAN. L. REV. 759, 763–64 n.37 (1992).

40. ACKERMAN, supra note 9, at 16, 319–22. For the notion of "temptation," see ROBERT H. BORK, THE TEMPTING OF AMERICA (1990).

41. ACKERMAN, supra note 9, at 15–16.

42. On one interpretation, which I offer below, these provisos in Article V entrenched compromises with our constitutive principles. On another interpretation, which underscores the injustice of the original Constitution, these provisos entrenched two of our constitutive principles: the fundamental right of slaveholders to property in slaves and structural protections of states' rights. John Finn suggested the latter interpretation to me (without endorsing it).

43. See RICHARD B. MORRIS, THE FORGING OF THE UNION: 1781–1789 at 281–87 (1987). See also RICHARD B. BERNSTEIN (WITH JEROME AGEL), AMENDING AMERICA: IF WE LOVE THE CONSTITUTION SO MUCH, WHY DO WE KEEP TRYING TO CHANGE IT? 20–22 (1993).

44. See, e.g., FINN, supra note 26, at 179–93; KOMMERS, supra note 26, at 36–39, 52–55.

45. Here I mean to echo the title of a fine collection of essays. See RESPONDING TO IMPERFECTION: THE THEORY AND PRACTICE OF CONSTITUTIONAL AMENDMENT (Sanford Levinson ed., 1995). Ackerman might concede this point yet still contend that it cuts in favor of dualism that the American founders did not entrench unalienable rights. One response is that they did, for example, in the Preamble, the First Amendment, the Ninth Amendment, the Declaration of Independence, and the structural implications of the constitutional order. See, e.g., HARRIS, supra note 32, at 164–68, 191–201 (analyzing "the limits of textual amendability" and "a hierarchy of amendment sequences" that distinguishes between the limits on amendability through Article V and the greater revisability of the polity through Article VII); Akhil Reed Amar, *The Consent of the Governed: Constitutional Amendment Outside Article V*, 94 COLUM. L. REV. 457, 504–5 (1994) (emphasizing the Declaration of Independence, the Preamble, and the logic of a system of republican self-government in suggesting that "not everything is properly amendable," for certain higher law principles, including popular sovereignty and perhaps liberty of conscience, frame Article V itself); Akhil Reed Amar, *Philadelphia Revisited: Amending the Constitution Outside Article V*, 55 U. CHI. L. REV. 1043, 1044–45 n.1 (1988) (arguing that "the First Amendment may itself be a seemingly paradoxical exception to the general rule that amendments must not be unamendable"); Walter F. Murphy, *The Art of Constitutional Interpretation: A Preliminary Showing*, in ESSAYS ON THE CONSTITUTION OF THE UNITED STATES 130, 150–51 (M. Judd Harmon ed., 1978) (suggesting that the First Amendment may be an "unamendable constitutional provision"); Jeff Rosen, Note, *Was the Flag Burning Amendment Unconstitutional?* 100 YALE L.J. 1073, 1084–89 (1991) (arguing that there are natural rights limitations on the amending power, derived from the history and structure of the Constitution as a whole, that are expressed in the Declaration of Independence and the Ninth Amendment).

Another response is that the American founders did not need explicitly to entrench unalienable rights. See, e.g., Freeman, supra note 21, at 41.

46. CONSTITUTIONAL STUPIDITIES, CONSTITUTIONAL TRAGEDIES, supra note 10, at 170–71 n.25.

47. Dandridge v. Williams, 397 U.S. 471 (1970); San Antonio v. Rodriguez, 411 U.S. 1 (1973); Harris v. McRae, 448 U.S. 297 (1980); DeShaney v. Winnebago County Dep't of Social Servs., 489 U.S. 189 (1989).

48. There already are cracks in the wall, but it has not yet collapsed.

49. Dred Scott v. Sandford, 60 U.S. (19 How.) 393 (1857); Plessy v. Ferguson, 163 U.S. 537 (1896); Korematsu v. United States, 323 U.S. 214 (1944).

50. Slaughter-House Cases, 83 U.S. 36 (1872); Bowers v. Hardwick, 478 U.S. 186 (1986). *Bowers* was overruled by Lawrence v. Texas, 539 U.S. 558 (2003).

51. Buckley v. Valeo, 424 U.S. 1 (1976).

52. See *Constitutional Stupidities: A Symposium*, 12 CONST. COMM. 139 (1995), *reprinted in* CONSTITUTIONAL STUPIDITIES, CONSTITUTIONAL TRAGEDIES, supra note 10.

53. In giving an account of a constitutional tragedy, one might also ask how it compares with a literary tragedy. It might seem promising to draw on formulations of the elements of tragedy in Greek, Elizabethan, or modern drama. See, e.g., A. C. BRADLEY, SHAKESPEAREAN TRAGEDY (2d ed., 1905); RAYMOND WILLIAMS, MODERN TRAGEDY (1966). But that effort is stymied by the lack of agreement about what those elements are and by the difficulty of translating from those genre to the discourses and dilemmas of constitutional law.

54. See ROBERT M. COVER, JUSTICE ACCUSED: ANTISLAVERY AND THE JUDICIAL PROCESS (1975).

55. It may seem jarring to speak of happy endings in the context of an analysis of the right to die, including the right of persons to author their own tragic endings. By "happy ending," I refer to the notion that the Constitution, rightly interpreted, is consistent with what justice or sound political philosophy requires. By no means do I intend to suggest that persons' tragic endings will be happy.

56. Letter from Felix Frankfurter to Harlan Fiske Stone regarding Minersville Sch. Dist. v. Gobitis, in WALTER F. MURPHY, JAMES E. FLEMING, SOTIRIOS A. BARBER & STEPHEN MACEDO, AMERICAN CONSTITUTIONAL INTERPRETATION 1267–69 (3d ed. 2003); Minersville Sch. Dist. v. Gobitis, 310 U.S. 586, 594 (1940). Frankfurter was wrong to conceive that case as illustrating a clash of rights, as Justice Robert H. Jackson effectively retorted in the second flag-salute case: "The sole conflict is between authority and the rights of the individual." West Virginia v. Barnette, 319 U.S. 624, 630 (1943). See chapter 8. Still, Frankfurter's formulation of a "tragic issue" may be helpful in thinking about what constitutes a constitutional tragedy. For the idea of "tragic choices," see GUIDO CALABRESI & PHILIP BOBBITT, TRAGIC CHOICES (1978).

57. 79 F.3d 790 (9th Cir. 1996) (*en banc*), *reversed sub nom.* Washington v. Glucksberg, 521 U.S. 702 (1997). I shall put to one side all of the difficult issues concerning whether there are crucial distinctions between the right to die conceived as the right to refuse unwanted medical treatment and the right to die conceived as the right to physician-assisted suicide. I believe that Judge Reinhardt convincingly showed that many proffered distinctions of this sort, although familiar, are distinctions without a difference. Id. at 820–24. I also believe that Reinhardt persuasively argued that state interests, such as avoiding the involvement of third parties, and precluding the use of arbitrary, unfair, or undue influence, do not justify a total ban on physician-assisted suicide, although they do justify the creation of procedural safeguards. Id. at 825–27, 832–33. See James E. Fleming, *Constitutional Tragedy in Dying: Responses to Some Common Arguments against the Constitutional Right to Die*, 24 FORDHAM URBAN L.J. 881 (1997).

58. 80 F.3d 716 (2d Cir. 1996), *reversed*, Vacco v. Quill, 521 U.S. 793 (1997).

59. See RONALD DWORKIN, LIFE'S DOMINION 217 (1993) [hereinafter DWORKIN, LD]. See also Ronald Dworkin, Thomas Nagel, Robert Nozick, John Rawls, Thomas Scanlon & Judith Jarvis Thomson, *Assisted Suicide: The Philosophers' Brief*, reprinted in N.Y. REV. BOOKS, Mar. 27, 1997, at 41.

60. Cf. Planned Parenthood v. Casey, 505 U.S. 833, 928 (1992) (Blackmun, J., concurring in part, concurring in the judgment in part, and dissenting in part) (arguing that "[b]y restricting the right to terminate pregnancies, the State conscripts women's bodies into its service"). I realize that some will object that the state does not compel terminally ill persons to do anything, much less conscript them into involuntary servitude. In particular, they may contend that the state does not forbid such persons from committing suicide, it simply prohibits them from getting physicians' assistance in doing so. But that claim does not defeat the analogy to involuntary servitude, any more than a similar claim would defeat the analogy between involuntary servitude and the forced continuation of a pregnancy. It would be absurd to say that the Constitution protects the right of women to decide whether to terminate a pregnancy, but does not protect the right to physician-assisted abortion (as if the right to abortion embraced only self-performed abortion). It would be equally problematic to say that the Constitution protects the right of terminally ill persons to decide whether to terminate their lives, but does not protect the right to physician-assisted suicide (as if the right to die encompassed only self-performed suicide). As for the tirelessly repeated claims that there is a fundamental difference between "passive" and "active" euthanasia, I have nothing to add to Judge Reinhardt's powerful rejection of those claims. See *Compassion in Dying*, 79 F.3d at 820–24.

61. See Pierce v. Society of Sisters, 268 U.S. 510, 535 (1925) (stating that "[t]he child is not the mere creature of the state"). For an assertion to the contrary, see Stephen L. Carter, *Rush to a Lethal Judgment*, N.Y. TIMES, July 21, 1996, at 28

(Magazine) (approvingly stating that the laws in England and America that prohibited suicide "reflected a strong belief that the lives of individuals belonged not to themselves alone but to the communities in which they lived and to the God who gave them breath"). See also Michael J. Sandel, *Last Rights*, THE NEW REPUBLIC, Apr. 14, 1997, at 27, reprinted in MICHAEL J. SANDEL, PUBLIC PHILOSOPHY: ESSAYS ON MORALITY IN POLITICS 113 (2005).

62. See DWORKIN, LD, supra note 59, at 217.

63. Cf. CATHARINE A. MACKINNON, *Privacy v. Equality: Beyond* Roe v. Wade, in FEMINISM UNMODIFIED 93, 100 (1987) (arguing that the right to privacy may readily prove, for women, to be "an injury got up as a gift"). Similarly, Judge Reinhardt criticized the district court decision invalidating Oregon's Death with Dignity Act because it "treats a *burden* [prohibition of physician-assisted suicide] as a *benefit* and a *benefit* [the right to physician-assisted suicide] as a *burden.*" *Compassion in Dying*, 79 F.3d at 838 (criticizing Lee v. State of Oregon, 891 F. Supp. 1429, 1438 [D. Or. 1995], *vacated and remanded* by Lee v. State of Oregon, 107 F.3d 1382 [9th Cir. 1997]).

64. See chapter 5.

65. *Casey*, 505 U.S. at 848–49, 901 (joint opinion).

66. Although the Supreme Court unanimously reversed the Ninth Circuit, that is not to say there is no support among the justices for the constitutional right to die. In *Glucksberg*, Rehnquist framed the asserted right highly abstractly, as "a right to commit suicide which itself includes a right to assistance in doing so." *Glucksberg*, 521 U.S. at 723. See chapter 6. All nine justices rejected any such abstractly, absolutely, and categorically formulated right. Arguably, five of the nine justices have given indications that they would accept a more narrowly formulated right to die, expressed in more specific formulations that have greater support in our traditions, whether those traditions are understood as historical practices or aspirational principles. See Ronald Dworkin, *Assisted Suicide: What the Court Really Said*, N.Y. REV. BOOKS, Sept. 25, 1997, at 40. For example, Justice Breyer framed the asserted right in concurrence as "a right to die with dignity" (which he characterized as "a different formulation, for which our legal tradition may provide greater support"). *Glucksberg*, 521 U.S. at 790 (Breyer, J., concurring). Justice Stevens objected in concurrence that, even if "[h]istory and tradition provide ample support for refusing to recognize an open-ended [or 'categorical'] constitutional right to commit suicide," our Constitution protects a "basic concept of freedom" that "embraces not merely a person's right to refuse a particular kind of unwanted treatment, but also her interest in dignity, and in determining the character of the memories that will survive long after her death." Id. at 740, 743 (Stevens, J., concurring).

67. See DWORKIN, LD, supra note 59, at 199–213.

68. WILLIAM SHAKESPEARE, THE TRAGEDY OF KING LEAR act V, sc. iii, 314–16 (cited in *Compassion in Dying*, 79 F.3d at 821).

69. PLATO, THE LAWS bk. vii, at 817b (A. E. Taylor trans.), in THE COLLECTED DIALOGUES OF PLATO (Edith Hamilton & Huntington Cairns eds., 1961).

70. See Meyer v. Nebraska, 262 U.S. 390, 401–2 (1923) ("[The] ideas touching the relation between individual and state [in Plato's ideal commonwealth, which 'submerge the individual and develop ideal citizens'] were wholly different from those upon which our institutions rest").

71. I allude, of course, to BRIAN CLARK, WHOSE LIFE IS IT, ANYWAY? (1980). But Levinson has written, "In answer to the question asked by playwright Brian Clark some years ago, *Whose Life Is It, Anyway?*, almost no one is truly willing to say, 'The person's own, to do with as he or she wishes.'" Sanford Levinson, *The Court's Death Blow: Is the Supreme Court's Decision on Assisted Suicide to be Lauded or Condemned?* THE NATION, July 21, 1997, at 28, 29.

72. See DWORKIN, LE, supra note 7, at 176–275; DWORKIN, AMOP, supra note 7, at 146–66.

73. For a work that seems to revel in the evil that the Constitution might be interpreted to permit, see J. M. Balkin, *Agreements with Hell and Other Objects of Our Faith*, 65 FORDHAM L. REV. 1703 (1997).

74. See DWORKIN, LD, supra note 59, at 119, 126–29.

75. See James E. Fleming, *Fidelity to Our Imperfect Constitution*, 65 FORDHAM L. REV. 1335 (1997). This article appears in *Symposium: Fidelity in Constitutional Theory*, 65 FORDHAM L. REV. 1247 (1997).

# Index